Jacques-Louis David
and
Jean-Louis Prieur

Revolutionary Artists

D0912384

Jacques-Louis David

and

Jean-Louis Prieur

Revolutionary Artists

The Public, the Populace, and Images of the
French Revolution

Warren Roberts

STATE UNIVERSITY OF NEW YORK PRESS

Published by
State University of New York Press, Albany

© 2000 State University of New York

All rights reserved

Printed in the United States of America

No part of this book may be used or reproduced in any manner whatsoever without
written permission. No part of this book may be stored in a retrieval system or transmitted in any form or by any means including electronic, electrostatic, magnetic tape,
mechanical, photocopying, recording, or otherwise without the prior permission in
writing of the publisher.

For information address
State University of New York Press, State
University Plaza, Albany, N.Y., 12246

Production by Dale Cotton and Michael Haggett
Marketing by Fran Keneston

Library of Congress Cataloging-in-Publication Data

Roberts, Warren, 1933–
    Jacques-Louis David and Jean-Louis Prieur, revolutionary artists :
the public, the populace, and images of the French Revolution /
Warren Roberts.
        p.   cm.
    Includes bibliographical references and index.
    ISBN 0-7914-4287-X (alk. paper). — ISBN 0-7914-4288-8 (pbk. :
alk. paper)
    1. David, Jacques Louis, 1748–1825—Criticism and interpretation.
2. David, Jacques Louis, 1748–1825—Political and social views.
3. Prieur, Jean-Louis—Criticism and interpretation.   4. Prieur,
Jean-Louis—Political and social views.   5. Tableaux historiques de
la Révolution française.   6. France—History—Revolution, 1789–1799—
Art and the revolution.   I. Title.
ND553.D25R54   1999
759.4—dc21
    [B]   99-37078
                                                              CIP

10 9 8 7 6 5 4 3 2 1

Contents

Figures

Preface

A book on Jacques-Louis David and Jean-Louis Prieur, contemporary artists who were drawn into the French Revolution but moved in completely different spheres, requires explanation. Why bring together in one study artists of such disparate importance?

David, incomparably the greatest French artist of his generation, achieved stunning successes in the salons of the 1780s in paintings whose themes of patriotic sacrifice and stoic resolution related uncannily to the ideals and conflicts of the French Revolution and made him appear as one of its prophets. He identified with the Revolution from the beginning and lent his brush to the new order as a patriot artist. He served the Revolution as an artist, and, as a devoted follower of Maximilien-François Robespierre, he orchestrated revolutionary festivals whose purpose was to mobilize popular support for the Revolution. He was elected to the Convention in September 1792, served a one-month term as president on a rotating basis, and sat on the Committee of General Security and the Committee of Public Information. While he sat on the Revolutionary Tribunal, he signed at least 406 warrants, including the death orders for Louis XVI and Marie-Antoinette. As an artist he received commissions from the government to paint heroes of the Revolution, Louis-Michel Lepeletier de Saint-Fargeau and Jean-Paul Marat, whose images were placed in the meeting hall of the Convention, on a wall behind the president. In August 1793, he presided over the dissolution of the Academy, within which he had achieved fame, but whose leadership he had come to resent bitterly in the years just before the Revolution. A year later he was in prison. In the entire annals of Western art, there is no story quite like that of Jacques-Louis David, for in the span of ten years, extending from 1784 to 1794, he not only created his breakthrough Salon painting, the *Oath of the Horatii*—whose greatness even rivals in the academy had to concede—but he also was imprisoned after the fall of Robespierre.

As an illustrator Jean-Louis Prieur occupied a much lower place in the hierarchy of artistic prestige than David did as an academic artist.

With one known exception, his only works are the sixty-nine drawings he did for the *Tableaux historiques de la Révolution française*, deluxe prints offered for sale to a public that wanted to purchase images of the French Revolution.[1] Prieur drew important events of the Revolution and someone else, Pierre-Gabriel Berthault, engraved them. His drawings were not self-contained artistic statements and were not exhibited during his lifetime; they fell from sight after the Revolution, surfaced in 1900, and are now housed in the Musée Carnavelet. His illustrations have been studied by only a handful of specialists, and have never been reproduced in their entirety in a single publication. Prieur moved within a different orbit than David during his lifetime, and, when his illustrations are reproduced in books on the French Revolution, they are sometimes not even identified as his. By contrast, David's importance, paramount during his lifetime, has never been questioned, and since 1989, the Bicentennial of the Revolution, he has been the object of renewed interest, so much so that he has become a growth industry of sorts among both art historians and historians.[2]

So why write a comparative study of these two artists, of such disparate importance? One answer to that question lies in the differences between their images of the French Revolution. David viewed the Revolution from the elevated perspective of a history painter, and his style, his language, was that of someone thoroughly schooled in academic technique. His images of the Revolution are those of an artist who was trained in the Academy and saw the world nobly, in the manner of a history painter. As an illustrator Prieur drew from a different reservoir of techniques and the techniques served a purpose congruent with the project he was associated with, the *Tableaux historiques de la Révolution française*

From the beginning, contemporaries understood the importance of the Revolution, and wanted a pictorial record of the events that changed their world so dramatically. In the absence of the camera, prints provided that record. Of the various publishing ventures that offered prints, illustrating the leading events of the Revolution to the public, the *Tableaux historiques* was arguably the most important. As the first illustrator for that venture, Prieur provided illustrations of the Revolution for the period June 1789 to September 1792. His perspective, unlike that of David, was at street level: he did sixteen illustrations of the Paris Insurrection of July 12–14, 1789, of which nine were of the first day.

During the three-year period for which Prieur illustrated for the *Tableaux historiques*, David painted but one revolutionary event, the *Tennis Court Oath*, a twenty feet by thirty feet canvas that he never completed. For a pictorial record of the Revolution one must turn to other artists, illustrators such as Prieur, whose images portrayed its leading events. Prieur not only offered a pictorial record of the first three years of the Revolution, but also one that was done in a different style and language than that of David. The differences between the two artists are at the heart of this study.

The story of David and Prieur is not just one of differences: Both artists moved with the Revolution as it turned to the Left, both became Jacobins, both sat on the Revolutionary Tribunal, and both were arrested and incarcerated after the fall of Robespierre.[3] The well-connected David was released and lived another thirty years, but Prieur went to the guillotine. As fellow jurors on the Revolutionary Tribunal, the two men attended sessions together, but there is no documentary evidence that they exchanged words. Part of the interest in David and Prieur, for me, lies in their commitment to the Revolution, both as artists and radical Jacobins who not only ended up as instruments of the Terror, but also sat together on the Revolutionary Tribunal. Similar as they were in their politics, their images of the Revolution were strikingly different, in terms of number, subject, perspective, and style.

This study examines the revolutionary images of Jacque-Louis David and Jean-Louis Prieur as if they were documents, evidence used by the historian to understand the past, and it tries to place them in context. In placing the images of David and Prieur in historical context, I have employed a conceptual scheme used by historians who have moved away from the Marxist interpretation of the French Revolution. In this conceptual scheme, the public and populace have replaced the bourgeoisie, a category of central importance to Marxist analysis.[4] How I have used the public and the populace will become apparent as the reader proceeds through the book. It is not the first study to use the public as a historical construct and to shed light on the art of David, but it is the first to examine Prieur's revolutionary images within the context of the populace.[5] The book is a comparative study of David and Prieur, the Revolution's greatest artist and its leading illustrator, and it is about the French Revolution. It is about a Revolution that was saved by the people in 1789 but whose subsequent dilemmas and tragedies were bound up with their appearance on the historical stage.

Part One is on Jean-Louis Prieur. It begins with a chapter on the Paris insurrection of July 12–14, 1789 and is followed by a chapter on Prieur's tableaus illustrating that episode. The people of Paris who rose up in this crucial three-day period saved the Revolution but at the same time cast it in a different mold. The unexpected directions the Revolution would take after a period of initial calm have many causes; among them was a climate of fear in Paris, politicization of the people, and their continued intervention in revolutionary politics. Prieur's pictorial record of the Revolution ended with the Storming of the Tuileries and the September Massacres; it does not show the *journées* of May 31–June 2, 1793 and September 4–5, 1793, nor does it show the savage political infighting within the revolutionary leadership and the bloodletting of the Terror. What Prieur's sixty-nine tableaus do show is the forces that were released so unexpectedly and explosively in Paris in the summer of 1789 and the direction events would take in the course of the next three years. Chapter 2 covers the period from August 1789 to September 1792.

Working my way through Prieur's tableaus was like taking a tour through the first three years of the Revolution, with him as my guide. He did not offer an objective account of what happened, but put his spin on the events he illustrated. Far from being a detached observer, he was caught up in the sound and fury of the French Revolution, and in the struggles of the people. More particularly, as illustrator for the *Tableaux historiques*, he was engrossed in the struggles of the people of Paris in the three-year period between two Paris insurrections, those of July 12–14, 1789 and August 10, 1792.

Part Two is on Jacques-Louis David, but begins with a chapter on Robespierre and the people. Of all the Revolution's leaders, none sided earlier and more resolutely with the people than Maximilien Robespierre, and it was through sans-culotte intervention that he became the Revolution's dominant political figure. Yet to achieve his high-minded goals, Robespierre ended up silencing the sans-culottes and suppressing the popular movement. Sympathize with the people and their plight as he did, Robespierre was ultimately a member of the eighteenth-century public. The same may be said of his devoted follower, Jacques-Louis David. Like Robespierre, David was swept into the dilemmas and tragedies of the Revolution, from which he was fortunate to escape with his life. Having already written a book on David, I limited myself in this book to themes that connect him to Robespierre, to his revolutionary ideas, to his strategies to bring them to fruition, and to the ultimate collapse of his program. The argument on David is set forth in two chapters, one on his grand—but unfinished—painting of the *Tennis Court Oath*; the other is devoted to the revolutionary festivals that he orchestrated in collaboration with Robespierre.

As central as the public and populace categories have been to the post-revisionist analysis of the French Revolution, historians have used them for the most part to explain the outbreak of the Revolution, not the Revolution itself. By placing the images of David and Prieur within the context of the public and the populace, I have tried to extend analysis of these categories into the eddies and currents and storm-tossed waters of the Revolution; I have tried to offer a new perspective on David; I have presented the first systematic study of Prieur's images of the French Revolution. A comparative study of these two artists within the context of the public and the populace has furthered my understanding of them and their art, and it has enlarged my understanding of the French Revolution. I hope readers will share in that understanding.

Acknowledgments

I have expressed my indebtedness to undergraduate students at the State University of New York at Albany who took my Culture and the French Revolution course several years ago in an article in the "Teaching Innovations" column in *Perspectives*, the newsletter of the American Historical Association (April 1997). In this piece, "Teaching as Scholarship, Scholarship as Teaching: A Case Study," I described what happened when I assigned drafts of two chapters I had written on Jean-Louis Prieur's illustrations for the *Tableaux historiques de la Révolution française* to my students. Discussing Prieur's drawings with students, both in class and in my office, resulted in the revision of my two Prieur chapters. The chapters were different at the end of the semester than at the beginning, thanks to exchanges with students and in a couple of instances thanks to their papers. If undergraduate students were responsible for changes in my manuscript, graduate students have played a direct role in the thinking and writing that went into the manuscript. It is to my students that I dedicate this book.

Other debts should also be acknowledged: Barry Shapiro and Ian Germani for reading and commenting on chapters; James A. Leith who has helped me in ways too many to recount; Claudette Hould, who offered invaluable suggestions on the manuscript at several stages, and made available to me the text of the *Tableaux historiques*; Sue Welsh Reed for giving me access to the 1802 edition of the *Tableaux historiques* and other materials in the prints and drawings collection of the Museum of Fine Arts, Boston; Gerald Zahavi for helping me with technical matters that proved indispensable for the two Prieur chapters; John Monfasani for help in a key Italian translation; H. P. Salomon for help in translating French verse; Charles Hartman for directing me to the State University of New York Press; unnamed readers of the State University Press who critiqued the manuscript; Priscilla Ross, Jennie R. Doling, Dale Cotton, Michael Haggett and Lani Blackman, all of the State University of New York Press, and all, in their different ways, helpful and impeccably professional. And to Debbie Neuls, who turned my untidy handwritten pages into clean word processed pages, and saw it through more revisions than I would have thought possible, I owe particular thanks.

Introduction
The Public and the Populace

The public, does it exist? What is the public?
Where is it? By what organ does it manifest its will?
     —*Louis Sébastien Mercier*, Le Tableau de Paris, *1783–1787*

Our investigation is limited to the structure and function of the *liberal* model of the bourgeois public sphere, to its emergence and transformation. Thus it refers to those features of a historical constellation that attained dominance and leaves aside the *plebeian* public sphere as a variant that in a sense was suppressed in the historical process.
     —*Jürgen Habermas*, The Structural Transformation
of the Public Sphere, *1962*

"What is the public?" If Louis-Sébastien Mercier found the "public" that he referred to in the first of the above quotes elusive, he was convinced of its importance. The same may be said of a generation of post-revisionist historians who have tried to reconceptualize the French Revolution since the meltdown of the Marxist paradigm. In the conceptual framework constructed by historians to explain the French Revolution, the public has assumed an importance comparable to the bourgeois category in the Marxist scheme. Ironically, the work that was instrumental in formulating the concept of the public, Jürgen Habermas's *The Structural Transformation of the Public Sphere*, rested on Marxist foundations and gave prominence to the bourgeois category that was a central component of the Marxist conceptual scheme. For Habermas the public sphere was a bourgeois public sphere, a feature that made it compatible with the Marxist system. Giving primacy to economics and class conflict in their theory of history, Marxists saw the rising bourgeoisie as a dynamic force of change during the early modern period and they saw it as a driving force behind the French Revolution.[1] Among the works that contributed to a weakening of the Marxist theory of the Revolution was a 1967 article published by George V. Taylor, when the struggle between Marxists and revisionists was in full swing; it traced the flow of bourgeois capital at the end of the eighteenth century into the time-honored channels of offices, land, and aristocratic marital alliances.[2] If Taylor's analysis undercut the idea of a rising bourgeoisie tearing down the ancien régime to make the world safe for capitalism, it also devalued economics as the main determinant in the behavior of the group he studied. Status was at the core of the value system of a bourgeoisie that continued to fit into the ancient régime social order; culture prevailed over economics.

Habermas's pioneering study appeared in 1962, two years before the publication of Alfred Cobban's *The Social Interpretation of the French Revolution*, the first major blow aimed at the Marxist interpretation of the Revolution.[3] Cobban criticized the categories that were an integral part of the Orthodox Marxist scheme and suggested others that he felt fit more closely with actual change in eighteenth-century France, as he understood it. Some of Cobban's categories have proven useful to historians, some have not, but it was not his intention to replace one framework with another; essentially *The Social Interpretation of the French Revolution* was a work of demolition, not one of synthesis, as indicated by its call for detailed research on which more solid structures could be built. That Cobban focused so closely on categories, and offered some of his own, would suggest that he recognized the importance of a conceptual scheme to explain the French Revolution. At no point did he mention the category of the public, or public sphere, that Habermas articulated in his landmark work. Cobban did not refer to Habermas's *Structural Transformation*, and there is no indication that he had read it when he published his *Social Interpretation*. A conceptual scheme that gives prominence to the public and has been taken up by post-revisionist historians of the French Revolution can be traced back to a work that not only preceded the assault on the Marxist interpretation, but also rested in some measure on Marxian premises.

The dissolution of the Marxist paradigm took place when historians came to feel that it was at variance with the changes it purported to explain. Having concluded that the Revolution was not a collision between a rising bourgeoisie and the feudal monarchy, historians had to relocate the lines of conflict, and in doing so Habermas's public, or public sphere, was rich in interpretive possibilities. For Habermas a public sphere emerged out of a new space formed by the bourgeois family and out of a literate stratum of informed readers that learned to think independently and critically. This sphere was autonomous and separate from the monarchical state.

Habermas's *Structural Transformation* did not have an immediate impact on French Revolution historiography. Only as revisionist historians did battle with Marxist historians and dismantled their categories did Habermas's public sphere become a prominent analytical tool for post-revisionist historians. One might say that with the adoption of the Habermas public sphere model, French Revolution historiography shifted from a revisionist to a post-revisionist stage. Keith Michael Baker was one of the key figures in this shift in a series of papers written in the 1980s, by which time revisionists had for the most part rejected the bourgeois category as an analytical tool to explain the French Revolution.[4] When Baker adopted the Habermas public sphere model, he also adapted it to the current thinking among historians about the Revolution. The public sphere that figured so prominently in his analytic scheme was shorn of its bourgeois component; in effect, it was de-marxified. For Baker what was important about the public sphere was that it was an autonomous space separate from the state, and within which there were discourses that were part of an ongoing power struggle in the politics of contestation in eighteenth-century France. Baker argued that discourses within the public sphere made the Revolution a conceptual possibility, and by tracking those discourses he was able, as an historian, to construct, or invent, the French Revolution.

Baker constructed three ancien régime discourses: one of will, with Jean-Jacques Rousseau as its leading proponent, one of reason, with Anne-Robert-Jacques Turgot baron de l'Aulne as the principal voice; and one of justice, with Louis-Adrien Le Paige, a highly influential Jansenist lawyer, and a parlement polemicist, as advocate. The first three months of the Revolution, for Baker, became an epic struggle between these discourses, with September 11 as the crucial moment when the National Assembly opted for a suspensive veto, in effect affirming the notion of popular sovereignty. This represented a victory for the Rousseauist discourse of will over the rival discourses, and it crystallized the Revolution in a form it would retain through the Reign of Terror.

Other historians, most notably François Furet and Marcel Gauchet, also employed discourse analysis to explain the French Revolution.[5] As illuminating as the studies of these historians were, it is

possible, at this remove, to examine them critically, as Robert Darnton
has in *The Forbidden Best-Sellers of Pre-Revolutionary France* (1995).
According to Robert Darnton, "By imposing a discursive model on the
flow of events," these historians "left no room for contingency, accident, and the revolutionary process itself." Darnton argued that the
Revolution was not an abstract process but was driven by events that
produced unintended consequences; it "became increasingly radical in
response to events that occurred after 1789: religious schism, war,
counter-revolutionary uprisings, pressure from the Parisian Sections,
and economic disaster.[6] An additional criticism that Darnton might
have made was the type of revolution Baker invented using September
11 as the defining event in his discursive model.

    According to that model, the decisive change took place within the
legislature. The fact is that however the debate between Rousseauists
and Montesquieuists turned out in the legislature, the members of that
body were not free, as time would tell, to act independently. As important as September 11 was as a moment of crystallization, one could
argue that the Paris Insurrection of July 12–14 was the decisive event
of the 1789 Revolution. The Paris uprising not only saved the Revolution, but also cast it in a form that had profound influence on the
Rousseauist legislature. Moreover, the Paris uprising was followed by
the *journées* of October 5–6, when some twenty thousand Parisians,
mostly women, compelled the King and Queen to take up residence in
Paris, where they were soon joined by a legislature that was never free
from popular pressure. As Darnton stated, it was not discourses that
determined the direction the Revolution would take, and the problems
it would encounter, but the real struggles and conflicts carried out by
real people. Yet, when arguing against the discourse analysis historians, Darnton directed attention to the "events that occurred after
1789"; he did not examine the Paris uprising of July 12–14 and the insurrection of October 5–6.

    Why, one might ask, did Darnton, who emphasized the real events
of the Revolution that lay beneath the abstract analyses of the discourse historians, overlook the crucial role of the people of Paris in
1789? Perhaps the answer to this question lies in the central thesis of
his book. For Darnton, public opinion was the key to the Revolution,
and the public opinion model he constructed encompassed everyone,
from the highest nobility to people in the street, from Versailles to
Paris taverns, and as such it explained the complete collapse of monarchy in 1789.[7] Nobles, bourgeois, and ordinary people, those of all stations, were no longer loyal to monarchy, and together they brought
down the curtain on the ancien régime. Public opinion was more important than the public sphere in Darnton's conceptual scheme; more-

over, he was critical of Habermas's bourgeois public sphere category: "Since 1962, when Habermas originally published his thesis, historians have generally abandoned the notion of a rising bourgeoisie as an explanation of the French Revolution. Why should they adopt the rise of the 'bourgeois public sphere' in its place?"[8] Darnton explained that while there was no "bourgeois public sphere," there was a grouping that was socially heterogeneous but culturally homogeneous, a convergent elite that became the dominant political force in the nineteenth century, the Notables.

The origins of that grouping are to be found in the eighteenth-century public. How that group came together is one of the most important problems for the historian of ancien régime France; there is clearly a place in revolutionary historiography for the public as a theoretical construct. Yet for that model to achieve full effectiveness for historians seeking a conceptual framework for the Revolution, it should be complemented by one that is based on the populace.

In the second of the quotes at the head of this chapter Habermas relates "Our investigation is limited to the *liberal* model of the bourgeois public sphere," and that it "leaves aside the *plebeian* public sphere as a variant that in a sense was suppressed in the historical process." Arlette Farge has reasoned that if a plebeian public sphere was suppressed, it must, by definition, have existed, and in *Subversive Words: Public Opinion in Eighteenth-Century France*, she has attempted to articulate a popular public sphere.[9] Through diaries, news sheets, chroniclers, police records, illegal pamphlets, and Bastille records, Farge has tried to fill in an historical void, to formulate a popular public sphere that Habermas maintained had been suppressed. What makes Farge's popular public sphere a useful analytical tool is that it lays bare the most important division within ancien régime society, which was between those who did and did not work with their hands. Farge's popular public sphere is a theoretical construct derived from her reading of the materials she has examined; those materials tell us what this diarist or that journalist said about ordinary people; what transgressions led to their imprisonment; or what police spies heard them say in the streets or taverns of Paris. Farge's materials do not contain the actual voices of the people; rather, they are a record of what officials who served the state or writers who belonged to the public sphere thought and said about ordinary Parisians.[10] The materials Farge has used capture with much accuracy and a wealth of detail a mounting restlessness within the populace, disrespect for the king, and a spirit of insubordination that made the authorities uneasy. In fact, what Farge reveals is not only a popular sphere that was removed from the public sphere but public and official fear of the populace.

Antoine Furetiére's *Dictionnaire universel* (1690) said: "The *peuple* is *peuple* everywhere, that is, stupid, turbulent, eager for novelties. He is from the dregs of the *peuple*. The little *peuple*, the mean *peuple*, the common *peuple*, is cunning and seditious."[11] Abbé Coyer, writing in 1755, was well aware of a devaluation of the people that was codified in the *Dictionnaire universel*: "The people was at one time the most useful, the most virtuous and consequently most respectable part of a nation. It was composed of farmers, artisans, merchants, financiers, men of letters and men of law."[12] As Coyer understood, those with social pretensions had—over time—withdrawn from the people and merged with what came to be regarded as polite society. This included men of letters who, according to Coyer, separated themselves, "in the manner of Horace," from the people. It was, of course, in Renaissance Italy that men of letters—humanists—first emulated Horace and other Roman authors whose works they admired and whose values and social attitudes they absorbed. This included contempt for plebeians. As F. R. Cowell wrote: "Despite the fine sentiments he was fond of uttering about the dignity and brotherhood of mankind, Cicero, the most urbane of men (to use a favorite word of his own invention), in his more intimate and candid moments called the masses the scum of the earth."[13] The Roman world was dominated by a narrow elite that regarded the considerable emoluments of offices they held as theirs by natural right. In their largesse they provided cheap food and entertainments to the masses, which Cicero regarded as a "wretched starveling mob, the bloodsucker of the Treasury."[14] The Graeco-Roman elite was a "wellborn" few that according to Peter Brown was educated in a system designed to establish social distance between them and the uncultivated society of their inferiors. In screened-off classrooms boys were absorbed into a peer group of those with similar status. "A literary education was considered part of a more intimate and exacting process of moral grooming. It was firmly believed that the meticulous internalization of the literary classics went hand in hand with a process of moral formation: correct forms of verbal interchange manifested the upper-class citizen's ability to enter into the correct form of interpersonal relations among his peers in the city. A studied control of deportment, quite as much as of language, was the mark of the wellborn on the public stage."[15]

The role of Renaissance humanism in the shaping of elite values and attitudes in early modern Europe has not received the attention it deserves. As humanists retrieved the classical legacy, they restored the elevated social perspective of the elite that was an integral part of that legacy. By the time the classical legacy was assimilated, a social wall arose throughout Europe separating the elite from the unwashed and crude people. Two Italian writers, Niccolò Machiavelli and Baldesar Castiglione, exposed the mind-set of an elite whose norms and models came out of the classical past. Machiavelli was not a humanist in the strict sense of the word, but he was steeped in the thought of antiquity and he drew repeatedly from classical texts in his political writings. He expressed scorn for the multitude in *The Prince* when he said "the masses (*vulgo*) are always impressed by the superficial appearance of things . . . and the world consists of nothing but the masses."[16] That Machiavelli used the word *vulgo* rather than *popolo* is noteworthy; it was a way to drive home the point that the people were vulgar. Once a powerful force in Italian politics, the *popolo* had undergone an internal change during the Renaissance that left it very different from what it had been at the end of the thirteenth century.[17] Merchants and financiers that had been part of the *popolo* fused with the *grandi*, forming a cultured patriciate that was removed from a truncated and devalued *popolo*.

Baldesar Castiglione, a contemporary of Machiavelli, offers a unique picture of the dynamics of social differentiation in Renaissance Italy in *Il Cortegiano* (1528). Written in dialogue form, *Il Cortegiano* is presented as a series of conversations at the court of Urbino in the early sixteenth century. In one conversation Signor Gaspar Pallavicino relates that in his Lombard country "we do not stand on ceremony. On the contrary, there are many young gentlemen who, on festive occasions, dance all day in the sun with peasants, and play with them at throwing the bar, wrestling, running, and jumping."[18] Federico Fregoso considers mixing with peasants in this way undignified, and as a general rule he recommends "shunning the crowd, especially the ignoble crowd."[19] Throughout *Il Cortegiano* advice is offered on the cultivation of proper behavior that marked one as refined, polished, and polite. This includes advice on dancing, horsemanship, musical performance, exercising, the art of conversation, and the correct use of language. One courtier, aware of how the Italian language had changed, states, "among wellborn men versed in the usages of courts, in arms, and in letters, a concern arose to speak and write more elegantly than in that first rude and uncultivated age when the fires of calamity set by the barbarians were not yet extinguished."[20] Proper use of language requires the elimination of low and common words that "have remained with the peasants, and are rejected by [the polite] as words that have been corrupted and spoiled by age."[21] That Castiglione's *Il Cortegiano* was translated into French and other European languages and appeared in many editions in the sixteenth and seventeenth centuries is one index of its importance. Another is that in the course of the seventeenth century it was absorbed into courtier's books, etiquette books, treatises on civility, novels, plays, and the actual social life of the polite world.

"A slow, powerful and deep-seated movement seems gradually to have twisted and transformed the societies of the Mediterranean between 1560 and 1600. It was a lengthy and painful metamorphosis. The general and growing malaise was not translated into open insurrection; but it nevertheless modified the entire social landscape. This was an upheaval of unquestionably social character," Fernand Braudel wrote. The bourgeoisie not only withdrew from the people but also strove to enter the higher world of the nobility. A once resilient society that sanctioned contact between the high and the low and offered spaces and ceremonies for interplay between people of all stations became more rigid and aware of group differences. If a cultured elite despised the common herd, the people undoubtedly resented the privileges of the few and the contempt toward themselves of their betters. "There can be no doubt," Braudel continued, "that society was tending to polarize into, on the one hand, a rich and vigorous nobility reconstituted into powerful dynasties owning vast properties and, on the other, the great and growing mass of the poor and disinherited, 'caterpillars and grubs', human insects, alas too many. A deep fissure split open traditional society, opening up gulfs that nothing would ever bridge . . . "[22]

Braudel wrote: "There was no real sophistication of eating habits in Europe before the fifteenth or sixteenth centuries."[23] Predictably, it was in Italy that fine culinary tastes appeared first. They then spread, along with other cultivated social forms, to France and elsewhere in what Norbert Elias, in his magisterial study of the modern system of manners, has called the "civilizing process."[24] Manners were a device by which refined people separated themselves from the low, the coarse, and the commonplace, ultimately from a crude and vulgar populace. Out of the civilizing process came a polished elite that observed proper forms of behavior, cultivated exquisite culinary tastes, followed the latest fashions in literature and the arts, and spoke a purified language from which colloquialisms and low, ordinary words, the vocabulary of the street, had been purged. If one impetus behind the civilizing process was self perfection, an aesthetic goal, another was disdain for a crude populace that by the end of the seventeenth century was beyond the civilized pale. Furetière's 1690 definition of the word *peuple* codifies this state of mind.

Elite attitudes to the people that took shape in the seventeenth century, as indicated by Furetière's 1690 definition, carried over to civilized members of the eighteenth-century public. Voltaire called the people fanatic, inconstant, and "a ferocious and blind monster" in the *Henriade* (1717–21),[25] and he wrote in *Le Christianisme dévoilé* (1767) that "the people neither read nor reason. They have neither the leisure nor the capacity to do so. Books are made only for that portion of a nation which its circumstances, its education and its feelings raise above crime."[26] Voltaire felt the "fickle, riotous, misguided people" should not exercise political power.[27] Denis Diderot wrote that superstition was declining, but only among the enlightened. The people was "too idiotic—*bête*—too miserable," and too busy with ordinary matters to shake free from its dumb habits of mind.[28] The Baron Paul-Henri-Dietrich d'Holbach associated the people with crime and "shocking excesses," and felt they were such a destructive force they should not have a political voice: "A multitude knows no moderation."[29] The Abbé de Morellet, an habitué of the salon of Mme Marie-Thérèse Geoffrin and a regular at evenings held by the Helvétiuses, baron d'Holbach, and the Neckers, disdained *le peuple* and believed that "a multitude without learning, without education, without morality, without property," should not participate in politics.[30] Even Rousseau, the "great democrat," as Peter Gay describes him, despised the *canaille* (riffraff) and scorned the multitude. Their condition was one of "ignorance and torpidity," and in politics they were not to be trusted.[31] "Wise men, if they try to speak their language to the common herd instead of its own, cannot possibly make themselves understood. There are a thousand kinds of ideas, which it is impossible to translate into popular language. Conceptions that are too remote are equally out of its range."[32] Rousseau would not give power to the populace. Nor did the philosophes regard the people as a constructive force in antiquity, to which they frequently turned for political wisdom—and lessons.

Baron de La Bréde et de Montesquieu, in his *Considérations sur les causes de la grandeur des romains et leur décadence*, regarded the senatorial party in Republican Rome as one of moderation and the popular party as one of jealousy, envy, and bloodthirstiness. It was the people in early Republican days who craved war, and it was when leaders curried popular favor that Rome's decline began. This was the accepted wisdom of the time. Most philosophes would have had some variant of the senatorial order—progressive, enlightened, judicious, responsible, and dedicated to the commonweal—serve, advise, and correct those who ruled. Baron Anne-Robert-Jacques de Turgot, the key figure in the reform movement at the beginning of Louis XVI's reign, was such a person. Determined to sweep away the dead wood of the past and open the doors of change, Turgot was a member of the eighteenth-century elite in his attitudes to the people. He wrote that the people, hardened by misery, were "almost indifferent to life" and approached death "without emotion. No matter what is said, the sentiments of nature are much less alive among it than among men of a higher station."[33]

Marie-Jean-Antoine-Nicolas Caritat, marquis de Condorcet, mathe-
matician, scientist, and apostle of progress, shared Turgot's view of the
people. He wrote that a spirit of compassion was beyond the capacity
of someone occupied with base work; material conditions among laborers resulted in a "habit of callousness [that] produces [a] penchant
for violence."[34]

Between the men cited above—Voltaire, Diderot, d'Holbach, Morellet, Rousseau, Turgot, and Condorcet—there were major differences
of outlook, attitude, and opinion on a wide range of issues. They fought
bitterly amongst themselves and aired their differences publicly. One
of them, Turgot, was not part of the eighteenth-century public according to the Habermas construct: as an official under Louis XV and Louis
XVI, he was a servant of the state that was removed from the public
sphere. In fact, reforming officials in state service were as forward
looking, progressive, liberal, and enlightened as philosophes who
presided over the Republic of Letters. Reformers in state service such
as Turgot moved in polite society, had ties with salons, and broadly
speaking were part of the educated public. There was a division between monarchy and the eighteenth-century public, but it was far from
absolute. Those on both sides of the divide inhabited a mental landscape with many shared contours.[35] All were part of a cultural bloc
that was separate from the populace.

But the public, or public sphere, is not just a cultural bloc. If that
were the case, the term elite, or educated elite, could be used to identify
the group. Differences between seventeenth and eighteenth-century
salons highlight a structure of change within the French elite that un-
derlay the formation of the eighteenth-century public.

The first of the great Paris salons was that of Marquise Mme de
Rambouillet, who left the court in 1607 and soon thereafter began
weekly gathering in her *chambre bleue* that lasted until the 1660s and
spawned similar groups that also met in Paris and contributed to the
rule of good manners.[36] Mme de Rambouillet was born in Rome and
her mother descended from a distinguished noble family. Jean Reg-
nault de Segrais, a member of Mme de Rambouillet's salon, wrote that
she was "mild, kind, gracious, and had an equitable and just mind. It
was she who corrected the ill-natured customs that had prevailed. She
formed her mind reading the right Italian and Spanish books and
taught politeness to all those of her time who frequented her gatherings."[37] Mme de Rambouillet offered a setting for polite conversation
and refined social behavior, she brought together nobles and non-
nobles who, in spite of differences of birth, shared common pursuits,
and she presided over a circle that achieved cultural leadership to an
extent that the duc de Richelieu found bothersome. The exquisite

ideals of the seventeenth-century salon were far removed from the democratic sociability that took shape in the evolved milieu of the eighteen-century salon that became a mainstay of the Republic of Letters and was an integral part of the public sphere.

For Dena Goodman, the Republic of Letters played a key role in the formation of the eighteenth-century public sphere.[38] Rising up within the monarchical state, the Republic of Letters saw itself as universal, liberal, and progressive; unlike the Academy, it has no ties to the state but was independent and autonomous. At the same time, it had its own base, the salon, within which conversation was open, free, and egalitarian in the sense that ideas counted for more than birth or pedigree. Eighteenth-century salon conversation was more than brilliant repartee; it doubted, probed, criticized, and called everything into question. Philosophes became ornaments and fixtures in the salons, particularly after 1750, giving them a heightened sense of their importance. As philosophes entered the salons the ground rules of this civilized world changed; meetings took place not in the evening but at 1:00 P.M., and the serious and independent exchange of ideas replaced polite parlor games. Within the autonomous space of the salon, there was not only a probing and critical spirit but a democratic sociability. Yet, this was a highly exclusive, sophisticated, and cultured sphere, far removed from the populace. The salon was an integral part of the public sphere, separate from the monarchical court and at the same time cut off from what Habermas called the "plebeian sphere."

The salons that Voltaire frequented as a young man were centers of politeness and literary interest, and as such they looked back to their seventeenth-century predecessors. The literary ambitions of young Voltaire were synchronous with the ideals of the salon world at the end of Louis XIV's reign, and during the Regency, but by the time he returned to Paris in 1729, after three years of enforced exile, Voltaire had become a *philosophe*. He had read John Locke even before going to England, but being in England enlarged his outlook and was instrumental in his conversion from a versifier, whose ambition was to establish a literary reputation, to an embattled *philosophe* who took up public causes. Writing in 1750, Voltaire said the French nation, "having had enough of verse, tragedies, comedies, operas, romances . . . and theological debates and convulsions turned at last to discoursing on corn . . . useful things were written on the subject of agriculture; everyone read them save for the farmers."[39] If the ironic tone was typical of Voltaire, the observation was serious, and it expressed not only a personal change within Voltaire but also within the educated public. It was change that took place within what one might call a "public sphere."

Mona Ozouf wrote that the word public "carried a polemical charge," particularly in the second half of the eighteenth century.[40] For David A. Bell an oppositional public began during the 1720s, when the parlements collided with the monarchy over a crisis that resulted from the bull *Unigenitus.* [41] Combating that bull, Jansenist barristers appealed to a "public" that was composed of "citizens." The collisions of the 1720s were followed by others, with religion continuing to define lines of conflict, but in ways that had consequences far beyond the contested issues. In the conflicts of the 1720s, the parlements claimed to be the representatives of an ancient *curia regis*, and as such protectors of the fundamental laws of the kingdom. This changed in the 1750s, when the parlements, drawing from the ideas of Montesquieu, redefined themselves as a *corps intermédiares* between the king and people. A leading voice of the parlementary cause, Montesquieu maintained in *L'Esprit des lois* (1748) that monarchy was corrupt when a prince deprived his subjects of their "hereditary employments [*fonctions naturelles*] and gives them arbitrarily to others." Once monarchy became despotic it was by definition corrupt; the "principle of despotic government is ceaselessly corrupt, because it is corrupt by its very nature."[42] One of the most influential books of the French Enlightenment, Montesquiru's *L'Esprit des lois* enunciated principles that gave the high moral ground to the parlements in conflicts with monarchy in the second half of the eighteenth century. In the struggle against "despotism," the parlements engaged in a publicity campaign to defend the rights of the people against the demands of the monarchical state. Protesting against the "continual encroachments by the clergy on the temporal power," the parlements sold over twenty-thousand copies of the Grand Remonstrances of 1753 in less than a week in its struggle against the Church, with which the monarchy was allied. Out of parlementary remonstrances came a flow of ideas that helped shape public opinion and contributed to an oppositional public sphere. The Parlement of Rouen stated in 1760: "It is the essence of a law to be accepted. The right of acceptance is the right of the nation." In 1763, the Parlement of Toulouse announced that the law depended on "the free consent of the nation." The Parlement of Rouen declared in 1771 that fundamental laws were "the expression of the general will," and in 1788 the Parlement of Rennes proclaimed that "man is born free, that originally men are equal," and, "One of the first conditions of society is that particular wills should always yield to the general will."[43]

That the language of Rousseau found its way into parlementary remonstrances is part of a larger structure of change in the forging of an oppositional public sphere. One might say that a *parlementaire* discourse was superseded by a Rousseauist discourse. To understand

Rousseau's influence on the public sphere it is necessary to look be-yond the direct impact of his writings on the audiences he addressed. A series of crises in the last several decades of the ancien régime created fierce debate, and it was into that debate that the ideas of Rousseau were introduced. Of these crises the most important was the "Mau-peou Revolution," as Durand Echeverria has called it, of 1770–1774.[44] The destruction of the parlements, and the creation of a new judicial system at the end of Louis XV's reign, was countered by an outpouring of oppositional pamphlets. The *patriotes*, who opposed the Maupeou courts, took their case to the court of public opinion in a publicity campaign that denounced the despotism of the Maupeou ministry. The 167 publications that appeared between 1770–1774 stirred public dis-cussion and contributed to the political education of the nation. The Comte Graf Florimund Mercy d'Argenteau wrote Maria Theresa, "Now that everyone has become thoroughly revolted by all that is hap-pening, the public is unrestrained in its discussion. Political questions have become almost the only topics of conversation at the Court, in society, in the city, and indeed in all the kingdom."[45] Pierre Victor, Baron de Besenval de Bronstadt, wrote in his *Mémoires* that "the [Mau-peou] edict caused the greatest sort of ferment . . . . In conversations and at supper parties no one talked of anything else. These social gath-erings became miniature States General . . ."[46] Montesquieu provided the *patriotes* with much of their vocabulary, but radical *patriotes* were drawn to Rousseau and invoked his ideas in the anti-Maupeou campaign. Among the tenets of *patriote* constitutionalism were three Rousseauist propositions: sovereignty of the Nation, a national gen-eral will, and a contract between the nation and the people. Nineteen years before the 1789 Revolution *patriotes* called themselves "citi-zens," meaning that they saw themselves as members of a sovereign nation. Liberal and dedicated to liberty, *patriote* constitutionalism was not egalitarian. Anti-Maupeou polemicists used the word people theoretically; people who worked with their hands were outside their concept of the political nation. G. J. B. Target, one of the more vocal anti-Maupeou polemicists, wrote, "I should like to see only one na-tion, one family of brothers who have essentially the same interests and the same rights—the interests and rights to preserve what we hold in common: as men, our lives and our liberty; as citizens, our honor, our estates, and our properties, and as subjects, our government and our prince."[47] Jacques-Claude Martin de Mariveaux, another anti-Maupeou polemicist, wrote, "Laws . . . are acts of the general will. . . . The legislative power belongs to the people. . . . The effective will of the prince or the magistrate is or should be simply the general will, that is, the law."[48]

It has often been noted that the *Social Contract* was not widely read before the Revolution. Nonetheless, Rousseau's ideas in that work did enter into public discourse in the last several decades of the ancien régime; they did so during the publicity campaign that resulted from the Maupeou Revolution and in political exchanges that continued down to the crisis of 1787–1789. Within those exchanges the monarchy was set apart rhetorically from an oppositional public that embraced ideas that were congruent with those of Rousseau's *Social Contract*.

The Rousseauist discourse that undermined monarchy was paralleled by an underground *libelliste* discourse that passed through different channels. Among the categories of illicit literature that Robert Darnton studied in *The Forbidden Best-Sellers of Pre-Revolutionary France* were pornographic novels that portrayed the world of high society, and the court in particular, as corrupt and depraved. The 1775 *Anecdotes sur Mme la comtesse du Barry*, probably by Matthieu-François Pidansat de Mairobert, was written as if it were a true history scrupulously compiled after exacting research. It purported to give a candid, accurate account of a prostitute who became the king's *maîtresse en titre* at the time of the Maupeou Revolution, and who supported the King's "despotic" minister. According to Darnton, best-selling forbidden novels of this type, along with an outpouring of *libelles* that flooded Paris and France in the last several decades of the ancien régime, helped destabilize and delegitimize monarchy.

The negative image of high society projected by the *libellistes* was confirmed in real life by a succession of highly publicized scandals at the end of the ancien régime.[49] Of these scandals, the most spectacular was the 1785 Affair of the Necklace, in which Marie-Antoinette, though innocent, was found guilty in the court of public opinion. That verdict was rendered in what one might call the full court of public opinion. Yet, within the court of public opinion there was a higher court and a lower court. The higher court was that of the eighteenth-century public, the lower court was that of the populace. In a discussion of public opinion, Roger Chartier makes a clear distinction between the public and the populace. "Lexical contrasts show this particularly forcefully: Condorcet contrasted 'opinion' with 'populace'; Marmontel opposed 'the opinion of men of letters' and 'the opinion of the multitude'; d'Alembert spoke of 'the truly enlightened public' and 'the blind and noisy multitude'; Condorcet, again, set 'the opinion of enlightened people which precedes public opinion and ends up by dictating to it' against 'the popular opinions'." Continuing his analysis, Chartier writes: "Public opinion, set up as a sovereign authority and a final arbiter, was necessarily stable, unified, and founded on reason. The universality of its judgments and the constraining self-evidence of its decrees derived from that unvarying, dispassionate constancy. It was the reverse of popular opinion, which was multiple, versatile, and inhabited by prejudice and passion."[50]

The value of Chartier's analysis of public opinion lies in its retaining the division between the educated elite and the people, which has disappeared from Robert Darnton's public opinion model. Of course, Darnton recognizes that public opinion was anything but monolithic, and that its internal rifts and divisions reflected the highly differentiated groups contained within the communication circuit. Drawing from reader response theory, he explains that individuals place information within their own schemes, and as a cultural historian he understands full well how differently people at opposite ends of the ancien régime social spectrum processed information.

However, even that did not affect the main thrust of his argument, which he drives home in the final chapter of *The Forbidden Best Sellers*, "Public Opinion." By the end of the ancien régime, monarchy had lost the support of the people of France. The regime stood condemned because it lost the final round in the long struggle to control public opinion; it lost legitimacy among people of all stations. All conspired in the overthrow of a discredited regime. But if public opinion condemned monarchy in 1789 it did so by stages, in two episodes, one in June, at Versailles, the other in July, in Paris. The public spoke with one voice and the populace with a different voice in 1789, and while they agreed on the overthrow of the ancien régime they did not agree, as time would tell, on other issues.

PART ONE

Jean-Louis Prieur, the Populace, and Images of the French Revolution

Chapter 1

The Paris Insurrection

A riot that would turn into an uprising is morally impossible [in Paris].
The surveillance of the police, regiments of Swiss and French guards,
billeted [close by] and everywhere ready to march, the King's bodyguard, the fortresses that surround Paris, without even considering the
immense number of men attached by interest to the court, all these
factors together make the chances of a serious revolt most unlikely.
> —*Louis-Sébastien Mercier. Le Tableau de Paris, 1783.*

To arms! to arms! . . . Yes, it is I who call my brothers to freedom.
> —*Camille Desmoulins, speech of July 12, 1789*
> *at the Palais-Royal.*

Kiss papa! Kiss papa!
> —*Chant of the crowd on July 22, 1789 as the head of Foulon*
> *is held on a pike before his son-in-law, Bertier de Sauvigny.*

The first of the passages quoted above, from Louis-Sébastien
Mercier's *Le Tableau de Paris*, maintained that rioting in the streets
of Paris was a "moral impossibility." Yet, as Mercier reflected further, he
decided that if the people of Paris were caught up in the frenzy of riot the
results could be explosive. "Once the people of Paris are freed of restraint, once they are no longer held back by the police, foot or mounted,
and are no longer under the scrutiny of the *commissaire*, they would recognize no measure in their disorder. The populace, released from its ac-
customed control, would be all the more cruel because they would not

know when to stop." The occasion for Mercier's ruminations on rioting was the Gordon Riots in London, an explosion of urban violence in 1780 that lasted a week and during which much of the city was in the hands of a mob that burned and pillaged. "Any attempt at sedition [in Paris] would be known and snuffed out. . . . The sedition led by Lord Gordon in London is unimaginable to Parisians." Mercier felt that in Paris the forces of order held the people in check: "If the Parisian, in a moment of excitement, were to riot, he would soon find himself inside the immense cage in which he lives, refused bread, and when he no longer had anything to eat he would immediately plead misery and beg to be pardoned."[1]

The Paris Insurrection of July 12–14, 1789 showed how right and how wrong Mercier was in his discussion of riots. He was wrong in his prediction that riots such as those that convulsed London in 1780 could not happen in Paris, but he was all too accurate in his observation that should rioting take place it could be attended by cruelty. As someone who walked the streets of Paris, from commodious sections in the west to the dense and crowded inner city in the center of the capital to artisan sections in the east, Mercier was keenly aware of material and cultural differences among Parisians. He was struck by the poverty and callousness he encountered in the working-class sections of Paris, and by the contrast between those sections and the polite neighborhoods inhabited by the affluent. "There is more money in a single house of the faubourg Saint-Honoré than in the entire faubourg Saint-Marcel or Saint-Marceau," Mercier wrote. Equally telling is his comment that "Sedition and rebellion have their origins concealed in this place of obscure misery." The inhabitants of these districts, he continued, "wander, taking their miserable possessions from refuge to refuge. One sees no shoes in their lodgings; one hears only the sound of wooden clogs in the stairs. The children are naked and sleep helter-skelter." Entire families occupied a single room, beds had no covers, and kitchen utensils were piled up with chamber pots. The smells and noise of these people was unbearable: "A frightening and confused noise, a foul odor, everything keeps you from this horribly crowded place, where the populace, engaged in pleasures suitable for it, drinks a wine as disagreeable as everything else." In a telling remark Mercier said the people of the faubourg Saint-Marcel "have no connection with the Parisians."[2] Many had recently arrived in the capital and taken up residence in working-class sections, hungry, penniless, desperate, subject to laws designed to regulate them and keep them under control. Tensions were inherent in the very circumstances under which people lived in the working-class sections of Paris, and as an observer of that scene Mercier saw within it a capacity for violence.

Paris in 1700 encompassed some 1,000 hectares but in 1790, after a period of unprecedented growth, it had expanded to some 3,400 hectares.[3] The expansion took place principally in two stages, from 1700 to 1730, and from 1760 to 1790. Military expenditures between 1730 and 1760 would seem to have been a brake on urban growth, but from the end of the Seven Years' War to the Revolution expansion moved ahead, in spite of official efforts to stem the tide of growth. If the city of Paris pushed outward in all directions, the growth was not contiguous but followed a patchwork pattern of developed areas interspersed by open spaces. In the west of Paris there were open, agreeable spaces in the midst of fine *hôtels* and mansions, but at the opposite end of the city, in the eastern, working-class suburbs, tenements rose up in the midst of fields or semi-rural patches of land. The greatest concentration of people, by far, was in the dense and crowded inner city, whose narrow and irregular streets continued to bear the stamp of a much earlier medieval city. Spacious quarters in the west of Paris, on both the left and right banks of the Seine, were inhabited by merchants, the professional classes, and members of the nobility, civilized members of an eighteenth-century public who lived in tasteful *hôtels* with inner courtyards that formed a private space set apart from the street.[4] The contrast between these quarters and artisan sections at the opposite end of Paris, such as the faubourg Saint-Antoine, whose boundaries were relentlessly extended to the east, could hardly have been more striking.

The French economy underwent major expansion in the eighteenth century. Foreign trade is said by some historians to have increased from 215 million livres in 1716 to 900 million livres in 1750, and by others to have quintupled by 1789.[5] Economic growth was greatest from 1764 to 1770, and continued for another five to eight years, after which there was a period of decline that lasted to the time of the Revolution.[6] Even during the period of expansion, it was those with property who derived the benefits, not those at the bottom of the socioeconomic order, small farmers and sharecroppers in the countryside and those dependent on wages in towns. Moreover, wages did not keep up with inflation: overall, wages rose 22 percent between 1730 and 1789 while prices rose 65 percent during the same period. The time of greatest hardship was from 1775 to 1790, when France was hit by periodic bad harvests, falling commodity prices, such as wine, and a general crisis in agricultural profits. What intensified the dislocation caused by economic contraction and the agrarian crisis was a population increase from some twenty million to twenty-eight million in the course of the eighteenth century. Rural France was barely able to feed the populace in the best of times, and the pressures of a rising population and the economic contraction of 1775–1790 created a crisis from which those who were most vulnerable found no escape.[7]

An impoverished rural population roamed the countryside, hungry, desperate, sometimes organized into gangs of lawless brigands.[8] Parts of that population moved to towns and cities, above all to Paris, into grim tenements without amenities or privacy. From 1750 to 1790, seven thousand to fourteen thousand migrants passed from rural France into Paris every year. Huddled together in working-class districts, this hungry and often desperate transient population was an ongoing problem for the authorities. As a rule, only one-third of those who ran afoul of the law were born in Paris; two-thirds were from a population of recently arrived transients. Similarly, 65 percent of those arrested for rebellion from 1785 to 1789 were also recently arrived transients. Workers, according to the observations of contemporaries, were often found in enclaves defined by their trade and place of origin, but whatever their place of origin, hardship was commonplace:

> [The watercarriers] are mostly from Auvergne, whence they return to the bosom of their families with a small accumulation of capital after twenty hard, frugal years. They gather together in large groups and rent large or small apartments or stalls in the quarters which they supply with water. Here they sleep at night ten to twenty at a time on straw or mattresses. The oldest man of the group is the advisor and judge, and they hold as strongly to the maintenance of decency and order among themselves as do the Savoyards.
>
> Some [streetporters] wander about the streets of Paris and look through garbage; others go to the promenades and to the livelier places and look for pins, hairpins and similar things [that may have been lost]; others look through the gutters in the middle of the streets to find pieces of iron or brass that may have fallen from horses, harnesses or carriages. So as not to dirty their hands and arms they use a long stick with which they rake through the puddles of water and can detect things as easily as snails can with their antennae. Others gather up in the markets leaves of cabbage, unripe vegetables and bits of straw and get money by selling this to people who keep rabbits, for example. These people never know, when they get up, what they will live on during the day, but comes evening they have eaten and drunk. Only in this city, amongst such a crowd of inhabitants, where everything is sold and must be paid for can people of this sort survive.[9]

Newcomers who arrived in Paris were struck by the filth and squalor. What Rousseau expected before his arrival was quite different from the reality of what he saw.

> How different was the sight of Paris from what I expected. . . . I had imagined a town as beautiful as it was large, with a most imposing aspect in-

cluding nothing but superb streets, palaces of marble and gold. Coming in through the Faubourg Saint-Marceau, I saw only dirty, stinking alleys, ugly black houses, an air of filth and poverty, beggars, carters, mending women. The cries of women selling their herb tea and old hats. I was so struck by all this at first that all the truly magnificent things I have since seen in Paris could not efface this first impression, and I have been left with a secret distate for life in this capital city . . .[10]

Visiting Paris in 1764 with his eight-year-old son, Leopold Mozart wrote:

You will hardly find any other city with so many miserable and mutilated persons. You have only to spend a minute in a church or walk along a few streets to meet some blind or lame or limping or half-putrefied beggar, or to find someone lying on the street who has had his hand eaten away as a child by the pigs, or someone else who in childhood fell into the fire and had half an arm burned off while the foster father and his family were working in the fields. And there are numbers of such people, whom disgust makes me refrain from looking at when I pass them.[11]

A German traveler who visited Paris in 1791 wrote the following description of the inner city:

The closer one gets to the center of the city the narrower and, therefore, the dirtier the streets become. Here are the Rues de la Pelleterie, de la Draperie, du Moulin, in which not a single sunbeam penetrates all year long . . . and if one set down a blindfolded foreigner in this network of mainly short, narrow, black, dirty streets and then took the blindfold off and let him guess where he was, it would be impossible for him to know that he was standing in the middle of the finest capital in the world, until he heard the ragpickers and beggarwomen around him addressing one another as Monsieur and Madame.[12]

Streets in the poorer sections of Paris were unpaved and had ditches running down their center for rain. Rubbish was collected but irregularly, and, adding to the stench, was urine and excrement from people and animals as well as rotten vegetables from food stalls and the blood of animals slaughtered in front of butchers' shops. The cries of street hawkers contributed to the coarse texture of the street. Out of the Paris population of 650,000, a disproportionate part lived in the medieval quarters of the ancient city, where there was an average of 900 to 1,000 persons per 2.5 acres. This made it one of the most densely populated urban spaces in eighteenth-century Europe. Paris was not rigidly separated into elite and working-class neighborhoods; there were sections where such a division was pronounced, but in older sections such as the Marais, the well-to-do lived alongside people who worked with their hands. Often they lived in the same buildings, those with incomes occupying the lower floors and those dependent on wages occupying the upper floors. Even when the public and the populace lived in the same section of Paris, and occupied the same buildings, they were separated by what one might call a "vertical principle," determined by where they lived in multiple-floor buildings. Also, the public and populace were horizontally separated, the former inhabiting fashionable quarters to the west of the city and the latter congregating in tenements at the opposite end of the capital.

Order was maintained in eighteenth-century Paris by a police of some fifteen hundred men.[13] The word *policer*, from which police is derived, is a clue to the mental world of those who exercised authority. *Policer* has two separate but related meanings: "To establish law and order," and "to civilize, to polish, to refine." The world *poli*, which means, "polite, civil, refined," also indicates order, and the civilized and polished social forms that are at the core of the word's meaning imply a carefully defined and ordered social life. The Paris police force, founded in 1667, was equated with civilization itself. Where there was police there was civil society; without it there was barbarism. Before 1750 the word police referred not to a group of men but to a set of functions. If there was no police force per se, there were people in authority who had to address a wide range of problems rooted in poverty. So severe was the problem of poverty that extraordinary measures were necessary, according to the wisdom of the authorities. The *Encyclopédie*, a good indicator of the public mind-set, maintained that people wanted comfort and order, and that achieving it was the responsibility of the police: ". . . a comfortable and tranquil life, despite the work of error and the disturbances of selfishness and passion."[14]

Beggars and vagabonds that poured into Paris threatened the tranquility that was essential to civil society; from the viewpoint of the authorities something had to be done. Out of that perceived need came two periods of repression, one from 1724 to 1733 and the other from 1768 to 1789. The decision was made to forbid begging and to institutionalize paupers unable to maintain themselves, people whose distress and physical presence the authorities found dismaying.[15] In the first period of incarceration, 1724–1733, paupers were placed in municipal hospitals, *hôpitaux*, and in the second, 1768–1789, they were put in workhouses, *dépots de mendicité*. A 1724 royal declaration declared that "public order and the general good in our Realm" required "severe" measures to deal with the problem of "criminal idleness." Programs to address the related problems of mendicity, begging, and criminality were not successful; ultimately there were more beggars and vagrants to be confined than there were facilities to accommodate them. Moreover, the authorities found it easier to confine the docile poor than willful idlers and criminals who often remained at large. One thing the government's efforts seem to have achieved was increasing public awareness of the poor and the problems they posed to civil society.

The Paris police was not a commanding presence in the capital. Fifteen hundred men in a city of six hundred and fifty thousand was hardly enough to maintain order by means of force, but that was not the objective. The police did not carry arms. Control was maintained by surveillance more than coercion, the principal instrument being a highly developed system of spies who reported to inspectors, of which there were twenty, each responsible for a district. By the end of the eighteenth century, this system was so efficient that it was admired outside France. Another measure, adopted in 1781, that furthered control of the populace was requiring workers to obtain passbooks—*livrets*—to get work. As effective as the police were in maintaining order in eighteenth-century Paris, fifteen hundred men, augmented by one hundred and fifty watchmen, were not enough to put down a major uprising. Additional forces were also at hand should they be needed, perhaps the most important being the regiment of *gardes-françaises*, three thousand six hundred professional soldiers that were part of the Royal Household and stationed in Paris; however, they were not on permanent military duty. In addition to the *gardes-françaises*, there were Swiss guards stationed at Versailles as well as other units stationed outside Paris that could be summoned to the capital if necessary. For major uprisings foreign mercenaries were deemed indispensable, as the authorities feared French units would side with the people. This included the *gardes-françaises*, soldiers who had served in other units, and when stationed in Paris were put on reduced wages which required them to find additional employment as cobblers, tailors, upholsterers, and the like. Many were married and had families; living amid the local population, they formed roots in the districts in which they were housed. Some of the *gardes-françaises* were older but many were young and from provincial towns, particularly in the north, such as Amiens, Caen, and Lille. Lowly paid and often dependent on wives who supported them, conditions among the *gardes* were ripe for insubordination.[16]

On May 1, 1750 some *gardes-françaises* opposed the arrest of Paris children by the police and drew their swords in protest; they intervened against the police a few weeks later when there were additional arrests and several days of rioting. The Children's Riot was precipitated by a 1749 edict ordering the arrest and imprisonment of "all beggars and vagrants found in the streets of Paris . . . of whatever age or sex."[17] There had been considerable growth of beggars in Paris for several decades, and edict after edict had been passed to deal with the problem, but to no avail. The 1749 edict was a response to the feeling of insecurity caused by rootless, drifting vagabonds, some of whom put themselves outside the law.[18] In enforcing the edict, six children playing in the street were arrested and sent to the Châtelet, "to make an example of them."[19] Rumors began to spread of the indiscriminate arrest of children by the police. Out of the fear fed by these rumors came the riot of May 22 and 23. Altogether there were a few kidnappings, a police spy was lynched, some shots were fired, and three youths were hung. The 1750 Children's Riot was not large-scale, but observing its dynamics Marc René, Marquis de Voyer de Paulmy d'Argenson wrote in his journal that "a disturbance can become a rebellion and a rebellion, total revolution."[20] Fear of crowds increased after 1750 in response to more frequent strikes in Paris and to what seemed to have been a rising spirit of insubordination within the populace.[21] A police report indicated the official reaction to popular restiveness:

> Who then are these instruments of public calamity and disaster? They are always men whose names and addresses one does not know; individuals and strangers in the very town which provides them with their means of subsistence; creatures of the moment who disappear with the same ease as they appeared in the first place. In short, they are the sort who stick to nothing, who are without property and who take flight with the speed of lightning.[22]

Beyond official fear of a restive populace, there was a weakening of the moral bond between the king and his subjects. Among the rumors that circulated during the Children's Riot of May 1750 were those of a leprous prince who required baths of human blood—of children. D'Argenson reported in his journal that people said Louis XV was that prince. The King was stung by charges against him, including one that "the wicked people . . . are calling me a Herod."[23] The lawyer Le Paige, commenting on the events of 1750, sympathized with parents who lost their children and predicted that "streams of blood will flow."[24] Louis XV was said to be bored by private pleasures, and he was criticized for laziness and idleness. D'Argenson said the people no longer loved the King. Jean-Jacques-François Barbier wrote that according to rumor "he only waged war on deer,"[25] and there were complaints that the king and queen did not give alms to fishwives as Louis XIV had. These and other remarks were reported by police spies who gathered information from the street and deposited it in files that month-by-month recorded a street discourse—a *mauvais discours*—that exposed a fraying of the moral bond that traditionally bound the King to his subjects. For his part, Louis XV was so disturbed by the Children's Riot that he ordered construction of a road in 1753, the *route de la révolte*, that bypassed Paris when he traveled from Versailles to Fontainebleau.

The street discourse recorded by the police at the time of the May 1750 riot was one of several *mauvais discours* that extended from the first half of the eighteenth century down to 1789 and contributed to de-sacralization of the monarchy.[26] If the popular discourse was fed by the price of bread, taxes, and economic misery, other discourses that issued from different sources had different causes, one of which was a bitter struggle in the 1750s between rival coalitions of parlements and Jansenists on the one hand and *dévots* and Jesuits on the other. When parlements supported Jansenists, they claimed they were, as Alfred Cobban wrote, "guardians of the fundamental laws of the kingdom."[27] They set themselves up as defenders of Gallican liberties and oppo-nents of Jesuit ultramontanism, and while they expressed loyalty to monarchy they opposed a clergy that they maintained took its cues from Rome. Among those affected by the parlement / Jansenist *dis-cours* was a servant whose daughter was arrested in the vanishing Children's Riot of 1750. This servant, Robert-François Damiens, posted a threatening letter to the lieutenant of police, demanding the release of his daughter. It was in that same year, 1750, that the Arch-bishop of Paris, Christophe de Beaumont, withheld sacraments from Jansenists, a measure that drew a series of protests from the par-lements and resulted in a crisis that peaked in 1753, when the king ex-iled members of the Paris Parlement. Most of the exiled magistrates re-signed in December 1756, after several years of demonstrations and small-scale riots. Less than a month later, in January 1757, Damiens, waiting in the château courtyard at Versailles, struck at the king with a dagger as he descended a stairway. The trial of Damiens revealed him as well-informed on public issues, a strong supporter of the par-lements, and openly hostile to priests.

Damiens' execution in the Place de Grève on March 28, 1757 be-fore an immense crowd followed the same procedures that were ap-plied in 1610 to François Ravaillac, the assassin of Henry IV. A naked Damiens lay strapped down as slow torture was applied that began with placing his right hand in burning sulfur, proceeded to the pouring of boiling liquid in holes cut in his flesh, was followed by the removal of his entrails, and ended with his being drawn and quartered. The horses that were to pull his body apart found it more than unusually resistant, and to facilitate that stage hangmen loosened his joints with knives. It was only in the last stages of a prolonged execution that Damiens finally expired. Roger Chartier has argued that his execution was an exhibition of the sovereign's power to punish, and at the same time "a clear indication of the rift between the king and his people."[28] Spies reported street mutterings after Damiens' execution and police were obliged to remove seditious placards that were posted surreptitiously in the aftermath of the public event. Among those arrested was Moriceau de la Motte, a bailiff in a complaint's court, for remarks spies overheard him make in a Paris inn. According to Barbier, who reported the episode in his journal:

> Sieur Moriceau de la Motte, bailiff of the *requêtes de l'hôtel* [a court that handled complaints concerning royal secretaries, etc.], a hot-head fanatic, and a captious critic of the government—a man at least fifty-five, and who married his mistress eight months ago—took it into his head, a month or two ago, to go dine in an inn on the rue Saint-Germain-l'Auxerrois at a *table d'hôte* for twelve. There, having turned the conversation to the terrible Damiens affair, he spoke heatedly about the way in which the trial had been conducted, against the government, and even against the king and the ministers.[29]

Moriceau was arrested, placed in the Bastille, and interrogated under torture. According to Barbier:

> It is rumored that placards were found among his papers that were posted at the gates of public gardens and other [places] before and after the attempted assassination of the king. He was asked where he had gotten the posters, to which he replied that he had torn them down, but the posters were neither glued nor pierced with holes from having been torn off.[30]

Found guilty of the charges against him, Moriceau received the death penalty, which was carried out, as with Damiens, in the Place de Grève. Barbier said of the execution:

> There was a great crowd of people assembled along his route and at La Grève. Some were saying that you don't put people to death for words and simple writings; others were hoping he would have his pardon; but they wanted to make an example using a bourgeois of Paris—a man who held a [public] office—in order to repress the license of a number of fanatics who are speaking out too boldly about the government.[31]

The Place de Grève was adjacent to the Hôtel de Ville, the center of municipal government.[32] It was surrounded by one of the most densely constructed areas of Paris, and flanked by gabled buildings that extended almost to the strip of beach along the Seine where boats were moored. The word *grève* has two meanings: one is "strand, beach of sand," while the other is "strike of workmen." Workers went to the

Place de Grève, hoping to find work; it was here that they organized strikes. The history of popular collective action and the Place de Grève are bound together in a common script. This most popular of public squares was also a center of political disturbances. It had been a focal point of the Fronde, and it would seem to have been a contested space.

The Place de Grève was a place for public parades and festivals, officially ordered and given for state purposes, and it was a place for public executions, where nobles, rebels, traitors, famous brigands, assassins, heretics, and ordinary criminals met their end. Claude le Petit wrote in his *Chronique scandaleuse ou Paris ridicule* that the Place de Grève was an "unhappy piece of ground consecrated to the public where they have massacred a hundred times more men than in war."[33] He himself was executed at the Place de Grève in 1662 for *lèse majesté* and *écrits séditieux*. His right hand was amputated, his property confiscated, and his ashes thrown to the wind after he was burned alive. Executions in the Place de Grève were public for a reason: justice was to be exemplary. Jacques-Louis Ménétra wrote, in the aftermath of the Children's Riot, "Three poor fellows were hanged in the Place de Grève for the sake of the Parisian state of mind."[34] Ménétra's ironic comment indicated that he understood full well that the execution did not necessarily produce the desired effect, and he was right: the 1750 public executions led to several incidents in the Place de Grève that were part of a larger response which included the posting of placards and mutterings that police spies overheard in the street and in taverns; they were part of a *mauvais discours* within a Paris that was not impervious to discontent.

Mauvais propos continued in the 1760s; street mutterings became more frequent as parlementary opposition increased, the burdens of the Seven Years' War were felt, and popular discontent focused on a king who failed to provide effective leadership. Sébastien Hardy wrote in his journal after the death of Louis XV in 1774: "The people, far from seeming affected by the death of this naturally good but weak king, who in recent years, had unfortunately become the unhappy prey of an inordinate passion for women encouraged in him by villainous courtiers intent on fanning his distaste for work in order to become more powerful themselves, gave somewhat unseemly evidence of its satisfaction in having changed masters."[35] Six thousand masses had been requested when the king became seriously ill at Metz in 1744, six hundred at the time of his attempted assassination in 1757, and three at the time of his death in 1774. Louis XVI was more popular than Louis XV, but the queen was hated; she was the subject of *mauvais propos*, as were the king's younger brothers and the court itself, which was rocked by a series of scandals at the end of the ancien régime. Thus, a series of discourses, popular and public, passed through the second half of the eighteenth century that suggest dissatisfaction with an unpopular king and even desacralization of monarchy. While Louis XVI was outwardly popular in 1789 and widely praised in the *cahiers de doléances*, the institution of monarchy had weakened. There had been a subterranean shift of thought and attitude, a fraying of loyalty that became part of the revolutionary dynamic and contributed to the explosive events that shook France in the summer of 1789.

Behind the facade of order in eighteenth-century France there was mounting unrest that weakened the foundations of the ancien régime. An impoverished rural population roamed the countryside, hungry, desperate, sometimes organized into gangs of lawless brigands. Parts of that population moved to towns and cities, above all Paris, into whose working-class districts there was an influx of rootless, unemployed poor. Revealingly, when discussing the possibility of sedition in Paris, Mercier said the authorities of that city had to protect it from peasants who "assembled in great number." What added to a collective feeling of insecurity was eruptions of violence among unemployed poor, some of whom were organized into gangs. Mobs attended public festivals, such as the 1781 birth of the dauphin, making the task of maintaining order more difficult for the authorities. Unrest resulted in a demand for order, to which the police responded without full understanding of the social dynamics that caused the unrest. Seeing workers in the mass as an untamed mob, the authorities imposed measures that kept them under control. When Mercier said that Parisians lived in a huge cage, he was not wide of the mark; his prediction that if by some chance there was unrest, and the people were to achieve some slight successes violence could erupt, suggests how accurately he took the popular pulse. Outwardly, order was imposed, but behind the surface of order there was seething discontent that only needed the politically explosive circumstances of 1789 to turn into the *journées* of July 12–14.

The second quotation at the head of this chapter, "To arms! to arms! . . . Yes, it is I who call my brothers to freedom," is from a speech given by Camille Desmoulins standing on a table in front of the Café de Foy in the Palais-Royal on July 12, 1789, the first day of the Paris Insurrection. Other orators in the Palais-Royal were holding forth at the same time, addressing crowds that were gathered within an urban space that was immune to police authority because it was owned by a prince of the blood, Louis-Philippe-Joseph, the duc d'Orléans.[36] Ostensibly open only to the aristocracy until 1780, it had in fact become a meeting place for all Parisians before it was officially opened to the public in that year. Eager to gain economic advantage from his property, Orléans installed shops of every type, several théâtres, an opéra, cafés, restaurants, and an annex for Curtius' wax museum, whose main salon was in the rue du Temple. The Palais-Royal attracted all manner of popular entertainers that performed before large and socially varied audiences, itinerant peddlers hawked fruit, lemonade, pheasants, partridges, even stolen dogs, and prostitutes carried on a brisk traffic just as they did along the boulevards that they also frequented. Contemporaries were well aware of the mixing of high and low within this urban space, within which the architect Louis Victor made many innovations. Frénilly, a contemporary observer, said of the Palais-Royal that it was "turned into a market place, red heels gave way to shops, swords to tax measures, and the reign of democracy began in the city of Paris."[37] Mercier wrote of "the confusion of the estates, the mixture, the throng," in the Palais-Royal, and another commentator François Marie, Mayeur de Saint-Paul said, "All the orders of citizens are joined together, from the lady of rank to the dissolute, from the soldier of distinction to the smallest supernumary of farms."[38] *Musées* dedicated to the advance of knowledge held meetings in the Palais-Royal, as did clubs, some highly select, others less so. A Masonic lodge met within the precincts of the Palais-Royal and writers gathered there, some in the employ of its politically ambitious owner.

As head of a lateral branch of the ruling family, the duc d'Orléans did not hesitate to fish in troubled waters.[39] He had been humiliated and disgraced at the battle of Ushant in 1778 when he had failed to follow orders and attack. Despised at the court, he in turn hated the King and Queen. The Palais-Royal was called the "Palais-Marchand," and Louis XVI quipped on one occasion that his cousin was a shopkeeper and that Sunday was the only day he could get off. For his part Orléans was a leader of the parlementary opposition during the fiscal crisis of 1787, and when a flustered Louis XVI tried to impose a tax measure on the Parlement of Paris on November 19, 1787, it was he who called it illegal, for which he was sent into temporary exile. Orléans called on the King to summon the Estates-General, and threw his considerable influence and resources behind the campaign to achieve that goal. He hired pamphleteers who showered Paris with Orléanist reform plans, as well as scurrilous *libelles* that held the court up to ridicule. Among those with ties to Orléans or in his pay were Pierre-Ambroise-François, Choderlos de Laclos, Jacques-Pierre Brissot de Warville, Bertrand Barère de Vieuzac, Honoré-Gabriel Riqueti, Comte de Mirabeau, Emmanuel-Joseph Sieyès, Camille Desmoulins, George-Jacques Danton, Adrien-Jean-François Duport, Charles-François Dumouriez du Pèrier, and Jean-Paul Marat, all future revolutionaries. The Palais-Royal can be regarded as a seedbed of revolution during the crucial years 1787 to 1789, and it was a space, a politicized and protected space in the heart of Paris, where the worlds of high culture and popular culture fused. Just how politicized this space became after the King summoned the Estates-General and Paris was inundated with pamphlets is indicated by an entry on June 9, 1789, in Arthur Young's journal.

> The business going forward at present in the pamphlet shops of Paris is incredible. I went to the Palais-Royal to see what new things were published, and to procure a catalogue of all. Every hour produces something new. Thirteen came out to-day, sixteen yesterday, and ninety-two last week. . . . Is it not wonderful, that while the press teems with the most levelling and even seditious principles, which put in execution would overturn the monarchy, nothing in reply appears, and not the least step is taken by the court to restrain this extreme licentiousness of publication? It is easy to conceive the spirit that must thus be raised among the people. But the coffee-houses in the Palais-Royal present yet more singular and astonishing spectacles; they are not only crowded within, but other expectant crowds are at the doors and windows, listening *à gorge déployée* [enthusiastically] to certain orators, who from chairs or tables harangue each his little audience: the eagerness with which they are heard, and the thunder of applause they receive for every sentiment of more than common hardiness or violence against the present government, cannot easily be imagined. I am all amazement at the ministry permitting such nests and hot-beds of sedition and revolt, which disseminate amongst the people, every hour, principles that by and by must be opposed with vigor, and therefore it seems little short of madness to allow the propagation at present.[40]

When Desmoulins addressed a crowd in front of the Café de Foy on July 12, a crisis was at hand. The King had transformed the Estates-General into a National Assembly but also ordered troops from provincial outposts to march on Versailles and Paris in an apparent plan to dismiss the newly reconstituted representative body. Louis XVI may have decided to dissolve the Estates-General on June 23, before he yielded to the demands of the Third Estate on June 27 to form a National Assembly. Without declaring his intentions, he took measures that pointed towards a coup d'etat that would restore power to its proper monarchical source. To that end he put the Baron de Besenval, a foreigner—he was Swiss—in command of the troops in Paris, and orders went out summoning regiments stationed outside Paris to the capital. From mid-June on there had been fear of an aristocratic plot, and when troops began to appear on June 26 the worst rumors seemed to have been confirmed. The king carried out the coup on July 11 by dismissing Jacques Necker, a favorite of the people, along with two of his supporters, Armand Marc, Comte de Montmorin Saint Hérem and François Emmanuel, Comte Saint-Priest. Henceforth there would be no "official minister," although Louis Auguste Le Tonnelier, Baron de

Breteuil, as head of the *conseil des finances*, would act in that capacity. Noted for will and energy, Breteuil was expected to bring resolution to a new and more conservative ministry that resulted from the clean sweep of July 11.

Among the newly appointed officials was a wealthy financier, François Foulon de Doué, a favorite of the daughters of Louis XV. Foulon was intensely disliked by the populace, in contrast to Necker, some of whose functions Foulon would assume. It was not just Necker's dismissal that was provocative but also the clean sweep of his ministry and the appointment of more conservative ministers by the king to carry out his designs. News of Necker's dismissal reached Paris on Sunday, July 12, and the stage was set for Desmoulins' speech in the Palais-Royal. Violent speeches had been made in the Palais-Royal on July 6, which caused such unrest that the duc d'Orléans had to intervene personally to get the crowd to disperse, which he was able to do only after summoning troops. On July 8 a police spy got someone arrested in the Palais-Royal but he was seen doing it and a crowd chased him, caught him, and cut off an ear. A woman accused of spitting on a portrait of Necker was publicly whipped, also in the Palais-Royal. Pressures building for weeks were ready to explode.

The *journées* of July 12–14 were carried out by crowds drawn largely from working-class districts, most notably the faubourgs of Saint-Martin and Saint-Denis to the north and Saint-Antoine, Saint-Marcel, and Saint-Victor to the east.[41] Of the 954 persons who received the title of *vainqueur de Bastille* in June 1790, the great majority of those whose place of residence can be identified lived in the faubourg Saint-Antoine (425 out of 602), and fifty from the faubourg Saint-Marcel. All of the demonstrators seemed to have been Parisian and to have lived within two kilometers of the Bastille, but many were recently Parisian. Three hundred forty-five of the six hundred two *vainqueurs* from the faubourg Saint-Antoine were born in the provinces. Mercier wrote that the people of the faubourg Saint-Marcel went into the center of Paris on Sundays to visit the cabarets, and so, too, did the inhabitants of other working-class faubourgs.

In the several weeks before Sunday, July 12, Paris had been swept by rumors of plots, treachery, and troop movements. After a disastrous harvest in 1788, bread prices soared, reaching a peak in July 1789. Seen against this background, the decision to sack Necker on Saturday, July 11, could hardly have been more ill-timed, but the government was desperate. News of Necker's being sacked began to circulate by 9:00 A.M. July 12, and Parisians, eager for news, flocked to the Palais-Royal, where orators held forth before agitated crowds. The orator, who seems to have drawn the largest audience, Camille Desmoulins, called the people "to arms," and he urged them to close the théâtres: "No théâtres! No dancing. This is a day of mourning." It was the latter part of Desmoulins' speech to which the crowd in the Palais-Royal responded first. Moving to the east, it came to the Opéra, located a few blocks from the Palais-Royal, which it forcibly entered, "uttering fearsome cries," and shut down. The crowd continued to move in an easterly direction until it came to the boulevard théâtres on the rue du Temple, which it also closed down. While passing along the rue du Temple the crowd came to Curtius' wax museum, which some people entered, and from which they took busts of Necker and the duc d'Orléans, both popular favorites. Carrying the wax busts, which were draped in black, a symbol of mourning, and joining other crowds from the rue Saint-Martin and the rue Saint-Denis, the procession moved west on the rue Saint-Honoré until it came to the place Louis-le-Grand (Place Vendôme), where it encountered a detachment of dragoons.

The Prince de Lambesc, stationed in the Place Louis XV with the Royal-Allemand regiment, rode with his men to the Place Louis-le-Grand to rescue the dragoons who were unable to cope with the crowd, and then returned with the dragoons to the Place Louis XV, followed by the crowd. It was a Sunday afternoon and Parisians who had been walking in the Champs-Elysées were passing through the Place Louis XV as another crowd entered the same space from the rue Saint-Honoré, and, caught in a press of people, Lambesc and his men clashed with the converging crowds as bystanders pelted the German Guards from the Tuileries. Under orders from Besenval, Lambesc then tried to clear the Tuileries, but was unable to do so when Parisians, lined up on a wall above them, threw whatever missiles were at hand at Lambesc's guards and forced them to withdraw. With the clash between civilians and soldiers in the Place Louis XV and the Tuileries the Paris Insurrection can be said to have begun.

To understand the dynamics of the Paris Insurrection one should pay attention to the geographical field on which it unfolded. As we have seen, the crowd that set out from the Palais-Royal to close down théâtres proceeded first to the Opéra, which had been relocated a few blocks to the east, after a fire burned down the Opéra on the rue de Richelieu, just west of the Palais-Royal in 1781. Having closed the Opéra, the crowd continued moving to the east, towards the boulevard théâtres on the rue du Temple. The crowd then moved down the rue du Temple to the rue Saint-Antoine, where it turned west (just beyond the Place de Grève it became the rue Saint-Honoré) and continued westward until it came to the Place Louis-le-Grand and the Place Louis XV. Had the crowd crossed the rue Saint-Antoine rather than turning to the right, it would have come to the Place de Grève and the Hôtel de Ville,

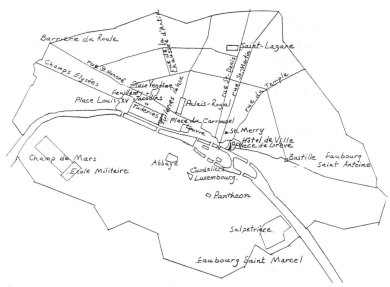

Revolutionary Paris. Source: Map by Warren Roberts (author)

which occupied the space between the end of the rue du Temple and
the right bank of the Seine. The Place de Grève and the Hôtel de Ville
became a focal point of the Paris Insurrection on July 13 and even more
on July 14, but it was not within this space in the center of the ancient
city of Paris that the crowd gathered on July 12. Instead the crowd
walked west until it came to Paris' two finest public squares, the Place
Louis-le-Grand and the Place Louis XV, ordered spaces based on design
concepts that passed from Italy to France in the seventeenth and eighteenth centuries.

Of these, the last to be constructed, and the grandest, was the Place
Louis XV (now the Place de la Concorde).[42] The Bureau des Marchands
petitioned the King in 1748 for permission to erect a statue in his
honor, but they did not choose a site for the square within which it
would be placed. A competition was held for designs that proposed lo-
cations in various parts of the capital, one of which was the Place de
Grève. The Esplanade was chosen, a plot of land west of the Tuileries,
and in 1753 Jacques-Ange Gabriel was awarded the commission. Work
on the public square began in that year and continued into the reign of
Louis XVI; for the most part the project was completed in 1772 when
an *arrêté* was issued authorizing the pavement of the royal square.
Construction costs were enormous. The machine used to transport
and raise the Louis XV equestrian statue cost twenty thousand livres.
Barbier described the inauguration of Edme Bouchardon's statue in
February 1763:

On the 23rd of this month, the equestrian statue of the king was placed on the pedestal in the new square across from the Pont-Tournant of the Tuileries. It took three days to transport the statue from the workshop, which was at Roule. There was a great crowd to see the mechanics of this operation, supervised by a builder from Saint-Denis, a man of great skill. The governor of Paris, the prévôt des marchands, and the city fathers were under tents [with] Madame la marquise de Pompadour, M. le duc de Choiseul, the prince-marshal de Soubise, and others. But, as in a crowd there are always trouble-makers and ill-intentioned people, it was reported that along the way and in the square several persons were arrested for proffering indecent remarks about why the statue was advancing so slowly. They were saying that the king was going along the way he was led; that they would have a hard time getting him past the Hôtel de Pompadour; that he had to be held up by four grues [cranes; prostitutes] to be lowered on the pedestal, along with allusions to the ministers and several other *mauvais discours.*[43]

The *mauvais discours* that swirled about the Louis XV equestrian statue at the time of its inauguration did not end after it was officially installed. On the contrary. The statue became, as Robert Isherwood stated, "a cynosure of public scorn and was regularly covered with epigrams and graffiti."[44] Municipal authorities had to organize cleaning crews to remove the visible evidence of a *mauvais discours* that passed into the finest of public spaces in eighteenth-century Paris.

Construction of the Place Louis XV began in the same year, 1753, in which Parlement issued the Grand Remonstrances, a vociferous protest against the "despotism" of the government. This was in the aftermath of the Children's Riot of 1750 that helped crystallize ill feeling toward the King. Hardly one to help his own cause, in 1754 Louis XV purchased the hôtel and gardens of Louis-Henri de La Tour d'Auvergne, comte d'Evreux, in the fashionable Saint-Honoré quarter west of the Esplanade and gave the property to his mistress, Mme de Pompadour. The Hôtel d'Evreux, which would become the residence of the Presidents of the Republic, had been built in 1714 and was purchased in 1754 for 730,000 livres. Mme de Pompadour redecorated the interior, which was splendidly furnished and hung with Gobelin tapestries. She entertained Louis XV in this hôtel, which Barbier referred to in his description of the raising of the Louis XV equestrian statue.

When the procession, conveying the Louis XV equestrian statue, made its way from Roule (to the west of Paris) to the Place Louis XV it passed by the Hôtel de Pompadour (as it was then called), and it was there, as someone said, that it had trouble getting past the residence of the King's mistress. In 1757, the same year in which *lettres patentes* were issued authorizing transfer of the title of the land for the Place

Louis XV to the city of Paris, a would-be regicide suffered excruciating torture before a huge crowd; at the other end of the capital work proceeded on a public square in honor of a King whose private life was seen as scandalous in the streets of Paris. People murmured not only against the King in the aftermath of Damiens' execution but of Mme de Pompadour as well. Raising funds for the Place Louis XV was difficult given the fiscal hardship facing the government during the period of its construction, which largely coincided with the Seven Years' War. The city of Paris had no alternative but to shoulder most of the expense; it had to finance construction of a public square in honor of a King who was far from popular in the capital.

If construction of the Place Louis XV began under unfavorable circumstances in the 1750s, this public square was to be the scene of real tragedy in 1770 when a festival was staged to commemorate the marriage of the dauphin to the Austrian princess, Marie-Antoinette. The wedding took place at Versailles on May 16, and to celebrate it in Paris a fête was held on May 30 in the Place Louis XV, where special pavilions were constructed, along with a temple of marriage and a long colonnade that was adjoined to Bouchardon's equestrian statue. Accounts differ on what happened in the Place Louis XV, on the number of people who died as a result of a terrible disaster, and who was at fault. According to one version those responsible for orchestrating the fête built a storage house for a bouquet that was to be the climax of a fireworks display, but during the festivities a rocket landed on the storage house that ignited the bouquet and caused the crowd to panic.[45] Another explanation was that when the fireworks display was over people began to leave the Place Louis XV at the Rue Royale as a crowd was trying to push its way into the Place Louis XV from the opposite direction. Carriages also tried to force their way into the Place Louis XV, and in the crush of people and carriages panic broke out, the crowd stampeded, and by the time the episode ended bodies littered the space where the tragedy had taken place.[46] Various estimates of the number of dead were made, from the 688 noted by Sébastien Hardy, who cited a police report as the source of his information, to the figure of 132 given by the lieutenant of police. Hardy wrote that eleven cars were needed to remove the bodies. The dauphin and his teenage bride could hardly be held responsible for the tragedy, and both contributed money "to help the unfortunate." However, Marie-Antoinette, who became Queen four years later, was the object of intense public hostility. That the 1770 tragedy took place in the Place Louis XV when Parisians first met a teenage bride they would come to hate added to the negative associations they attached to this public square.

The ordered classical spaces of Paris' two finest royal squares, the Place Louis-le-Grand and the Place Louis XV, were given over to seasonal fairs in the last several decades of the ancien régime. For centuries fairs had been installed around Paris, on the periphery of the city and in surrounding villages. The two most popular fairs were those of Saint-Germain on the south side of Paris and Saint-Laurent between the faubourgs of Saint-Denis and Saint-Martin. Joachim Neimitz said of the fair of Saint-Germain that everyone went there "helter-skelter, masters with valets and lackeys, thieves with honest people. The most refined courtesans, the prettiest girls, the subtlest pickpockets are as if intertwined together. The whole fair teems with people from the beginning to the end."[47] Members of the public and the populace mingled in the crowded space of the fair and gave themselves over to a show, as Robert Isherwood said, "in which everyone participated in derisive laughter at the behavior of civil society and in which the entertainments incorporated the songs and cries of the people, their gestures and postures, their language, and their aspirations and fears. Audiences and entertainers profaned and satirized the accepted standards of etiquette and decency, helping to create a familiarity in the fairs among people often separated by occupations, wealth, age, and sex."[48]

After flourishing in the first half of the eighteenth century, the fairs of Saint-Germain and Saint-Laurent underwent decline in the second half of the century.[49] New places of entertainment installed along the boulevards in the center of Paris drew spectators away from the fairs, and in 1762 one of the main attractions of both fairs, the Opéra-Comique, merged with the Comédie Italienne. Deprived of that théâtre, the fairs lost an important magnet. In that same year the Saint-Germain fair was destroyed by fire, and, while partially rebuilt, it never recovered. The decline of Paris' two leading fairs did not mean that the taste for popular spectacles was at an end, for that taste continued to flourish, but in a different venue. The Saint-Ovide fair had been installed by the Capuchins in the place Louis-le-Grand, which was in close proximity to their quarters, towards the end of the seventeenth century, but it was only in the 1760s that it began to prosper. All manner of shops were installed in the place Louis-le-Grand for the Saint-Ovide fair, and in 1766 there were twenty-three different entertainments, including a portable théâtre installed by Jean-Baptiste Nicolet, an entrepreneur who had built a wooden théâtre on the rue du Temple, and the Hall of Great Dansers in 1764. Only forty feet by thirty-six feet in size, that théâtre seated socially mixed audiences of four hundred who bought inexpensive tickets to see pantomimes. Nicolet's théâtre in the rue du Temple entertained audiences with satire and ridicule, sometimes at the expense of well-known actors. Nothing was sacred in this théâtre, in which ribaldry was given full reign and upper-class, elite types were pilloried by pantomimes. Also, tough-talking comic, popular characters appeared in plays that Nicolet mounted in the years just before the Revolution. Among those plays was *Le Père Duchesne, ou la mauvaise habitude*, performed in 1789, whose gruff, ill-mannered hero, a stove setter, delivered sentences laced with coarse, vulgar words. It was to capitalize on the interest in his productions that Nicolet set up a portable théâtre for the Saint-Ovide fair, first in the Place Louis-le-Grand and then in the Place Louis XV.

In effect, the Paris Insurrection on July 12 followed a theatrical route, from the Palais-Royal (which itself had théâtres) to the Opéra, to the boulevard théâtres on the rue du Temple, and then back to the sites of the fair théâtres in the Place Louis-le-Grand and the Place Louis XV. Nicolet's théâtres were not standing in either of the royal squares on July 12, so the crowds that entered these public spaces on that day did not do so to close them down. Yet they, and the fairs with which they were associated, had been magnets for several decades drawing Parisians of all stations and from all parts of the capital to the royal squares in which they were situated. The Place Louis-le-Grand and the Place Louis XV had become public spaces, and it was in these spaces that a public protest turned into an insurrection on July 12. According to Colin Lucas, crowd action in eighteenth-century Paris was localized and connected to the places where incidents occurred that caused disturbances.[50] This had been true in 1750 in the Children's Riot, it was the case in the disturbances of August–September 1788 when crowds rioted in the Place Dauphine and Pont-Neuf as the government clashed with Parlement, and it was the same with the Réveillon Riot in April 1789 in the faubourg Saint-Antoine when workers protested in the very neighborhood that was the locus of their grievances. Workers were not bound together as workers, but were made up of enclaves defined, in large measure, by the *quartiers* in which they lived.[51] As local as ties were in eighteenth-century Paris, workers did move to other parts of the city, as on Sundays, when they frequented taverns and dancing halls in the center of Paris; they went to fairs in royal squares in the west end of Paris and mingled with others of different stations; and they attended public festivals in those same royal squares. Also, Parisians of the lower orders from the faubourgs that lay to the east of the city went to the Palais-Royal, located a short distance from the Place Louis-le-Grand and the Place Louis XV. It was in the last several decades of the ancien régime in particular that the populace became familiar with the two royal squares in the affluent neighborhoods in the west of the capital, and were drawn to the Palais-Royal, which was opened to the public, regardless of rank or station.

When the crowd turned right on the rue Saint-Antoine, just before
it came to the rue Saint-Honoré, after closing down the boulevard
théâtres on the rue du Temple, it came within a few hundred feet of the
Place de Grève, which would become the center of bloody deeds on
July 14 and again on July 22, when Parisians exacted vengeance on the
enemies of the people. With completely different symbolic associations than the royal squares to the west, the Place de Grève became a
center of popular retribution during the Paris Insurrection, but on July
12, before a political protest turned into an uprising, the crowd was
drawn to the Place Louis-le-Grand and the Place Louis XV. It was the
king who had dismissed Necker; the problem was at Versailles, where
Louis XVI, on the previous day, had seemingly undone the recent victory of the Third Estate by jettisoning Necker and appointing a conservative and hardline ministry. It was the public squares in the west of
Paris, the Place Louis-le-Grand and the Place Louis XV, that had symbolic associations with monarchy, and it was to these spaces that the
crowd moved on July 12, after closing down the théâtres along the rue
du Temple.

The Paris uprising began when the crowd swamped Lambesc's
troops in the Place Louis-le-Grand and fighting broke out on the edge
of the Place Louis XV adjacent to the Tuileries. From that point on se-
curing arms was most important, and throughout the day on Monday,
July 13, crowds searched for weapons. The seizure of muskets and cannon at the Invalides on July 14 virtually guaranteed the success of the
Paris Insurrection. All the crowd needed was gunpowder, which was
stored in the Bastille. The oft-told story of the siege and fall of the
Bastille does not require yet another narration here.[52] Rather than
looking at the episode as a whole, our vantage point will be inside the
Hôtel de Ville, from which a total of four delegations were sent to the
Bastille in an effort to persuade the Comte Bernard Jordan de Launay,
the military governor, to surrender the fortress. Inside the Hôtel de
Ville was a certain Pitra, born in Lyons but a resident of Paris since
1766, and an elector for the Estates-General. He wrote a detailed account of the day, which Jacques Godechot considered "quite devoid of
any critical sense."[53] Its value was not in its accuracy or critical perspective, but in the sense of atmosphere that it captured, as well as the
descriptions of people milling about awaiting news from the crowd at
the Bastille.

> I cannot attempt to describe the scene in the main hall. The amphitheatres
> and the rows of seats all round it were filled by a crowd of people armed
> with guns, pikes, swords and even sticks with knives fastened to them;
> others, who by their atrocious expressions even more than by their dress

resembled the brigands we had disarmed only the day before, filled the centre of the hall; they were armed, for the most part, with old-fashioned or foreign axes which they had taken from the Garde-Meuble; some of them, shoeless and almost without breeches, were armed only with stonemasons' hammers. They were loudly clamouring for the electors, who stood in a tiny group at the far end of the hall, unable to find seats, and trying in vain, through this terrifying tumult, to obtain silence.[54]

Clearly, Pitra, a draper and professional journalist, an elector and chair of a temporary police committee that included Jean-Sylvain Bailly, the mayor of Paris, was profoundly uncomfortable in the presence of rough Parisians with their guns, pikes, axes, and knives, and so, too, was the permanent committee that sent one deputation after another to work out a surrender agreement with de Launay. Having described the discomfort of the permanent committee while it awaited the return of its deputations, Pitra decided to give "some account of what had taken place in the Bastille." One group that lay siege to the fortress was a "disorderly rabble," another was a "multitude, armed only with pitchforks, scythes and other implements," and yet another was "a disorderly and unarmed mob . . . surging around the Bastille on almost every side." If Pitra was uneasy in the company of armed Parisians and increasingly nervous as one deputation after another returned from the Bastille without having come to terms with de Launay, Jacques de Flesselles, the *Prévôt des marchands*, was even more apprehensive. When a crowd appeared at the Hôtel de Ville earlier in the day demanding arms, de Flesselles said he would send for them and hand them out later, but when the crowd returned all he was able to offer was the 360 muskets stored at the Hôtel de Ville, not any additional ones. De Flesselles ordered cases of weapons from the arms factory at Charleville, but when opened they contained nothing but rags. He then said guns and ammunition could be found at a Carthusian monastery near the Luxembourg, but none were there and when a crowd returned empty-handed to the Hôtel de Ville there were cries of treachery. That cry was heard often on July 14, and it was a cry that expressed mounting anger.

Pitra wrote that "While the attack on the Bastille was proceeding and the life of the *Prévôt des marchands* hung in the balance, I had gone to my own district; I had found it in a state of extreme ferment; the news of the first civilian casualties had just reached it; people wanted to set forth immediately to be avenged on the Governor for his perfidy in firing on those to whom he had opened the *avancée* [drawbridge] under pretext of giving them arms." In fact, de Launay had not opened the drawbridge to the outer courtyard, and he did not lure besiegers there under the "pretext of giving them arms." Shots were fired, and men in the exposed courtyard were killed, but not because of perfidy on the part of de Launay. Rumors of treason spread because people within a crowd did not know what others had done—in this case that two Parisians broke into a guardhouse and lowered the drawbridge—and also because of a deep distrust of the authorities that was combined with not only a collective fear that had been gathering force for weeks, but also when the extraordinary circumstances of July 14 came to a head.

Far from trying to slaughter those laying siege to the Bastille, de Launay wanted as much as possible to avoid conflict. More determined to resist, and willing to fire on the crowd, was Louis Deflue, a lieutenant who had recently arrived with thirty Swiss mercenaries to shore up the defense of the Bastille. The regular garrison, made up of eighty-two "invalids"—soldiers unfit for regular duty—had little appetite for battle with the crowd; they urged de Launay to surrender, as he finally did by 5:30 P.M., after *gardes-françaises* arrived with four cannon. When the second drawbridge was lowered, and the crowd swarmed into the Bastille, de Launay was arrested, and amid cries of "*A mort!*" he was taken to the Hôtel de Ville, protected by two men who led the final stage of the siege, Pierre-Augustin Hulin and Jacob Elie. Along the way crowds that lined the street shouted insults at de Launay and lashed out at him in anger. Near the church of Saint Louis a crowd tried to kill him, but Hulin and Elie intervened. Back at the Hôtel de Ville, Pitra described the scene when news arrived of the fall of the Bastille. "I must observe that at this moment, the memory of which will never fade from my memory, when the universal cry 'The Bastille has fallen!' echoed through the great hall, I saw the *Prévôt des marchands* turn pale and almost tremble." Soon the angry mob from the Bastille was before the Hôtel de Ville, with their prisoners.

> It was amidst these cries of victory, or rather amidst the confused noise of a hundred thousand voices surrounding or filling the Hôtel de Ville, that we saw the Conquerors of the Bastille enter, or rather rush into, the great hall. This horde of men of all conditions, armed in such diverse manners, all breathing vengeance and carnage, were dragging with them thirty or forty pensioners or Swiss guards and shouting: "Hang them! death! no quarter!" These men, whose faces and eyes blazing with anger were as terrifying as their cries, were followed by a crowd of citizens mingled with *gardes-françaises*, bearing brave Elie aloft in their arms.[55]

The crowd did not kill the captive soldiers from the Bastille, but it did take vengeance on two men, de Launay and de Flesselles, who were suspected of treason. As de Launay's captors held him in front of the Hôtel de Ville and debated what to do with him, Desnot, a pastry cook, said he should be taken inside. Weary of his ordeal, de Launay cried, "Let me die!" and kicked Desnot in the groin. He was instantly run through with a sword and shot and stabbed repeatedly. Desnot then cut off de Launay's head with a knife and put it on a pike. Incriminating notes were found that made de Flesselles appear a traitor and he, too, was shot and decapitated. The two heads were paraded together in the streets of Paris.

Eight days later, on July 22, amid a chant of "Kiss papa! Kiss papa!" (the third and last quote at the head of this chapter), another macabre scene unfolded as heads were again stuck on pikes. Bread prices had soared and a hungry people vented their anger on Joseph François Foulon de Doué, a landlord and government contractor who had been appointed Controller of Finances after Necker's dismissal. Already unpopular, Foulon was thought to have said years earlier, in the 1775 food crisis, that if the people were hungry they could eat hay. Anxious for his life, Foulon went into hiding outside Paris but was recognized and captured. He was made to walk to Paris behind a cart, with a crown of thorns on his head and a bundle of hay on his back. To quench his thirst he was given vinegar laced with pepper. Back at the Hôtel de Ville, Bailly, and Lafayette tried unsuccessfully to save him from the crowd. He was taken to a lamppost in the Place de Grève to be hung, which was successful only on the third try. He was then decapitated and his head put on a pike with straw stuffed in its mouth.

On the same day another band of revolutionaries apprehended Foulon's son-in-law, the intendant of Paris, Louis-Jean Bertier de Sauvigny, at Compiègne and placed him under arrest. News reached Paris that he was on his way and by the time he arrived, conveyed to the capital in a carriage whose top had been torn off, he was met by a throng that danced, shouted, carried placards and pikes, and brandished on a pike the head of his father-in-law. The crowd chanted "Kiss papa! Kiss papa!" as the procession worked its way to the Hôtel de Ville. It was there that Bertier de Sauvigny was killed, his heart torn out and thrown towards the center of municipal government, and his head cut off. The crowd then, with Foulon's and Bertier's heads on pikes, paraded through the streets of Paris. The chant "Kiss papa! Kiss papa!" confirms the observations of Louis-Sébastien Mercier that if the forces of order were to break down and the people were "caught up in the frenzy of riot" their "violence" would be cruel.

Mercier was by no means alone in his belief that the people were a potentially anarchic force. Within the educated public of eighteenth-century France, and most importantly among *philosophes* and reform-minded officials, there was a sustained debate on the people. That debate revealed a deep ambivalence not only towards fear and disdain of the people, but also concern and hope for improvement through policies that were intended to achieve greater national wealth from which the people would ultimately derive benefit. In 1789, the people freed themselves from the discourses in which they had been the object of so much thought and attention. They were no longer a subject only to be discussed. They were a force. None of the eighteenth-century discourses on the people suggest that even the most progressive thinkers were prepared for the political realities that presented themselves with such suddenness in the summer of 1789, and from the spasms of July 12–14 to the bloodletting of 10 Thermidor the people were a powerful force in the Revolution. While a few eighteenth-century observers considered the possibility of revolution in France, they did not contemplate a popular revolution. The Abbé Gabriel Bonnot de Mably's *Des Droits et des devoirs du citoyen*, written some time after 1758 but not published until 1789, explained that sovereign power originally resided in the people and that if France were to recover its liberty it had to "choose between a revolution and slavery."[56] Mably regarded traditional bodies of government that had atrophied under the monarchy a seedbed of liberty, and particularly the Estates-General, which he believed should be strengthened. He predicted, with uncanny accuracy, conflicts between the parlements and crown that would result in summoning of the Estates-General, after a thousand pamphlets would "instruct the public in its interests." This was precisely what happened between August 1788 and May 1789. The successful parlementary campaign was what Mably meant by *"une Révolution ménagée,"* managed, as Keith Michael Baker said, "in the sense that it would be sparingly carried out, according to orderly principles, and not in the name of 'a licentious liberty' that would lead to violence."[57]

When Mably wrote that pamphlets would "instruct the public in its interests" after the summoning of the Estates-General he had in mind members of the educated public. The traditional view, as expressed by Jacques-Bénigne Bossuet, had been that the king alone was a public person and that there was no public apart from the person of the king. By the middle of the eighteenth century, the thought of the Enlightenment with its rational inquiry, critical spirit, and readiness to challenge established verities, religious and secular, made Bossuet's concept of the public, and the premises on which it rested, untenable. An oppositional public had coalesced, made up of those who were educated, aware of public issues, and thought in terms of the nation as a whole.[58] Drawn from the aristocracy and the urban bourgeoisie, those belonging to this stratum were internally differentiated, but as an educated elite, as the public, they were, as we have seen, separated from the populace. The populace, for its part, was also diversified, if anything even more than the public.

The peasantry inhabited a different world than that of urban workers, and geographical and linguistic differences contributed further to the patchwork character of a rural populace that lived much as it had through the centuries and was all but untouched by the ideas that circulated within the public. It was not just that peasants from one region of France worked under a different agrarian regime than peasants from some other region, and that they spoke a different dialect, or that urban workers identified themselves as water carriers, stonemasons, bakers, street sweepers, building laborers, porters, coal heavers, and the countless trades by which they made, or tried to make, a living. Many were unemployed. Some took to the road and became a floating population of beggars or vagabonds. Within the artisanate some earned good wages, others earned bare subsistence wages; some were unable to feed their families when the price of grain rose. What characterized people who lived under these highly varied conditions, those who made up the populace, as J. F. Bosher has written, was "an inability to rise above their differences, or to see public issues, or to discuss projects for improvement, or to collaborate with others for the common good."[59]

Daniel Roche in his book, *The People of Paris*, showed that literacy increased markedly in working-class sections of eighteenth-century Paris. In Saint-Denis, an artisan section, 86 percent of the men and 73 percent of the women whose marriage contracts Roche examined signed their names. By 1780, 35 percent of the popular classes in Paris owned some books, according to items listed in wills. Yet the books that would have occupied the shelves or cupboards of working-class Parisians were not works of learning, erudition, or sophistication but religious stories, fables, fairy stories, and fantasies available in cheap editions of the blue library. Parisians, who could sign their name and were sufficiently literate to read inexpensive books intended for a popular audience, were far removed from the educated elite whose mental world was the product of a different educational and cultural system. While devotional literature and the traditional fare of the blue library constituted the main reading material of the groups Roche studied, "A popular public was awakening, thirsting for news, hungry for discussion, easily roused to enthusiasm and, in some cases, to action."[60] A flood of subversive, scurrilous literature that inundated Paris in the second half of the eighteenth century, according to Robert Darnton, crossed the divide separating the public from the populace and reached a popular audience. This literature, unlike economic treatises, philosophical writings, and sentimental novels written for an elite audience, was in some measure accessible to the populace.

Entering the mental world of the eighteenth-century populace presents the historian with formidable problems. What the authorities feel and think about the people can be established with reasonable assurance, and what their material conditions are like—wages, rents, the cost of bread—can be determined and even charted, but with a few exceptions their actual voices are not to be heard. The most notable exception is the *Journal of My Life* by Jacques-Louis Ménétra, a Paris glazier, born in 1738, who began committing the story of his life to writing in 1764 and continued working on it down to 1803. Ménétra's *Journal*—it is more of an autobiography than a journal—is written without paragraphs and even without punctuation.

The author was literate, had considerable powers of observation, could tell a good story, but spelled phonetically, was often unclear about his meaning, and did not obey the proper rules of grammar. One might think that with effort he could have remedied his writing deficiencies, but the fact is that he did not. He may simply have thought the task too great, beyond his capacity, or he may have preferred writing as he did as a class statement, but whatever the reason the very writing form in which he committed his story about himself separates it from the autobiographies of contemporaries who inhabited a different cultural sphere. Among those who come to mind in this connection is Jean-Jacques Rousseau, an older contemporary, whom Ménétra met, had dinner with at the Café de la Régence, played checkers with (Rousseau won; he wanted to play chess, but Ménétra did not know how), and whose breadth of knowledge, Ménétra felt, created a distance between the two men that was "like night and day."[61] Even though Rousseau was from an artisan background (his father was a watchmaker) and had little formal education, he absorbed elite culture and in his *Confessions* wrote a work that laid out his life story, with all of its detours, conflicts, reversals, and successes, stage by stage; it revealed the author's inner life as it proceeded. The story was told with artistry, polish, sophistication, and an agenda: his own vindication. Rousseau amused, delighted, and shocked his audience; always, the audience was in mind; always Rousseau the wordsmith and manipulator, arranged the story to suit his authorial purposes.

By contrast, Ménétra's *Journal* is without Rousseau's artistry and sophistication. It is not only the form that connects Ménétra's *Journal* to the artisan world from which it issued but the absence of perspective, of a shaping vision, even of chronology. Except when particular events are identified, the reader has no sense of the temporal framework within which Ménétra's life took place (a stock phrase is "at about this time"). Acutely aware of change within his world, Rousseau's *Confessions* relates his experience to the historical transformations taking place within it. In Ménétra's *Journal* there is no awareness of this, no overview, no historical consciousness. Rather, he tells of his work as a glazier, of his travels through France as he went from job to job, his escapades along the way, his sexual exploits (of which there were many), his scrapes with the law, his pranks, his quarrels, his marriage at age twenty-seven, his fragmented and unhappy family life, and at the end of his story, his role in the Revolution as an active sans-culotte. The story unfolds seamlessly and episodically; the stories he tells about himself do not issue from any psychological premises or purpose; they have no inner plan; and some of them would seem to have been lifted from broadsheets or a rich oral storytelling tradition to which he, as a worker, is directly connected. In this respect, his *Journal* reads like a picaresque novel.

Ménétra is seen at fairs, carnivals, Nicolet's popular théâtre, and public executions; he meets with actors, knows Sanson, the official executioner, whom he sees "do a job," goes to cabarets where he drinks with male companions and meets women he has sex with and whom he shares with friends and chance acquaintances; he stumbles over people copulating when walking through woods, sees people urinating in streets, is robbed, is himself involved in some fifty fights, and inhabits a world that is pervasively violent. The violence is sometimes accompanied by pranks and mirth and followed by bouts of heavy drinking; life for Ménétra is not only at once hard, but also convivial, punctuated by "good times" (one of his favorite terms), laughter, macabre humor, and entertainments. In all of this there is something Rabelaisian: priests are objects of scorn and butts of jokes, humor is coarse, class feeling intense, and violence capable of erupting at any moment. In Ménétra's *Journal* life is raw, it is loud, and it smells. For all of its limitations, this unique work takes us into the world of the eighteenth-century populace as does no other; it offers a unique view of someone who lived within that stratum.

The mental world of the populace, both rural and urban, was utterly different from that of the public, which by definition was educated and elite. Efforts to get at something as intangible as a collective mentality are inherently difficult, and to do so for groups as distant in time as the eighteenth-century French populace is fraught with risk. Yet, if the Paris *journées* of July 12–14 are to be understood, the risk must be taken. Economic conditions—wages that did not keep up with inflation, bad harvests, the high price of bread—help explain the Paris uprising. So, too, does the atmosphere of fear that was fed by rumors of treason in late June and the early part of July. While these conditions help explain why the populace rioted, they do not explain the dynamics of the insurrection. If that aspect of the episode is to be understood, it is necessary to get inside the minds of the working-class Parisians who took to the streets. Robert Darnton's "Great Cat Massacre" essay says much about the mental world of urban workers whose *journées* were at the center of the popular revolution in July 1789.[62] The execution of cats on the rue Saint-Séverin that Darnton analyzes took place some five decades before the 1789 Revolution, but it reveals a mode of behavior that would be funneled into the larger dynamics of the Paris Insurrection.

Those who committed the bloody execution of cats in the rue Saint-Séverin in the late 1730s were journeymen in a printshop who seethed with resentment and bitterness against their master and his wife, who adored her well-fed gray cat. Through a well-scripted strategy, the journeymen prodded the master into ordering them to get rid of neighborhood cats that made sleeping impossible. The first cat they seized, before carrying out the wholesale slaughter, was the gray cat so beloved of the master's wife. To explain the meaning of this grim episode, Darnton takes his reader into the symbolic world of the urban worker, with its rites, rituals, superstitions, cruelty, and violence. Darnton's workers were dominated and exploited by a master against whom they could not retaliate directly, but against whom they could achieve a measure of satisfaction through their wickedly clever scheme. If the modern reader finds it difficult to see humor in an episode whose comic point turned on the killing of cats, it is because he / she inhabits a different mental and emotional realm than the journeymen of rue Saint-Séverin.

Those journeymen were part of a populace whose blunt, plain language reflected the hard world they inhabited. It was a world in which executions were public, animals were strangled as a matter of course, manners were rough, thievery common, and violence a fact of life.[63] There was little room for the squeamish in this world. The authorities were well aware of how hard material conditions were, and how resentment was unavoidable in a society marked by sharp distinctions of wealth and in which language, manners, clothing, and the many rituals of daily life separated people of breeding, refinement, leisure, and property from the populace. Public ceremonies that reached back to the Middle Ages acted as a safety valve, a way for people to let off steam, to turn the world upside down, and then to return to the world as it was. Humor was an essential part of festivals that were repositories of *gauloiserie* (coarse jokes), a comic tradition that was part and parcel of popular culture in ancien régime France.[64] This culture was potentially explosive and within its folds lay comic opportunities that, when acted out, could turn into cruelty and erupt in violence. This was true of popular culture throughout the ancien régime. That culture helped define not only the world of the rue Saint-Séverin workers, who settled accounts with their master and his wife in the late 1730s, but it also helped define the world of the working-class districts of Paris whose uprisings in the summer of 1789 put the French Revolution on a completely different course.

The vanishing Children's Riot of 1750 revealed a symbiosis of politics, popular culture, and violence in eighteenth-century Paris. A drummer from the *gardes-françaises* saw Labbé, a constable, try to take an eleven-year-old youth from the Pont-Marie; the drummer sounded the alarm. A crowd intervened and after freeing the youth it gave chase to Labbé, who escaped twice but was seen entering a building where he was discovered hiding under an attic bed. Guards protected him from immediate lynching and put him in a carriage, but the crowd tore down the carriage gates. The Watch then held the people at bay with bayonets and Labbé was taken to a nearby room and placed in custody, but, after shots were fired, the crowd seized Labbé while a small group of officers, sensing their danger, stepped aside. Labbé briefly freed himself from the crowd but was run down, beaten, and stoned to death. His body, which "no longer had a human face," was then dragged to the house of Lieutenant General Berryer, the official whose measures had been responsible for the riot. When archers carried Labbé's body to the morgue on a ladder that night, a crowd followed behind in mocking silence. The next night a crowd appeared outside the house of Labbé's mistress, where he also had lived. The crowd cut a cat's throat and then performed a travesty of a religious ceremonial that included blessing the cat with water from the gutter, singing the *De Profundis* and *Libera Nos*, and throwing the cat into a fire amid jeers and threats that police spies could "end up like this cat."

While some bourgeois were in the crowd during the two days of rioting, their response for the most part was to withdraw from scenes of violence and from the populace. As Arlette Farge and Jacques Revel said, the "bourgeoisie were aware that during the height of the revolt they had rubbed shoulders with a profoundly alien culture, which in the cold light of day they found deeply threatening."[65] French society was divided before the Revolution, and when France was swept by rural and urban uprisings in the summer of 1789 that division did not go away. On the contrary, the entire subsequent history of the Revolution reflected that division.

Two journals kept from 1718 to 1789 offer a continuous narrative of the mounting tensions within Paris that came to a head in the insurrection of July 12–14.[66] Edmond-Jean-François Barbier, born in 1689, was a lawyer who lived all his life in the rue Galande. He began his journal, which in manuscript ran to seven volumes, in 1718 and continued it down to the time of his death in 1763, when a bookseller, Sébastien Hardy, whose shop on the rue Saint-Jacques was close to Barbier's rue Galande, took up the narrative and continued it to the first year of the Revolution. Barbier's first mention of conflict between Parisians and the authorities was in 1720, when a disturbance took place in the faubourg Saint-Antoine over the severities of the Parisian Watch. His narrative for the 1730s included disturbances, resulting from the struggle between the parlements and the government over the Jansenist issue that would prove so disruptive in decades to come. In the 1740s, Barbier described conflicts between Parisians and the authorities over efforts to control beggars and to round up stray children who could be conscripted into the army and thereby removed from the streets. These efforts fed into the Children's Riot of 1750, for which Barbier compiled a detailed account. Then, in the 1750s, his narrative returned to the struggle between Parlement and the government over Jansenism, which sowed additional seeds of popular unrest. When Hardy took up the chronicle in 1764, the year after Barbier's death, he began a narrative that would fill eight manuscript volumes. The Seven Years' War had just ended, leaving fiscal problems that would never be resolved, that would be exacerbated by France's financial support of the American Revolution, and would result in the crisis of 1787 that set in motion the chain of events culminating in the Revolution.

Between the Children's Riot of 1750 and the fiscal and political crisis of 1787 only one uprising had broken out in Paris, the Flour Riot of 1775. With the 1787 crisis, long simmering discontents erupted in a series of Paris uprisings that are an integral part of the 1787–1789 pre-Revolution. Hardy wrote in his entry of August 19–20, 1787: "Rage stifled the Parisians' usual lightheartedness, even in public." Several hours after Hardy made this comment, a disturbance, the Tounneau Riot, broke out in the Marais when an angry crowd tried to find and punish police spies, the hated *mouchards*. For Thomas Manley Luckett much of the importance of this episode was manifested in popular hatred of spies who had penetrated their lives so pervasively. The very fact that police spies were so effective helps explain the hostility that surfaced on this occasion; precisely because order had been imposed on eighteenth-century Paris, the underlying resentments were that much greater. The Tounneau Riot of 1787 was followed by two other popular disturbances, one in 1788 and another in 1789, for which Hardy gives detailed accounts.

In the twenty-six-year period of his narrative, Hardy describes the escalating tensions between Parisians and the authorities. Of particular interest is his commentary on two incidents that took place at the base of the Henri IV equestrian statue on the Pont-Neuf, and in the adjacent Place Dauphine, one at the beginning of Louis XVI's reign and the other on the eve of the Revolution. When Louis restored the parlements in 1774, a crowd celebrated the decision by burning an effigy of René-Nicolas-Charles de Maupeou with a head representing the fallen chancellor and a body made of a laundry can stuffed with straw and decked out in judicial robes. Two days later a new mannequin of Maupeou was burned at the base of the Henri IV equestrian statue, this time having been filled with fireworks. Shortly thereafter, in another mockery of official ceremony, a crowd burned an effigy of Abbé Joseph-Marie Terray in the same place and held a grotesque funeral for its remains in the Place Dauphine. Popular rejoicing broke out again twenty-four years later, in August 1788, when Louis XVI dismissed his Finance Minister Étienne-Charles de Loménie de Brienne and recalled Necker, a popular favorite. Festivities included three days of fireworks in the Palais-Royal and the burning of an effigy of Brienne at the base of the Henri IV equestrian statue.

In his description of this incident, Hardy wrote that on August 27, "After carrying the mannequin to the equestrian statue of Henri IV, and after having pushed him down on his knees before the statue, they carted him all around the square. Then, after reading him his death sentence, and making him ask forgiveness of God, the King, the judiciary, and the nation, they lifted him into the air at the end of a pole so everyone could see him better, and finally threw him onto an already lighted pyre." The watch tried to block the entrance to the Place Dauphine on August 28, which led to a violent confrontation that left fifty wounded and three dead. Hardy wrote that on the next day, August 28:

> Toward seven o'clock at night, the Foot Watch and the Horse Watch having been ordered not to appear in the palace quarter, the rowdy youngsters, backed by the populace, who had planned to come declare a sort of open war on the watch, were emboldened by their absence. The youngsters began to gather on Pont-Neuf and at the Place Dauphine, within which people had to close all the shops and illuminate all the facades of all the houses, along with those of the rue du Harlay. Toward nine o'clock the populace of the faubourg Saint-Antoine and the faubourg Saint-Marcel came to swell the number of the local smart alecks. The disorder grew and grew; instead of sticking to lighting firecrackers, which were already bothersome enough to the inhabitants, they then lit a big fire in the middle of the Place Dauphine. They fed the fire with anything they could find in the vicinity, such as the sentinel's guardhouse from the Pont-Neuf near the statue of the bronze horse, the stands of orange and lemon merchants in the same place, which were made of simple planks, and the grills of poultry merchants from the Quai de la Vallée, all at the risk of burning the

nearby houses. On that fire they burned the effigy of Monseigneur de Lamoignan, the current French minister of justice, after having him do public penance for his wrongdoing.[67]

Having destroyed the Pont Neuf guardroom the crowd gave itself over to rioting in other parts of Paris. That night they destroyed six additional guardrooms. "The tumult did not end until past three in the morning, and most of the brawlers did not go home until they had set fire to everything they could," Hardy wrote.[68]

Stirred by events and encouraged by Parlement, Parisians had become a volatile force by the end of 1788. The flood of pamphlets that soon inundated the capital further politicized the people, as did elections for the Estates-General. A week before deputies descended on the Palace of Versailles for the opening of the Estates-General a riot broke out in the faubourg Saint-Antoine that can be seen as a measure of how restive workers in this section of Paris had become. Jean-Baptiste Réveillon a wallpaper manufacturer, one of the largest employers of workers in the capital, had tried to hold down wages, but at the same time he strove to maintain the price of bread at the current level. Whatever his intentions may have been, he was seen as an exploiter of the people, and after angry workers gathered on the night of April 26–27, 1789 they mobilized for action. Having heard about a disturbance that was breaking out in the faubourg Saint-Antoine, Hardy left his bookshop to go there and witness whatever was taking place. In his account of the episode, he described the rush of people heading toward the scene of disorder:

> In the afternoon, the Parisians were much affrighted, even shutting up their shops in some places, by a sort of insurrection that spread through the Saint-Antoine faubourg to the vicinity of Notre-Dame. It involved a considerable portion of the workers supposedly of that faubourg, whom some rogues had stirred up against a man named Réveillon, a wealthy manufacturer of printed wallpapers, and another man, also quite rich, named Hanriot, a saltpeter manufacturer, the two men being friends and living in the same part of town. The workers were marching, armed with sticks, and doing no harm to anybody; I met a detachment of about five or six hundred of them on the rue de la Montagne-Sainte-Geneviève, heading . . . toward the Saint-Marceau faubourg with just one drum; one of the men was carrying a gibbet over his shoulder, from which hung the effigy of a man painted on a piece of cardboard.[69]

By the time the riot was over, a mob looted Réveillon's house, drank the wine in his cellar, and fought the *gardes-françaises* sent to restore order. When the fighting ended, some dozen soldiers and many civilians, perhaps several hundred, were dead. In the midst of the riot the duc d'Orléans appeared, after having been at the races. He gave a speech to the people in the street and gave out money to the assembled crowd. Two of the rioters, a roofer named Gilbert and a street porter named Pourrat, were hanged on a gibbet erected at the foot of the Bastille, which was at the west end of the faubourg Saint-Antoine, on April 30. Hardy wrote of the two accused that:

> They were escorted by substantial detachments of the foot and mounted Watch. . . . Some people, seeing them go by, observed that the roofer, who was said to have a wife and four children, wore a resolute and insolent air; he stared boldly at the onlookers and took no notice of the priest, who was talking to him about eternity. He appeared to be about forty-five or fifty; but the other man, much younger, kept well-hidden in the vehicle so as to be seen by nobody; every aspect of him denoted suffering and repentance. The moment they reached the gallows, without having asked to go up to the Chamber [to make any last confessions], they were executed in turn, and their bodies removed an hour later, with the gallows."[70]

Five other workers found drunk in Réveillon's cellar were sent to the galleys. Orléans, who sided with the crowd, was playing a more dangerous game than he realized. So was Parlement, which incited the crowd to action in shows of force during the crisis of 1787–1789. Both Orléans and the parlements used the people to further their agendas and both succumbed to the Revolution they helped bring about. Their actions fed into the revolution Abbé Mably had predicted decades earlier, but it was not the "managed revolution" he had anticipated.

Those responsible for the "managed revolution" at Versailles in May and June of 1789 were unable to control the forces that were unleashed in Paris and throughout France in the month of July. During that month a popular revolution took place that, as time would prove, was so explosive as to drive events in new and unexpected directions. Throughout much of the eighteenth century, the parlements presented themselves as champions of liberty and defenders of the people's rights against royal despotism. By circulating preambles to Remonstrances the parlements contributed to political ferment, and precisely as Mably predicted, after the crown summoned the Estates-General, France was flooded with pamphlets that "instructed the public in its interests." One of these pamphlets proclaimed that "we will all be happy" when everyone, "from the highest princes to the lowest artisans, enjoy the happiness to which their condition entitles them," and that "each man must forget himself, see himself only as a part of the whole [nation] of which he is a member, detach himself from his individual existence, renounce all esprit de corps, belong only to the great society, and be a child of the patrie."[71] Besides pamphlets that trumpeted the virtues of patriotism and proclaimed the rights of man, Paris was flooded by *libelles*, subversive pamphlets that denounced and defamed a court that was the center of government. The Palais-Royal, protected from the police, was one of the sources of these publications. Moreover, leaders of the parlementary opposition used the people as a weapon against the crown in the campaign to summon the Estates-General. Prodded by the parlements, the people took to the streets in Paris and in the provinces in the critical period 1787–1788, and it was shows of force, and violence, that compelled the government to capitulate.

When the "managed revolution" that followed that capitulation was followed by a popular revolution the response, in the main, was one of euphoria. Yet, the violence of July 12–14 did cause uneasiness. Officials in Paris, already apprehensive over maintaining public authority on July 11, the day before the uprising began, petitioned the National Assembly for the formation of a *garde bourgeoise* that could control unruly crowds, and one consequence of the Paris Insurrection was the creation of a National Guard. According to Colin Lucas, "one of the principal 'revolutionary' conseqeunces of crowd action in mid-1789 was to stimulate the crystallization of new municipal governments and national guards that were intended to control the crowd."[72] The very first measure adopted by the permanent committee that came to power as a result of the Paris Insurrection was the formation of a *milice* (militia) and the forbidding of crowds. In the opinion of Jean-Sylvain Bailly, "by their courage and activity, the electors saved the city of Paris,"—not from the enemies of the Revolution but from the people who had just risen. The day after the murder of Foulon and Bertier de Sauvigny, Thomas-Arthur, Comte de Lally-Tollendal tried to persuade members of the Assembly that what had just happened should not be condoned.

A fellow delegate, Antoine-Pierre Barnave, responded: "Gentlemen, there are those who would attempt to elicit our sympathies in favor of the blood spilt yesterday in Paris. Was that blood therefore so pure?"[73] Deeper waters had been stirred than Barnave was able, at the moment, to understand. Passionately dedicated to the Revolution in 1789, his political views began to change in 1790 as he came to regard democratic demands as a danger, and in 1791 he entered into secret correspondence with Marie-Antoinette in a futile effort to retain monarchy as an institution of government. Incriminating papers were discovered in the Tuileries on August 10, 1792, and Barnave was arrested five days later. Before he was executed at age thirty-two on November 29, 1793, he wrote an *Introduction to the French Revolution*

(his title of the work was simply *Introduction*). At the end of the manuscript, Barnave considered the possibility that events might have
taken a different and perhaps better course: "What might have been
done by the government was done without it and against it. The com-
munes, tired of so much inaction and sensing the support of popular
opinion, organized and in doing so declared that they represented the
nation. From then on they were the only power, and from then on the
fate of the revolution was almost a foregone conclusion."[74] Throughout his *Introduction*, Barnave was aloof and looked at the history he
had helped make from a critical distance. Even as he was in prison
awaiting his death he contemplated with "patrician detachment"
(Furet's phrase) a Revolution that had become a Reign of Terror.

Historians have always recognized the centrality of violence to the
Revolution, but they have not been, and are not now in agreement on
its meaning. A critique by Brian C. J. Singer of George Rudé's *The
Crowd in the French Revolution* provides a useful focus for some of the
underlying problems.[75]

Rudé's crowd was made up of craftsmen, artisans, shopkeepers,
petty tradesmen, and the like, humble but respectable people who
knew hunger and hardship first hand. They were, in the main, neither
unemployed nor criminal, but stable, law abiding, and bent upon pre-
serving or reclaiming traditional rights that were imperiled by government ministers, reformers, and capitalists. The motives of revolutionary crowds were archaic but reasonable. There was popular violence,
but when heads were counted the extent of violence was minimal, certainly by twentieth-century standards, but even by those of the eighteenth century. The Gordon Riots claimed more lives than the Paris Insurrection of July 12–14, and for that matter so did the Réveillon Riots,
which erupted in Paris in April 1789, a week before the summoning of
the Estates-General. Singer maintained that Rudé made the revolutionary crowd rational; he also maintained that Rudé lifted the people
he studied out of their own culture and failed to see them within their
actual contemporary context. The perception of the time was that the
revolutionary crowd was dangerous and unstable; there were stereo-
types and prejudices, and people who made up the crowd were part of
this system. Prejudice, Singer believed, had a social dynamic of its own,
independent of discrete events. Rumors, usually false, set crowds in
motion and drove them with whirlwind force to deeds of violence. Even
if the head count was small in the tumultuous days of the July 1789
Paris Insurrection, the meaning of the violence was profound. Singer
was concerned not with the number of lives lost as much as the chore-
ography of violence, the symbolic field on which it was acted out. The
popular violence of July 1789 made a spectacle of victims, whose de-

capitated and, in some cases, eviscerated bodies were dragged through the streets as grim trophies of victory over the people's enemies. The typical course of events was for crowds, stirred by rumors, to meet in the street and for someone suspected of treachery to be seized and threatened with popular justice, which often meant being hung from a lamppost. Someone tries to reason with the crowd, usually an official of some type, but he is ignored or shouted down and leaves. The crowd then makes good its threat. The poor wretch is put to death, hung or otherwise, his head is separated from the body, which is eviscerated, and both the head and various organs are put on pikes.[76] Then there is a macabre procession of the body and its removed parts through the streets with special visits to places that were of particular significance to the victim. These visits reveal a macabre humor that gives the spectacle an element of festivity. In fact, these processions, fully to be understood, should be seen against the background of a popular culture that in some ways had been attenuated in the eighteenth century but in others had been vitalized.[77]

A tradition of gallows humor was an essential part of that culture. And cruelty. After a crowd broke into the monastery of Saint-Lazare on July 13, they made monks serve them food and drink and give them money. For every part of the ritual, which in effect this was, there was symbolic meaning, which was projected by sardonic humor. A sacrilegious masquerade was then organized that set out for the Halles with anatomical skeletons propped on carts alongside pillaged wheat. The monks of Saint-Lazare were made to sit beside the skeletons with empty pitchers of wine. During the night, the monastery cellars had been raided, their wine casks broken open, and the next day drunken rioters were found drowned in the wine that flooded the cellar floor. Others had fought over loot and been killed by their comrades. One way to understand this episode was to see it against the background of Carnival, a potentially explosive festival with its excesses of food and drink, its mockeries, and the sardonic humor of *gauloiserie*.

In a July 13 entry in his *Journal* Sébastien Hardy wrote, in the full heat of the Paris uprising, "One was surprised to see that a day that should have been a day of public mourning seemed to be a day of rejoicing, judging by the shouts and indecent laughter on every side, and by the shenanigans people were performing in the street, as if it were a day of carnival." The chant of the crowd to Bertier de Sauvigny on July 22 to, "Kiss papa! Kiss papa!" was a perfect example of that humor. The spectacle of violence in the summer of 1789 was an acting out of an ancient popular culture on a new historical stage. Even as the Paris Insurrection drove the Revolution into the uncharted waters of modernity, it did so by acting out a symbolic system that was buried in the

past. The Revolutionary elite did not grasp the full meaning of the
Paris Insurrection, and even today historians are divided in their responses to the spectacle of popular violence.

The Paris Insurrection was part of a larger urban protest movement
throughout France, whose explosiveness resulted from conditions peculiar to the summer of 1789 and tensions and conflicts deeply embedded in the mental and material world of the eighteenth-century French
urban populace. And a combination of conditions particular to the
summer of 1789 and long buried resentments within the peasantry
brought about rural protest, the Great Fear. This was not the managed
revolution that Mably had predicted decades earlier. A pamphlet published in 1789, part of the flood of pamphlets that Mably had predicted
would appear after the summoning of the Estates-General, maintained
that all would be happy, "from the highest princes to the lowest artisans," when they fused together in the nation. "Each man must forget
himself, see himself only as a part of the whole of which he is a member, detach himself from his individual existence, belong only to the
great society, and be a child of the patrie." A society that was divided
into an educated public and a populace separated by a wall of fear and
anger could not achieve this goal; it could not achieve the unity to
which patriotic pamphleteers aspired on the eve of the Revolution.
Unity was a high-minded goal that liberal members of the revolutionary leadership would embrace, but it was impossible to achieve. The
Paris Insurrection saved the Revolution but at the same time cast it in
a new mold. The Revolution was never able to resolve conflicts that
surfaced in the summer of 1789. If all agreed on overthrow of monarchy, disagreements were present from the beginning, disagreements
that reflected a fundamental division between an educated public and
a populace that worked with its hands.

FIGURE 1. J.-L. Prieur, *The Intendant Bertier de Sauvigny, led to the Hôtel de Ville, recognizes the Head of Foulon,* July 22, 1789, Musée Carnavelet, Paris

Chapter 2

Jean-Louis Prieur and the *Tableaux historiques*
Images of the Paris Insurrection

Jean-Louis Prieur's drawing in black chalk, stump, point of brush, and black ink, *The Intendant Bertier de Sauvigny, led to the Hôtel de Ville, recognizes the Head of Foulon*, (fig. 1), portrays a spasm of violence in Paris on July 22, 1789, eight days after the fall of the Bastille. Two heads in the drawing are prominent, those of the decapitated Foulon, whose mouth is stuffed with straw and whose neck shows the jagged marks of the knife that severed it, and that of Bertier, who turns away in horror. Other figures also emerge as distinctive individuals, particularly the bearded man with an ax on his shoulder who leads the procession, but also the men—*gardes-françaises* and Parisians—who follow him. Pierre de Nolhac has identified the man with the ax in other drawings by Prieur, an indication that the artist observed directly, at least in some cases, the scenes he portrayed. And immediacy is certainly one of the most striking features of this drawing.[1] It captures in a wealth of concrete detail a scene of popular violence in the aftermath of the Paris Insurrection of July 1789. It also captures the gallows humor of the episode. The crowd chants: "Kiss papa! Kiss papa!" However, the dead mouth of Foulon is stuffed with straw. Ironically, and mordantly, Prieur portrays the procession as it passes the church of Saint-Merry in the rue Saint-Martin, and directly behind the decapitated head of Foulon are medieval sculptures, saints who stare out from a Christian past on the grisly carnivalesque scene, replete with children in tattered clothing who participate in the macabre festivity. The church, bathed in light, is in contrast to the dark tones of the figures who lead the procession. Another contrast is between the orderly divisions of the church, a series of vertical lines that provide a rational background, and the press of figures in the foreground. Rising out of the sea of figures standing in front of the church are muskets, bayonets, and pikes that charge the atmosphere with a sense of violence. This is a drawing that captures both the popular anger that was unleashed during the Paris Insurrection and the macabre humor that accompanied the anger. Prieur has succeeded, as an artist, in projecting the ritualistic dimension of a Paris *journée*.

The Intendant Bertier de Sauvigny was one of sixty-nine drawings done by Prieur for the *Tableaux historiques de la Révolution française*, deluxe full-page engraved folio illustrations offered for sale to the public. From the beginning of the Revolution, the people of France were aware that they were living through a time of momentous change, and, realizing how keen that feeling was, publishers wanted to reach what they calculated was a sizeable market for prints of revolutionary events. The *Tableaux historiques* was the most ambitious and successful of these commercial undertakings. Altogether, the *Tableaux historiques* issued 144 prints, covering the period June 1789 to 18 Brumaire, of Year VII (1799) in the revolutionary calendar. Prieur was the first illustrator for the *Tableaux historiques*, and did drawings for sixty-seven of the first sixty-eight prints, as well as two drawings that were not engraved. Pierre-Gabriel Berthault engraved all of Prieur's illustrations that were included in the *Tableaux*. The prints were offered for sale to the public in sets of two, with accompanying commentaries by Abbé Claude Fauchet and Sébastien Roch Nicolas de Chamfort. Fauchet provided the commentaries for the first two installments and Chamfort wrote commentaries for other tableaus for which Prieur provided illustrations. Prints in the *Tableaux historiques* sold for six livres per installment, far more than six sous that the least expensive revolutionary prints sold for, but, compared to the competition of the *Tableaux*, it was not out of line. It has been estimated that throughout the Revolution the average selling price of a print was six livres, the same price as two prints with accompanying text, issued by the *Tableaux historiques*.[2] The 1791 prospectus of the *Tableaux* emphasized the "superfine woven paper" of the prints and "the consummate beauty of Didot's typesetting."[3] Clearly, the intended audience of the *Tableaux historiques* was well-to-do. The six livres selling price would have constituted something like several days wages for a manual laborer; there can be no question that the market for these deluxe prints was the educated public. At the same time, it was a much broader audience than one that had the means to purchase paintings. To purchase a painting of almost any type would have required greater outlay than for a print, and to buy a work by a known artist would have been beyond the means of all but wealthy connoisseurs. Deluxe prints, by contrast, were affordable to people of taste and discernment but less than great wealth. Broadly speaking, those limits presumably defined the audience for which the *Tableaux historiques* was intended.

Biographical information on Prieur is scanty. One source is a brief notice written in 1809 by E.-J.-L. Barillet, years after Prieur's death.[4] He explains that Prieur was born in Paris in 1759, his father was a "Sculptor for the King," he spent some of his early years in the Temple, where his father had taken refuge because of debts he had incurred, he was received in polite circles, achieved some success in the liberal arts, and was a skilled violinist.

Prieur's father, Jean-Louis Prieur the elder, was a sculptor, designer, and engraver who did some decorations for the coronation of Louis XVI. He was also a member of the Academy of Saint-Luc before it was suppressed in 1777. Jean-Louis Prieur the younger grew up in a world of design and decoration, but it was a tier below the more prestigious world of the Academy. To belong to the Academy of Saint-Luc, as Prieur the elder did, was to inhabit a lesser sphere than that of artists belonging to the Academy. As far as can be determined, Prieur the younger never enrolled as a student in the Academy, and he certainly never won the Prix de Rome, which would have led to a period of study in Rome and set the stage for him to become a member of the Academy. He may have studied under Charles-Nicolas Cochin and Jean-Michel Moreau the younger. As illustrator for the *Tableaux historiques*, his drawings covered the period from June 20, 1789 to September 2–3, 1792. With one known exception, his only works were his illustrations for the *Tableaux*, five of which have been lost.[5] When Prieur left the *Tableaux*, he was actively involved in revolutionary politics. He was a Jacobin and active member of the Revolutionary committee in the Poissonière section, and in September 1793 he was appointed to the Revolutionary Tribunal. As a member of that body, he was present at the trials of Mme Elisabeth and Danton, and he is said to have sent sixty people to their death.[6] He was arrested after the uprising of 12 Germinal (April 1, 1795) and went to the guillotine with Antoine-Quentin Fouquier-Tinville and fourteen others on May 7, 1795.

A resumé was drawn up at the time of Prieur's trial that claimed: "He prided himself on having voted the death of Frettau. When the latter was initially acquitted he said, 'We will get him anyway! Fouquier (-Tinville) ordered his arrest; he will be guillotined in a week's time; having sat on the Constituent Assembly, he is a dead man. We give the death sentence to all who are identified with a certain mark next to their name. I don't care if former nobles and priests are guilty of the charges against them; they are not good republicans; all we have to do is declare them guilty.' " The marks next to the names on lists of the accused referred to in the above passage would appear to have been made before the accused were tried. Decisions had already been made about the accused, for whatever reason, and so far as Prieur was concerned he only had to scrutinize the lists for the marks to decide on guilt or innocence. Prieur was also reported to have said, "rather publicly," that "This one (an accused person) is anisette de Bordeaux, that one is liqueur de madame Amphoux." By calling those condemned to death by different types of drink, he was clearly ridiculing them. Prieur had, it would seem, a sharp tongue, and he was given to mockery and derision towards those he sent to the guillotine.

During Prieur's trial, the clerk-recorder of the Revolutionary Tribunal, Wolff, accused him of bloody-mindedness (*le caractère le plus sanguinaire*) and gave evidence to substantiate the claim. He said, Prieur insulted those he condemned and, during the hearings, he did not bother to listen but drew the heads of the accused, which were completely covered with blood. Prieur replied that he had been calumnied and that he took notes on whoever might have appeared before him. As to the other charge, he said, "Sometimes I drew caricatures, beastly little things (*cochonneries*), small trifles (*petites bêtises*), that is all."[7] The caricatures have been lost, but a drawing in the Royal Collection, Windsor, could be a sketch made by Prieur while he sat on the Revolutionary Tribunal.[8]

Prieur was not the only person associated with the *Tableaux historiques* who went to the guillotine. The first two commentators, Abbé Fauchet and Chamfort, suffered the same fate. Fauchet was a leading figure in the *Cercle Social*, a liberal, progressive group that initially looked to La Fayette for leadership. Chamfort belonged to the Club of Thirty, along with Emmanuel-Joseph Sieyès, Comte de Mirabeau, and Charles-Maurice Talleyrand, as France made ready for the elections to the Estates-General, and in 1790 he joined the *Société de 1789*, a group made up largely of political moderates. Fauchet's and Chamfort's commentaries do not refer to Prieur's illustrations, except indirectly, but to the events they portrayed. In effect, the commentaries were a running narrative of the Revolution, including observations that reflect the political views of the authors.[9] Written after Prieur made the illustrations, the commentaries offered an interpretation of the Revolution that accompanied Prieur's visual account. The two accounts of the Revolution, the verbal account presented in the commentaries and the pictorial account contained in Prieur's illustrations, were not always in agreement. This is not surprising, given the apparent political differences between Prieur and the commentators. Fauchet and Chamfort both developed ties with Girondins who were lined up against the Montagnards as France headed towards the Reign of Terror, for which they paid with their lives. Prieur, by contrast, moved with the Revolution through its more radical stages, and as a Jacobin and member of the Revolutionary Tribunal he participated in the Terror. He was executed after the Terror as a terrorist.

Both Fauchet and Chamfort were part of the crowd that stormed the Bastille. Having been actively involved in the most important episode of the 1789 Revolution, they praised the people for their historic achievement. Yet they were uneasy over the excesses they witnessed. Chamfort made a distinction between the "enlightened" citizens of Paris and the populace, and he made a further distinction between Parisians who worked, had families, and were settled, and "a throng of brigands under the name of workers" who were "without domicile, vagrants (*sans aveu*), without jobs, menaced the capital . . . [and] used their freedom to carry out every excess and licence" (commentary for tableau 10). Chamfort felt the Paris Insurrection delivered France from despotism, but that it unleashed forces that could be dangerous unless contained. He felt a need for imposed order and saw the National Guard as a direct response to that need. The problem was to contain the "brigands," the rootless, violent, destructive elements that made an unwanted appearance in the Paris uprising. Strongly supportive of the popular revolution, Chamfort was disposed to blame vagabonds and brigands for the excesses he had witnessed. This perception did not tally in all cases with the pictorial record of the Revolution presented by Prieur.

Pricur left behind a detailed pictorial account of the Revolution during the period covered by his illustrations, June 1789 to September 1792, and he brought to his tableaus a distinctive and personal style. His account was sometimes narrative and descriptive but could be subjective and interpretive; he did not hesitate to take liberties, to embellish freely, and to invent if doing so served his purposes. He identified with the Revolution and particularly with the popular revolution, and was fascinated with crowd scenes, mob violence, deeds of cruelty and the macabre humor that accompanied those deeds. His work, to be certain, was variable, and if he was uninspired by some scenes, he was stirred by others, and his illustrations reflect those responses. At his best his *tableaus* captured revolutionary conflict and above all the determination, anger, and volatility of the populace.

Prieur's drawings are a superb record not only of important events of the Revolution but also the city of Paris at the end of the eighteenth century. As a skilled illustrator he was well equipped to draw architecture, and it is the buildings of Paris that dominate many of his tableaus. At first glance, it might appear that the architecture in

Prieur's tableaus is presented neutrally, but this is far from the case. The Church of Saint-Merry in *The Intendant Bertier de Sauvigny* is an example of how Prieur used architecture to convey a message.

Having fled Paris, when Bertier de Sauvigny returned to the capital from the north, escorted by captors, he did so at the Porte Saint-Martin. He then proceeded along the rue Saint-Martin, which ended at a cluster of buildings adjacent to the Place de Grève. It was along this route, at the Maubuée fountain, according to Michelet, that Bertier saw the head of Foulon on a pike.[10] This is not where Prieur showed the encounter between Bertier and the decapitated head of his father-in-law. Rather, he showed the encounter at the Church of Saint-Merry, which was also on the rue Saint-Martin. Without documentary evidence it is difficult to prove precisely where the two processions met, one brandishing the head of Foulon, the other escorting Bertier de Sauvigny to the Place de Grève. What makes the most sense is that Prieur chose to set the event against the backdrop of the Church of Saint-Merry because that was what served his purposes. What supports this reading was the composition of Prieur's tableau; he did not just show the church in the background but created an ironic effect by placing a saint on the church directly behind the severed head of Foulon, along with two other saints that frame the scene.

The saints in Prieur's tableau do not correspond to those on the Church of Saint-Merry. In Prieur's illustration, the figures are separated by expanses of undecorated wall that are not to be found on the Church of Saint-Merry, not on the west end that faces the rue Saint-Martin which is dominated by a portal, and nowhere else on the building. The saints in Prieur's tableau are similar to those on the Church of Saint-Merry, but they have been arranged by the artist to achieve the effect he sought. Moreover, the vertical lines that run along the wall in Prieur's tableau are at variance with the masonry of the Church of Saint-Martin. There are no expanses of unrelieved wall on the church, and the masonry is not rectilinear. To create contrast between the tumultuous scene in the street and the church in the background Prieur has altered both the wall of the church and the location of the sculptures. In addition, the crowd that is seen in front of the church could not have occupied the space within which it has been placed. The rue Saint-Martin is far too narrow to have accommodated the jeering mob that witnesses the encounter between the two processions.

Superb as the tableau is, it is far from an accurate portrayal of the event it depicts; much of the tableau's effectiveness is achieved through Prieur's scripting of the event. By showing Bertier recoiling from the decapitated head of his father-in-law against the background of a church, he creates an incongruity that served his rhetorical objec-

This photograph, taken by the author, shows how Prieur's depiction of Saint-Merry is not accurate. The saints are similar to those on the church, but the vertical lines that articulate the wall surface are freely invented by the artist. The rue Saint-Martin, where Saint-Merry is located, is too narrow to get a photograph of the entire facade; this photograph covers the full extent of the building that faces the street. The expanse of wall seen in Prieur's drawing is not to be found on the church.

tives; the crowd that brandished pikes and axes is in grotesque counterpoint to the ordered architecture of the Gothic church in the background. What is ironic, and mordant, is the contrast between the Christian saint directly behind the severed head of Foulon, the two saints who frame the scene at opposite ends of the illustration, and the procession in the street below them. The architecture in this tableau has become part of Prieur's message; it furthers his agenda. The same is true over and over in Prieur's illustrations. Sometimes monumental architecture that had clear associations with the monarchy offers an ironic backdrop to the seizure of power by the people of Paris, or to scenes of violence driven by popular fear or popular anger. Sometimes the angle of vision affects the way one responds to architecture or public spaces and the events that take place in their midst. Typically, Prieur views the scenes he portrays from afar. The distant perspective he favors allows him at once to give prominence to architecture and the public spaces of Paris and to show large crowds participating in those events. The perspective is so distant and the crowds are so large in most of Prieur's drawings that individual figures do not, as a rule, stand out.

FIGURE 2.   J.-L. Prieur, *The Tennis Court Oath*, Tableau 1, June 20, 1789, Musée Carnavelet, Paris

Prieur's first illustration for the *Tableaux* is a drawing of the *Tennis Court Oath* (tableau 1, fig. 2). Viewing the event from a distance, Prieur depicts two groups of figures, those on the floor who swear the oath and those in a gallery above. The figures within these groups are minute, and they are seen against a large expanse of wall. Some figures can be identified, Bailly obviously, standing on a table, but also Jean-François Goupilleaux de Fontenay in an armchair and Maupetit de la Mayenne in a sedan chair. These two deputies are singled out not for their political significance but for their narrative value. They add descriptive detail to a scene that is descriptive in character. It is a work without ideas, without an underlying conception. To move from Prieur's *Tennis Court Oath* to J.-L. David's more famous version of the same historic event is to enter a completely different world. David's *Tennis Court Oath* (fig. 3), like his earlier masterpieces in the Salons that catapulted him to greatness, is an idea painting. It is the product of reflection. It is not a work that merely shows a group of men gesturing with their arms to someone standing on a table; it celebrates the birth of a nation. The descriptive character of Prieur's drawing is in definite contrast to the high rhetoric of David's finished study that he did in preparation for an immense painting of the *Tennis Court Oath*.

FIGURE 3.   J.-L. David, *The Tennis Court Oath*, Musée National du Château, Versailles

A seemingly plausible explanation for the differences between David's and Prieur's renderings of the *Tennis Court Oath* was their training. As an academic artist, David had acquired techniques for history paintings, for serious works of art, and he employed these techniques in the *Tennis Court Oath* much as he had in his earlier masterpieces, such as the *Oath of the Horatii*, with which this work had so many affinities. By contrast, Prieur, as a mere illustrator, did not apply those techniques in his *Tennis Court Oath*. Hence, the argument might go, the merely narrative quality of his version.

Yet Prieur's compositional approach in *The Intendant Bertier de Sauvigny* is much the same as that of David's painting. As in David's *Tennis Court Oath*, Prieur's field of vision in *The Intendant Bertier de Sauvigny* is from below and from the exact center of the scene. The saint in the background dissects the space into equal parts, just as Bailly does in David's *Tennis Court Oath*. Prieur's saint serves a completely different purpose, however, than Bailly does in David's work. Its purpose is not to create unity, but incongruity. The saint stands behind and solemnly above the marching soldiers, the open carriage that conveys Bertier, and the decapitated head of Foulon; the saint is in sharp contrast and ironic counterpoint to the scene below, the procession of a jeering, angry populace and those on whom they wreak vengeance. *The Intendant Bertier de Sauvigny* is carefully thought out and it uses compositional techniques that project and dramatize the artist's conception. The point is that there is a conception, and in this respect it can be compared to David's *Tennis Court Oath*. Stylistically different as these works are, they can be regarded as the two outstanding artistic statements of the two revolutions that set France forever in a new historical direction in 1789, the constitutional revolution of June at Versailles and the popular revolution in Paris in the following month.

A comparison of Prieur's *Paris guarded by the People on the Night of 12–13 July* (tableau 11, fig. 4) and Charles Thévenin's *Storming of the Bastille* (fig. 5) suggests some of the stylistic differences between an illustrator and an academic artist. In these two works, there is a similar balance between the figures in the foreground and the architecture behind them. If the figures in Prieur's and Thévenin's illustrations are on much the same scale and the architecture occupies about the same amount of pictorial space, the works otherwise are strikingly different. It would not be incorrect—or off the mark—to say that these works are done in different languages. One is done in the elevated language of the Academy, the other in a lower and more ordinary language that is free of grand gestures and high rhetoric. In Thévenin's *Storming of the Bastille* insurgents, who are furious with de Launay for supposedly ordering his soldiers to fire on the crowd, apprehend him and hold

FIGURE 4.   J.-L. Prieur, *Paris guarded by the People on the Night of July 12–13*, Tableau 11, July 12–13, 1789, Musée Carnavelet, Paris

FIGURE 5.   Charles Thévenin, *Storming of the Bastille*, Musée Carnavelet, Paris

him at gunpoint. Of particular interest is the figure seen from behind that holds his gun with one hand and de Launay with the other hand. Thévenin was at pains to put the splendid anatomy of this figure on display because of the heroic quality it adds to the scene. This figure is done in the grand manner, and as such it draws from the long tradition of academic art. Other figures draw from the same tradition, such as the soldier who arrives with the white flag. There is something theatrical about the gesture of this soldier, which is underscored rhythmically by the sweep of the flag. At his right is a group of two more figures, one seated and injured, and a compatriot who offers support. These figures are done in an appropriate expression for their role in the illustration. All of the figures seem to have been done according to a particular expression: righteous anger, fear, terror, stoic acceptance, pathos, suffering, compassion; the figures are properly expressive and correctly take their place within the drama of the scene. Thévenin's *Storming of the Bastille* is an assured, accomplished, fine illustration that puts a wealth of technique on display. And well it should.

Thévenin was a student of François-André Vincent, a distinguished member of the Academy, whose grand, elevated manner he appropriated. The high rhetoric of this work connects it to the language of the Academy. It might be noted in this connection that Thévenin exhibited both his drawing and etching of the *Storming of the Bastille* in the Salon of 1793 and then did a painting of the same scene, which he exhibited in the Salon of 1795.

Prieur's *Paris guarded by the People* lacks the virtuosity of Thévenin's illustration. It does not achieve its effect by grandiloquence and theatricality; individual figures do not stand out and there is little variety of expression. The figures in the crowd move together in a common purpose and all are done in the same manner. It is clear that Prieur's objective is to show the people of Paris guarding the city; they move in unison with guns and pikes held at the same angle to underline a sense of common purpose. This aspect of the work is in sharp contrast to the broad spectrum of attitudes and gestures in Thévenin's *Storming of the Bastille*. Also different is the way Prieur draws his figures. It is not just that they lack the bravura display of Thévenin's figures. They move stiffly and even a bit awkwardly, as if they lacked the grace and ease of manner of refined people. There is something archaic about their appearance and their manner, a quality that connects them to their milieu, to the popular culture in which their life is embedded.

Prieur did thirty-two illustrations for the period June to October 1789 and nine for just one day, July 12. His identification with the 1789 Revolution is obvious and undeniable; what needs to be explained is how he responded. Tableau 2, *The People delivering the gardes-françaises detained at the Abbaye Saint-Germain* (fig. 6), helps

Figure 6. J.-L. Prieur, *The People delivering the gardes-françaises detained at the Abbaye Saint-Germain*, Tableau 12, June 30, 1789, Musée Carnavelet, Paris

define his perspective. The incident he illustrated in this tableau, which took place on June 30, shows a crowd of Parisians freeing *gardes-françaises* from detention. In the unfolding saga of the Paris In- surrection that took place two weeks later, the alliance between the people and the *gardes-françaises* was to be of critical importance, and in this illustration Prieur set the stage for what was to come.

On June 30 *gardes-françaises*, dressed as civilians, had gone to the Assembly at Versailles to denounce their commander, Florent-Louis- Marie, the duc du Châtelet.[11] The *gardes* were arrested and put in the Abbaye prison until a crowd freed them later that day, along with other *gardes-françaises* who had been detained in the Abbaye on June 28. The *gardes-françaises* had joined the Swiss Guards and fired on the people during the Réveillon Riots in April 1789, but the officer who gave the order to fire on the crowd, the duc du Châtelet, was publicly disavowed by fellow officers, and from this time on members of the *gardes- françaises* began to criticize the government.

On June 24 two companies of *gardes-françaises* refused to obey or- ders when they were told to repress a possible Paris uprising, and four days later other *gardes* assured a crowd at the Palais-Royal that they would not use their arms against the people. The duc du Châtelet ar- rested the fourteen grenadiers he regarded as the ringleaders and placed them in the Abbaye prison, where they were joined two days later by the officers who denounced their commander when they appeared be- fore the National Assembly. By the time a crowd freed the *gardes* from detention in the Abbaye on June 30, a bond had been established be- tween the *gardes* and the Paris populace. Hardy noted in his *Journal* a few days before the Paris Insurrection: "Soldiers of the *gardes- françaises* from several barracks in the faubourg Saint-Marcel declared their intention of deserting." And Desmoulins wrote his father: "The *gardes-françaises* would all sooner be hanged than fire on a citizen."[12] The *gardes-françaises* sided with the people in the insurrection of July 12 and played a decisive military role in the conflict with foreign regi- ments that were under the command of the Baron de Besenval. In tableau 2, *The People delivering the Guards*, Prieur portrayed the al- liance between the people of Paris and the *gardes-françaises* that was to be of crucial importance in the Paris Insurrection.

The first of Prieur's nine illustrations of the July 12 *journée*, *Camille Desmoulins making a Motion at the Palais-Royal* (tableau 3, fig. 7), shows the fiery young orator holding forth on a table in front of the Café de Foy before an agitated audience.[13] Desmoulins was one of several orators in the precincts of the Palais-Royal who spoke out in protest at news of Necker's dismissal, which began to circulate through Paris around nine in the morning. "To arms! To arms! Let us

FIGURE 7.   P.-G. Berthault engraving of Prieur drawing, *Camille Desmoulins making a Motion at the Palais-Royal*, Tableau 3, July 12, 1789, Bibliothèque Nationale, Paris

all wear cockades of green, the color of hope. . . . The infamous police are here. They can take a good look, observe me closely." Brandishing a pistol, as seen in Prieur's illustration, Desmoulins exclaims, "At least they will not take me alive, and I shall know how to die gloriously. . . . No théâtres! No dancing! This is a day of mourning."[14] The crowd that Desmoulins addresses, judging by types of clothing in Prieur's illustration, is socially mixed but predominantly bourgeois. Most figures are attired in knee breeches, long coats, vests, three-cornered hats, and wigs. Mingled among well-dressed bourgeois are a few men who wear shirts and trousers and plain round hats. They carry sticks, in contrast to the canes held by bourgeois members of the crowd, and they move differently. They run rather than walk towards the crowd, and one is seen climbing onto a chair. At his left a woman in fine dress and fancy hat holds her child, and behind her a husband and wife, clearly refined types, leave with their son, the only members of the crowd to do so. The husband points away from the crowd, as if to say this is not where we belong, and the wife looks at him and holds onto his arm. Already in this drawing Prieur has brought out differences within a Paris crowd.

Responding to Desmoulins's call, "No théâtres!," a crowd of over three thousand appear before and force its way into the Opéra, "uttering fearsome cries." This is the subject of Prieur's next drawing, *The People closing the Opéra after the dismissal of Necker* (tableau 4, fig. 8). In the drawing, people in the street push forward and move into the Opéra while members of the audience stand outside on a balcony. A carriage has arrived outside the Opéra to remove a civilized member of the audience from the pandemonium of the street. The crowd is made up of some who are well attired and others dressed in trousers and plain shirts, but it is the latter who are now most numerous. The social composition of the crowd has changed since the previous scene at the Palais-Royal, and already in this depiction of a crowd in action there are signs of militancy conveyed by sticks held up in protest and by workers who run forward to join the crowd. The elite gathering from the Opéra drawn to the balcony by the crowd below them does not, with the exception of two figures, look down but rather to the left, at the crowd that moves toward the Opéra from the Palais-Royal. Those

FIGURE 8.   J.-L. Prieur, *The People closing the Opéra after the dismissal of Necker*, Tableau 4, July 12, 1789, Musée Carnavelet, Paris

on the left of the balcony lean forward, in the direction of the crowd that heads their way, but those at the far right are huddled together, as if in a defensive posture. The response covers a spectrum from curiosity to guardedness, in contrast to the agitation and militancy of the people in the street below.

Having closed down the Opéra, a crowd moved to the rue du Temple, along which boulevard théâtres were situated, and where Curtius' wax works museum was also located. Entering it, the crowd demanded the bust of Necker, which the owner promptly gave over, along with the bust of the duc d'Orléans. Carrying their trophies, the crowd marched along the rue Saint-Honoré until it came to the Place Louis-le-Grand (Place Vendôme), where they encountered a detachment of dragoons that was under orders to use only the flats of their swords and was swamped by the crowd. Accounts of this episode vary, but apparently one *garde-française,* who had defied orders and left his barracks, was killed in the melée. The Prince de Lambesc, commander of the Royal-Allemand regiment, who was stationed in the Place Louis XV, heard that his detachment in the Place Louis-le-Grand was unable to cope with the crowd and rode with his men to rescue the beleaguered soldiers; both units returned to the Place Louis XV. The crowd that had been in the Place Louis-le-Grand passed into the rue Saint-Honoré and joined by others headed toward the Place Louis XV.

An illustration in the Musée Carnavelet by Nicolas Pérignon (fig. 9) of the Place Louis XV showed the geographical space within which the next episode took place. One crowd passed into the Place Louis XV

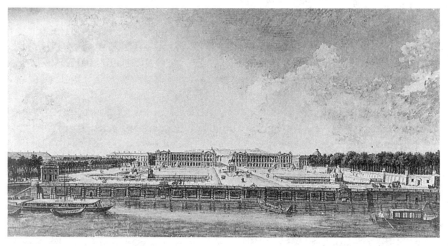

FIGURE 9.   Nicolas Pérignon, *The Place Louis XV*, Musée Carnavelet, Paris

from the rue Royale directly behind the equestrian statue in the center of the square as Parisians returned from their afternoon walk in the Champ-Elysées to the left of the Place Louis XV. The convergent crowd clashed with Lambesc's German Guards at the east end of the Place Louis XV, in Pérignon's illustration to the right of the equestrian statue and in the space between it and the Tuileries. A peddler, François Pépin, who was carrying the bust of the duc d'Orléans, was seized and dragged behind a horse to the equestrian statue of Louis XV, where he was stabbed in the breast and killed. Standing above the clash of soldiers and civilians, on the wall at the west end of and inside the Tuileries, were Parisians drawn there by the fighting, and from that position they pelted the German Guards with stones and whatever other missiles that were at hand from a nearby construction project. At this point, the Baron de Besenval, who received a report of the clash at his headquarters in the Champ de Mars, ordered Lambesc to clear the Tuileries. To do so, Lambesc had to ride with his men over the swing bridge, the Pont Tournant, that connected the Place Louis XV to the Tuileries. As the German Guards entered the circular area inside the Tuileries, they came under another barrage of missiles from the crowd above them, and, unable to carry out his orders, Lambesc ordered his men to withdraw to the Place Louis XV, but, as they did so, they clashed with civilians inside the Tuileries; they did so again when they reached the Pont Tournant on the way back to the place Louis XV.

Lambesc's men used their swords against the crowd, several civilians were injured, and one old man may have been killed, but Jacques Godechot, who has sorted the evidence carefully, said, "There is no proof of this."[15] Thus, according to the standard accounts of the first violence of the Paris Insurrection, someone, perhaps a *garde-française*, was killed at the Place Louis-le-Grand; civilians clashed with German Guards at the far end of the Place Louis XV and inside the Tuileries; the peddler François Pépin was dragged to the royal equestrian statue, where he was killed; and an old man might have been killed when Lambesc tried to carry out Besenval's order to clear the Tuileries.

Within the large output of illustrations depicting the Paris Insurrection, the clash between Lambesc's German Guards and civilians was among the events portrayed most frequently. A Bibliothèque Nationale Catalogue of revolutionary images issued in 1990 includes thirty-two illustrations depicting this episode, of which two are by Prieur: tableau 5, *The Busts of the duc d'Orléans and Necker are carried in Triumph and broken in the Place Louis XV* (fig. 10), and tableau 7, *The Prince de Lambesc enters the Tuileries* (fig. 11).[16]

Prieur's tableaus offer a different pictorial record of the clash between the German Guards and Parisians than that of other artists.

FIGURE 10.   J.-L. Prieur, *The Busts of the duc d'Orléans and Necker are carried in Triumph and broken in the Place Louis XV*, Tableau 5, July 12 , 1789, Musée Carnavelet, Paris

Only Prieur shows the clash in the Place Louis XV; all other artists show it taking place inside the Tuileries. In the first of Prieur's two tableaus that portray the event, tableau 5, *Busts carried in Triumph*, fighting between Lambesc's German Guards and Parisians takes place at the base of the Louis XV equestrian statue. Prieur's perspective is from the east—the Tuileries are behind him—as the fighting spills across the Place Louis XV to the west end of the public square.

That he chose this vantage point had much to do with the effect he wished to achieve. To have foreign mercenaries, armed and on horseback, swinging away at civilians under the statue of a king around whom scandal had swirled for decades, and from which popular graffiti had regularly to be cleaned, was perfect in its irony. Moreover, Prieur showed the king looking down at the carnage, as if he were issuing orders to the soldiers who slashed away at Parisians, his own people. The people did not run from their tormentors; rather they fought back with the only arms they had, pikes and axes. That Parisians would have had as many of these implements on a Sunday afternoon as shown in

Figure 11.   J.-L. Prieur, *The Prince de Lambesc enters the Tuileries*, Tableau 7, July 12, 1789, Musée Carnavelet, Paris

Prieur's drawing was improbable, and no other illustrations showed the people brandishing arms.

   In all other depictions of the clash between the German Guards and civilians, Parisians run from armed soldiers, but in Prieur's version the people fight back, and with good effect. One German Guard has been dislodged from his horse and behind him stands a Parisian, a worker, judging from his attire, who raises an ax overhead to finish off the helpless soldier. A Parisian jabs a pike into the body of another German Guard, in an attempt to bring him down from a rearing horse, and to the left a *garde-française*, who has sided with the people, fires at a mounted German Guard. Next to him is a Parisian who picks up a stone that he will use against the enemy. The people fight back fiercely against armed soldiers, and on even terms. A worker behind the *garde-française*, who shoots at a German Guard, raises a pike towards, and looks in the direction of, the Louis XV equestrian statue, as if in defiance.

   Prieur chose the middle of the Place Louis XV in tableau 5 because it allowed him to show fighting next to the Louis XV equestrian statue;

FIGURE 12.   J.-F. Janinet,
*Charge of the Prince de
Lambesc,* Musée Car-
navelet, Paris

he inflated the violence and most importantly he showed Parisians offering fierce resistance to the German Guards. In all other illustrations
civilians run from German Guards; in all other illustrations only civilians lie on the ground. Only Prieur showed German Guards being dislodged from their horses and lying helpless before Parisians with raised
axes. In what surely were more accurate renderings of the fighting between German Guards and Parisians, those of J. F. Janinet and J. B.
Lallemand (figs. 12–13), soldiers were seen riding after civilians with
raised swords, as men and women fled from their charge.

In tableau 6, *Gardes-françaises protect the duc du Châtelet from
the Crowd* (fig. 14), the scene shifted from the Place Louis XV to the
barracks of the *gardes-françaises* on the boulevard de la chaussée d'Antin, three-quarters of a mile to the north. Uncertain of the loyalty of
the *gardes-françaises,* Besenval had ordered them to remain in their
barracks, and with the exception of a few men, who joined the crowd,
the *gardes* had obeyed orders.

FIGURE 13.   J.-B. Lallemand, *The Charge of the Prince de Lambesc at the Tuileries*, Musée Carnavelet, Paris

FIGURE 14.   J.-L. Prieur, *Gardes-françaises protect the duc du Châtelet from the Crowd*, Tableau 6, July 12, 1789, Musée Carnavelet, Paris

According to Chamfort's commentary for this tableau, the duc du Châtelet was recognized and followed "by the people. Where, might one think, would he seek refuge? At the very *dépôt* of his soldiers, on the boulevard de la chaussée d'Antin. He believed them capable of a generous sentiment, and he was not mistaken" (commentary, tableau 6). The duc du Châtelet apparently sought the protection of his men when pursued by a crowd, but, according to an illustration by A.-L.-F. Sergent (B.N. cat. no. 762–66), the incident took place not on July 12 and in front of the dépôt of the *gardes-francaises* but on July 13 and in front of the Invalides.

That Prieur and Sergent chose to illustrate *gardes-françaises*, protecting their commander from an angry crowd, was not because the incident had political or military importance, but to place the *gardes-françaises* in a favorable light. The duc du Châtelet, known for being harsh to his men, had ordered the *gardes* to fire on the people during the Réveillon Riots in April, and since then he and his men had clashed repeatedly. In Prieur's *Gardes-françaises protect the duc du Châtelet*, the hated commander was protected from an angry crowd by the men he had oppressed; in a time of crisis he sought refuge with the very soldiers he had persecuted. The thin figure of Châtelet was seen between two of his men, both larger than he, who protect him without the use of weapons.

Châtelet holds his hand on his chest, as if pleading innocence, but Parisians gesture angrily and wave pikes at the hated commander. The guard to the right of Châtelet holds back someone who, it seems, would like to get his hands on an enemy of the people. In this illustration the *gardes-françaises* are seen as generous to the commander who persecuted them, and, while their sympathies were with the people, they remain in their barracks, as ordered by the Baron de Besenval.

In tableau 7, *The Prince de Lambesc enters the Tuileries* (fig. 11), the scene shifts back to the Place Louis XV, where the Prince de Lambesc, following Besenval's order, rides at the head of the German Guards into the Tuileries. It is this order, according to Jacques Godechot, "which was to turn the demonstration into an insurrection."[17] In Prieur's tableau, Lambesc rides at the head of his men with upraised sword at a male civilian who tries to protect three women who have panicked and gotten on the wrong side of a fence that separates the soldiers from the crowd. Behind the fence are men, some barefoot, most of them workers who brandish pikes in angry protest. One member of the crowd picks up a stone as he looks at Lambesc, who holds his sword over the civilian who tries to rescue the fleeing women. People are lined up at the base of the terrace with raised pikes awaiting the Royal-Allemands, while the crowd above prepares to unleash a volley of missiles.

Once inside the Tuileries, the German Guards clash again with civilians, this time in the circular space beyond the Pont Tournant. As we have seen, other artists portray the German Guards running down civilians, and civilians trying to defend themselves with chairs, but Prieur does not include that scene in his visual account of the Paris Insurrection. Rather, in tableau 8, *The gardes-françaises attack the Royal-Allemands* (fig. 15), the scene shifts back to the boulevard de la chaussée d'Antin, and to the barracks of the *gardes-françaises*, where the French Guards are seen putting the German Guards to rout.

According to Chamfort's commentary for this tableau, Lambesc sent a detachment of German Guards to be certain that the *gardes-françaises* remained within their barracks, and it was here that the French Guards and German Guards are said to have fought. This is not an accurate account of the episode as best as can be determined. While some of the *gardes- françaises* appear to have remained in their *dépôt* at the beginning of the Paris Insurrection, others escaped and went into the center of Paris; it was there, in the Tuileries according to Godechot, that they fought the German Guards.

FIGURE 15.   J.-L. Prieur, *The gardes-françaises attack the Royal Allemands*, Tableau 8, July 12, 1789, Musée Carnavelet, Paris

By depicting the *gardes-françaises* fighting German Guards in front on the boulevard de la chaussée d'Antin, in front of the *dépôt* of the *gardes-françaises*, the German Guards are seen to have taken the initiative; they have sought out the *gardes-françaises*, who have obeyed their orders and have remained in their barracks until they are confronted by Lambesc's German Guards. In Prieur's tableau, three steadfast rows of *gardes-françaises* fire at the mounted German guards who are shrouded by a cloud of gunsmoke. A barely discernible Royal-Allemand fires in the direction of his own men as he falls backward from his horse, discharging a puff of smoke as he does so. Crowds to the side of and behind the *gardes-françaises* cheer them on, and two unarmed Parisians, heedless of the risk, seize a mounted German guard who raises his sword against them.

By the evening of July 12, Besenval decides to move Swiss regiments stationed at the Champ de Mars since June 5 to the Place Louis XV. This is the subject of Prieur's next drawing, *Troops on the Champ de Mars cross to the Place Louis XV* (tableau 9, fig. 16). Tents are lined up in parallel rows that extend from one end to the other of the vast space of the Champ de Mars, and through the middle of that space cavalry, infantry, and cannons move in a long column. Prieur shows neither the beginning nor end of the file of soldiers. The impression is one of an endless procession, and the numbers are, in fact, so great, nine thousand men in all, that it requires several hours to complete the operation. Troops crossed the Seine in boats mounted with guns for protection against *gardes-françaises* on the right bank. The crossing is made and the Swiss troops join Lambesc's beleaguered men at the Place Louis XV. Then, after having been fired on by *gardes-françaises* lined up in adjacent boulevards, Besenval's massed forces abandon their position in the Place Louis XV and withdraw to camps on the right bank. The center of Paris is now in the hands of the people.

Prieur's last two illustrations of the July 12 *journée* show Paris after the breakdown of order. In one, *Burning of the Barrière de la Conférence* (tableau 10, fig. 17), a crowd sets fire to one of the hated customs posts that ringed the capital. In 1785, the architect Claude-Nicolas Ledoux had been commissioned by the King to build fifty-five customs houses connected by a wall that radiated around Paris.

Ledoux worked with Antoine-Laurent Lavoisier, the renowned chemist who was a tax farmer and in that capacity had conducted a study to determine the loss of tax revenues to smuggling in the capital. Lavoisier recommended the construction of a wall and fifty-five customs houses, the *barrières*. Charles-Alexandre Calonne approved the project, and by the time Louis XVI gave official approval in 1785 construction had already begun. Completed in 1787, the *barrières* were

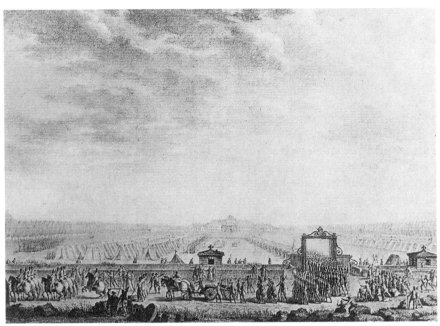

FIGURE 16.   J.-L. Prieur, *Troops on the Champ de Mars cross to the Place Louis XV*, Tableau 9, July 12, 1789, Musée Carnavelet, Paris

FIGURE 17.   J.-L. Prieur, *Burning of the Barrière de la Conférence*, Tableau 10, July 12, 1789, Musée Carnavelet, Paris

controversial from the beginning and a source of widespread resentment. The *Mémoires secrètes*, published in 1785, called the *barrières* "a monument of slavery and despotism," a comment that reflected with undoubted accuracy a widely held feeling about a project whose purpose was to increase tax revenues.[18] Parisians put forty of the fifty-five customs houses to the torch on the first night of the Paris Insurrection, of July 12–13.

In Prieur's drawing of the *Burning of the Barrière de la Conférence*, flames pour from the building and a cloud of smoke lines the sky. The crowd is not content to burn the customs post but also pillages it, smashes and burns furniture, and destroys a sculpture by an adjacent gate. This is an angry but jubilant crowd. In the space beneath the burning building rioters hold their hands upward in gestures of triumph and others stand on the roof of the *Conférence* customs post waving scythes and pikes. Even as fire pours from the building, a rioter, who stands on a fence, leans against the building with a torch in his hand.

Chamfort's theory of the Paris crowd was developed most fully in his commentary for this tableau, *Burning of the Barrière de la Conférence*. A "crowd of brigands under the name of workers" from the faubourgs took advantage of the breakdown of order and burnt the *barrières* in a night of "bizarre incidents" that Parisians painfully discussed the next day and then forgot in the following week, for the capital was shaken by a succession of disturbances. "Yet in the midst of this chaos the principal inhabitants, the good people (*honnêtes hommes*), and all those who had something to lose, joined together to prevent, as much as was possible, the brigandage and devastation" that followed the collapse of order (commentary, tableau 10).

In Prieur's illustration of the *Burning of the Barrière de la Conférence*, the crowd acts collectively and with a sense of united purpose; the sense of the tableau is not one of brigands but ordinary Parisians who destroy one of the customs posts that had recently been built, for the people resented paying higher taxes in order to pay for the recently constructed *barrières*.

In his commentary for tableau 11, *The People Guarding Paris*, Chamfort explained that patrols of men and even women appeared in the streets of the capital armed with guns, swords, and axes, after brigands had become masters of the city on the night of July 12–13. Carrying torches, they appeared to threaten the capital more than protect it; they "inspired more fear than confidence" (commentary, tableau 11). This interpretation of the patrols that guarded Paris on the first night of the insurrection can be compared to an aquatint illustration by Antoine-Louis-François Sergent for the *Tableaux des Révolutions de*

Paris, French Citizens demonstrating in the Streets of Paris on the Night of 12–13 July (fig. 18).

Sergent shows Parisians and *gardes-françaises* in the street and a woman in a window above them peering down at a scene that from her viewpoint was presumably not reassuring. This is not how Prieur portrayed the night of July 12–13. Discussed above (fig. 4), this is the tableau in which a crowd is seen from a closer perspective than in any of Prieur's previous tableaus, and in which men, women, and *gardes-françaises* guard the capital. Prieur's crowd is not one that inspires fear from Parisians who have something to lose but one that has suddenly, and abruptly, appeared on the historical stage. The focus is not, as in Sergent's illustration, on the tension between the crowd and an apprehensive woman standing behind a window but on the crowd itself, and its sense of common purpose. The crowd in Prieur's drawing, unlike the one in Sergent's illustration, does not have guns, swords, and axes. With a few exceptions, the Parisians in Prieur's tableau have only

FIGURE 18.   A.-L.-F. Sergent, *French Citizens demonstrating in the Streets of Paris on the Night of July 12–13, 1789,* Musée Carnavelet, Paris

pikes, which they hold at the same angle, underscoring a sense of common purpose. Pikes have already become symbols of popular militancy on the first night of the Paris uprising in Prieur's tableau 11, and, held at the same angle, they convey a sense of popular unity.

Chamfort's commentary for tableau 12, *Pillaging the Monastery of Saint-Lazare* (fig. 19), described the "dark event" it portrayed as a "disastrous precursor of the Revolution" and one that occurred "under the most sinister auspices." With the *barrières* burning in the faubourgs and "most citizens having returned to their homes," brigands gathered together behind the *moulin des dames* on Montmartre, held council, and decided on their next exploit. After considering several possibilities, they decided on the monastery (*maison*) of Saint- Lazare. Arriving unannounced at its doors at 3:00 A.M., the signal was given and the "brigands" forced their way into the monastery, where a "masquerade mixed with the horrors of a revolting scene" took place (commentary, tableau 12). Already discussed in the previous chapter, the pillaging of the monastery of Saint-Lazare was a scene of sacrilegious masquerade, mockery of the clergy, drunkenness, and looting. Besides drowning in a cellar inundated with wine from smashed caskets, rioters were poisoned by drugs they foolishly took from a pharmacy they raided. Others fought over loot and killed their own comrades. In his illustration of the event, Prieur did not show the scene inside the monastery, where the worst excesses took place, but views the scene from the street.

A large crowd has gathered outside the monastery where it observes compatriots, who are inside the building, dropping whatever they have found into the street below. Tables are carried and stacked and bags of wheat are piled up. The street turbulence is in striking contrast to the stateliness of the monastery, which also served as a prison in the eighteenth century. Architecturally, Saint-Lazare is not unlike *hôtels* of powerful families in the finest neighborhoods of Paris. Nothing about the building suggests it is a monastery; everything about it exemplifies power and affluence, and, judging from what was confiscated, appearances were not deceptive. Over one hundred *muids* (hogsheads) of wine were on reserve, one *muid* being equal to 268.2 litres, plus large supplies of bottled wine, beer, cheese, olive oil, butter, wheat, vinegar, silver, books, and furniture, most of which was consumed, smashed, or confiscated. Fifty-three cartloads of wheat were taken to the Halles out of concern for the welfare of the people.

The overall impression of Prieur's tableau, portraying the event, is of an angry crowd that vents its anger on a center of wealth. Members of the crowd, standing before the building, hold pikes, swords, and muskets in gestures of defiance and wrath. Judging from clothing, the

FIGURE 19. J.-L. Prieur, *Pillaging the Monastery of Saint-Lazare*, Tableau 12, July 12, 1789, Musée Carnavelet, Paris

crowd is made up largely of workers, but not entirely. Also included are men who wear long coats and triangular hats, and they, too, raise their hands upward in gestures of support. Perhaps the most revealing touch is the cart filled with sacks of wheat, on which a monk kneels, his head lowered in humiliation or prayer. One man points at him accusingly from the rear of the cart, and at the other end two more men point muskets in his direction. The monk could well have been one of the clergy who went from Saint-Lazare to the Halles in a sacrilegious masquerade with anatomical skeletons, empty pitchers of wine, and carts filled with sacks of pillaged wheat. Directly below the cart in Prieur's tableau, members of the crowd hold swords, pikes, and muskets, also pointed toward the monk. A woman with an empty basket and a child in her arm looks at the cart laden with sacks of wheat. Prieur's perspective does not appear to be at one with the printed description that accompanied his tableau. He portrays the scene not as "sinister" and a "disaster" but as an expression of popular anger directed at a bastion of wealth and privilege, and the appropriation of wheat for a hungry populace.

For the Paris Insurrection to succeed, the people needed to secure arms, and Prieur's next two tableaus showed their efforts to achieve that goal. The first, *Arms taken from the Garde-Meuble, Place Louis XV* (tableau 13, fig. 20), portrayed a scene after the pillaging of Saint-Lazare, on the same day. Various attempts were made to get arms, including repeated efforts at the Hôtel de Ville, which as we have seen in the previous chapter were unsuccessful. Also abortive was a foray to the Arsenal, whose arms and powder had been sent to the Bastille. Raids on armorer's shops yielded only a few weapons, and the next target was the Garde-Meuble, which did have weapons, but they were museum pieces of little or no use to the people who seized them. In Prieur's depiction of the Place Louis XV in front of the Garde-Meuble, a suit of armor was held up as a trophy and a cannon was carried away in the midst of an agitated crowd that brandishes pikes and muskets. The contrast between the crowd in the Place Louis XV and the stately magnificence of Gabriel's Garde-Meuble was certainly striking. This was a crowd with a keen sense of purpose, as indicated by the pikes held overhead, some of which carry *bonnets rouges*, already in Prieur's illustration symbols of patriotic dedication.

Chamfort's commentary for this tableau was not inconsistent with Prieur's visual depiction of the event. Nor did the commentary for the next tableau, *Taking of Arms from the Invalides* (tableau 14, fig. 21), diverge from Prieur's illustration, which showed the people forcing their way into the École Militaire on July 14, to secure arms. Baron de Besenval had ordered all thirty-two thousand of the guns stored in the

Figure 20.   J.-L. Prieur, *Arms taken from the Garde-Meuble, Place Louis XV,* Tableau 13, July 13, 1789, Musée Carnavelet, Paris

École Militaire put out of action. The twenty pensioners entrusted with removing hammers and unscrewing ramrods were sympathetic to the people who sought arms, and, in the six hours they spent responding to orders, they dismantled only twenty guns. Moreover, Besenval's orders to defend the École Militaire were not carried out; according to John Jay, who witnessed the scene, "5,000 foreign troops, encamped within 400 yards, never stirred."[19] A crowd simply poured into the École Militaire and seized muskets that were theirs for the taking. Prieur's tableau showed the crowd, for the most part without arms, forcing its way into the building. All the crowd now needed was powder, and it was to secure powder later in the day that the crowd laid siege to the Bastille.

In his visual record of the Paris Insurrection up to this point— tableau 14, *Taking of Arms from the Invalides*—Prieur illustrated scenes for the most part from the west of Paris. He began the sequence at the Palais-Royal, followed the crowd to the Opéra a short distance to the east, and then showed it at the Place Louis XV beyond the Tuileries. The crowd had moved eastward to the rue du Temple and at one point it had come within a few hundred feet of the Hôtel de Ville, but

Figure 21.   J.-L. Prieur, *Taking of Arms from the Invalides*, Tableau 14, July 13, 1789, Musée Carnavelet, Paris

rather than occupy the space next to the city hall, the Place de Grève, the crowd turned right at the rue Saint-Antoine and proceeded along the rue Saint-Honoré to the grand public squares in the west of the capital, and it is there, in Prieur's third illustration of the Paris Insurrection, that he showed a clash between the crowd and Lambesc's troops in the Place Louis XV. The next nine illustrations all portrayed events that took place in the west of Paris or in outlying parts of the capital. Only with tableau 15, *The Death of de Flesselles*, did the scene shift to the east, to the Place de Grève in the center of old Paris.

Prieur's next three illustrations, tableaus 15–17, which portray the culmination of the Paris Insurrection, did not follow the actual sequence of events. Rather than showing the siege of the Bastille as the first part of the sequence, Prieur began with the murder of Jacques de Flesselles, the *Prévôt des marchands*, in front of the Hôtel de Ville. That episode took place after the siege of the Bastille and the capture of de Launay, governor of the Bastille, the subjects of tableaus 16 and 17. After his capture, de Launay was escorted to the Hôtel de Ville by Elie, a lieutenant, and Hulin, director of the Queen's laundry, who protected him from a crowd that attacked him several times, shouted imprecations, and spat at him. Finally, having arrived at the Place de Grève adjacent to the Hôtel de Ville, de Launay was stabbed repeatedly, shot, and decapitated. It was after the crowd dispatched de Launay that de Flesselles walked out of the nearby Hôtel de Ville, where he was recognized, shot, and decapitated.

The events leading up to the scene portrayed by Prieur in tableau 15, *The Death of de Flesselles*, (fig. 22) have already been touched upon in the previous chapter. Pitra, an elector of the Estates-General, described the scene inside the Hôtel de Ville earlier in the day as Parisians from working-class districts milled about inside the great hall. An official and member of the elite, Pitra was surrounded by a crowd so frightening that it was difficult for him "to describe the scene." One group of "people armed with guns, pikes, swords and even sticks and knives fastened to them sat in rows of seats," while others with "atrocious expressions" and "armed, for the most part, with old-fashioned or foreign axes," taken from the Garde-Meuble, filled the center of the hall. Pitra was profoundly uneasy in the presence of these people, who "resembled the brigands we had disarmed only the day before," and now clamored loudly for the electors who gathered in a tiny circle at the end of a hall. For their part, the electors tried "in vain, through this terrifying tumult, to obtain silence." The crowd had tried to secure arms the previous day and again on July 14, and been sent hither and thither by de Flesselles on what they came to suspect were fools errands. Pitra said he "saw the *Prévôt des marchands* turn pale and almost tremble" when the cry was heard that the Bastille had fallen. Soon the conquerors of the Bastille appeared at the Hôtel de Ville with thirty or forty Swiss Guards shouting, "Hang Them! death! no quarter." These men, [with] "faces and eyes blazing with anger, were as terrifying as their cries." It was this crowd that shot and decapitated de Launay and then did the same to de Flesselles.

Prieur's *The Death of de Flesselles* shows the moment when the *Prévôt des marchands* is shot at point-blank range in front of the Hôtel de Ville and recoils from the force of the charge, which is dramatized by a large puff of smoke. One man kneels to the left of de Flesselles holding a document that brands him a traitor, and at the right a man with another document makes the same charge. On all sides the crowd points accusingly at, rushes toward, and shouts at de Flesselles. The crowd is made up largely of Parisians whose working-class attire is contrasted to the elegantly dressed de Flesselles, who wears a long coat, silk stockings, a flowing white neckpiece, and lace cuffs. Pikes, swords, bayonets, scythes, and pitchforks rise up from the crowd, investing it with a sense of violence that compares pictorially with Pitra's verbal description of the crowd. In fact, Prieur's drawing cap-

FIGURE 22. J.-L. Prieur, *The Death of de Flesselles*, Tableau 15, July 14, 1789, Musée Carnavelet, Paris

tures superbly the anger of the crowd that comes through also in Pitra's eyewitness account of the July 14 *journée*. The one thing Prieur's illustration is unable to convey is the noise, the "terrifying" cries that Pitra described in his account of the scene shortly before the crowd killed, beheaded, and mutilated de Launay and de Flesselles. To grasp the scene at the Hôtel de Ville, one must try to imagine the noise, not only the decibel level but also its social or class character. Pitra describes the "confused noise of a hundred thousand voices," and Prieur shows a scene that accords with the written account. In his superb illustration, he shows men "whose faces and eyes blazing with anger were as terrifying as their cries."

By showing the killing of de Flesselles on the steps in front of the Hôtel de Ville, Prieur's vantage point is from the Place de Grève, and it is from the Place de Grève that popular anger issues. Set against the cobblestone pavement is the ordered classical architecture of the Hôtel de Ville, over whose entrance a lantern hangs. Other artists, who portrayed the death of de Flesselles, do not show a lantern above the entrance to the Hôtel de Ville, nor do contemporary illustrations of that building do so. Prieur put the lantern there for a reason. The lantern became a symbol of revolutionary justice—Desmoulins wrote a *Discours de la lanterne aux Parisiens* in the summer of 1789—and it was from lampposts that the people hanged—*lanterné*—their enemies. As the watchmaker Morin shoots de Flesselles in Prieur's tableau, a Parisian who stands on a ledge of the Hôtel de Ville points at a lantern that hangs directly over the *Prévôt des marchands*, an enemy of the people, underscoring the type of justice, popular justice, that is being administered.

A comparison of Prieur's *Death of de Flesselles* with Jean-François Janinet's illustration of the same event in the *Gravures historiques principaux événements depuis l'ouverture des États-Généraux de 1789* (fig. 23) brings out the distinctiveness of Prieur's approach. Both artists show the watchmaker Morin shooting de Flesselles on the steps of the Hôtel de Ville, but Prieur's perspective is frontal whereas that of Janinet is diagonal. Running across the length of Prieur's illustration is a massed crowd that rushes towards the *Prévôt des marchands* and from which a forest of arms rises, charging the tableau with a sense of militancy. Only a handful of men are seen at the entrance of the Hôtel de Ville in Janinet's color print, and they occupy the lower third of the illustration, most of which is taken up by the fine architecture that provides a stately backdrop for the violent episode. The lantern that hangs above the entrance to the Hôtel de Ville in Prieur's illustration, a symbol of popular justice, is not seen in Janinet's color print. Men hold swords, but inconspicuously, at least in comparison to the raised

Figure 23.   J.-F. Janinet, *The Assassination of de Flesselles,* Musée Carnavelet, Paris

arms in Prieur's illustration. Moreover, there is no dynamic interplay between the figures in Janinet's illustration and the unseen crowd in the Place de Grève, no sense, in fact, that the figures in the illustration are part of a larger crowd. In Prieur's tableau, a figure to the right of de Flesselles holds two incriminating letters charging him with treason, one in each hand. This figure points the letters accusingly at de Flesselles while he looks toward the crowd in the Place de Grève. He is one of two figures that face in this direction. The other is a *garde française* who points accusingly at de Flesselles and at the same time looks and shouts at the crowd in front of him. This gesture, underscored by other figures that also point at de Flesselles, conveys an impression of dynamic interplay between the crowd in Prieur's illustration and an unseen crowd in the Place de Grève. The figures that rush forward from the Place de Grève toward the Hôtel de Ville increased a sense of crowd participation in the event he has portrayed in this tableau. The illustration is heavy with rhetorical touches broadly applied by Prieur to heighten the effects he strove to achieve and to portray the event in a manner that suited his purposes. The liberties he takes in this tableau are at one with the rhetorical touches; both underscore the crowd's vengeance against an enemy of the people.

In Prieur's tableau 16 (fig. 24), *Storming the Bastille*, the scene shifts some 1,200 metres to the east of the Hôtel de Ville, where a crowd, brandishing pikes, muskets, and a cannon pushes its way through a double drawbridge between the Bazinière and Comté towers of the fourteenth-century fortress that held two hundred fifty barrels of gunpowder and in the popular imagination had become a symbol of monarchical despotism. Moving away from the crowd, in the foreground, is a wounded insurgent, carried on a litter. Men on the roof of a building between the crowd and the Bastille shoot at its defenders as others, armed not with guns but axes, are tearing down the building they stand on, as if in anticipation of the destruction of the hated fortress in the background which is about to fall and whose demolition would begin almost immediately. In all illustrations and paintings of the storming of the Bastille, the perspective is from the outside, usually at the entry between the double drawbridge between the Bazinière

FIGURE 24.   J.-L. Prieur, *Storming the Bastille*, Tableau 16, July 14, 1789, Musée Carnavelet, Paris

and Comté towers, the scene of Prieur's tableau. No artist observed the event from the heights of the Bastille, looking down from above at the crowd below. Had the outcome been different, had de Launay's men prevailed and the Paris Insurrection been suppressed, artists could have put a completely different spin on the events of July 14. They could have showed an untamed mob on the rampage and going down to deserved defeat, but to the victors go the rights of pictorial representation, and Prieur's *Storming of the Bastille*, like the illustrations of other artists, portrays the victory of the people. Like other artists, he heightened and dramatized the event by making the fortress appear larger than it actually was. Hubert Robert, in his *Demolition of the Bastille*, actually went farther than Prieur in showing the fortress out of scale.

The title of Prieur's next tableau, *The Death of de Launay* (tableau 17, fig. 25), is misleading. The title was changed in the 1802 edition of the *Tableaux historiques* to *The Arrest of de Launay*, the actual subject of Prieur's illustration. De Launay's arrest was one of the most frequently illustrated events of the Paris Insurrection. The Bibliothèque

Figure 25.   G.-B. Berthault engraving of Prieur drawing, *The Death of de Launay*, Tableau 17, July 14, 1789, Photothèque des Musées de la Ville

Nationale catalogue of images of the French Revolution lists forty illustrations of an episode that began with de Launay's arrest and ended
with his death in the Place de Grève. Thirty-six of these illustrations
show the arrest of de Launay, either inside the Bastille or somewhere
outside the fortress; three show de Launay being led by a crowd towards the Hôtel de Ville; and one, that of J. F. Janinet (B.N. cat. no.
1124–25), shows a crowd in the Place de Grève as it makes ready to
dispatch de Launay. Many illustrations show the head of de Launay on
a pike, along with that of de Flesselles. Among the illustrations showing the arrest of de Launay, Prieur's is distinctive in a number of respects. In most other versions, the crowd that apprehends de Launay is
on one side of the pictorial space, or there are two separate crowds.
Only rarely is a crowd shown across the entire length of the pictorial
space. One example that follows this pattern is an anonymous print,
Taking of the Bastille, 14 July 1789 (B.N. cat. no. 1069–78), which
shows de Launay being led from the Bastille by his captors in a procession that passes through a gate on the right-hand side of the composition. The crowd in this illustration is a thin file of men and only here
and there are pikes and other arms displayed. The crowd in Prieur's
tableau dominates the scene, it is dense, and it is rendered in the distinctive way of this artist, with pikes, axes, scythes, swords, and guns
held aloft. In some illustrations, pikes and the other patriotic weapons
are sparse; in some they are prominent, but it is in Prieur's tableau that
they are most conspicuous and invest the work most vividly with a
sense of popular militancy. Looking back from the figure of de Launay,
there is a forest of pikes. Two captors hold de Launay in their grip and
at the same time protect him from a furious crowd. For his part, de
Launay holds his right hand outward in a defensive gesture. The
ground is covered with debris—a broken barrel, a broken wheel, fragments of wood—and cannon are to the right of the scene, with a fallen
body and cannonballs under one of them. A woman leans on a cannon
and mourns for a dead insurgent as men behind her raise their hands
upward in triumph, brandishing the weapons that helped the people
achieve a signal victory. Behind the crowd is a building with people
hanging from windows and looking at the scene below. At the head of
the crowd that moves away from the Bastille are Parisians who hold
flags, the trophies of victory. Unlike Thévenin's depiction of the same
event (fig. 6), discussed above, the overall sense of Prieur's illustration
is that of a people united in victory. Thévenin divides his composition
into two parts, with de Launay and his captors on the left and a uniformed figure with a flag on the right, and separates them by figures in
shadow. By contrast, Prieur places de Launay in the center of his composition and shows him in the midst of a crowd that celebrates its hard

earned and costly victory. Clouds of smoke billow upward in the background and towering above the scene is the Bastille.

With the fall of the Bastille, the Paris Insurrection had run its course, but this was not evident to Parisians in the capital or to the King at Versailles. Louis XVI had not yet abandoned the possibility of a counter offensive, and on the night of July 14 rumors circulated of an attack from Versailles.

Prieur's *Alert at the Porte Saint-Denis* (tableau 18, fig. 26) illustrates one response to those rumors. Carrying torches and fully armed with rifles and cannons, the crowd prepares itself for a show of force. The next tableau, *Cannons of Paris transported to Montmartre by the People* (tableau 19, fig. 27) shows the people taking further measures on July 15 to safeguard the victories of the previous day. Long files of armed men move along paths leading from the base of Montmartre to the top of the hill, wheeling cannons that would be used were the King to send troops into Paris. No such orders were given.

News of the people's victories on July 14 reached the King at Versailles on July 15, but the full impact of what had happened was slow to sink in.[20] What the King did not grasp initially was the collapse of military authority in Paris. Willing to make concessions, Louis ordered troops to withdraw from Paris on July 15, but in his own mind he was not yet defeated. A council attended by the Queen and the Counts of Provence and Artois urged the King to resist, but leaders of the Assembly called on him to meet with his ministers and recall Jacques Necker, the people's favorite. The Minister of War, Marshal Victor-François, duc de Broglie, informed the council that troops were no longer loyal, he explained that retaking Paris was militarily impossible, and suggested to the King that he withdraw with loyal troops to a provincial capital. Louis considered following this advice but decided against it. That night, July 16, his brother the Comte d'Artois left Paris with his wife, mistress, and friends. For his part, Louis accepted his defeat and resigned himself to the grim trip from Versailles to Paris, which he made on July 17, after recalling Necker. It is the end of that trip, as the King in his royal carriage rolls up to the Hôtel de Ville, that Prieur depicted in *The King at the Hôtel de Ville after the recalling of Necker* (tableau 20, fig. 28).

The setting of Prieur's *The King at the Hôtel de Ville* was the Place de Grève, within which an altogether new historical script was unfolding. The Place de Grève, as we have seen, had long been used by the authorities for their purposes: to impose public order through official ceremonies and celebrations and, rather differently, to administer exemplary justice by means of public executions. But the Place de Grève had also been a place where workers gathered in an effort to get

FIGURE 26.   J.-L. Prieur, *Alert at the Porte Saint-Denis*, Tableau 18, July 14, 1789, Musée Carnavelet, Paris

FIGURE 27.   J.-L. Prieur, *Cannons of Paris transported to Montmartre by the People*, Tableau 19, July 15, 1789, Musée Carnavelet, Paris

FIGURE 28.   J.-L. Prieur, *The King at the Hôtel de Ville after the recalling of Necker*, Tableau 20, July 17, 1789, Musée Carnavelet, Paris

jobs and to devise strategies, including strikes, that would work to their advantage. A spirit of resentment, and protest, was not alien to this ancient urban space. It is against this background, and the violence of July 14, that Prieur's superb illustration, *The King at the Hôtel de Ville*, must be seen.

Soldiers with weapons have cordoned off a protected space through which the King passes in his carriage, escorted by troops. Lined up in the Place de Grève, and looking down from the roof and windows of the Hôtel de Ville, is a huge and restrained crowd that observes the remarkable spectacle of the King coming to accept the Paris Insurrection as an accomplished fact. It was within this very space that violence had erupted three days earlier. The King's carriage could not have been far from the place in the Place de Grève where de Launay had been murdered and decapitated; it is heading directly towards the very Hôtel de Ville in front of which de Flesselles had been shot before being decapitated. A jubilant crowd had carried their grim trophies on pikes within the space through which the King now passes, having completed the trip to Paris from Versailles. The magnificent architecture of the Hôtel de Ville in Prieur's drawing and the ordered crowd in the Place de Grève can, and should, be seen within the context of the bloody events that had transpired three days previously.

If someone standing in the Place de Grève at the point from which Prieur viewed the event he portrayed in *The King at the Hôtel de Ville* were to turn around and face in the opposite direction, buildings on both sides of the rue Mouton would have come directly into view. The area around those buildings, located at the northwestern end of the Place de Grève, is the setting for Prieur's tableau 21, *The hanging of Foulon at the Place de Grève* (fig. 29). In *The King at the Hôtel de Ville* the crowd is unarmed and restrained by troops, but in Prieur's next illustration, *The hanging of Foulon*, it brandishes pikes and muskets, moves about at will, and carries out its own type of justice. The Place de Grève is filled with a crowd that has again risen, on July 22, and whose murder of an enemy of the people is cheered from the street and from the windows of buildings on both sides of the rue Mouton. The Place de Grève had been a center of public justice under the ancien régime and it was where the people administered their justice on July 14 and again on July 22.

The spectre of famine had hung over France since the spring of 1789, bread prices rose steadily in June and July, and reached a peak on July 14. As so often in the past, rumors circulated of conspiracies engineered by rich monopolists who controlled the grain trade and were ready to starve the people to further their own greedy ends. It was widely felt that some officials sided with the people and others were their enemy. The most popular official was Necker, who had extended credit to the state to the extent of two million livres, half of his fortune, and stood behind the loan even after his dismissal. By contrast, the man who briefly became Finance Minister after Necker's dismissal, Joseph-François Foulon de Doué, a speculator, financier and contractor, as well as a former member of the Royal Council, was hated by the people. At age seventy-four, he had acquired the reputation of despising the people and was thought to have said, years earlier, in 1775, "If they are hungry, let them browse grass. Wait till I am minister, I will make them eat hay: my horses eat it."[21] The people had not forgotten this remark reportedly made fourteen years earlier. Foulon was unfortunate to have had a name that appeared to underscore his reputation for rapacity: *foulons*, "let us trample," as on the people. To make matters worse, for him, he had built a splendid hôtel on the rue du Temple, which could all too easily be seen as the product of ill-gotten gains achieved at the cost of the people.

FIGURE 29. J.-L. Prieur, *The hanging of Foulon at the Place de Grève*, Tableau 21, July 22, 1789, Musée Carnavelet, Paris

Aware of popular feeling against him, Foulon spread rumors that he had not wanted to be finance minister, that he had fallen ill, and finally, that he was dead. A funeral was announced, and he was supposedly buried, but it was a servant who had just died whose remains were committed to the earth. Foulon fled Paris and moved in with his friend, Antoine-Gabriel de Sartine, a former Lieutenant General of the police, a few leagues outside the capital at Viri, in whose garden he was found on July 22: "You want to give us hay, you shall have some yourself."[22] As we have seen, a bale of hay was attached to his back, which he was obliged to take with him to the Hôtel de Ville. To heighten the comic and festive dimension of the episode, Foulon wore a nosegay of nettles and a collar of thistles and was given vinegar laced with pepper to relieve his thirst. By the time of Foulon's arrival at the Hôtel de Ville, the Place de Grève was filled with a crowd that had heard of his seizure. He was taken inside the Hôtel de Ville, where a crowd shouted, "Hang him! Hang him!" However, Jean-Sylvain Bailly, mayor of Paris, insisted that he be judged. According to Colin Lucas, while inside the Hôtel de Ville, the crowd adhered to at least a semblance of legal procedures by calling for a trial and choosing judges, not men from their own ranks but those associated with public office, a former *échevin*, a *juge-autiteur*, a *procureur de roi*, and a *greffier*.[23] Only when these men procrastinated did the crowd take matters into their own hands and administer their own type of justice. Unwilling to temporize, the crowd inside the Hôtel de Ville seized Foulon and took him outside, where the Place de Grève was filled with an angry crowd bent on retribution.[24]

The scene that unfolded in the Place de Grève should be seen within the context of this particular space and its symbolic associations. This was where the authorities had administered official justice, and now, under rather different circumstances, the people would dispense popular justice. Crowds in the Place de Grève had called for pardons when criminals were executed, and now that the tables were turned there were again to be no pardons.

Réstif de la Bretonne wrote of Foulon, "His only crimes were his continuous good fortune, his ambition to be minister, and his immense wealth . . . which could not save him."[25] In the Place de Grève, Foulon tried to mount a box to address the crowd but, according to Réstif, someone grabbed him and "flung him into the midst of those who were waiting for him." He was dragged "half dead" to the lamppost at the corner of the rue Mouton, ordered to demand pardon of the nation, and strung up. The rope broke twice, someone fetched a new one, and on the third attempt Foulon was hanged. He was then decapitated and his head put on a pike and carried through the streets of Paris as a trophy.

The background for Prieur's *The hanging of Foulon* is the imposing buildings in the northeast corner of the Place de Grève opposite the Hôtel de Ville. The cobblestone street below the buildings is occupied by a crowd that pushes in on Foulon from both sides and from the rue Mouton behind him. Observers in the street and in buildings above it point at Foulon, dramatizing his grim fate. Mounted on a wall behind the lamppost from which Foulon hangs is a sign that reads, ironically, "Fabrique du chocolat."

Prieur's next drawing, *The Intendant Bertier de Sauvigny* (fig. 1), is a sequel to the *Hanging of Foulon*. Louis-Benigne-François-Bertier de Sauvigny (1737–1789), the intendant of Paris, was the son-in-law of Foulon.[26] He belonged to a family of royal officials that had served the monarchy for generations, and he and his father, Louis-Jean Bertier de Sauvigny (1709–1788), had undertaken a massive cadastral survey of land holdings in eighteen hundred parishes between 1771 and 1789, to achieve greater administrative efficiency. Devoted to the monarchical state, the two Bertiers were also swept up in the reform movement. When they drew up assessments for tax purposes in the *généralité* of Paris, they submitted them to landowners and tenant farmers for scrutinizing, anticipating the deliberative principle introduced by Necker's Provincial Assemblies. According to Peter M. Jones, Bertier *fils* was among a small group of "intendants who became impatient with the stop-go politics of reform. Rather than wait upon events, they pushed on with practical measures, hoping to convert ministers along the way."[27]

Among the projects undertaken by Bertier *fils* were helping establish *dépôts de mendicité* (workhouses), which were to serve as instruments of rational social policy.[28] The poor presented a problem of ever-increasing proportion as the eighteenth century ran its course, manifested by vagabonds, beggars, derelict children running loose, and the constant threat of rioters. One response to this problem was the creation of *dépôts*, to which beggars would be forcibly committed. In debates among state officials over how the *dépôts* should be organized, Bertier took a moderate line, favoring a combination of mild, humane treatment of inmates with an imposed regime of work. Looking at the problem of mendicity publicly, Bertier favored a systematic response to a systemic problem; the poor lacked discipline, making it necessary to "inspire fear . . . because of their slothfulness." To understand Bertier's position, it is useful to see it within the context of contemporary public debate on the problem of beggars.

In 1777, the Academy of Châlons-sur-Marne sponsored a prize essay contest on, "How to make beggars useful to the state without making them unhappy?" The prizewinning essay recommended putting beggars to work. Only by imposing discipline, according to this line of thinking, could those unable to fend for themselves become citizens capable of making a contribution to society and as a result reap the benefits of regular employment. Bertier's thinking was congruent with this type of reasoning, and the *dépôt* at Saint-Denis that he supervised represented his attempt to translate a reasoned position into a workable and practical result. Funding the *dépôts* was an ongoing problem, and while some ministries were prepared to support them others were not. The Brienne ministry of 1787–1788 withdrew support and removed Bertier as general supervisor of the *dépôts*. Assemblies for the Estates-General debated the *dépôts*, and in some cases denounced them as "Bastilles for the people."

As someone who was associated with the *dépôts*, Bertier came under attack, and he was on a proscription list drawn up at the Palais-Royal on July 13, along with Foulon, his father-in-law. What further compromised Bertier at the time of the Paris Insurrection was the role he played deploying troops in and around Paris before the King sacked Necker. As intendant of the *généralité* of Paris, it was his responsibility to carry out this measure. Bertier not only urged the King to remove troops from the capital in the aftermath of the Paris Insurrection in an attempt to restore calm, but also he tried to secure food provisions for Parisians who suffered from severe shortages. Apprehensive after the Paris uprising, he fled the capital for Soissons on July 18, and then went to Compiègne, where he was recognized and detained by members of a local surveillance committee.

When his captors drew up charges against him, he requested that one of the Paris electors escort him to the Hôtel de Ville. He entered the city from the north by the Porte Saint-Martin in a cabriolet whose top had been broken off so he could be seen. Seated next to Bertier was Etienne de la Rivière, an elector, who shielded him from the blows of a crowd that lashed out in fury at the hated intendant of Paris, the corrupt official responsible for their hunger. The crowd that lined the streets on the way to the Hôtel de Ville taunted Bertier and carried placards that read: "He has robbed the King and France"; "He has devoured the substance of the people"; "He has been the slave of the rich and the tyrant of the poor. He has deceived the King. He has betrayed the King. He has devoured the substance of the people."[29] The crowd danced in front of the carriage, as if it were a popular festival of sorts, and threw black bread into the carriage: "Take that, brigand, that is the bread you made us eat."[30]

Passing along the rue Saint-Martin, the procession encountered another crowd heading in the opposite direction from the Place de Grève, carrying the head of Foulon, Bertier's father-in-law. "Kiss papa!" "Kiss papa!" was the crowd's response to the encounter. What underscored the gallows humor of the crowd's chant was the hay that was stuffed in the dead mouth of Foulon. Taken to the Hôtel de Ville, the same script unfolded as earlier in the day when Foulon had been murdered. Officials tried to protect Bertier from a furious crowd; efforts were made to send him as a prisoner to the Abbaye; the authorities were unable to hold off the crowd; and finally the crowd seized him and lynched him in the Place de Grève.

According to Réstif de la Bretonne's account, "The noose was slipped around his neck and he was lifted up. He tried to support his body's weight with his hand. A soldier went to slice off his hand, and cut the cord. The victim fell, lunged at the executioner's cheek and scratched it. He was hoisted up again. But the rope snapped a second time and he was slaughtered at the foot of the lamppost; his belly was slashed open, and his head cut off."[31] The decapitated head of Bertier was then put on a pike, another trophy of popular justice. As seen in a drawing by Girodet, *Decapitated Heads of marquis de Launay, Foulon, and Bertier de Sauvigny* (fig. 30), Bertier's head, which was stuck on a pike, was without a face. Girodet's drawing also shows Bertier's heart impaled on a pike, Foulon's head stuck on a pike with straw stuffed in its mouth, and de Launay's head stuck on a pitchfork.

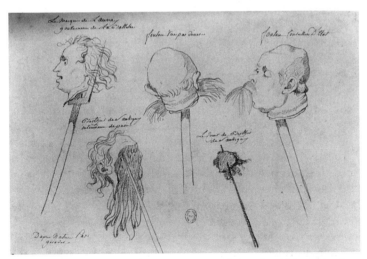

FIGURE 30.   A.-L. Girodet, *Decapitated Heads of Marquis de Launay, Foulon, and Bertier de Sauvigny*, Bibliothèque Nationale, Paris

George Rudé has written that the violence of July 14 and July 22 has, "of course, been picked upon to discredit the captors of the Bastille and to represent them as vagabonds, criminals, or a mercenary rabble hired in the wineshops of the Saint-Antoine quarter. This is a legend that dies hard."[32] Brian C. J. Singer feels that Rudé has tried to normalize the Parisians who carried out the deeds of July 14 and July 22 by seeing them within the context of their trades and occupations, rather than within their own cultural context. The "body count" of these *journées*, as Simon Schama has put it, might have been small but the significance of the violence was profound. "It was what made the Revolution revolutionary."[33] One of the most interesting eyewitness accounts is that of François-Noël Babeuf, who saw the murder of Foulon and Bertier and reflected on the violence in a letter to his wife:

> Our punishments of every kind, quartering, torture, the wheel, the stake, and the gibbet, and the multiplicity of executioners on all sides, have had such a bad effect on our morals! Our masters, instead of policing us, have made us barbarous, because they are barbarous themselves. They are reaping and will reap what they have sown.[34]

Having witnessed barbarity, Babeuf considered what brought it about; he did not try to normalize the violence. Another eyewitness of Bertier's murder, Réstif de la Bretonne, also reflected on those who committed the deed: "Oh men of France! Oh, my fellow citizens of Paris! What monster's black soul raged in you during those moments? Ah! You would never of yourselves have committed such atrocities worthy of cannibals!"[35] Yet another contemporary response to the murder of Foulon and Bertier was that of the journalist Elysée Loustalot, whose *Révolutions de Paris* was the most popular of all the revolutionary newspapers that appeared in the summer of 1789. Loustalot wallowed in the violence: The severed head of Foulon, with hay stuffed in its mouth, "announced to tyrants the terrible vengeance of a justly angered people." When Bertier was confronted with the spectacle of his father-in-law's head, he "shuddered and for the first time, perhaps his soul felt the twinges of remorse. Fear and terror seized him." Capturing the festive character of the procession that led Bertier to the Hôtel de Ville, Loustalot said it was accompanied by fifes and drums that declared "the cruel joy of the people."[36] Reaching a conclusion similar to that of Babeuf about Bertier's murder, although couched in rather different language, Loustalot wrote of the just wrath of the "barbarian" who tore the palpitating heart from the "monster" Bertier de Sauvigny.

> Already, Bertier is no more; his head is nothing more than a mutilated stump separated from his body. A man, O gods, a man, a barbarian tears

out his [Bertier's] heart from his palpitating viscera. How can I say this? He is avenging himself on a monster, the monster who had killed his father. His hands dripping with blood, he goes to offer the heart, still steaming, under the eyes of the men of peace assembled in this august tribunal of humanity. What a horrible scene! Tyrants, cast your eyes on this terrible and revolting spectacle. Shudder and see how you and yours will be treated. This body, so delicate and so refined, bathed in perfumes, is horribly dragged in the mud and over the cobblestones. Despots and ministers, what terrible lessons! Would you have believed that the French could have such energy! No, no, your reign is over. Tremble, future ministers, if you are iniquitous. . . .

Frenchmen you exterminate tyrants! Your hatred is revolting, frightful . . . but you will, at last, be free. I know, my dear co-citizens, how these revolting scenes afflict your souls . . . but think how ignominious it is to live as slaves. Think what punishments should be meted out for the crime of lèse-humanité. Think, finally, what good, what satisfaction, what happiness await you and your children . . . when the august and holy temple of liberty will have set up its temple for you.[37]

Prieur's tableau, *The Intendant Bertier de Sauvigny*, is another contemporary account—visual, to be certain—of an event about which there was disagreement at the time and still invites disagreement. It is a freely invented account, as we have seen; by setting the encounter between Bertier and the procession that brandished Foulon's head in front of the church of Saint-Merry, Prieur has brought out a dimension of the event, its macabre, festive quality, that comes through also in Loustalot's journalistic account.

Prieur's drawing, *The Intendant Bertier de Sauvigny*, like Babeuf's letter to his wife, and Loustalot's journalistic account, is the result of reflection. This is not an objective account but a commentary. Every detail has been thought out, nothing has been left to chance, and the setting is staged for effect by having Bertier encounter the head of Foulon in front of a church. It is not by accident that a Christian saint, sheltered under a canopy, is in the exact center of the drawing. Other saints in the background also stand above the crowd that passes along the cobblestone street on its way to the Place de Grève, the scene of popular justice. The saint in the central niche and in the center of the drawing appears to be looking at the head of Foulon stuck on a pike, and at Bertier de Sauvigny, who turns away in horror. Seated next to Bertier is Etienne de la Rivière, who covers his eyes with his hands. The incongruity between the religious statuary of the church and the macabre festivity in the street is most striking. So, too, is the contrast between the vertical lines of the church that invest the background with a sense of order and a foreground that bristles with guns, pikes, and an ax. Between the Christian past represented by the church and the revolutionary *journée* in the street there is a chasm of history. Also noteworthy, and at the center of Prieur's conception, is the gallows humor that his drawing captures. This is a revolutionary event, a *journée*, in which the people make an altogether new appearance on the stage of history; as actors on that stage they draw from their own cultural repertoire and its comic and festive forms. As an illustration of a Paris *journée* it is without equal in the visual record of the French Revolution. Yet it was not included in the *Tableaux historiques* and offered for sale to the public. It is one of two of Prieur's drawings that suffered this fate, the other being his very last work, an illustration of the September Massacres. These drawings are among Prieur's finest; the decisions not to include them in the *Tableaux historiques* could not have been made on the basis of artistic merit. Why those decisions were made will be considered in the next chapter.

Chapter 3

Jean-Louis Prieur and the
Tableaux historiques
August 1789 to September 1792

*P*rieur's first illustration for the *Tableaux historiques* after his *Intendant Bertier de Sauvigny* portrays a funeral service that took place on August 5 in a parish church in Paris in honor of patriots who lost their lives during the storming of the Bastille. The date of the funeral service, August 5, is noteworthy: it was on that same day, the night of August 4–5 to be exact, that the National Assembly passed laws that swept away the ancien régime. The decision to show Parisians commemorating fallen patriots rather than portray members of a legislative body enacting laws is consistent with the selection of subjects for the *Tableaux* when Prieur served as illustrator.

The emphasis was on the convulsions of the Revolution, and on patriotic ceremonies and celebrations, largely in Paris. Of Prieur's sixty-nine illustrations, sixty portrayed events that occurred in Paris or Versailles; only nine portrayed events outside those locales. Prieur's pictorial record of the Revolution was Paris-centered, its point of departure was the Paris Insurrection of July 12–14, and it took little cognizance of debates in the National Assembly. He did but one illustration of the National Assembly, *Women Artists offering their Jewels at the National Assembly at Versailles* (tableau 26, fig. 31).

What is striking about this work is the indifference of the deputies to the women who made patriotic gifts to the nation on September 7, 1789. The deputies sit idly, their legs crossed, they talk to one another, they lean on their elbows, they do anything but direct their attention to women patriots. Prieur's depiction of the National Assembly is less than heroic in this illustration, and, judging from the rest of his work

FIGURE 31.   J.-L. Prieur, *Women Artists offering their Jewels at the National Assembly at Versailles*, Tableau 26, Musée Carnavelet, Paris

for the *Tableaux*, he does not seem to have been particularly interested in the Revolution's legal and constitutional achievements.

Tableau 22 (fig. 32), *Funeral Service for French Citizens who died during the Storming of the Bastille*, shows Abbé Claude Fauchet, who provided commentaries for the first two installments of the *Tableaux*, delivering a fiery sermon on August 5 in the Church of Saint-Jacques de l'Hôpital to a crowd that filled the interior of the building.

Fauchet, a leader in the storming of the Bastille, proclaimed, "by risking similar danger" to those being honored, that he had "shown the same braveness and fearlessness." The funeral service for which Fauchet delivered the sermon was ordered by a National Assembly that urgently wanted to restore calm to a Paris that had just experienced massive convulsions, and through which rumors of conspiracy continued to pass. Staging a grand funeral at the parish Church of Saint-Jacques de l'Hôpital was a calculated effort by the Assembly to bring down the political barometer in Paris.

In his illustration of the scene, Prieur shows Fauchet standing at a pulpit and holding forth with outstretched arm: "Citizens of Paris, my

FIGURE 32.   J.-L. Prieur, *Funeral Service for French Citizens who died during the Storming of the Bastille*, Tableau 22, August 5, 1789, Musée Carnavelet, Paris

brave brethren, you have raised high the banner of liberty; glory be unto you! And you, fearless victims who have sacrificed yourself for the good of the homeland, receive in heaven, with our tears of gratitude, the joy of your victory!"[1] A crowd of men, women, and children that fills the church in which they are assembled to overflowing looks up at Fauchet as if hanging on his every word. Some kneel in prayer, and others hold up their hats in salute. One woman supports another who succumbs to grief over a fallen patriot.

The National Assembly had every reason to be apprehensive over the Paris populace. Forces had been unleashed in July 1789 whose political outcome no one at the time could predict, forces that blew away the old municipal government of Paris and indeed the entire ancien régime and its institutions. The Paris Insurrection had saved the Revolution but also redefined it completely. After the Paris *journées* of July 12–14, political leaders in the Assembly were acutely aware of pressure from the Paris populace. Just how real that pressure was is superbly documented by Prieur in illustrations 23–31 in the *Tableaux* that cover the period August 6, 1789 to October 6, 1789. It was Necker's dismissal on July 11 that triggered the Paris Insurrection, and on July 17 the King recalled him in an effort to restore stability. The people's favorite was triumphantly welcomed in Paris on July 29, but instantly popular acclaim turned to popular hostility. On the day of his arrival in Paris, Necker delivered a speech in which he called for steps necessary for the establishment of a "perfect and durable order" that would allow peace to descend upon a city and nation that had just experienced momentous changes and whose well-being now required calm and stability. Important as economic considerations were, Necker said, he felt obliged to turn to "a greater concern which is weighing on my heart and oppressing it": he pleaded with those he addressed to "consult nothing but your hearts," to honor "this quality of kindness, justice, and mildness which distinguishes the French Nation," and to "make the day of indulgence and forgiveness arrive as soon as possible." He pleaded with his audience for moderation: "In the name of God, gentlemen, no more proscriptions, no more bloody scenes."[2]

Necker had been the first victim of the July 11 coup and was driven from a state to which he had offered his service, and to which he had loaned a substantial part of his fortune; however, now it was time to forgive those who had been commissioned to carry out the coup. In the context of July 30, when he delivered his speech, this meant forgiving the Baron de Besenval, who had fled the capital and been apprehended at Villenauxe 100 miles east of Paris as he headed for Switzerland. Besenval was sent back to Paris on July 30, the day after Necker returned to the capital. Bailly, the mayor of Paris, feared that Besenval would suffer the same fate as Foulon and Bertier eight days earlier if the people were to get their hands on him. Bailly met with the Police Committee to keep Besenval's arrival in Paris "secret so the people would not be warned of his arrival, thereby allowing the prisoner to be brought in safely." Necker shared this concern: "I prostrate myself, I throw myself on my knees in order to ask that no one treat Monsieur de Besenval or anyone else in a manner in any way comparable to the scenes which have apparently been recently enacted."[3] Taking a conciliatory stand, he called for Besenval's pardon and beyond that act of forgiveness he urged a general amnesty.

Necker's mind-set was that of the eighteenth-century liberal elite, forgiving, moderate, accommodating. His call for amnesty and the pardoning of Besenval was consistent with his principles, and, while members of the political leadership such as Bailly shared it, many in Paris emphatically did not. To those inclined to discover conspiracies, Necker's support of Besenval meant that the two men were in collusion, and that they were enemies of the people joined together in criminal intrigue. While Necker could well say that this charge was rubbish and that he was in fact generously supporting a man who carried out orders of which he was a direct victim, he was unable to retain popular support after calling for Besenval's pardon. Between his idea of justice and that of the Paris populace there was a deep gulf, and from this time on Necker ceased to be a popular favorite. He was able to carry the day in the Hôtel de Ville, when he addressed moderate Représentants who shared his tolerant views, and the order for Besenval's release was quickly signed. An escort set out for the Swiss border to guarantee Besenval safe passage, and believing that a crisis had been averted Clermont-Ferrand, a moderate, wrote that "the Revolution was over."[4]

This was far from the case. As news of Baron Besenval's pardon and release spread, a crowd gathered at the Place de Grève, and within three hours, according to a contemporary account, "the entire capital has risen, the multitude had assembled, and the placards announcing a general amnesty had been torn down."[5] There were cries to burn down the Hôtel de Ville, so furious was the crowd with the Représentants who pardoned Besenval and issued a general amnesty. The popular idea of justice was less yielding, more punitive than that of elite officials. Besenval's release was called "illegal," and so great was the outcry that new orders were issued calling for his arrest. He was apprehended at Brie-Comte-Robert twenty-five miles east of Paris and held there as the Assembly decided what to do. Troops dispatched to take Besenval in custody arrived at Brie-Comte-Robert on August 10, 1789, and plans were made for his trial, which began in November and resulted in his acquittal in January 1791.

Prieur illustrated four tableaus portraying the period that followed Necker's July 29 call for Besenval's pardon and the arrival of troops at Brie-Comte-Robert to take him in custody on August 10. The first of these illustrations we have already discussed, *Funeral Service for French Soldiers who died during the Storming of the Bastille.* The storm of anger that resulted from Necker's speech was the background against which Fauchet's August 5 sermon in a parish church can be viewed. Inside the church, fallen patriots were honored and expressions of patriotic sacrifice were made. Outside there was collective anger, driven by rumors of conspiracy that swept Paris. On August 6, the day after Fauchet's sermon, rumors circulated that Antoine-Laurent Lavoisier, the *régie des poudres*, had removed gunpowder stored at the Arsenal. Lavoisier was charged with a conspiracy to prevent Paris the means to defend itself, arrested, and taken to the Hôtel de Ville. It turned out that gunpowder had been moved, but only because it was of poor quality; room was needed for good battlefield powder. Before the

FIGURE 33.   J.-L. Prieur, *Popular Tumult at the Port Saint-Paul on the Occasion of the Arrival of Ship with Powder*, Tableau 23, August 6, 1789, Musée Carnavelet, Paris

true facts were known, gunpowder was dispatched to the Port Saint-Paul to enable the capital to defend itself against those who, according to rumor, threatened its overthrow. This is the subject of Prieur's tableau 23, *Popular Tumult at the Port Saint-Paul on the Occasion of the Arrival of Ship with Powder* (fig. 33). As the gunpowder was unloaded, people on both sides of the Seine raised their hands in triumph: Paris now had the needed gunpowder to defend itself.

Tableau 24, *Cannons arriving from Chantilly* (fig. 34), shows crowds cheering the arrival of artillery on August 9 that would further bolster the defense of Paris. This is the first of Prieur's illustrations that shows a crowd raising tree branches upward in gestures of patriotic celebration. The figure who holds the largest tree branch is in the center of the drawing, seated on a cannon that is drawn by a horse into Paris to defend the capital from its enemies. This figure looks straight ahead, at an unseen crowd that faces him and presumably joins in the celebration. Two groups of men convey additional cannon and raise their hands upward in gestures of victory, as do figures behind them on

FIGURE 34.   J.-L. Prieur, *Cannons arriving from Chantilly*, Tableau 24, August 9, 1789, Musée Carnavelet, Paris

a rampart. With one exception all of these figures brandish swords or pikes. The exception is a figure on the rampart who stands above the others and holds the branch of a tree in a gesture of celebration. This connects him to the figure on the cannon and to those who not only precede him but also carry tree branches. How are the tree branches to be understood?

When Camille Desmoulins addressed a crowd at the Palais-Royal on July 12, at the beginning of the Paris Insurrection, he stuck a green ribbon in the band of his hat, calling it a cockade; then he gave ribbons to others until he had no more. Parisians then broke twigs or branches from trees and called them "cockades." The tricolor soon replaced the twig as the revolutionary cockade, but the tree twig, or tree branch, became a revolutionary symbol in itself. Already at the Palais-Royal, following Desmoulins's example, people in the crowd broke off twigs or branches from nearby trees, and along with the cockade, the pike, *bonnet rouge*, and the Liberty Tree, the tree branch came to have symbolic importance, expressing patriotic dedication to the Revolution. Tree branches reappeared in Prieur's later tableaus, as we shall see.

For Prieur's next tableau, *Besenval detained at Brie-Comte-Robert* (tableau 25, fig. 35), the scene shifts to the village twenty-five miles east of Paris where soldiers take Besenval in custody on August 10. In his illustration of Besenval's detainment, the general is forced to join soldiers that are formed in ordered lines as people behind him brandish swords, pikes, and scythes. Besenval's rough treatment by the troops, who detain him, is improbable. Troops are sent to take Besenval in custody, not for punitive reasons but in response to popular pressure in the capital. This tableau and the others discussed above offer an edited version of what transpired in early August, in the aftermath of the Paris Insurrection and the Great Fear. Standard histories of the Revolution tell a different story than that projected by the *Tableaux historiques*. They describe the sweeping away of the ancien régime on the night of August 4–5, and the political debates that followed in the Assembly. The *Tableaux historiques* casts its eye in a different direction, not at Versailles where legislators are gathered but at the city of Paris where dead patriots are honored and where the populace takes measures to defend itself from its enemies. Yet the influence of the Assembly can be felt in Prieur's visual narrative.

FIGURE 35.   J.-L. Prieur, *Besenval detained at Brie-Comte-Robert*, Tableau 25, August 10, 1789, Musée Carnavelet, Paris

The funeral service at Saint-Jacques de l'Hôpital was ordered by the Assembly in an effort to placate *le peuple,* and the detainment of Besenval was a response to the popular anger that followed the announcement of his pardon. The wrath directed at Besenval at Brie-Comte-Robert was the displaced anger of Paris; the soldiers who seize him forcefully in Prieur's illustration in fact put him in civilized confinement where he enjoyed the amenities of a person of his station. If Prieur's narrative of the period from August 5 to August 10 brought out the popular anger in Paris that followed Besenval's pardon, it did so selectively; it did not show massed demonstrations in the Place de Grève, or the tearing down of placards announcing a general amnesty but a patriotic *peuple* defending themselves against their enemies. Tableaus 23 and 24 portrayed events that were driven by rumors of conspiracy that had no basis in fact, but the fear that gripped Paris was real and illustrations that dramatized it were part of the actual history of the Revolution. As such, these tableaus have definite documentary value.

Paris was a tinderbox. Rumors of conspiracy continued to sweep the capital in August and the price of bread, after going down in late July, rose again, creating hardship that in turn created desperation. A bookseller in Paris commented that there was constant talk of lynching: "The lamppost; everyone called an aristocrat is threatened with it; and the aristocrat is a name for anybody you don't like. Imagine the alarm in certain circles, people of wealth, title, or ability, everybody in fact whom the populace and others once feared or envied. Fear of the lamppost stops the plotting of a few mischief-makers, but it also terrifies many honest folks who pass for enemies of the new order of things but really are not."[6] Fear of the populace by "respectable" Parisians, those of means who wanted stability, led to the formation of the "bourgeois guard" on July 15; they were soon renamed the National Guard. It was Emmanuel-Joseph Sieyès who invented the name National Guard, a citizen militia whose function was to harness the forces of disorder; Lafayette was appointed commander.

Lafayette had already assumed that position when he met Louis XVI in Paris on July 17, and rode before the King's carriage, dressed as a private person, not in military uniform, as the King's carriage made its way to the Hôtel de Ville. Having arrived at the Hôtel de Ville, the King was offered a cockade, already a symbol of the Revolution, which he placed in his hat. Originally red and blue, the colors of Paris, Lafayette added the white of the Bourbons in an attempt to establish unity. That Lafayette invented the tricolor cockade in this way, trying to join symbolically the city of Paris and monarchy, exemplified his politics and leadership style. As a moderate he wanted stability, which he hoped to achieve through a policy of reconciliation, by charting a middle course through troubled waters with extremist groups lined up on both the left and the right. As it turned out, he was unable to achieve this objective, but, for something like two years, he was the leading political figure of the Revolution, throughout the period during which a Fayettist coalition held sway. The balance he maintained was precarious. Never accepted at Court, he was also suspect in the Paris Sections and among left factions in the National Assembly. Yet moderates, who dominated the Assembly, were attuned to his policies and shared his wish for stability.

Prieur's tableau 27, *Benediction of the Flags of the National Guard in the Church of Notre Dame* (fig. 36), begins a sequence of illustrations covering the period September 27, 1789 to September 18, 1791 during which the Fayettist coalition maintained a leadership position. The thirty tableaus in this sequence give prominence to the National Guard; they offer a visual record of the crises with which the National Guard was confronted; they portray the successes of Lafayette and his

FIGURE 36.   J.-L. Prieur, *Benediction of the Flags of the National Guard in the Church of Notre-Dame*, Tableau 27, September 7, 1789, Musée Carnavelet, Paris

policies; and they reveal the instabilities within France that ultimately broke the Fayettist coalition apart and drove the Revolution in new directions. The tableau that begins this series, *Benediction of the Flags of the National Guard in Notre-Dame*, receives little if any attention in standard histories of the French Revolution. It shows sixty companies of the National Guard, one from each of the Paris districts, lined up with their flags in the interior of Notre-Dame where they are blessed by the Archbishop of Paris, "in the name of the God of Justice." Lafayette, his right hand held upward in a gesture of leadership, is in the center of the cathedral nave and he is symbolically in the center of the composition. Men are gathered around him and look to him, it would seem, for direction. Ordered rows of guardsmen are lined up on both sides of the nave with muskets as the flag-blessing ceremony is under way.

Tableau 28, *Orgy of the Guards in the Versailles Opéra* (fig. 37) could hardly be in greater contrast to tableau 27. This tableau illustrated a banquet held on October 1 at Versailles in the *grande salle des spectacles* for the King's *corps de garde* of the Flanders Regiment that had been summoned, with the approval of the Assembly, to protect the King and his palace. At the banquet, "The table setting was splendid. The music . . . delighted the ear, and when it died down the room was filled with the sound of toasts proposed by the soldiers."[7] The King Louis XVI and Queen Marie-Antoinette appeared at the banquet, the company drank toasts to their health, and after they departed there were many more toasts. The Flanders Regiment became unrestrained, and this is how they were seen in Prieur's tableau. They were seen in drunken abandon, in an orgy at Versailles that was in striking contrast to the hunger that gripped Paris. People in the capital were starving while soldiers and members of the court abandoned themselves to excesses. The revelry in the *grande salle des spectacles* was framed by splendid columns with Corinthian orders and a fine curtain, and inside the stage, where the banquet tables had been placed and the soldiers toasted the King and Queen, there were candled chandeliers that contributed to an impression of courtly magnificence. News of this scene reached Paris the next day. Reports circulated in the press that drunken members of the Flanders Regiment trampled on the patriotic cockade and embraced the white of the King and Queen. This news had an electric effect on Paris, and particularly on women who were unable to feed their children, owing to the high price of bread.

A crisis was at hand; pressure that had been building in Paris throughout the summer was close to the breaking point. A crowd of somewhere between two hundred and fifteen hundred had attempted a march on Versailles on August 30 to prevent acceptance of a royal veto,

FIGURE 37. J.-L. Prieur, *Orgy of the Guards in the Versailles Opéra*, Tableau 28, October 1, 1789, Musée Carnavelet, Paris

but Lafayette and the National Guard prevented the unarmed crowd from leaving the Palais-Royal, its gathering place. There was talk of dissolving the Assembly and bringing the King to Paris; anger remained high after the march on Versailles was thwarted. In response to daily rioting, the Commune increased the number of guards to six hundred to protect the wheat market on September 10, and on the following day the Assembly granted the King a suspensive veto. On September 16 the first issue of Jean-Paul Marat's *Ami du Peuple* appeared with an attack on the Assembly. The publication of Marat's radical newspaper at this time was another index of the political volatility in the capital. The October 1 banquet of the Flanders Regiment at Versailles led to rumors that the King intended to launch a coup d'etat, and in a meeting of the Cordeliers Danton urged the people to take up arms. On the morning of October 5, market women led a crowd of some six or seven thousand to the Hôtel de Ville; muskets and two cannons were appropriated, and the crowd set off for Versailles, followed later by Lafayette and the National Guard.

Lafayette opposed sending the National Guard, fearing that by joining the crowd, they would be seen as coercive. Concerned with sta-

FIGURE 38.   J.-L. Prieur, *The Women of la Halle go from Paris to Versailles,* Tableau 29, October 5, 1789, Musée Carnavelet, Paris

FIGURE 39.   J.-L. Prieur, *The King promises to go to Paris with his Family*, Tableau 30, October 6, 1789, Musée Carnavelet, Paris

bility, Lafayette did not want to antagonize the King and the National Assembly, but *garde-francaise* members of the National Guard were insistent, and reluctantly Lafayette gave marching orders. Upon arriving at Versailles after midnight, Lafayette told the King he was prepared to die at his feet, but added that might not be necessary if Louis were to reside in Paris, "in the palace of his ancestors at the Louvre."[8] Before Louis agreed to return to the capital, an angry crowd broke into the Cour de Marbre and ran up stairs in search of the royal apartments. The royal family barely escaped the fury of the armed crowd, and, having survived the ordeal, the King announced that he would move to Paris.

In his first tableau illustrating these events, *The Women of la Halle go from Paris to Versailles* (tableau 29, fig. 38), Prieur shows women, two of whom are astride a cannon, leading the procession to the royal palace. The crowd marches with pikes and raised swords and is followed by soldiers with muskets. The second tableau, *The King promises to go to Paris with his Family* (tableau 30, fig. 39), shows a salvo of artillery in front of Versailles as files of National Guardsmen

FIGURE 40.   J.-L. Prieur, *The King and Royal Family led to Paris by the People*, Tableau 31, October 6, 1789, Musée Carnavelet, Paris

are lined up and the crowd makes ready for the journey to Paris. The last illustration, *The King and Royal Family led to Paris by the People* (tableau 31, fig. 40), shows the royal family in a carriage, surrounded by the crowd and followed by the National Guard. People are lined up on a wall, cheering, waving, and holding pikes aloft. At the far right-hand side of the scene, a man sits on a lantern, an ironic and menacing commentary on the anger and vengeance of the people, to whom the King and Queen had been forced to submit when they made the trip to Paris. Another figure has climbed a pole next to the lamppost, and holds a tree branch upwards in his right hand. The tree branch intersects the space between the pole and the lamppost, thereby bringing together two patriotic symbols of the Revolution. Figures on a cart laden with sacks of grain that heads the procession into Paris also hold tree branches, as do people who line the road to Paris; they wave at the royal carriage as it passes by. Tree branches are mingled with pikes, axes, and scythes, all symbols of patriotic dedication. Adding to the array of patriotic symbols are *bonnets rouges* placed on pikes and held aloft by the people who stand below the wall that frames the background of the procession. As a result, the royal carriage passes through a space that is charged with symbolic meaning provided by the patriotic objects held aloft by the assembled crowd. The most menacing of the objects is the lamppost, a symbol of popular justice, at the far right with the seated figure who looks at the royal carriage below him, conveying the King and Queen into the capital after the people have exercised their will. To reinforce the point of popular militancy, an ax is seen against the door of the royal carriage and a woman gestures angrily at the King and Queen.

Prieur's illustrated narrative of the October *journées* left out the eruption of violence at Versailles on August 6 that repeated the bloodletting of July. Columns of people passed through the mysteriously open chapel gates in the early morning and poured into the palace courtyard. The King had issued orders to troops not to use force, but, if need be, to expose themselves to force. Following orders, they did not fire a shot. Unable to defend themselves, the guards were swamped by a rampaging mob that swept into the palace in search of the Queen. Once inside the palace the mob ran down helpless guards, two of whom were killed. Their bodies were taken outside to the courtyard where they were decapitated and the heads stuck on pikes amid loud cheering. This scene could hardly stand in greater contrast to the one illustrated by Prieur in tableau 30 that showed ordered lines of soldiers and the firing of salvos as preparations were made for the King and Queen to go to Paris. The jubilation in Paris shown in tableau 31, the last of the three-part sequence, illustrating the October *journées*, offered Prieur the opportunity to apply his own personal touch. He did this by showing a man seated atop a lantern at the far right-hand side of the tableau, expressing emblematically the popular idea of justice.

In contrast to Prieur's restrained version of the October 5–6 *journées* was the record compiled by other artists. Jean-François Janinet showed Lafayette's men entering the courtyard at Versailles as they fire muskets in an attempt to establish order (B.N. cat. no. 1770–72); he showed Parisians killing a guard outside the Queen's apartment (B.N. cat. no. 1794–96); and he showed the King on a balcony in the *cour de marbre* (court of marble) as National Guardsmen try to hold an agitated crowd below in check. Other illustrations showed a woman stabbing a National Guardsman (B.N. cat. no. 1780–81); Marie Antoinette taking flight from the mob (B.N. cat. nos. 1800–06); women brandishing heads on pikes (B.N. cat. nos. 1778–79, 1839–46); the riotous arrival of the King and Queen in Paris at the barrière de la Conférence (B.N. cat. no. 1895–99); and a crowd assembling in the Place de Grève, displaying the heads of two guards on pikes on the afternoon of October 6 (B.N. cat. no. 1916–20). Prieur did not depict the violence of the October 5–6 *journées;* he did not portray the Queen's peril; and he did not show crowds brandishing heads on pikes.

Lafayette's thwarting of the August 30 march on Versailles had aroused popular feeling against him, and, when he returned to Paris with the King and Queen on October 6, he was seen by some as a friend of the Court and an enemy of the people. Yet this episode gave Lafayette a political ascendancy that he would exercise for something like the next two years. Both the King and Assembly were now in Paris, thanks in part to his efforts; he had exercised moderation at Versailles; and he had consolidated his position politically. As a patriot he was allied with leaders of the Revolution; he was willing to talk to *monarchiens,* but increasingly found such efforts futile. Curious as it might seem, calm followed the October *journées* and the King and Queen were never more popular, at least among moderates. The excesses of the October *journées* had caused apprehension and even revulsion among "respectable" patriots and the prospects of monarchical government under liberal Fayettist leadership seemed favorable.

After his tableaus of the October *journées,* Prieur did no more illustrations for the remainder of 1789. His next tableau, *Lafayette has 200 Soldiers disarmed at the Champs-Elysées* (tableau 32, fig. 41), showed Lafayette putting down a plot on January 12, 1790 in which recruits in the National Guard were involved. According to the com-

FIGURE 41.   J.-L. Prieur, *Lafayette has 200 Soldiers disarmed at the Champs-Elysées,* Tableau 32, January 12, 1790, Musée Carnavelet, Paris

mentary in the *Tableaux historiques*, two hundred soldiers of the National Guard had been bribed by Philippe Egalité, duc d'Orléans, and gathered with a mob in the Champs-Elysées. Warned the previous day of a plot against the government, Lafayette surrounded and arrested the soldiers and declared them unworthy of the uniform they wore.

Prieur's next tableau, *The Commune of Paris bestows a Sword and Civic Crown on the Englishman C. J. W. Nesham* (tableau 33, fig. 42), portrayed a response of the Fayettist regime to one of the many crises with which it was confronted. Food riots had broken out throughout France in January 1790, and in the village of Vernon, a representative of the Commune of Paris responsible for provisioning the capital, tried to prevent a crowd from blocking a shipment of grain to Paris. A crowd seized him and dragged him to a lamppost, where he was to receive popular justice. He was saved, according to the commentary in the *Tableaux*, from a "frenzied multitude" by "a young man, a foreigner, an Englishman," who shielded him with his body and helped him escape (commentary, tableau 13). It was this Englishman, Nesham, who

FIGURE 42.   J.-L. Prieur, *The Commune of Paris bestows a Sword and Civic Crown on the Englishman C. J. W. Nesham*, Tableau 33, January 15, 1790, Musée Carnavelet, Paris

was shown in Prieur's tableau, receiving a sword and civic crown in Paris on January 15, 1790 in the great hall of the Hôtel de Ville.

Prieur's tableau 34, *The Agasse Brothers on the way to their Execution* (fig. 43), showed two men carted to the Place de Grève on February 8, 1790. This episode demonstrated the principles of impartial justice that resulted from liberal legislation in the Fayettist Assembly. On January 20, Father Papin had requested of the Assembly that executed criminals be permitted normal burial and that their families be allowed to claim their bodies; the Assembly passed decrees, assuring that the execution of criminals was not to involve families in any loss of civil rights or blemish them in any way. As Papin had requested, normal burial of criminals was guaranteed.

The Agasse brothers in Prieur's tableau that are being conveyed to the Place de Grève on a cart are evidence of the tolerant and rational justice administered by the Fayettist government. On the day of the execution, members of the Saint-Honoré district invited an uncle of the Agasse brothers to take up his duties again, to prove that "a bar-

FIGURE 43.   J.-L. Prieur, *The Agasse Brothers on the way to their Execution*, Tableau 34, February 8, 1790, Musée Carnavelet, Paris

barous prejudice, born in an age of ignorance, can have no effect on the hearts of free, enlightened men."[9] In Prieur's tableau, the two Agasse brothers, who were guilty of trading false bills of exchange in London, are barely discernible in the cart that takes them to the Place de Grève. The illustration is dominated by the Conciergerie and Palais de Justice on the opposite side of the Seine. The cart with the condemned criminals is followed by ordered files of soldiers and proceeds along a stretch of pavement that is guarded by another row of troops. Men and women in working-class dress wave at the Agasse brothers and run in front of the cart, presumably to watch the execution.

It is useful to bear in mind that the cart with the condemned men was headed toward the Place de Grève, the scene of popular justice administered by furious crowds in the previous summer. Not content to execute their enemies, those crowds had mutilated the bodies of those they had murdered. These acts of vengeance expressed vividly, specifically, and graphically the anger of a crowd swept up by the floodtide of revolutionary fervor. Undoubtedly François-Noël Babeuf's reflections on these atrocities, which he witnessed, shed light on the crowd's urge for vengeance. The monarchy had been barbarous to the people and the people in turn were barbaric. Babeuf lamented the savagery but felt those who carried it out were giving back what they had received. It was this vicious cycle that the legislation enacted in the Assembly wanted to end through liberal, impartial justice carried out in the name of the law. Prieur's superb drawing, which portrays a scene that came out of this legislative episode not only captured its essential meaning, but also the tensions that were bound up in its enactment.

If the overall sense of the tableau is one of official order and solemnity, there are also sparks of popular spontaneity not only in the crowd that runs ahead of the cart with the Agasse brothers toward the Place de Grève where they will be executed, but also figures in the right foreground that lean forward and gesture at the condemned men. The group that runs in front of the crowd is made up of workers, as are the figures who gesture at the Agasse brothers. By contrast, the well-dressed spectators stand upright; their body language indicates a different response to the event they observe than that of the people.

Tableau 36, *M de Favras makes honorable Amends at Notre-Dame* (fig. 44), illustrated an event that took place on February 19, 1790. Thomas de Mahy, Marquis de Favras of this tableau was a royalist conspirator who had been arrested on December 25, 1790, after his plot to spirit the King and Queen out of France had been discovered. He was placed on trial in January 1790, when the trial of Besenval was also being held. That Besenval was freed and Favras executed was not inconsistent with the evidence used against them, but the managing of the trials says

FIGURE 44.   J.-L. Prieur, *M de Favras makes honorable Amends at Notre-Dame*, Tableau 36, February 19, 1790, Musée Carnavelet, Paris

much about the political methods of the Fayettist government. Favras' death sentence was announced at the same time that Besenval went free, a calculated scheme by the liberal leadership to mollify *le peuple*. The shared feeling in the government was that the people needed a victim, and that if given one, Favras, it would be possible to free the other, Besenval. What complicated things was Favras' offer, on the eve of his execution, to name his accomplices. Up to this point, he had maintained an honorable silence, but, faced with the finality of death he had second thoughts and tried to bargain for his life. Anxious as the authorities were to get the names of Favras' fellow conspirators, they decided not to bargain. A crowd had already begun to gather at the Place de Grève, eager for the execution of an enemy of the people. The crowd had to be placated, so the execution went on as scheduled. According to Jules Michelet, the procession, taking Favras to the Place de Grève, was "long and cruel" and the execution was attended by mirth and mockery. "Saute, marquis, saute marquis," the crowd jeered, a double entendre that alluded to Favras' loss of status—he was the first aristocrat to be hanged rather than beheaded—and to the "jump" of the rope. As his body twitched there were cries of "bis, bis" (encore, encore).[10] The macabre circumstances of the execution of Favras was a striking contrast to the stately scene in front of Notre-Dame on the previous day when Favras made amends for his deeds. In Prieur's tableau, guards kept a large crowd at a distance from the condemned man, who displayed public fortitude as he did penance for his crime.

Prieur's illustration of *Favras making Amends* was preceded and followed by tableaus that showed scenes of popular unrest in the south of France. Taken together, they set the stage for a set of four tableaus, illustrating the July 14, 1790 *Fête de la Fédération*, a grand Fayettist patriotic celebration. Behind the July 14 festival that proclaimed the unity of France was the reality of conflict within an increasingly divided nation. Prieur's tableau 35, *Pillaging the Arsenal of Lyons* (fig. 45), showed a patriotic protest in Lyons that resulted in the overthrow of the consulate, a municipal government headed by Jacques Imbert-Colomès, a counterrevolutionary who was in communication with emigrés in Turin headed by Charles Philippe, the Comte d'Artois, later Charles X.[11] What precipitated the protest in Lyons was the refusal of young volunteers who supported the local National Guard unit to participate in a confederation festival in Valence to celebrate liberty. That festival was organized by National Guardsmen in the south of France, and was part of a larger confederation effort that culminated in the *Fête de la Fédération* on July 14, 1790.

The suspicion among patriots in Lyons was that the young volunteers, of which there were between seven and eight hundred, were op-

FIGURE 45.   J.-L. Prieur, *Pillaging the Arsenal of Lyons*, Tableau 35, February 7, 1790, Musée Carnavelet, Paris

posed to the Revolution, and that their refusal to attend the confederation festival in Valence proved it. In fact, counterrevolutionaries did try at this time to capture municipalities in the south of France by infiltrating National Guard units with young volunteers. Persuaded of the duplicity of their own young volunteers, Lyons patriots demanded that they never again be entrusted with guarding the arsenal. When some three hundred volunteers arrived for the changing of the guard at the arsenal on February 7, a crowd insulted, threatened, and forced them to withdraw, but not before the volunteers fired some shots into the crowd. "Then the multitude became furious, cried out 'To arms!,' attacked, got over the walls, broke down the doors of the arsenal, and took possession of forty thousand muskets."[12]

Prieur's tableau was a pictorial narrative of that event. Some of the young volunteers were thrown into the Rhône and the municipal government headed by Imbert-Colomès was overthrown. Driven from Lyons, Imbert-Colomès, working in concert with emigrés in Turin, threw himself into plans to foment civil war in the south of France. Out of these efforts came the Languedoc Plan, which strove to pit Catholic workers against Protestant employers in towns such as Montauban. That Protestants, who constituted one-sixth of the Montauban population, was overrepresented in the National Guard made Catholics suspicious and resentful. Against this background, a riot that left five dead and sixteen injured erupted on May 10, 1790 when an order went out to make an inventory of five religious houses. This was seen as a step toward giving churches back to Protestants that had been taken away in 1685 at the time of the Revocation of the Edict of Nantes.

In his illustration of the May 10 Catholic riot, tableau 37, *Massacre of the Patriots of Montauban* (fig. 46), Prieur shows a Catholic with a white flag, at this time the flag of revolt, who cries according to the commentary, "Down with the Nation and the national cockade."[13] In the foreground, a priest stands above the crowd, exhorting it to deeds of vengeance as he holds a sword in one hand and a crucifix in the other. Furious Catholics are not reluctant to answer his call. A man, standing below the priest and under his sword, raises an ax as he makes ready to cut down a guardsman. To his left, a woman holds another guardsman by the ear and forces him to look up at the ax that is about

FIGURE 46.   J.-L. Prieur, *Massacre of the Patriots of Montauban*, Tableau 37, May 10, 1790, Musée Carnavelet, Paris

to dispatch him. Men on horses fire pistols and swing swords as they slaughter Protestants whose bodies cover the ground. At the far right, a priest with a knife in his hand, seizes a Protestant from someone who tries to protect him. The scene of violence is shown against a backdrop of churches whose towers carry crosses that are connected pictorially to the cross in the hand of the priest who presides over the scene of violence.

Prieur's next four tableaus, 38–41, portrayed preparations for the July 14 *Fête de la Fédération*, the festival itself, and patriotic celebrations that took place afterwards. The origin of this event started on November 29, 1789, when some twelve thousand National Guardsmen from Vivrais and the Dauphiné pledged a bond of mutual brotherhood. After the fall of the Bastille, France had been swept by a wave of patriotic loyalty to the *patrie*, and a spirit of fraternity was channeled into festivals that drew from a wellspring of popular support for the Revolution. It was National Guardsmen who organized ceremonies of confederation in which young and old marched together, ministers of rival faiths celebrated together, weddings and baptisms were solemnized anew on patriotic altars, and ordinary people experienced patriotic brotherhood. After the November 29, 1789 ceremony, organized by National Guardsmen from Dauphiné and Vivrais, festivals were held in the following spring in Marseille, Lyons, La Rochelle, Troyes, and Strasbourg.

The July 14 *Fête de la Fédération* that commemorated the fall of the Bastille was a logical outgrowth of the federation movement that originated in provincial France and passed to Paris in the grandest of all patriotic festivals. Also, it was an ideal occasion for Lafayette to add to his popularity and, at the same time, to enter a plea for national unity that was his most essential political objective. After Charles-Maurice Talleyrand celebrated a High Mass that was followed by songs and salvos of gunfire, Lafayette dismounted, walked to the patriotic altar constructed on the Champ de Mars, and swore on behalf of the military and citizen-militia to "remain united with every Frenchman by the indissoluble ties of fraternity."

The Assembly approved the *Fête de la Fédération* on June 21, allowing a mere three weeks to prepare for the huge task of making the Champ de Mars ready for the grand event, which was to accommodate some four hundred thousand people.

Prieur's tableau 38, *Work on the Champ de Mars for the Fête de la Fédération* (fig. 47), shows thousands of men and women digging, pulling wheelbarrows, pushing carts, standing on scaffolding, performing all of the laborious tasks necessary for staging the patriotic event. The overall sense of the tableau is one of activity and energy, which is

FIGURE 47.   J.-L. Prieur, *Work on the Champ de Mar for the Fête de la Fédération*, Tableau 38, July 4, 1790, Musée Carnavelet, Paris

conveyed not only by groups of workers scattered across the expanse of the Champ de Mars, but also by mounds of dirt, irregular terrain, and construction that is under way. The teeming energy of this tableau is in contrast to the unity of tableau 39 (fig. 48), *Fête de la Fédération*, which shows lines of soldiers and spectators spread along the length of the Champ de Mars, which is now a regular, ordered plane rather than the irregular space of the previous tableau. Out of the people's work and energy has come unity and power, underscored by salvos of cannon. For this tableau, Prieur has chosen a vantage point at the far end of the Champ de Mars, beyond the triumphal arch built for the festival. Prieur's perspective, which places the patriotic altar so far in the distance that it is hardly distinguishable, is unusual. Other illustrators frequently have given greater prominence to the patriotic altar than Prieur. To understand his decision to view the event as he did, one can compare this tableau to an earlier one, tableau 9, *Troops of the Champ de Mars cross to the Place Louis XV* (fig. 17), which shows long, seemingly endless rows of troops marching on July 12, 1789, almost exactly a year earlier, with cannon, from the Champ de Mars to

Figure 48.   J.-L. Prieur, *Fête de la Fédération,* Tableau 39, July 14, 1790,
Musée Carnavelet, Paris

the center of Paris. The Paris Insurrection has broken out, and Besenval has given orders to Swiss guards to move from their encampment
on the Champ de Mars to the opposite side of the Seine. As they pass
under an ornamental gate and turn left (right for them) they would
seem, given their numbers, to have had an overwhelming advantage
over the unarmed crowds backed up by the *gardes-françaises* that they
would soon face.

For his illustration of the *Fête de la Fédération,* Prieur has chosen
the same vantage point as when he showed Besenval's troops depart on
a mission that would end in ignominious failure. He again looks across
the Champ de Mars and at the École militaire at the far end; what he
shows in the foreground is a commentary on the earlier illustration.
Before the foreground had been occupied by a file of soldiers ordered to
put down the popular insurrection; now, in the same space, he shows a
triumphal arch, emblematic of the people's victory over despotism,
through which files of National Guardsmen pass and on top of which
people wave in gestures of patriotic enthusiasm. To the right of the
arch, a crowd can be seen on specially built stands cheering as they pro-

FIGURE 49.   J.-L. Prieur, *Celebration of the Memory of the Fête de la Fédération on the Seine*, Tableau 40, July 18, 1790, Musée Carnavelet, Paris

tect themselves with umbrellas from rain. Just as the National Guardsmen who pass into the Champ de Mars suggest a commentary on Besenval's foreign mercenaries, who moved in the opposite direction on July 12, 1789, so are salvos from cannons in the foreground a reminder of the cannon in the earlier illustration that would not be fired.

Tableaus 40 and 41, *Celebration of the Memory of the Fête de la Fédération on the Seine* (fig. 49) and *Fête and Illumination of the Champs-Elysées* (fig. 50), show public celebrations four days later, on July 18. In one tableau, people on the banks of the Seine dance and wave at a fleet of barges on the river and in the other people dance, frolic, and climb flagpoles. The atmosphere in both of these tableaus is one of euphoria.

The euphoria portrayed in Prieur's tableaus 40 and 41 was undoubtedly an accurate record of the scenes he illustrated, and the sense of unity that he projected in tableau 39 surely captured the authentic feelings of the huge crowd that assembled on the Champ de Mars for the *Fête de la Fédération*, but the fact is that divisions within France,

FIGURE 50.　J.-L. Prieur, *Fête and Illumination of the Champs-Elysées,* Tableau 41, July 18, 1790, Musée Carnavelet, Paris

already portrayed in tableaus 35 and 37, wcre continuing to deepen. Prieur's tableaus for 1790 after the *Fête de la Fédération* series were a continuing record of those divisions.

An event that epitomized the mounting tensions within France was the August 1790 revolt of the Châteauvieux garrison stationed in Nancy. Military order was breaking down throughout France and the Fayettist Assembly took a firm line against rebellious units. Soldiers at the Nancy garrison, spurred on by National Guardsmen and Jacobins, had been requesting better pay and better treatment since May. Officers resented the claims of enlisted men and enlisted men were hostile to their superiors. The punishment of an enlisted man provoked the confiscation of regimental funds and account books by mutinous soldiers. Lafayette, concerned over a breakdown of military discipline, was determined to make an example of the soldiers in Nancy, and the Assembly took his side. It passed a decree that would be a "sanction to strike fear" into the mutinous soldiers. Those who incited the revolt were to be declared guilty of treason and punished with death. First, it was necessary to restore order, and to that end the chevalier Guyot de Malseigne was sent to Nancy, but efforts to negotiate with the mutinous soldiers came to an impasse when Malseigne treated them as criminals. Furious over their insubordination, Malseigne drew his sword, wounded several soldiers, and fled to Lunéville. At this point, the Assembly sent the Marquis François-Claude-Amour de Bouillé, La Fayette's cousin, to Nancy, and while two regiments accepted the harsh terms he imposed, the Swiss troops of the Châteauvieux regiment did not.

During the negotiations between Bouillé and the Châteauvieux regiment, Antoine-Joseph Désilles, an officer in the King's regiment of chasseurs (light infantry soldiers), pleaded with the extremists to end the mutiny. Addressing the fifty or so Châteauvieux hardliners, he said: "Don't shoot! They're your friends, your brothers, sent by the National Assembly; is the King's regiment to be dishonored?"[14] Désilles was a loyal officer who had sworn an oath of fealty to the King and Nation on July 14 at the Fête de la Fédération; he belonged to a regiment that had accepted Bouillé's terms, and in effect he had taken the side of the authorities when he appealed to the mutinous Châteauvieux soldiers not to fire. He positioned himself across two cannons that separated the rival soldiers, and for a half-hour he warded off the clash, until he was shot. Fatally wounded, he died on October 16, 1790. The bloody battle that erupted after his death resulted in the defeat and punishment of the Châteauvieux regiment. Some three hundred died in the fighting, and, to punish the mutinous men and make an example of them, thirty-three were broken on the rack wheel or hung and forty-one were committed to penal servitude.

The savage repression of the Châteauvieux regiment did not gain universal acceptance; some felt that the mutinous soldiers had legitimate grievances. Moreover, the Swiss guards had refused to fire on the people during the Paris Insurrection in July 1789, when they had been stationed in the capital. There was widespread support in Paris for the Châteauvieux regiment after the Nancy affair, and extremists such as Jean-Paul Marat said the wrong party had been punished; he maintained it was Bouillé and his men, creatures of the Assembly, who deserved the fate meted out to the patriot soldiers of the Swiss regiment. In time the supporters of the Châteauvieux regiment would prevail, and on April 15, 1792 a public festival was held in the regiment's honor. Soldiers sent to penal servitude were pardoned and welcomed as heroes at the Châteauvieux festival.

Illustrations of Désilles, trying to prevent bloodshed between Bouillé's men and the Châteauvieux regiment in the Bibliothèque Nationale catalogue, view the event in different ways and from different perspectives. Most illustrations show the event taking place against the backdrop of the Stainville gate leading into Nancy. In some the perspective is outside the gate, in others it is from the inside, and in a few cases the setting is within the city of Nancy. In all cases, Désilles tries to intervene between the hostile forces in an attempt to prevent violence. Sometimes shooting has not yet begun, sometimes the fighting has already erupted, and in one instance Désilles stands in front of the barrel to prevent it from being fired (B.N. cat. no. 17275). A comparison of two illustrations, Prieur's tableau 42, *Affair of Nancy: Death of Désilles* (fig. 51), and Jean-Jacques-François le Barbier's *Young Désilles at the Meeting of Nancy* (fig. 52), demonstrates how differently artists could portray the same event.

Barbier shows Désilles sitting on one cannon and shielding another as he gestures to the mutinous guards not to fire. The Swiss lunge at him and aim a rifle and point a bayonet at him, whereas Bouillé's men are lined up defensively. One of Bouillé's men, standing directly behind Désilles, holds up both arms, and pleads with the Swiss not to fire. In this highly dramatized version, there is no question that it is the Swiss guards who are the aggressors: Le Barbier's perspective is that of someone who portrays the Désilles episode to vindicate Bouillé and, by extension, the Fayettist Assembly that ordered him to Nancy. It was that same Assembly that requested le Barbier to memorialize the Désilles episode in his 10' × 15' painting, which was subsequently engraved.

For his part, Prieur shows Désilles pleading with the men of the Châteauvieux regiment to hold their fire after hostilities have already erupted. There is no way in this version to tell who instigated the fighting, but the bloodshed has begun and men lie on the pavement next to the cannon and below the soldiers who fire at Bouillé's men. Even as the Swiss guards fire at the enemy, one of them moves toward a group of civilians, including a woman and child, in a protective gesture, suggesting that even in the midst of bloody fighting, the Swiss guards are humane. Knowing what one does about Prieur, one would expect him to come down on the side of the Châteauvieux regiment, and this is what he would seem to have done. In his commentary for Prieur's tableau, Chamfort also sides with the Châteauvieux regiment.

The sequel to this tableau, *Funerary Festival at the Champ de Mars in Honor of the Victims of Nancy* (tableau 43, fig. 53), portrayed the funeral on September 20, 1790, organized by the Paris National Guard in honor of the men serving under Bouillé who had been killed at Nancy. By the time the event was carried out ceremoniously on the Champ de Mars, there had been demonstrations in the capital on Sep-

FIGURE 51.   P.-G. Berthault engraving of Prieur drawing, *Affair of Nancy: Death of Désilles*, Tableau 42, August 31, 1790, Bibliothèque Nationale, Paris

FIGURE 52.   Pierre Laurent engraving of J.-J.-F. le Barbier Painting, *Young Désilles at the Mutiny at Nancy*, Bibliothèque Nationale, Paris

FIGURE 53.　J.-L. Prieur, *Funerary Festival at the Champ de Mars in Honor of the Victims of Nancy*, Tableau 43, September 20, 1790, Musée Carnavelet, Paris

tember 2 and 3, in favor of the Châteauvieux's Swiss. The Nancy affair was deeply divisive and drove a wedge between the Fayettists and their adversaries. The King had congratulated Bouillé on September 4, the day after a demonstration for the Châteuvieux regiment. That the National Guard should hold a funeral on September 20 in honor of Bouillé's fallen soldiers did not settle well with Parisians who sided with the Swiss. Chamfort's commentary for Prieur's tableau of the funerary festival was highly critical of the event, which he contrasted to earlier festivals held within the same space. The soldiers being honored were "brave and credulous citizen soldiers, sacrificed to treason and intrigue, and had believed themselves to have given up their lives in defense of the law" (commentary, tableau 43).

　　In Prieur's illustration of the funeral, the patriotic altar of the Champ de Mars is surrounded by National Guardsmen with raised flags, by columns of guardsmen who stand at attention; it is ringed by stands in the distance filled with people. Officials have gathered on the patriotic altar to participate in the ceremony but the open field of the Champ de Mars is virtually free, except for the National Guardsmen and a handful of Parisians that guardsmen with guns chase from the scene. No one proceeds towards the altar; the sense of the tableau is that the guardsmen are shielding the patriotic altar from the people rather than participating with them in a patriotic celebration.

Prieur's illustrations after the Nancy affair portray events that are something like a catalogue of crises that contributed to the breakup of the Fayettist coalition. Tableau 44, *The Brest Affair* (fig. 54), shows a battalion of National Guardsmen arriving at the port city of Brest on September 17, 1790 to restore order after crews on two ships, the *Patriot* and *Léopard*, rebelled against their officers. A spirit of insurrection, fomented by Jacobin clubs and fed by the revolt of the Château-vieux regiment in Nancy, was passing across France.

Tableau 45, *The Mayor of Paris on his Way to the Law Courts to put Seals on Documents of the Parlement* (fig. 55), shows the official end on November 12, 1790 of the Parlement of Paris, "whose decrees could once stir up the entire populace and cause civil war . . ."[15] In Prieur's illustration, lines of ordered troops form a corridor through which the mayor passes as he heads toward the ornamental gate in front of the monumental Palais de Justice. The next tableau, *Pillaging*

FIGURE 54.   J.-L. Prieur, *The Brest Affair*, Tableau 44, September 6, 1790, Musée Carnavelet, Paris

FIGURE 55.   J.-L. Prieur, *The Mayor of Paris on his Way to the Law Courts to put Seals on Documents of the Parlement,* Tableau 45, November 13, 1790, Musée Carnavelet, Paris

the Hôtel de Castries (tableau 46, fig. 56), portrays an event that took place on the same day. The two tableaus could hardly offer a more striking contrast: one shows an official procession in front of the Palais de Justice and the other portrays a rampaging mob in a different part of Paris. The mob in Prieur's tableau 46 pillages the hôtel of an aristocrat, Augustin de la Croix, duc de Castries, who had wounded Charles de Lameth, a liberal, in a duel.

The duel resulted from a stratagem of the right to prevent Lameth from attending a session of the National Assembly, where a motion was presented to assign the King a military guard of six thousand men. After avoiding several taunts by political rivals, Lameth accepted Castries' challenge. When news spread that Lameth was wounded in the duel, a crowd marched to the hôtel de Castries, which it was told had been sold. Rather than burn the hôtel de Castries, the mob entered it forcefully and within an hour pillaged and destroyed it. Iron bars were used to smash windows, the Castries coats-of-arms were torn down

FIGURE 56. J.-L. Prieur, *Pillaging the Hôtel de Castries*, Tableau 46, November 13, 1790, Musée Carnavelet, Paris

and demolished, curtains were set on fire, mirrors broken, and furniture and household objects stolen or destroyed.

Prieur shows people throwing everything they can from windows to people in the street below who pile up the loot or smash it to bits with picks. National Guardsmen with Lafayette at the head, seen in Prieur's tableau with raised sword, arrive at the far left but make no effort to stop the pillaging. If the previous tableau shows an episode in the transfer of legal authority in front of the Palais de Justice, this one shows National Guardsmen under Lafayette standing passively by as a Paris mob goes on a rampage.

Lafayette came under heavy criticism for not imposing order when the mob pillaged the hôtel de Castries. He tried to justify himself by saying the looting lasted only a half hour, and added: "This was the only house in Paris devastated during my term of command, and it belonged to the very man among the emigrants whom I liked best."[16] If Lafayette liked Castries, who emigrated the day after the looting of his hôtel, he did not feel the same way about Charles de Lameth. In May 1790, Lameth's supporters had advanced him as Lafayette's successor as head of the National Guard, an ambition that Lameth claimed not to have. Even as Lameth denied aspiring to Lafayette's position, he found ways to insinuate that Lafayette had abandoned the people's cause, and, by the end of May 1790, a split within the *Patriot* ranks had developed, with Lafayette, Mirabeau, Sieyès, Le Chapelier, and Talleyrand on one side of the division and Barnave, Dupont, and Lameth on the other.

Lafayette's popularity was at a high point at the time of this division, thanks to his response to an incident on May 22 when a crowd killed someone accused of stealing a sack of oats on the Quai de la Ferraille. Lafayette, who was driving to the Hôtel de Ville, heard about the incident and despite warnings not to intervene leaped from his carriage and pushed through the crowd to the place where the man accused of stealing the sack of oats had been beaten to death. When National Guardsmen identified one of the perpetrators, Lafayette personally took him to the Châtelet and then went outside to face an assembled crowd. While National Guardsmen wanted to escort Lafayette through the crowd, he entered it alone and berated those responsible for the deed and called them dupes of troublemakers and brigands. Theatrical as Lafayette's role in this incident may have been, it added to his popularity. By November 1790, the time of the pillaging of the hôtel de Castries, there were internal rifts within the Fayettist coalition, and those who had turned against Lafayette used the incident to undermine his authority. Writing about the incident in a secret bulletin to the court, the Comte de Mirabeau said prophetically: "It is possible that the shame of tolerating insurrection when he has an army of thirty thousand men will ultimately lead M. de Lafayette to open fire on the people. In doing so he will only wound himself."[17]

Prieur's tableaus for the first half of 1791 show a continuing rise of the political barometer. Tableau 47, *Affair of la Chapelle between Patriots and the Chasseurs of the Barrières* (fig. 57), portrays an incident on January 24, 1791, in which armed toll agents are shown firing on an unarmed crowd identified in the commentary for the *Tableaux historiques* as "patriots." Toll agents had searched the house of an innkeeper of the La Chapelle district who was suspected of smuggling goods. As the toll guards were leaving, an alarm was sounded, a shot was fired, and a full-scale fight took place between toll agents and the crowd, which included members of the National Guard and some armed men. In Prieur's tableau only the toll guards have guns, and they slaughter helpless "patriots." Tableaus 48 and 49 portray political disturbances in two episodes that took place on February 28, 1791.

A royalist conspiracy had been uncovered in Lyons in December 1790; in January 1791 emigrés headed by the Comte d'Artois decided to leave Turin. Artois had been actively supporting Catholic forces in the

FIGURE 57.   J.-L. Prieur, *Affair of la Chapelle between Patriots and the Chasseurs of the Barrières*, Tableau 47, January 24, 1791, Musée Carnavelet, Paris

south of France, and the specter of counterrevolution was now becoming more ominous. On February 21 the King's aunts were allowed to begin a trip to Rome so they could meet with the Pope, which they did upon their arrival in April. Seeing their departure as part of a Catholic and royalist conspiracy, a crowd surrounded the King's brother in the Luxembourg on February 22 to prevent his departure for Rome, which according to rumor, he was about to undertake.

Against this background the Paris municipality voted a large sum to restore the donjon of Vincennes in order that it could accommodate prisoners from the Châtelet, which was filled to overflowing. Under these circumstances rumors of a plot, always ready to spread in times of fear, began to circulate in working-class sections of Paris. In the popular mind, Paris was covered with underground passages and subterranean cavities where dead bodies were buried and gunpowder stored. In July 1789, there had been rumors of underground passages connecting the Bastille and the donjon of Vincennes, and in February 1791 rumors circulated that there were passages connecting Vincennes and the Tuileries, and that the decision to restore the donjon at Vincennes was part of a plot to facilitate the King's flight from Paris. Responding to these rumors, a crowd of one thousand, largely from the faubourg Saint-Antoine, appeared at Vincennes to destroy a bastion of tyranny long associated with the Bastille. Hearing of the crowd's intentions, Lafayette rode at the head of a militia of National Guardsmen to Vincennes to prevent destruction of the donjon. Upon his arrival, he told his men to establish order, and sixty-four people were arrested.

In Prieur's illustration of the episode, tableau 48, *The Affair of Vincennes: Lafayette prevents Destruction of the Dungeon* (fig. 58), Lafayette addresses a crowd that is surrounded by armed soldiers. To heighten the sense of popular agitation, Prieur shows the crowd cheering and waving from walls and from the heights of the donjon itself.

After restoring order, Lafayette found the gates to Paris shut, and, when he threatened to open fire with cannon, he was allowed to enter the capital, but as he did so a volley of shots was fired at him in an apparent attempt on his life. By the time Lafayette reached the center of Paris, armed noblemen had forced their way into the Tuileries, presenting him with another crisis. He later claimed that the riot at Vincennes had been orchestrated by royalist conspirators who wanted to lure him and National Guardsmen outside Paris in order that they could spirit the King out of the capital, but this is far from certain. More probably, when the nobles who acted out the "day of the daggers" heard that Lafayette and National Guardsmen were at Vincennes, they became apprehensive over the King's safety and entered the Tuileries to offer needed protection, believing that another October 5 was taking

FIGURE 58.   J.-L. Prieur, *The Affair of Vincennes: Lafayette prevents Destruction of the Dungeon*, Tableau 48, February 28, 1791, Musée Carnavelet, Paris

place. When Lafayette reached the Tuileries, he thought he was confronted with an escape plot and ordered his men to restore order. Having arrested sixty-four rioters at Vincennes, he now arrested eight royalists at the Tuileries.

Prieur's tableau 49, *The Affair of the Daggers at the Château of the Tuileries* (fig. 59), portrays a scene of conflict and violence; while the conspirators have been apprehended and are being hauled away the sense of the illustration is one of disarray. Le Vau's monumental staircase with its ordered geometry is in strange counterpoint to the torrent of violence that sweeps through it. An intriguing question is this: What is the political perspective of tableaus 48 and 49? Depicting related events that took place on the same day, these tableaus chronicle one of the many crises confronting the government as Lafayette's political coalition breaks down. Presenting a visual narrative of the events of February 28 as he has, Prieur conveys an impression of instability, of forces that are difficult to contain.

Comte de Mirabeau delivered a speech in the National Assembly on February 28, the same day as the "day of daggers," in which he ar-

FIGURE 59.   J.-L. Prieur, *The Affair of the Daggers at the Château of the Tuileries*, Tableau 49, February 28, 1791, Musée Carnavelet, Paris

gued for freedom of individual movement. In the judgment of Simon Schama, the issue Mirabeau addressed was *"the* turning point of the Revolution."[18] The King's aged aunts, Adélaide and Victoire, had undertaken a journey to Rome for Holy Week, accompanied by a retinue of twenty, but they were detained at Arnay-le-duc. Mirabeau had urged the King not to allow his aunts to make the trip, recognizing that Louis would resent his advice. Even though Mirabeau had opposed the trip, once it was undertaken he believed in principle that it should not be obstructed. The Assembly debated a proposed law on February 28 that would restrict the movements of suspected emigrés, and it was to that measure that Mirabeau responded in his speech. This was a principle on which he had strong feelings; in a free society freedom of movement should not be abridged. By taking this line, he was in opposition to the Jacobins who favored the proposed law; he did not hesitate to dress down his rivals in the Assembly. They were stung by his verbal barbs, and that night, when he appeared at the Jacobins, he encountered a hostile response and charges of treachery. Himself a Jacobin, Mirabeau was at odds with those on its left, but he was also at odds with moderates, such as Antoine-Pierre Barnave. Nor was he on good terms with Lafayette. He received secret payment from the King but did not have his confidence; he wanted to strengthen monarchy, but the King's actions undercut that effort. When he died—aged forty-three—on April 2, the Revolution lost a man whose grasp of issues and powers of oratory had catapulted him to a position of leadership in the Assembly and made him a popular favorite. Even the Jacobins, who suspected him, supported the elaborate funeral attended by 100,000 in his honor on April 4, 1791; his remains were interred in the Church of Saint-Geneviève. He was the first hero of the Revolution to be pantheonized, but his remains would later be disinterred, after his secret correspondence with the King was uncovered.

Prieur's tableau 50, *Mirabeau's Funeral Ceremony at Saint-Eustache* (fig. 60), shows a stage of the funeral ceremony that ended up with Mirabeau's pantheonization at Saint-Geneviève. In Prieur's illustration, National Guardsmen are seen firing salvos inside the Gothic church of Saint-Eustache, in the center of which clergy have been gathered. What is visually striking about the tableau? The clouds of patri-

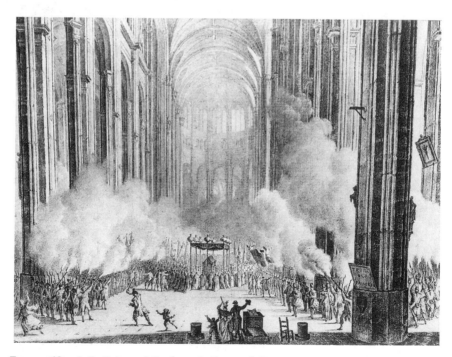

FIGURE 60.   J.-L. Prieur, *Mirabeau's Funeral Ceremony at Saint-Eustache*, Tableau 50, April 4, 1791, Musée Carnavelet, Paris

otic gunsmoke that billow within the vast Gothic interior of the Paris church. The remains of Mirabeau, under a canopy in the center of the building, are seen in contrast to the clouds of gunsmoke that issue from the muskets of National Guardsmen. By choosing this stage of the ceremony rather than the final one at Saint-Geneviève, Prieur charges his tableau with explosive patriotic energy, and he invests it with a measure of incongruity. A child in the foreground and a woman on the far left run from the thunderous volleys inside the Gothic church.

Prieur's tableau 51, *Mannequin of the Pope is burned at the Palais-Royal* (fig. 61), portrayed a crowd burning an eight-foot effigy of Pius VI in the Palais-Royal on May 3, 1791.[19] The Pope had condemned the Civil Constitution of the Clergy, and in protest Parisians made an effigy dressed in Papal attire, to which they attached posters with the words "civil war" and "fanaticism." According to some reports, the right hand of the effigy held a text of the papal condemnation and the left hand held a knife, but in Prieur's illustration of the scene the Pope held a staff in his right hand. People, who were assembled in the grounds of the

FIGURE 61.   J.-L. Prieur, *Mannequin of the Pope is burned at the Palais-Royal*, Tableau 51, May 3, 1791, Musée Carnavelet, Paris

Palais-Royal, pointed towards the Pope and threw their arms up in celebration as towering clouds of smoke issued from the papal bonfire.

The 1790 Civil Constitution of the Clergy arguably polarized France as did no other single issue. Obliged to accept this legislation officially, the King never accepted it in conscience. The trip to Rome for Easter by the King's aunts was seen, not incorrectly, as a sign of opposition by the royal family to the condition of the Roman Catholic Church under the Civil Constitution of the Clergy. The February 28 "day of daggers," widely regarded as an attempt to spirit the King and Queen from Paris, added to the perception of conspiracy against the Revolution and disloyalty within the royal family. On February 21, the Queen and royal children had received an ovation at the théâtre, but the events of February 28 stoked the fires of suspicion and resentment not only within the people of Paris but also the government. The National Assembly passed a decree on March 22, 1791 that stripped the Queen of regency power in the event of the King's death. Marie-Antoinette was understandably distressed by the decree. On April 18 the King and Queen intended to go by coach to Saint-Cloud, which they had been allowed to do in the previous year, but were blocked by a large crowd from reaching the carriages that lay in wait. Marie-Antoinette suggested they go instead in a nearby *berline* (traveling-coach), and Lafayette himself attempted to prepare a path to the vehicle. His own men shouted insults at him, and at the King and Queen, who had to suffer the abuse of the crowd for over an hour-and-a-half. The King asked why "He who gave the French nation its freedom should be denied his own." A member of the National Guard replied, "Veto."[20] Someone told the King he was a fat pig and the Queen, mortified and furious, listened helplessly at the crowd's mockeries. Unable to leave the Tuileries, the King and Queen returned to their apartments, more convinced than ever that they were prisoners in their own capital. By mid June, Marie-Antoinette—anxious to join loyal supporters beyond the frontier—persuaded the King to escape from Paris. On the night of June 20, they slipped out of the Tuileries in the abortive flight that ended at Varennes.

In his illustration of the King's capture in Varennes, *Arrest of the King at Varennes* (tableau 53, fig. 62), Prieur departs from his usual distant perspective and moves close to the scene he portrays, one of only four times in which he does so. In each of Prieur's four drawings with a close perspective a crowd with arms directs anger at enemies of the people, and in this instance the enemy is the King. Two members of the crowd carry torches that illuminate the dazed and corpulent monarch at the end of the table, whose large hat and private attire are disguises that add to the absurdity of his situation. Leaning back in his

FIGURE 62.   J.-L. Prieur, *Arrest of the King at Varennes*, Tableau 53, June 22, 1789, Musée Carnavelet, Paris

chair, the King recoils from the crowd that bursts into the room. At one end of the drawing is the inert, helpless figure of Louis XVI, and at the other end men charge forward with arms pointing accusingly at the monarch they have captured. One of Prieur's most freely invented tableaus, this illustration departs considerably from the actual circumstances under which the King was apprehended at Varennes.

News of the King's escape had reached Sainte-Menehould (on the road to Varennes) before the *berline,* carrying the King and Queen, arrived there, and members of the National Guard and local patriots were already on the lookout. The Postmaster Jean-Baptiste Drouet had seen the Queen before, while serving in the cavalry, and, believing it was she that he saw in the carriage, was able to identify the King by the simple expedient of comparing him to his printed image on a fifty-livre assignat. The travelers' papers were in order so they were allowed to ride ahead, but Drouet followed them on horseback, reached Varennes before the royal coach, and spread news of their arrival. The mayor was out of town, and it was the local *procureur,* Monsieur Sauce, who stopped the coach. The travelers' papers being in order, M Sauce was prepared to let them pass, but Drouet insisted that they were indeed the King and Queen and, if they were allowed to continue their journey, it would be treason. Under those circumstances M Sauce lodged them in his own house. The children were put to bed and at about midnight a local judge, Monsieur Destez, who had lived at Versailles, was taken to the King. When he bowed in the King's presence, Louis said, "Eh bien, I am indeed your King." In the early hours of the morning, two couriers from the National Assembly, who rode from Paris to Varennes, told the King and Queen they must return to the capital.

In his illustration, *Arrest of the King,* Prieur shows National Guardsmen and an angry crowd bursting into the shop of Monsieur Sauce, where the royal family is seated at a banquet table. Like other illustrators, who depicted the King's arrest at Varennes, Prieur turns the episode into a satirical portrayal of Louis XVI's legendary gluttony. "One primitive production in this vein," as Simon Schama has written, "strongly reminiscent of English satires, has Louis attacking a roast as the decree of his arrest arrives. 'Be damned with that,' he replies, 'let me eat in peace.' Marie Antoinette, admiring herself in the mirror, implores her husband, 'My dear Louis, haven't you finished your two turkeys yet or drunk your six bottles of wine, for you know we must dine at Montmédy'."[21]

Prieur's satire is less broad but no less pointed than that of the anonymous print. As armed men with torches burst into the room where Louis is seated at a dinner table, the King responds to his pathetic dilemma by clutching the side of his chair with one hand and grasping the nearest object available, a bottle of wine, with the other.[22]

In contrast to the spread of dishes on the table is an empty basket on a shelf behind the King. The light from the torches at the far end of the table illuminates the King, the Queen, and Mme Elisabeth, whose extravagant hats provide comic relief to the scene. The rough crowd that bursts into the shop where the King and his family eat dinner seems to have wandered into the drawing from Prieur's illustrations of Paris *journées*. They have the same facial expressions and body language, express the same righteous anger, and also brandish pikes and bayonets. That weapons would rise above the people inside a shop where the King is arrested as they do in Prieur's drawing is improbable, for men who carry pikes could hardly have walked unimpeded through the door of a local shop that deals in candles and provisions. Prieur has enlarged the doorway to accommodate the men with pikes who pass through it. The men carry pikes not for the sake of historical accuracy but to show the people as a militant and armed force acting against an enemy of the Revolution, for such is the guise in which Louis XVI is seen in this tableau. In fact, the scene depicted by Prieur never took place. A more accurate version is an engraving by J. G. Schultsz that shows a figure pointing at a portrait of Louis XVI that is exactly like the King who looks at his own image on the wall (B.N. cat. no. 5389–92) of Monsieur Sauce's residence.

Tableau 54, *Arrival of the King in Paris after returning from Varennes* (fig. 63) shows the King and Queen entering Paris after a three-and-a-half-day journey whose last stages were made at a walking pace to accommodate a crowd of six thousand that joined the escort of National Guardsmen. Prieur shows the procession entering Paris at the *barrière du Roule*, a tax station that is occupied by the people. It was not by chance that among the several *barrières*, illustrated by Prieur in the *Tableaux historiques,* this is by far the largest and most imposing. The Assembly had suppressed the tolls a month earlier, on May 1, the subject of Prieur's tableau 52, *Suppression of the Barrières* (fig. 64), in which he shows a crowd with animals and carts laden with goods passing unimpeded through the *barrière du Maine*, from whose toll houses people dance in celebration.

Tableau 54, *Arrival of the King in Paris*, is another scene of popular victory and again people stand triumphantly on a tollhouse, but on this occasion it is victory over the King and Queen that they celebrate. To drive home the point of popular victory over the King and Queen, Prieur has placed men on the roof of the royal carriage brandishing muskets, a scythe, a pike, and a raised sword. Almost surely Prieur has taken liberty placing the men on the roof of the carriage. Illustrations by other artists show guardsmen on the front and rear of the carriage to protect it, but no one celebrating on the roof.

FIGURE 63.   J.-L. Prieur, *Arrival of the King in Paris after returning from Varennes*, Tableau 54, June 26, 1791, Musée Carnavelet, Paris

To appreciate the distinctive qualities of Prieur's *Arrival of the King in Paris after returning from Versailles*, it may be compared to an engraving of the same subject, *The King arriving in Paris from Varennes* (fig. 65), after an aquatint by P.-F. Germain. In Germain's illustration three carriages pass through the Place Louis XV as they make their way to the Tuileries. Scattered figures in the foreground talk to one another and point at the procession of carriages, but most of the crowd in Paris' finest public square is gathered together in an ordered bloc between the Louis XV equestrian statue and the Pont Tournant that leads into the Tuileries. The people within that grouping do not gesture and do not brandish pikes or bear arms; the sense of the illustration is that of a silent crowd that observes the final stage of the King's four-day trip from Varennes back to Paris and to reimposed residence in the Tuileries. The three carriages are not highlighted but seen in the midst of the crowd, whose linear ordering adds to an overall impression of regularity. Germain's illustration is consistent with contemporary accounts of the King's arrival inside the city of Paris.

FIGURE 64.   J.-L. Prieur, *Suppression of the Barrières*, Tableau 52, May 1, 1791, Musée Carnavelet, Paris

The National Assembly had issued instructions for crowds to exercise restraint in the presence of the King and Queen; signs were posted throughout the capital that "Anyone who applauds the King will be beaten; anyone who insults him will be hanged." The silent passage of the royal carriage through Paris was in contrast to the journey that preceded it. At Sainte-Menehould a crowd halted the *berline*, and after it departed a noble, who wore the cross of Saint Louis and saluted the King, was shot in the back. Three members of the Assembly, Jérôme Pétion de Villeneuve, Antoine-Pierre Barnave, and Latour Maubourg, met the carriage outside Pont à Binson and rode with the royal family the rest of the way.

Pétion later described the crowd's hostility to the King and Queen, including an incident when fighting broke out among the people surrounding the carriage. Men with bayonets stared at the Queen, and "Soon they started swearing at her. 'Look at the bitch,' they shouted. 'It's no good her showing us her child. Everyone knows it isn't his.' " It was to avoid incidents such as this that the Assembly issued orders

Figure 65.   P.-F. Germain, *The King arriving in Paris from Varennes*,
Bibliothèque Nationale, Paris

that there were to be no signs of disrespect, on pain of death, when
crowds observed the carriage conveying the King and Queen. Thus, the
arduous return trip from Varennes included the three-and-a-half day
journey when crowds along the way vented their anger and, in the final
stage, the very different passage through Paris, when the carriage with
the King and Queen encountered funereal silence. To avoid hostile
crowds, the *berline* followed a circuitous route through Paris, moving
along boulevards and then looping back to the Tuileries after proceeding through the Place Louis XV. By selecting this scene for his illustration, Germain showed the royal carriage passing through an ordered
space, with National Guardsmen lining the way.

In his *Arrival of the King in Paris* Prieur showed National Guardsmen, escorting the royal carriage after it reached the west side of Paris,
before turning left at the *barrière de l'Etoile*. The *barrière du Roule*
was the last tollbooth before the *barrière de l'Etoile*, which lay at the
far end of the Champs Elysées, along which the *berline*, conveying the
King and Queen, would pass as it headed toward the Place Louis XV,
and toward its ultimate destination, the Tuileries.

In Prieur's tableau, the King's carriage stands out from a crowd in
the foreground that lines one side of the road and from another crowd
on the opposite side of the road. The crowd is not static as it is for the
most part in Germain's illustration, for they not only gesture and point

at the royal family in the carriage, but there are men on its roof. A child in the carriage, presumably the dauphin, leans out of the window and waves his hat at the crowd, while the men on the roof of the carriage, wave with a sword, a pike, a gun, and a scythe. Inside the carriage the King and Queen, attended by Barnave and Pétion, look straight ahead, as if to avoid the crowd. On the opposite side of the road a crowd is lined up in front of a wall and below the *barrière du Roule* and other buildings in the background. People not only stand on the roof and base of the *barrière du Roule,* but also sit and stand on the roofs of the other buildings. Like the crowds that line the road below, they wave with their arms and with tree branches, imparting a sense of activity and agitation as well as patriotic celebration.

Another contrast between Prieur's and Germain's illustration is the absence of arms in one and the prevalence of arms in the other. The people in the foreground of Prieur's tableau have the usual pikes, guns, and swords but even more striking is the rows of arms that rise above the crowd on the opposite side of the road. Accompanied by footsoldiers and mounted guards, the royal carriage passes through an armed and exercised crowd that lines both sides of the road that runs along the west side of the capital. The sense of popular militancy that comes through so strikingly in Prieur's tableau is utterly missing from Germain's illustration. So, too, is the impression of volatility imparted by the clouds on the far side of the road in Prieur's tableau. Presumably carriages and marching men and soldiers on horseback have stirred up dust, but if so it does not come directly from that source. Rather, it envelops the rows of armed bystanders lined up against the wall; it issues explosively from the crowd and helps invest the illustration with volatility. The clouds that issue from crowds that hold guns aloft in Prieur's tableau can be compared to the dust that rises from the dirt road in an illustration of the king's return to Paris by L. Lafitte (B.N. cat. no. 5457–62). The procession of soldiers, horses, and cannon would have stirred dust, and this is how it is seen in Lafitte's illustration. In Prieur's tableau, the impression is that of a cloud of gunsmoke, issuing from a crowd that discharges guns.

Another procession worked its way through Paris on July 11, a few weeks after the journey by the King and Queen on June 25. The July 11 procession was attended by 100,000 who turned out to observe the transfer of Voltaire's remains to the Panthéon, an idea advanced on November 11, 1790 by the revolutionary Marquis Charles de la Villette, in whose house Voltaire had died in 1778. The "deliberately stage-managed" apotheosis of Voltaire on July 11 emphasized Roman virtues in contrast to the discredited monarchy.[23] The apotheosis of Voltaire procession began at Rommilly-sur-Seine a mile outside Paris, to the west, and was received at designated stages by officials until it ended up at 10:00 P.M. at Saint Geneviève.

The first stage was the site of the destroyed Bastille, where Voltaire had been twice imprisoned, and from there it stopped at the scenes of Voltaire's triumphs, the Opéra and the Théâtre-Français. In Prieur's illustration of the procession, tableau 55, *Transferring Remains of Voltaire to the Panthéon: The Cortège at Pont-Royal* (fig. 66), the monumental chariot bearing Voltaire's remains is seen passing along the right bank of the Seine just before it reaches the Pont-Royal. Prieur's selection of this site for his illustration could not have been accidental.

He did not show the procession at any of the official stations for the event, but chose a location that had a rather different significance. Directly behind the chariot and its escorts was the Tuileries, within which Louis XVI was said to have been observing, surely with much discomfort, the procession below. How different this procession was from the one a few weeks earlier that ended where the King was now a furtive spectator and virtual prisoner, and how different this crowd was from the one that observed his return to Paris. When the King de-

FIGURE 66.   J.-L. Prieur, *Transferring Remains of Voltaire to the Panthéon: The Cortège at Pont-Royal*, Tableau 55, July 12, 1791, Musée Carnavelet, Paris

scended from his carriage on June 25 in front of the Tuileries, a cordon of guards had protected him from would-be assailants who wanted to strike out at the hated monarch. Now, on July 11, outside the Tuileries, a crowd was lined up along both sides of the Seine and across the length of the Pont-Royal, in spite of the rainy weather, to honor the immortal Voltaire. The crowd in this tableau held umbrellas as it observed a chariot with a statue of Voltaire on top of a colossal pedestal; by contrast, the crowd in the previous tableau held pikes and scythes as it observed a carriage with the King inside and armed men on its roof.

Two days after Voltaire's remains were placed in the Panthéon, the Assembly began a debate on the King's flight. Throughout its deliberations, the Assembly had worked under the premise that France was to be a constitutional monarchy, but with the King's attempted flight that premise was compromised. Latent republicanism surfaced, and petitions were sent to the Assembly calling for the end of monarchy. The Assembly denied the petitions as crowds gathered for another revolutionary festival, held as in the previous year on the Champ de Mars on July 14, although on a smaller scale. On July 15 and 16 further efforts were made to bring about the deposing of the King, and on July 17 a crowd gathered at the Champ de Mars to sign petitions drafted by the Jacobin and Cordelier clubs. The National Guard was summoned, and, at Lafayette's urging, Bailly declared martial law by raising the red flag of order. The crowd pelted the National Guardsmen with stones and apparently someone fired a shot. The guardsmen opened fire and by the time the massacre of the Champ de Mars ended the ground was littered with dead and wounded bodies.

This is the subject of Prieur's *Disorders when Petition is signed at the Champ de Mars* (tableau 56, fig. 67), which shows guards not only firing at defenseless civilians, but also cutting them down with swords. In the foreground, a soldier with a bayonet lunges at a woman as she raises her hands and tries to protect a child who clings to her back. To her left are officials who raise the red flag of order, calmly observing the slaughter they have brought about. The patriotic altar, the scene of celebrations three days earlier, is littered with fallen bodies and men and women who flee in panic from the withering fire of the guardsmen. Clouds of gunpowder that pour from the patriotic altar turn it into a sacrificial altar, at the summit of which a figure stands holding petitions heavenward. Files of soldiers on the left and right fire into the crowd with parallel guns that are in contrast to the waving crowd that stands on the altar and the dead bodies scattered across its steps. Mounted cavalry on the right slash away at helpless civilians with swords and behind the raised swords is a Liberty Tree with patriotic flags, rising incongruously from a cloud of gunsmoke.

FIGURE 67. J.-L. Prieur, *Disorders when Petition is signed on the Champ de Mars*, Tableau 56, July 17, 1791, Musée Carnavelet, Paris

For all practical purposes, the abortive flight of the King and the Massacre of the Champ de Mars brought an end to the Fayettist coalition. Lafayette was accused of complicity in the episode that ended ignominiously at Varennes, and, while there was no evidence to support the charges against him, he did not help his own cause by proposing the idea to the Assembly, which it adopted immediately, that the king had not attempted to escape but been abducted. Having tried from the time of his ascendancy to mediate between rival groups, polarization within France had made this strategy increasingly difficult, and with the King's attempted flight the strategy broke down completely. Even as Lafayette tried to rescue the King from the dilemma created by his flight, he called for careful surveillance of Louis XVI, which made the King resent him more than ever for his efforts. Circumstances forced Lafayette to resort to falsehoods that he hoped would enable the Assembly to complete the Constitution. Without a King there could be no constitutional monarchy, and within the Assembly no other form of government, at this stage, was acceptable. By opposing petitions for the end of monarchy, the Assembly was on a collision course with its opponents, the Jacobins and Cordeliers and the sans-culotte sections with which they were allied.

The Champ de Mars Massacre was the result of intractable differences between rival political groups. There was no evidence that Lafayette ordered troops to fire on the crowd at the Champ de Mars, but he was there, on horseback and at the head of his troops, and for many he was responsible for the massacre. While the Assembly was able to complete the Constitution, it did so under Lafayette's falsehoods that compromised it before it was decreed. The policy of mediation that he favored from the time of his ascendancy finally broke apart under the force of events over which he had no control. Utterly discredited by the Champ de Mars Massacre, Lafayette retired to private life after proclamation of the Constitution on September 18, 1791, but was persuaded by friends to run for mayor of Paris in November. Of the eleven thousand votes cast, he received only three thousand.

Prieur's final two tableaus for 1791 are a sequel to his illustrations of the King's flight and the Champ de Mars Massacre. In *Proclamation of the Constitution* (tableau 57, fig. 68), a crowd is seen in the Marché

FIGURE 68.   J.-L. Prieur, *Proclamation of the Constitution*, Tableau 57, September 18, 1791, Musée Carnavelet, Paris

des Innocents Square celebrating the newly proclaimed Constitution on September 18. The long row of buildings at the left of the illustration invest the scene with a sense of order, as do the rows of soldiers in the parade that celebrate the uniting of the King, the Nation, and the Law. Amid the public celebration, there are ironic touches that subvert the outer message of the tableau. People in buildings on the left wave at the procession below, as do men on the arched building at the right, but between the two groups there is a decided difference. Those in the building on the left are seen within the ordered architecture that frames them, and below them is the organized procession in the Marché des Innocents Square. Compositionally, the formalized procession is connected to the formalized architecture. By contrast, the people on the roof of the arched building on the right are free to wave with abandon, as they do, and below them a crowd rushes forward, underscoring the sense of agitation imparted by the figures on the roof. Thus, there is a sense of order on one side of the tableau and excitement on the other; files of uniformed people and horsemen are on one side, and people with pikes that hold *bonnets rouges* on the other. The contrast is between public order and popular enthusiasm. Rising above the people on the right is a Liberty Tree draped with patriotic flags. The tree occupies a place in this tableau similar to that of the Liberty Tree, also draped with patriotic flags, in the previous tableau, *Disorders when Petition is Signed in the Champ de Mars*, which shows soldiers slaughtering civilians who supported petitions to end the monarchy. The patriotic flag was not placed innocently in the Marché des Innocents Square. Carried over from the previous tableau, it is an ironic commentary on the proclamation of the Constitution, and its function is to subvert the tableau's outer meaning.

Tableau 58, *Death of Lescuyer in the Cordeliers Church in Avignon* (fig. 69), one of the nine tableaus by Prieur set outside Paris, was a vivid commentary on the failure of unity and the continued divisiveness and violence in revolutionary France. After patriots had taken control of Avignon in late August 1791, a counterrevolutionary crowd attacked Lescuyer, the secretary of the commune, and took him to the Cordeliers Church, where he was murdered. In Prieur's illustration, Lescuyer's assailants beat him and stab him to death directly under a statue of the crucified Christ. Priests, two in the foreground and one in a pulpit, are portrayed, raising crosses upward, as if they were blessing the bloody deed.

A patriot and official had been killed in a church by a reactionary crowd. This happened less than a month after the Constitution was proclaimed, and, judging from the printed commentary, Prieur's illustration depicted its shortcomings: "A monarchical Constitution, the

FIGURE 69.   J.-L. Prieur, *Death of Lescuyer in the Cordeliers Church in Avignon,* Tableau 58, October 15, 1791, Musée Carnavelet, Paris

guardianship of a false king, incomplete or perfidious laws that have already troubled both right and left *(les deux mondes)*, and seeds of discord between rival groups that soon erupted in other revolutions." (commentary, tableau 58.) The sequel to the event Prieur illustrated in tableau 57 was the slaughter of prisoners by patriots who took revenge on their enemies. A crowd of men broke into the Glacière prison the day after Lescuyer's murder, hauled dozens of prisoners from their cells, and beat and hacked them to death. They then buried the dead, sixty-one in all, in quicklime in a prison cell.

For 1792, Prieur did ten tableaus, nine of which were engraved by Pierre-Gabriel Berthault and included in the *Tableaux historiques.* Taken together they were a stunning record of the divisions within France and the pressures, political and military, that culminated in the explosive violence of August and September. Tableaus 59 and 61 illustrated two festivals, one organized by the Left and the other by the Right. The first, *Festival of Liberty in Honor of the Soldiers of Châ-*

teauvieux (fig. 70), portrayed an April 15 procession, commemorating the soldiers of the Swiss regiment that had been savagely repressed after they rebelled against officers; however, they were subsequently rehabilitated. For his tableau illustrating the day-long festival, Prieur chose the Place Louis XV as his setting. In the foreground were columns of the Garde-Meuble, and at its base a group of figures wave at the cart that passes by, pulled by a team of horses, and preceded by groups of patriots who commemorate the rehabilitated soldiers of the Swiss Regiment. That Prieur chose this space was far from accidental. It was in the Place Louis XV that the key events of the Paris Insurrection had taken place on July 12, 1789, and, by revisiting it in his illustration of the *Festival of Liberty in Honor of the Soldiers of Châteauvieux*, he connected it to an heroic episode in which the people of Paris fought back against the overwhelming advantage of foreign mercenaries in the pay of the monarchy. The soldiers of the Châteauvieux regiment had refused to fire on the people in the Paris Insurrection, and it is they who were now being honored.

The cheering crowds in the Place Louis XV join in the patriotic celebration of the Swiss soldiers who finally receive their just due. People

FIGURE 70.   J.-L. Prieur, *Festival of Liberty in Honor of the Soldiers of Châteauvieux*, Tableau 59, April 15, 1792, Musée Carnavelet, Paris

have climbed the Louis XV equestrian statue, and from it they wave at the groups marching below them in the patriotic festival. It was at the base of that royal monument that Prieur had shown the people clashing with German mercenaries on July 12 in the first violence of the Revolution.

Opposition to the festival in honor of the Châteauvieux regiment was fierce in the conservative press, the most scathing attacks coming from the poet and journalist André Chénier, whose brother Marie-Joseph-Blaise Chénier, the playwright, was one of the festival's organizers. André Chénier played an active role supporting a counter festival on June 3, 1792, the Festival of Simonneau, the subject of Prieur's tableau 61, *Festival in Honor of the Mayor of Etampes* (fig. 71), held in commemoration of the mayor of Etampes who had been killed in a food riot. One festival honored patriot soldiers crushed by the forces of order, while the other honored an official who was murdered by a mob. Prieur's illustration of the two festivals was less than evenhanded. The festival in honor of the mayor of Etampes began at the Bastille and ended up at the Champ de Mars, giving Prieur a wide choice of settings for his illustration of the event. He chose to set the procession against

FIGURE 71.   J.-L. Prieur, *Festival in Honor of the Mayor of Etampes,* Tableau 61, June 3, 1791, Musée Carnavelet, Paris

a fortress-like building with scaffolding that enclosed and confined the space through which the parade passed; it was in contrast to the open sweep of his tableau illustrating the Châteauvieux festival. A fence separated the procession, honoring the mayor of Etampes, from the handful of people who stood behind it. One person, a child, waved at the various groups in the procession while the others behind the fence stood by in apparent indifference.

Placed between tableaus 59 and 61, illustrations of festivals organized by the Left and the Right, was tableau 60, *Death of General Dillon in Lille* (fig. 72). France declared war on Austria on April 20, five days after the Châteauvieux festival and five weeks before the festival in honor of the mayor of Etampes. The vote in the Legislative Assembly was overwhelmingly in favor of war; only Lameth and his moderate supporters, and Robespierre, isolated on this issue in the Jacobins, opposed the declaration. Louis XVI favored war, hoping that Austria would defeat the Revolution's armies and deliver him from his bondage, and in the spring and summer of 1792 events seemed to justify his expectations. Nine days after the declaration of war General Comte Théobald Dillon was shot by his own soldiers in Lille, run through with a bayonet, and his body thrown in a fire.

FIGURE 72.   P.-G. Berthault engraving of Prieur drawing, *Death of General Dillon in Lille*, Tableau 60, April 29, 1792, Bibliothèque Nationale, Paris

Dillon had been ordered to simulate an attack on Tournai, in order to prevent the town's garrison from moving to Mons, which was under attack by an army under the command of General Armand Louis, Duc de Biron. Dillon's plan miscarried when his cavalry turned back and forced demoralized infantrymen to flee. Upon returning to Lille on April 28, the soldiers attacked their officers and shot their commanding officer and threw his body on a fire, after it had been hanged and a leg severed. Prieur's *Death of General Dillon* portrayed an early episode in the disastrous war declared by the Assembly that was a prelude to further military reversals. The worsening situation as spring passed into summer turned Paris—again—into a tinderbox.

Prieur's tableaus 62, 63, 65, and 66 are set in Paris and capture the collective fear and political anger that culminated in the storming of the Tuileries on August 10, the subject of tableau 67.[24] Tableau 62, *Journée of 20 June 1792* (fig. 73) portrays a dress rehearsal of the August 10 uprising. In this superb illustration, sans-culottes force their way into the Tuileries a year to the day after the King's attempted flight from Paris, and on the third anniversary of the Tennis Court Oath.

FIGURE 73.   P.-G. Berthault engraving of Prieur drawing, *Journée of June 20, 1792*, Tableau 62, June 20, 1792, Bibliothèque Nationale, Paris

Armed with pikes, axes, and pushing a cannon to the beat of a drum, the crowd passes through a courtyard and makes its way up a stairway. A placard in the midst of the crowd bears the inscription "Long live Liberty!"

After armed sans-culottes forced their way into the Tuileries, they found themselves in the presence of the King in the Salon de l'Oeil de Boeuf, where they taunted him and brandished swords and pistols in his face. Louis XVI calmly answered the taunts and when presented with a *bonnet rouge* he put it on and proposed a toast to the people of Paris and the Nation. An anonymous color engraving in the Bibliothèque Nationale shows the King taking the hand of a grenadier and placing it on his heart as he asks, "Do you think I am trembling?"

This illustration of the June 20 *journée* is in striking contrast to Prieur's tableau, which shows an armed crowd of sans-culottes forcing their way, with a cannon, into the Tuileries. Prieur's depiction of sans-culotte force rather than royal composure in the presence of sans-culotte anger is consistent with his visual rhetoric.

Prieur's tableau 63, *Commemoration of the Taking of the Bastille in the Champ de Mars* (fig. 74), shows a festival in the Champ de Mars held on July 14 to commemorate the fall of the Bastille. The setting is the same as for Prieur's illustrations of the 1790 *Fête de la Fédération* and the 1791 *Disorders when Petition is signed at the Champ de Mars*.

The 1790 tableau portrays an event whose theme is unity and whose purpose is to bring the Revolution to closure, whereas the 1791 tableau is a vivid commentary on the failure of that undertaking. Lafayette presides over both events, swearing an oath of allegiance to the *patrie* on the patriotic altar in one and standing at the head of soldiers that fire on a crowd, on that same patriotic altar, in the other. In the 1792 tableau, also set in the Champ de Mars, a crowd celebrates before a huge fire in which symbols of aristocracy are burnt. The flames that leap from the fire, and the smoke that pours forth, capture visually the volatility and explosiveness in Paris in the summer of 1792.

What added to a sense of crisis in Paris were reports of military defeat inflicted on France's revolutionary armies. The Assembly had declared the nation to be in danger on July 11 and on July 22 a ceremony was organized to call for volunteers. Prieur's tableau 65, *Proclamation of the Patrie in Danger* (fig. 75), showed a procession of armed men on the Pont-Neuf, part of a day-long ceremony to enlist support for the war against the Revolution's enemies. Two large processions wound their way through the streets of Paris, each headed by a National Guardsman who carried a banner proclaiming, "Citizens, the Nation is in Danger." The banners were placed at the Pont-Neuf and the Hôtel

FIGURE 74.   J.-L. Prieur, *Commemoration of the Taking of the Bastille in the Champ de Mars*, Tableau 63, July 14, 1792, Musée Carnavelet, Paris

de Ville, where they remained throughout the war. Eight makeshift buildings were set up to register the names of citizens who volunteered to fight in the Revolutionary army.

In Prieur's tableau, a press of citizens eager to join up are seen to the right of a registration booth on the Pont-Neuf, some of whom raise their hands upward in patriotic salute. At the left of the tableau is a Liberty Tree decked with tricolor flags, and in the center is the equestrian statue of Henry IV, surrounded by men who fire cannons. This is where demonstrations had been held in August 1788, on the eve of the Revolution, with the people burning effigies of their enemies. In Prieur's tableau, a cloud of smoke, issuing from cannon, invests the scene with patriotic volatility. At the far right a group of women and children wave at the men in the procession; next to them is a symbolically empty basket, a visible sign of popular hardship.

By the end of June, forges were installed in the Esplanade west of the Tuileries to make cannons. The manufacture of arms extended to the Seine, where boats with workshops that built badly needed guns

FIGURE 75.   J.-L. Prieur, *Proclamation of the Patrie in Danger*, Tableau 65, July 22, 1792, Musée Carnavelet, Paris

were tied up. Saltpeter was scraped from city walls in an effort to produce gunpowder for the war effort. On June 30, five hundred *fédérés* (confederates) from Marseilles arrived in Paris, singing the "Marseillaise" as they entered the capital.[25] Written within days of France's declaration of war against Austria, Rouget de Lille's patriotic song expressed in word and musical urgency the militancy of 1792. Rouget de Lille was, in fact, a monarchist army officer, and the "Marseillaise" expressed most directly his response to the threat of "The bloody prospect of tyranny" raised "against us" when war was declared. Originally entitled "Chant de guerre pour l'armée du Rhin," it became the "Marseillaise" as it spread to the south of France and took on new meaning among different groups who responded to its rousing militancy. The lilting optimism of the 1790 *Ça ira* was congruent with the early, optimistic stage of the Revolution, whereas Rouget de Lille's "Chant de guerre" with its steady, march-like rhythm, swelling notes, and fearful lyrics—"March on, march on, that impure blood will water our furrows"—captured a spirit of resolution within France in 1792 to fight to the death against the enemies of France.

If the original spirit of the song was military, it could easily take on broader patriotic meaning, and did precisely that. Adopted by *fédérés* of Montpelier and Marseilles, it became a rallying cry for those who would defend the Revolution, and, when *fédérés* of Marseilles marched into Paris in late July 1792, they sang it as they arrived. It was in their first night in Paris, June 30, that the "Marsellais" clashed with a regiment of guards, the National Guardsmen of Filles Saint Thomas, who were loyal to the King and sang "Long live the King, long live the Queen, long live Lafayette!" The *fédérés* from Marseilles clashed with the Guardsmen of Filles Saint Thomas when they held a banquet on the Champs-Elysées, the subject of Prieur's tableau 66.

In his illustration of this scene, *Disturbances in the Champs-Elysées after the Marsellais Banquet* (fig. 76), Prieur shows Marseilles *fédérés* slashing at the Guardsmen of Filles Saint Thomas with swords, shooting at them, and putting them to rout. To underscore their solidarity with sans-culottes, they are seen fighting together in a common

FIGURE 76.   J.-L. Prieur, *Disturbances in the Champs-Elysées after the Marsellais Banquet*, Tableau 66, July 30, 1792, Musée Carnavelet, Paris

cause, as they would in the Storming of the Tuileries, on August 10. In the foreground, two sans-culottes, fighting alongside Marseilles *fédérés*, beat and subdue Guardsmen of Filles Saint Thomas. The Marseilles *fédérés* had mingled with sans-culottes as soon as they arrived in Paris, and in Prieur's tableau they are seen fighting together against a common enemy. The stage is set for the storming of the Tuileries, the subject of Prieur's next tableau, *Siege and Capture of the Tuileries* (tableau 67, fig. 77).

When the tocsin sounded through the night of August 9–10, two thousand men, half of them the King's personal Swiss Guards, were stationed at the Tuileries. That another uprising was imminent had been apparent for weeks, and careful preparations were made for an assault that was certain to be directed at the King in the Tuileries. Guns had been placed on bridges to prevent sans-culottes and *fédérés* from the left bank from joining militants from the faubourg Saint-Antoine, but, after orders went out from the Commune in the early hours of August 10, the guns were removed. Jean-Antoine, Marquis de Mandat, commander of the National Guard, assembled men of loyal battalions

Figure 77.   J.-L. Prieur, *Siege and Capture of the Tuileries*, Tableau 67, August 10, 1792, Musée Carnavelet, Paris

in the extensive courtyards of the Tuileries, but he was ordered to the Hôtel de Ville, arrested, sent to the Luxembourg as a prisoner, and shot by a youth.

Jérôme Pétion, the mayor, was placed under protective arrest and taken from the Tuileries. By daybreak it was evident that the King's safety could not be guaranteed, and he, the Queen, and their retinue walked from the Tuileries to the nearby *Manège* (former riding school), where they placed themselves under the protective custody of the Assembly. Fighting broke out a couple of hours later. Swiss Guards, some of whom had put down their arms, fraternized with a crowd that was arriving in the courtyard outside the Tuileries; it would swell to twenty thousand, however, someone fired shots from the château into the crowd. Those fired upon believed they were witnessing a reprise of July 14, when shots were thought to have been fired treacherously into the crowd in the courtyard of the Bastille. Retribution was swift and terrible. By the time the savage fighting ended, some eight hundred of the King's men were killed, along with four hundred insurgents, of whom ninety were *fédérés* and three hundred sans-culottes from working-class sections of Paris. The furious crowd ran down and slaughtered the hated Swiss Guards, dismembered bodies, and stuffed anatomical parts in dead mouths or fed them to dogs.

In his illustration of the August 10 *journée*, Prieur looks across the Place du Carrousel courtyard where files of National Guardsmen fire on Swiss Guards who have fallen back to the entrance of the château. Apart from some handfighting to the right of the scene, the impression is one of formal battle between forces arrayed against one another in geometric regularity. The sense of violence that pervades the scene comes in large part from clouds of gunpowder and a building on the left that has been put to the torch. Only a few bodies litter the courtyard pavement. This is in striking contrast to Jacques Bertaux's painting, *Taking the Tuileries Palace on 10 August 1792* (fig. 78).

Unlike Prieur, Bertaux views the massacre in the Place du Carrousel up close. A sans-culotte in the foreground, among the most prominent of the figures, runs through a Swiss Guard with his lance while another sans-culotte raises a bloody sword, as he prepares to deliver another blow to the fallen soldier. To the left of this savage episode are dead bodies that litter the cobblestone pavements outside the château. Horses, too, have been cut down and the scene altogether is one of carnage. Throngs of sans-culottes and *fédérés* pass in waves into the scene of battle, firing guns and brandishing pikes, and between the groups of men, who enter the Place du Carrousel from the right, are cannons that blaze away, adding smoke, fire, and destruction to the scene. The pavement is covered with guns, pikes, axes, and bloody

Figure 78.   J. Bertaux, *Taking the Tuileries Palace on August 10, 1792,*
Musée National du Château Versailles

swords, and pools of blood flow from not only dead and wounded men
but also from fallen horses. The contrast between the spectacular violence and carnage of Bertaux's painting and Prieur's formalized illustration is certainly striking, and what makes the contrast all the more
noteworthy is knowing how adept Prieur was at portraying popular violence when he chose to. In this instance, he clearly chooses not to unleash a talent that if given full reign could have produced a scene of
truly grotesque savagery and carnage. In his cool, ordered, controlled
tableau, there is hardly a hint of the bloody violence that comes
through so vividly in Bertaux's painting. At the far right of Bertaux's
Taking the Tuileries an insurgent offers help to a fallen comrade blood-
ied by the fighting and suffering cruelly from his wounds; everywhere
men and horses writhe in pain. By employing an up-close perspective,
Bertaux shows the price in human and animal suffering of the August
10 uprising, whereas Prieur, by distancing himself from the fighting in
the Place du Carrousel, gives prominence to the monumental château,
which offers an almost stately backdrop to the formalized battle in the
foreground.

Other illustrations by different illustrators go beyond Bertaux in
depicting carnage in the Place du Carrousel on August 10. Bericourt's

version (B.N. cat. no. 2088–91) shows a crowd dragging and carrying bodies stripped of clothing and throwing them on a pile of burning corpses; a crude print (B.N. cat. no. 2132–33) shows the pavement of the Place du Carrousel littered with heads and dismembered bodies and sans-culottes hacking enemies to death as a building goes up in flames in the background and men in the foreground and right-hand side of the scene observe the slaughter; and two illustrations (B.N. cat. nos. 2138–39 and 2140–41) show sans-culottes and soldiers slaughtering Swiss Guards inside the Tuileries.

The formalized version of the August 10 *journée* by Prieur is in striking contrast to the violence of these and most other illustrations that portray the same episode. The most striking contrast of all is between Prieur's tableau and a crude print (B.N. cat. no. 2157–62) that shows butchery of every type, including a man who runs a woman through with a pike, children walking about with decapitated heads, and a woman, holding a fan, looks at severed body parts as a sans-culotte defecates on the principal part of a male torso.

Prieur's last published tableau, *Destruction of the Louis XIV Monument in the Place des Victoires* (tableau 68, fig. 79), portrayed a sequel to the August 10 *journée*. The people of Paris decided on August 11, the day after the savage fighting in the Place du Carrousel, to "take revenge on bronze kings," and tore down royal statues that occupied the public squares of the capital. That Prieur chose one of these incidents for his illustration would seem not to have been the result of chance. To show a crowd of Parisians pulling down a statue of Louis XIV in a square that honored his victories was perfect in its irony. This was a king who removed himself from Paris and its people, and during the longest reign in the history of France waged wars that resulted in crushing taxes and widespread misery. Isolated in the grandeur of Versailles, Louis XIV had separated himself from the people, and in this scene the people rendered their verdict.[26] Having the monumental bronze statue of the Sun King fall from its pedestal was Prieur's comment on the August 10 *journée*: he showed the people gathered together the next day in a public square dedicated to a king's victories celebrating the end of the monarchical order. Ironically, a lantern hung from a building at the left that frames the scene within the Place des Victoires, and below it people waved and cheered. Popular justice, it would seem, had many forms: in this instance it was expressed by pulling down a monument of a bygone and hated order.

Prieur's last illustration for the *Tableaux*, *Massacre of Prisoners at the Abbaye on the Night of 2–3 September 1792* (fig. 80), was not engraved and published. Of the Revolution's many episodes, the September Massacres was the one that historians are most likely to censure,

FIGURE 79. J.-L. Prieur, *Destruction of the Louis XIV Monument in the Place des Victoires*, Tableau 68, August 11, 1792, Musée Carnavelet, Paris

FIGURE 80.   J.-L. Prieur, *Massacre of Prisoners at the Abbaye on the Night of September 2–3 1792*, Musée Carnavelet, Paris

but this was not Prieur's response. He portrayed the scene as another Paris *journée*, with political violence carried out by an angry populace. To understand Prieur's perspective, it is instructive to compare his *Massacre of Prisoners* with Jacques-François Swebach-Desfontaine's *Massacre of September 2, 3, 4, 5, and 6* (fig. 81), which was engraved by Pierre-Gabriel Berthault and issued as number 72 in the *Tableaux historiques*. Swebach-Desfontaines showed the massacre of prisoners at the Abbaye, one of several Paris prisons where the people administered their own type of justice during the September Massacres. In *L'Ami du peuple*, Jean-Paul Marat urged "good citizens to go to the Abbaye, to seize priests, and especially the officers of the Swiss guards and their accomplices and run a sword through them."[27] Swebach-Desfontaines showed this in his illustration.

Prisoners are pushed through the door of the Abbaye and cut down as they enter the street. Corpses litter the pavement and, rising from the crowd, is the head of a victim of popular justice stuck on a pike. For all of the narrative detail of Swebach-Fontaine's illustration, for all of the evidence it presents of popular violence, it is surprisingly cool in appearance. It utterly fails to capture the sense of a Paris

FIGURE 81.   P.-G. Berthault engraving of J.-F. Swebach-Desfontaines illustration, *Massacre of September 2, 3, 4, 5, and 6*, Tableau 72, September 2–6, 1792, Bibliothèque Nationale, Paris

journée. Remove the dead bodies on the pavement and the head stuck on a pike, which is not conspicuous, and what is left is people milling about in the street in front of a row of buildings. When Prieur portrays a street scene, the people are seen in all of their raggedness and political anger, which their gestures and body language dramatize. They point accusingly at their enemies, they brandish pikes, axes, and guns, and they shout slogans and imprecations. None of this happens in Swebach-Desfontaines' *Massacres of 2, 3, 4, 5, and 6 September*. His crowd imparts no sense of righteous anger, and only here and there does a pike emerge from the crowd. Whether or not the detached quality of the work was the result of deliberate calculation or artistic predilection is a question that reasonably may be asked; probably it is a combination of both factors. Had Swebach-Desfontaines wished to dramatize the violence he portrayed, he could surely have done so more forcefully, but none of his works for the *Tableaux* suggest that he had the ability, or inclination, to portray street violence as vividly as Prieur. Had Prieur chosen to dramatize the butchery outside the Abbaye, his rendering of the scene would have had a different appearance and character than Swebach-Desfontaine's published illustration.

Prieur chose for his illustration of the September Massacre not the scene outside the Abbaye, but one presumably inside the same building. Because Prieur's drawing was not engraved and included in the *Tableaux,* it had no official title, but Pierre de Nolhac believes it portrayed the scene at the Abbaye on the night of September 2–3, and the presence of a torch indicated a nighttime setting.

On Sunday afternoon of September 2, several carriages delivered priests to the Abbaye de Saint-Germain des Prés, once an abbey seigneurial prison but converted to a military prison in the eighteenth century. After the Prussian victory at Longwy, news of which reached Paris on August 26, leaders of the Commune issued a call for popular justice, and the first victims were priests brought to the Abbaye. Of the twenty four priests pulled from carriages, nineteen were cut down by an angry crowd. After this spate of killing, the crowd moved to a nearby convent, the Carmes, which had been made into a prison, where some 150 priests were incarcerated. The butchery continued, under the supervision of the bailiff, Maillard, who set up a table and ordered "trials" to begin in the form of a popular tribunal which asked brief questions and administered swift justice; some of the prisoners tried to avoid the trial by running from the chapel. They were caught and cut down; so were those who were subjected to the mock justice of the tribunal. That night, after the butchery at the Carmes was completed, a crowd returned to the Abbaye, led by Maillard.

Perhaps it is he who stands in the center of the floor in Prieur's drawing. Wearing a hat with a rim, an ornamental sword, and flowing coat and sash, a person stands apart from ragged sans-culottes behind him and points accusingly at two men who bury their heads in their hands.[28] At their feet are two dead victims of popular justice, presumably two of the King's bodyguard, and behind them is a row of prisoners who either look dejectedly at their accusers, or avert their eyes from a scene too horrible to behold. One of these men is made to look at his accusers. A group of sans-culottes carry in a prisoner from the left and a group at the right brings forward another prisoner, whose captors grab him by the hair, raise a sword over his head, and hold him by a rope that binds his hands together.

Prieur's drawing is intense in his particular manner; the gestures of sans-culottes express popular anger forcefully, and, as in his other drawings of Paris *journées,* pikes, bayonets, and swords rise above the crowd. For all of the anger and violence expressed in the drawing, it is subject to controls imposed by the artist. Had Prieur wished to show mob butchery, he would not have shown the scene inside the Abbaye but what happened outside. The decapitated head would have been more conspicuous than in Swebach-Desfontaine's illustration, and the crowd less well behaved. The violence of the scene, only suggested by Swebach-Desfontaines, would have been brilliantly captured.

But Prieur chose not to portray that scene. To depict popular butchery was at odds with his essential purpose; he showed the right-eous anger of the people, not their savage excesses. Even though Swebach-Desfontaines chose a scene of mob butchery, replete with a head stuck on a pike, his illustration was so matter-of-fact, so de-tached, that he did not offend. His illustration was as cool as a photo-graph taken from a distance. Other illustrations of the September Mas-sacres, some of them artistically crude, were far more graphic in the depiction of violence than either Swebach-Desfontaines' tableau or Prieur's drawing.

One print shows the brutal slaughter of prisoners at the Abbaye (B.N. cat. no. 2236–37), two portray men dragging prisoners from the Châtelet, cutting them down with swords, and throwing their bodies onto piles of corpses (B.N. cat. no. 2252–55), and several show men stabbing and bludgeoning helpless women (B.N. cat. nos. 2238–40, 2242–43). Another print shows sans-culottes with raised swords mak-ing ready to cut down kneeling nuns (B.N. cat. no. 2265–66). Satirical prints, British and German, show the September Massacres being car-ried out in the name of Liberty (B.N. cat. no. 2283–90), as orgies with sans-culottes not only eating the eyes, hearts, and arms of the decapi-tated bodies they sit on, but also children eating human entrails from a pail (B.N. cat. no. 2291–97), and crowds dragging a decapitated and evis-cerated female body, whose head it brandishes on a pike, as men, women, and priests are about to be slaughtered after passing through a doorway over which religious statuary is placed (B.N. cat. no. 2303–09).

Within the context of illustrations of the September Massacres, the *tableaus* of Swebach-Desfontaines and Prieur are restrained, but in quite different ways. Swebach-Desfontaines shows bodies scattered on the pavement outside the Abbaye and a prisoner is being dispatched next to a doorway but men do not slash away with swords; dead bodies are fully clothed, and the distant perspective contributes to a sense of detachment. Swebach-Desfontaines has, in the literal sense of the word, distanced himself from the violence of the September Massacres. Prieur's perspective is different from that of Swebach-Desfontaines and indeed that of most other versions. Most illustrations show the slaugh-ter of prisoners in courtyards outside the buildings in which they had been incarcerated, but Prieur chooses an interior scene. Another print that employs an inside perspective may be compared to Prieur's version. In an anonymous print (B.N. cat. no. 2278–80) an official meets with sans-culottes to tell them about the distribution of arms, and, through a door of the building in which the meeting takes place, priests can be seen as they are thrown from windows to men below who hack them to death. Prieur also shows an official with sans-culottes inside a building, but the sense of the illustration is different from that of the anonymous print; the impression of Prieur's illustration is one of sans-culotte anger. Men angrily point at prisoners but they do not slaughter them. Two men lie on the floor, but there are no visible wounds, in contrast to prints that show piles of bodies, sometimes dismembered. Swebach-Desfontaines shows piles of bodies and a head on a pike, but his tableau is restrained to the point of coolness, whereas Prieur's drawing is intense in his particular way and conveys a sense of popular anger; sans-culottes brandish pikes and submit their enemies to rough treatment, but without savagery.

Why was Swebach-Desfontaines' illustration engraved and included in the *Tableaux historiques* rather than Prieur's version of the September Massacres? The decision could hardly have been made on the basis of artistic quality; between the two, Prieur's illustration is clearly superior. What makes more sense is Prieur's way of presenting the scene. Among the various illustrations of the September Massacres, his stands out in its depiction of the crowd as angry but not savage; it alone suggests the possibility of a just crowd. Was a visual interpretation of the September Massacres such as this what well-heeled buyers who purchased installments of prints issued by the *Tableaux historiques* wanted and expected? Was it what Prieur's associates in the publishing venture wanted?[29]

It is not known precisely when the decision was made not to include *The Intendant Bertier de Sauvigny*, but it was almost certainly sometime after the Storming of the Tuileries and the September Massacres. Installment numbers 7, 8, and 9 of the *Tableaux historiques*, including *tableaus* 13–14, 15–16, 17–18, were advertised in the *Moniteur* on July 21, 1792. There were no further advertisements until August 8, 1793, when installment eighteen was announced, containing tableaus 35 and 36. *The Intendant Bertier de Sauvigny* would have been tableau 22 had it been issued. From this information it is reasonable to conclude that the decision not to include it in the *Tableaux historiques* was made in the aftermath of the Storming of the Tuileries and the September Massacres. Why was that decision made? Given the absence of documents that contain the answer one can only speculate.

What seems plausible is that seen through the prism of August 10 and September 2–3, the graphic violence of Prieur's illustration of a crowd, carrying a trophy of popular justice on a pike, did not project an image of a revolutionary crowd that prospective customers might want to purchase. The recent spate of violence, far greater than that of July 1789, did not reassure those who sought stability, and it was politically divisive. As recently as June 20, 1792, Girondins had mobilized the sans-culottes in an invasion of the Tuileries, but after August 10 they feared the sans-culottes. August 10 changed the political landscape of the Revolution and left a legacy of factional strife and deeply divided perceptions of Paris sans-culottes. It was within this more troubled world that the decision was made not to include Prieur's *Bertier de Sauvigny* in the *Tableaux historiques*. Subsequently the decision was made not to include Prieur's illustration of the *September Massacres*.

Among Prieur's illustrations for the *Tableaux historiques*, there are none of military campaigns, but with his departure there was an immediate shift in that direction. Tableau 71 shows the taking of Verdun; Tableau 73 the taking of Speyer; Tableau 74 the bombardment of Lille; Tableau 75 the victory of Jemappes. From this time on, military campaigns that would eventually result in the conquest of Europe by the armies of France figure prominently in the *Tableaux historiques*. The very person who epitomized a shift within the Revolution from sans-culotte radicalism and Jacobinism to the conquest of Europe, Napoléon Bonaparte, is the subject of tableau 144, *18 Brumaire, Year VIII*, the last illustration in the *Tableaux historiques*. And it was Napoléon who put down the last of the Paris *journées*, that of 13 Vendémiaire (October 5) 1795.

A deluxe edition of the *Tableaux historiques* appeared in 1802 in three volumes, with a completely different text from that of Fauchet and Chamfort that accompanied the first sets of engravings. Of particular interest is volume three, which includes supplemental engravings that follow the 144 engravings contained in volumes 1 and 2. Volume 3 contains images of leading figures of the French Revolution, engravings of events associated with their lives, and short biographies.[30] Desmoulins was a "fanatical demagogue"; Pétion was "vain and mediocre" and a creature of the Orléanist faction; Orléans was a man of "ambition and vengeance"; "Marat! What a name, what a man . . . or rather, what a monster. What a flood of memories this ferocious person brings back . . ."; Jean-Baptiste Carrier was a "double outrage of nature," who "destroyed everything he encountered"; Robespierre was the "most execrable tyrant ever to burden this earth," and a man whose memory made the pen fall from one's hand. By contrast, Lafayette had suffered "long misfortunes" that made him an object of concern and respect; Condorcet was a "virtuous man"; Lavoisier had been proscribed by Robespierre but his "talents and virtues" assured the veneration of posterity; Louis XVI had been "seated on the throne at age nineteen," and as King he "showed a sincere desire to assure the happiness of the French, but the influence of perfidious councillors reduced his personal efforts to almost nothing"; and as for Marie-Antoinette, one could not think of her "without dwelling profoundly on human vicissitudes."

Marcel Roux said of the *Tableaux historiques*: "Revolutionary in the beginning, it progressively died out, and through a series of gradations, went from the most vivid red to an immaculate white."[31] In fact, the *Tableaux* was not red at the beginning of the Revolution and it was reactionary white only by the standards of a prospectus issued in conjunction with an 1817 edition published after the Bourbon Restoration. Looking back at the "long and terrible drama" of the Revolution at that point, after the return of the "august family of the Bourbons, who, for several centuries, occupied so gloriously the throne of France," the publishers of the 1817 edition of the *Tableaux historiques* did indeed render a negative verdict on the Revolution.[32] But this had not been the case in Year VIII, when the *Tableaux historiques* issued its first prospectus: "The genius of liberty awakens that of the arts, exalts its power, enlarges its domain, devotes its conceptions to the glory of the *patrie*, and celebrates its works for posterity. Citizen artists will engrave the great tableaus of our Revolution in a manner worthy of a free France, and of a Europe striving to become free, and moving toward that same goal. They have traced violent movements, terrible scenes, happy events, and prodigies of virtue."[33] An advertisement, published in the early part of 1791, claimed that those responsible for the *Tableaux historiques* were "eye witnesses to the upheavals of the Revolution," and that they "risked their lives for the cause."[34] It is safe to assume that when work on the *Tableaux historiques* began in 1789 those involved in the project were swept up in enthusiasm for the Revolution.

To say that those involved in the *Tableaux historiques* supported the Revolution is not to say that their responses were identical, or that they were on the same page politically. That there were differences among those attached to the project became evident as the Revolution headed in directions that no one in 1789 could have expected. Abbé Claude Fauchet, the first commentator, was caught up in the political dilemmas inherent in the revolutionary dynamic. Originally a Left-Fayettist, Fauchet drifted into the ranks of the Girondin Party opposition to Lafayette and his moderate government. He gave up his position in the Commune in October 1790 and organized the Social Club of the Society of the Friends of Truth, which held meetings in the Palais-Royal.[35] He had a large following at first, but events moved at a faster pace than his opinions, and the last time he carried the public was in a sermon delivered in Notre Dame on February 14, 1791. Allied with Jacques-Pierre Brissot by the time of the August 10 *journée*, he was elected to the Convention in October and served as its secretary until the *journée* of May 31, 1793. He went to the guillotine with Brissot and other Girondins in October 1793.

His successor in August 1791 as commentator for the *Tableaux*, Sébastien Roch Nicolas de Chamfort, was somewhat to the left of Fauchet politically. At one point, he was secretary of the Jacobin club, and like Fauchet he was caught up in the dilemmas of the Revolution. As commentator for the *Tableaux*, he was initially well disposed to Lafayette but he ended up criticizing him and his policies. In his commentary for tableau 46, *Pillaging of the hôtel de Castries*, he called the Jacobins the "mother of patriotism," but with the rise to power of Marat and Robespierre his devotion to Jacobinism wavered, and his caustic tongue did not spare the Jacobin-dominated Convention. Having been appointed director of the Bibliothèque Nationale by Jean-Marie Roland de la Platière, he was denounced by an assistant in July 1793, arrested, imprisoned, released, and threatened again by arrest. He attempted suicide with a pistol and sword, and though grievously injured he did not die at once. He wrote a statement in his own blood—in a clear hand—and lingered on until his death on April 13, 1794. His maxims, written earlier, had indicated concern for the populace: "Paris: a city of amusements, pleasures, etc., in which four-fifths of the inhabitants die of want"; "It is an undeniable fact that there are in France seven million men who beg for alms and twelve million with none to give them"; "The poor are the Negroes of Europe."[36] Having participated in the storming of the Bastille, his written narrative for the *Tableaux historiques* praised the "happy victory" and the "acts of virtue, magnanimity and grandeur of the historic event." His commentary also described the combination of "fierce passions" and "generous tenderness" with "terrible deeds" he had witnessed. Trying to strike a balance between the heroic and cruel, he said the greatness of the achievement overcame "the painful memory of the people's revenges."[37]

Commenting upon the impact of the Paris *journées* of July 12–14, Chamfort was aware of the problems facing the National Assembly in 1789: "The legislators must act like clever doctors, who, in treating the illness that is subsiding, administer tonics along with other palliatives."[38] A later remark was a mordant commentary on the failure of those tonics and palliatives: "I, Sebastien-Roche-Nicolas Chamfort, declare that I wish to die a free man rather than be taken to prison as a slave."[39]

Fauchet and Chamfort, the first two commentators for the *Tableaux historiques*, went to the guillotine during the Reign of Terror and Prieur, the first illustrator, succumbed to the same fate but after the Terror. The difference is noteworthy. Both Fauchet and Chamfort had been swept up by revolutionary enthusiasm in 1789, were active participants in the storming of the Bastille, and devoted themselves fully to the ideals and principles of the Revolution. As the Revolution entered its Jacobin phase, both Fauchet and Chamfort lined up with Girondins; both were moderates who fell victim to the Jacobin Terror. Prieur went the other way. He became a Jacobin and as a member of the Revolutionary Tribunal he was an instrument of the Terror, for which he was punished— after the Terror.

Two prints issued by the *Tableaux historiques* may be regarded as symptomatic of the change within the publishing project after Prieur left it to become a juror on the Revolutionary Tribunal. Tableau 103, *The Interior of a Revolutionary Committee* (fig. 82), illustrated by Alexandre-Évariste Fragonard *fils* and engraved by Berthault, is a commentary on the type justice that resulted from the Law of Suspects of September 17, 1793. According to that law, suspects were those who,

FIGURE 82.   P.-G. Berthault engraving of Fragondard *fils* illustration, *The Interior of a Revolutionary Committee*, Tableau 103, Bibliothèque Nationale, Paris

"by their conduct, relations, or language, spoken or written, have shown themselves partisans of tyranny or federation and enemies of liberty." The categories used to identify suspects were so broad that people of almost any type might find themselves compromised. In tableau 103 a well-attired couple and their child enter a room occupied by sans-culottes smoking pipes and holding pikes. The couple present papers to someone who receives them. Sheets of paper are on a table and someone seated at the far end is writing. No one pays any attention to a woman at the side of the table who has taken the precaution of placing a tricolor on her hat; all attention is directed at the couple. The sense of the tableau is that the rough men at the end of the table await the polite suspects with malicious eagerness. At the rear of the room, sans-culottes with pikes play a game on a counter, on which three bottles are placed. One of the sans-culottes puffs on his pipe as he considers what move to make. Presiding over these proceedings are busts mounted on the wall next to a window, presumably of Marat and Robespierre. Objects scattered on the floor next to an empty basket suggest that someone has eaten recently; they indicate disarray. This is a disorderly scene, not a proper setting for the dispensing of justice. The little girl who enters the room holds onto her mother and looks at a man sitting casually in a chair who holds a lance in one hand and a pipe in the other, and a dog is running from the man. Behind the mother is a standing sans-culotte who guards the door with a pike and looks at the suspects. The committee members gathered around the table await and gesture towards the suspects; all of the sans-culottes wear their hats, whereas the husband, who has removed his, hands a document to a committee member. The overall impression of the tableau is that of rough justice rendered by rough men.[40]

This is a scene that brings Prieur to mind. He himself, as a member of the Revolutionary Tribunal, rendered revolutionary justice. When he joined that body in September 1793 it was expanded to sixty; its composition changed as artisans were added to the list. Moreover, the portrayal of popular justice had been one of his distinctive themes as illustrator for the *Tableaux historiques*. The people in his tableaus administered very rough justice indeed when they killed their enemies by shooting them, stringing them up from lanternposts, chopping off their heads, and carring them on pikes. Now, in tableau 103, the people again administer justice, only those subject to its whims were ordinary citizens, a man, woman, and child who submitted papers to a revolutionary committee. The clear intent of the tableau was to expose the collapse of proper judicial forms under the Terror. Popular justice had been harrowing when administered by crowds in the full heat of their anger; now it was grotesque in its committee dispensations.

Figure 83.   P.-G. Berthault engraving of Girodet illustration, *Fouquier-Tinville before his Judges*, Tableau 114, May 1, 1795, Bibliothèque Nationale, Paris

Another tableau also summons memories of Prieur and revolutionary justice. Tableau 114, *Fouquier-Tinville before his Judges* (fig. 83), illustrated by Abraham Girardet and engraved by Berthault, showed the May 1, 1795 trial of the former head of the Revolutionary Tribunal. As an illustration for the *Tableaux historiques* there was nothing unusual about the print; like other tableaus it portrayed the Thermidorian reaction against the Terror. But among those who went to the guillotine as a result of that reaction was Jean-Louis Prieur, the first and finest illustrator of the very *Tableaux historiques* in whose pictorial record of the Revolution this print was placed. The same person, Pierre-Gabriel Berthault, who engraved Prieur's drawings, also engraved Girardet's illustration of the trial of Antoine-Quentin Fouquier-Tinville. What might Berthault have thought as he engraved Girodet's illustration of a judicial proceeding that resulted not only in the execution of the former head of the Revolutionary Tribunal, but also of an artist whose works he had known so well, as only an engraver can? Surely he thought of Prieur, but what did he think?

PART TWO

Jacques-Louis David and the Public

Rousseau, Robespierre, Revolutionary Images, and Revolutionary Festivals

Chapter 4

Robespierre and the People

It is necessary to remember that governments, of whatever type, are established by the people and for the people; that all who govern, including kings themselves, are only the mandatories and delegates of the people.

—Maximilien Robespierre, September 1789

*T*he above passage from a speech Robespierre had hoped to read to the National Assembly during the September 1789 debate on the royal veto question—he had it printed because he was unable to deliver it—can be broken into two parts. The first sets forth the idea of popular sovereignty: governments "are established by the people and for the people." This idea was accepted across a broad political spectrum within the Assembly, from royalists and moderate *monarchiens* to radicals on the far Left. François-Dominique de Reynaud, comte de Montlosier, a royalist, said that "all rights derive from the people," Emmanuel Mounier, a *monarchien*, maintained it was an "undeniable truth" that sovereignty resided in the nation, and the Abbé Jean-Siffresin Maury, a cleric on the Extreme Right said that "all powers derive from the people and belong to the people," a position he was subsequently to renounce.[1] In part, the acceptance of popular sovereignty among deputies was an acknowledgement, and a necessary one, that a revolution had taken place in France. Soon the term ancien régime would come into use, a historical category that consigned the old order to the past, including the theoretical base on which it had rested. The idea of popular sovereignty, which replaced the principle of divine right monarchy, had taken firm hold in France in the second half of the eighteenth century. Abbé Mably said it was in the people that "sovereign power originally resides,"[2] and parlementary remonstances enunciated the same position; in some measure, the idea of popular sovereignty grew out of the conflict between the parlements and monarchy, between a *corps intermédiare* that defended the rights of the people and the agents of monarchical "despotism." In the rhetorical struggles of the last several decades of the ancien régime, in the conflict between competing discourses, in the appeals to public opinion, it was monarchy that lost, and with that defeat the theoretical basis of government was redefined. The Revolution of 1789 confirmed the hegemony of popular sovereignty as an intellectual principle. So when Robespierre said that governments were "established by the people and for the people," he was setting forth a principle for which there was broad agreement among fellow deputies.

The second part of the passage from Robespierre's speech was more controversial. When he said that "all who govern, including kings themselves, are only the mandatories and delegates of the people," he was, in effect, arguing against a royal veto. As a mandatory of the people how could the king veto the work of another mandatory, the Assembly? In fact, Robespierre regarded the king as hostile to the Assembly, as a "powerful adversary" who would undermine the Assembly if he had veto power. When the argument was made that if the king were denied the veto he would be humiliated, Robespierre responded by saying the best way to deprive him the power to do harm was to deny him any veto power at all, including suspensive. As Norman Hampson said, according to the logic of that position, Robespierre should have dispensed with monarchy altogether, but given the shared assumption in virtually all quarters in the Assembly and across the nation that France would remain a monarchical state this logic was beside the point.[3]

The deputy Bertrand Barère de Vieuzac maintained on July 14, with unintended irony, that after a century of Enlightenment everyone knew what form the constitution would take; he predicted that the members of the Assembly could possibly draft it in a day. He and fellow deputies felt they should complete that task within a month or two, and would then be free to return to their homes. The Paris Insurrection and the Great Fear changed the ground rules of the debate within the Assembly, and, as discussion continued through August, there were fresh disturbances; those upheavals in Paris were of particular concern to the Assembly. On August 30 members of the National Guard prevented a group of men, who assembled at the Palais-Royal, from marching to Versailles to protest giving the King an absolute veto, which some deputies were known to favor. There had been talk of recalling some of the Paris deputies, forcing the Assembly to dissolve itself, and bringing the King back to Paris. The effect of pressure from Paris on the Assembly cannot be measured with any precision, but when votes were taken on September 10–11 on issues that had generated much controversy, the results were something of a surprise. The Right appeared to have had the best of the debate, and, just before the votes were taken, the Left was willing to offer a compromise that would have given Mounier, the leader of the *monarchiens*, most of what he wanted. He felt sufficiently secure to reject the offer. When the vote was taken on September 10 on the motion to create an Upper House the result was 89 for and 499 against, with 122 abstaining. On the next day 733 voted in favor of a royal veto and 143 against. In a follow-up vote, the veto was made suspensive rather than absolute by 673 to 329. It was a clear victory for the Left.

At one point in the debate within the Assembly over the contested issues , François, duc de La Rochefoucauld said, "Montesquieu will be opposed by Rousseau."[4] This was indeed the case, and the victory of the Left was a victory for Rousseau. Keith Michael Baker regarded the September 11 vote in favor of a suspensive veto as a defining moment of the Revolution, a crucial point at which the Revolution crystallized in a form that would have profound and lasting consequences. Perhaps it was Norman Hampson who has spelled out best what the victory of Rousseau over Montesquieu meant at this pivotal point. Urbane and cosmopolitan, Baron de La Brède et de Montesquieu "refused to identify himself with the self-interest of one particular society: 'If I knew of anything useful to my own nation that would be ruinous to another, I should not propose it to my prince, since I am a man before I am a Frenchman, or rather I am a man by necessity and a Frenchman by chance.' "[5] Careful to make distinctions, define limits, and allow for the contingent, Montesquieu resisted determinist reasoning. Good government was well managed and moderate, and those who shared in political power should exercise restraint: "I do not attach much value to the delights of furious disputation about affairs of state, to the endless repetition of *liberty* and the privilege of hating half of one's fellow creatures." No one, for Montesquieu, had a monopoly on truth; with a cast of mind such as his true believers were suspect: "Great God, how can we possibly be always right and others always wrong." Dedicated to political liberty, he felt it could be achieved only when "power checks power." Those who exercise power were inclined to abuse it, so a system of checks and balances was necessary for the preservation of freedom. "Every man with power is led to abuse it. He presses on until he encounters some limit. Who would have thought it, *vertu* itself needs limits."[6] As much as Montesquieu idealized the republican *vertu* of the ancient city state it was a thing of the past, to be studied and admired, but it was a chimera. The system of government he took as a given for his own time was monarchy, of which the British system with its mixed constitutional forms, as he understood them, was the finest example.

Robespierre took a firm line against the advocates of Montesquieuist mixed government in the September debates: "Don't quote me the example of England. . . . The representatives of the French nation . . . are not made for the servile imitation of an institution born in the days of ignorance, out of necessity and the strife of opposing factions."[7] Robespierre swept away the limits that were central to Montesquieu and his advocates; he rejected factions of any type.[8] In this he was a good apostle of Rousseau and the general will. For Norman Hampson the difference between Rousseau and Montesquieu was between will and circumstance. Rousseau, who gave primacy to the general will, said the individual had to transfer "his sense of identity to the community. In this way, each individual no longer believes himself to be single, but part of a unity and is aware only of the whole. A Roman citizen was neither Caius nor Lucias: he was a Roman."[9] The actual government of a state was merely the executive organ of the general will, and since politics was about morals the purpose of government was the transformation of human nature. Rousseau's religious conception of politics could not have been farther removed from Montesquieu's functional, pragmatic, and secular approach. If circumstances were central to the thought of Montesquieu, will, the *volonté générale*, was at the core of Rousseauist ideology. As a lawyer, a magistrate, and an eighteenth-century rationalist, Montesquieu saw government mechanistically; the art of politics was to achieve goals in the face of opponents who pursued different objectives. All of this was alien to Rousseau, whose starting point was virtue. For Rousseau the people were "never corrupted"; they "frequently are misguided, and that is the only time they appear to want what is evil." The people could never be corrupted because through the social contract they were joined together in a general will and the general will could never be in error. "The general will is always right and always tends toward public utility."[10] Once the people entered into the social contract the rule of virtue began: "Each man is virtuous," Rousseau wrote, "when his private will conforms totally to the general will."[11]

The general will, drawing from the moral influence of Rousseau, was part of the rhetorical baggage of late eighteenth-century political discourse, and was used by those on the Right as well as on the Left. For many its implications were not understood; for some it meant that governments should be responsible to public opinion, a position with which Montesquieu would have been in agreement. Baron Pierre-Victor Malouet, a moderate, who "studied facts rather than theories" and drew precepts from "history" rather than from "moralists," said at the end of 1788: "A power of reflection and feeling, unlike anything else, has been created in our midst. It is coordinated with the general will."[12]

In this instance, the general will was connected to the wave of enthusiasm that passed over France in response to the summoning of the Estates-General. It was when the idea of the general will, a "metaphysical concept" (Hampson), was placed in the service of debate within the political arena that complications arose. Boniface-Louis-André, the Marquis de Castellane said, "The people have invested us with its power. The general will is always wise and prudent."[13] Castellane used the general will to support the proposition that the National Assembly was infallible, an idea that would have elicited broad support among fellow deputies. Implicit within the general will concept was the sense of a new moral order based on common interest over sectional interests. The problem was that, while deputies felt they were working together in the creation of a new and better order, they did not agree on how to achieve that objective. The moral unity at the center of the general will idea was at variance with the reality of competing groups and interests in the Assembly.

A debate on mandates in July 1789 revealed fundamental differences between Right and Left deputies. The Right maintained that the Assembly's mandate from the people came through the *cahiers*; the Left argued that the autonomy of the Assembly transcended those limits. As debate continued through July, August, and September, differences between competing groups sharpened, and by the fall of 1789, after the *journées* of October 5–6 and the forced move of the Assembly from Versailles to Paris, some of the *monarchien* leaders wanted to leave the capital for their homes in the provinces; they were prevented from doing so by Left deputies who required them to request passports from the floor of the Assembly. However, only a few were willing to oblige. Within the brief span of four months a sense of deputies working together in a common cause was replaced by intractable differences between competing groups.

The differences had always been there, but debate sharpened them and created impassable barriers between deputies. For some on the Left, opposition to any aspect of Assembly policy, any measure adopted by the majority, was opposition to "the Revolution" and to the "sovereign people." In Rousseauist terms, opposition was wicked and illegitimate, and it could easily be seen as conspiratorial. Aware of the use to which the ideas of Rousseau had been put by deputies on the Left, Jean-Siffrein, Abbé Maury spelled out his objections:

> It is too easy to enthrone the general will in the place of legitimate authority and soon afterwards to substitute one's self for this pretended general will, while claiming to be its agent. No one can define popular sovereignty for us precisely since no one dares to admit that this pretended sovereignty is merely the right of the strongest. Remember that we are, in actual fact, representatives of the French nation and not Jean-Jacques Rousseau's plenipotentiaries; we have not submitted the Social Contract to the verdict of the electorate, as the measure of our power and the title of our mission.[14]

Mounier taunted his rivals on the Left when he said, correctly, that an elected Assembly could not be the custodian of the general will. In practice, the general will became a hammer used by the majority against their opponents; to oppose the majority in the Assembly was to be against the Revolution and against the people. Ideology—Rousseauist ideology—added to the difficulties of compromise between Left and Right.

Rousseau sympathized with *le peuple*, victims of the great and powerful, and he praised their simplicity. He described himself in the *Confessions* as a music copyist, someone who worked with his hands. He undertook his "reformation" by giving up his gold lace, white stockings, round wig, sword, and watch, and, in his chosen and humble "trade," he achieved a life of quiet and virtuous simplicity. If his work was "neither brilliant nor lucrative," at least it was "certain." This elaborately constructed persona was at variance with Rousseau's actual life. The reality was that he was lionized by aristocrats of fine pedigree who offered him housing in Paris or on their estates, and he discovered that by insulting them they were yet more generous in offers of hospitality. He dressed unconventionally in what he called his "careless style," with a rough beard or ill-combed wig or perhaps a Persian hat; he fabricated an image of honest simplicity that contemporaries—educated contemporaries—saw as a sign of virtue. The republican *vertu* in which he placed such value was an ethical ideal that applied only to a select few, and it was they, he felt, who should govern: "The best and most natural order is for those most wise to govern the multitude . . ."[15] This pronouncement was congruent with his statement quoted earlier that the position of the people was one of "ignorance and torpidity," and his belief that the people were not to be trusted in politics. For Rousseau there was a deep gulf between the educated public and the uneducated populace: "Wise men, if they try to speak the language of the common herd instead of its own, cannot possibly make themselves understood. There are a thousand kind of ideas which it is impossible to translate into popular language. Conceptions that are too remote are equally out of its range."

When Rousseau wrote in the *Social Contract*, "Never is the people corrupted," he meant an idealized people that was a product of his intellect. In this formulation "the people" was a mental construct that was far removed from *le peuple* in one of its several eighteenth-century usages that correlated the term with the populace.[16] For *le peuple* that contemporaries equated with the populace, Rousseau had more than a small measure of disdain, particularly the urban populace. Certainly the populace of eighteenth-century France, as seen by Rousseau, was unable to embrace the Spartan ideal of *vertu* that he espoused.

The National Assembly proclaimed in Article VI of the Declaration of the Rights of Man and Citizen on August 26, 1789: "Law is the expression of the general will. All citizens have the right to take part, in person or by their representatives, in its formation. . . . All citizens being equal in its eyes are equally admissible to all public dignities, offices, and employments, according to their capacity, and with no other distinction than that of their virtues and their talents."[17] Two months later, on October 29, 1789, the Assembly established two categories of citizens, active and passive, those with the franchise and those denied it, contravening Article VI of the Declaration of the Rights of Man and Citizen. Active citizens were males over twenty-five who paid the equivalent of three days unskilled labor in taxes, a measure that gave the vote, according to a 1790 estimate, to 4.3 million Frenchmen. Those who could hold office were much smaller. As William Doyle stated, "The deputies certainly did not intend to allow any say in political power under constitutional government to the sort of people who had come to their aid, but whom they had barely been able to control in July and the first few weeks of October."[18]

Robespierre was bitterly opposed to the limited franchise decreed by the Assembly; he argued that the Assembly should adhere to a principle it had already enunciated in the Declaration of the Rights of Man and Citizen: "Every citizen has an equal claim to representation, whoever he may be. Sovereignty resides in the people—that is, it is distributed among all individuals composing the people."[19]

The problem of the franchise illustrates some of the complications that arose when those in the political arena tried to adapt Rousseauist theory to the hard issues with which they were confronted. While deputies were in broad agreement that sovereignty resided in the people it did not necessarily follow for many—a majority, as it turned out—that all adult males should have the vote. Those opposing universal male suffrage could have argued that Rousseau was unclear on this issue in the *Social Contract*, that when its author became embroiled in heated controversies over Genevan politics in the 1760s he expressed no interest in those excluded from all voting rights, who comprised three-quarters of the population, and that, given his bias against the populace, it is questionable that he would have sided with Robespierre, his devoted follower, in the 1789 debate on the franchise.[20]

In his theoretical writings Rousseau thought in terms of the classical city-state or modern counterparts such as Geneva, which had a population of twenty-five thousand. Even in that context there were contradictions between his concepts and the political forms he discussed, as he was well aware. Democracy presupposed "a very small state," a "great simplicity of manners," a considerable "equality of rank and fortune," and "little or no luxury." In fact, the obstacles to democracy were insuperable: "True democracy has never existed and it never will"; "If there were a nation of Gods it would govern itself democratically. A government so perfect does not suit men."[21]

When Robespierre argued for universal male suffrage in 1789, he was acknowledging the crucial role of ordinary Frenchmen in the Revolution, from working-class districts in the capital to their urban counterparts throughout France, and to a peasantry that forced the measures of August 4 on the Assembly. Unlike many in the Assembly, Robespierre accepted the momentous changes wrought by the people in the summer of 1789, and from that point on, as a member of the radical Left, he sided with *le peuple*. More specifically, he sided with—in time he aligned himself with—Parisians in the working-class sections who would become the revolutionary sans-culottes. That he did so is a measure of how fully he grasped the changes wrought by the people and how completely he identified with the Revolution they had made. Even as Robespierre moved boldly beyond the social limits of his mentor Rousseau by siding with the people, it was he who embraced Rousseauist ideology most resolutely. What Robespierre did with unique consistency was to take the Rousseauist idea of a unitary *peuple* bound together by the *volonté générale* and use that model as a guide through the conflicts and struggles of the Revolution, through the vicissitudes of revolutionary circumstances; what Robespierre did was to impose a theoretical construct, the idea of a moral people, on the actual politics of the French Revolution. The controlling idea was that of a virtuous *peuple*, an idea that in the Rousseauist formulation was applicable to the citizenry of an ancient or modern city-state. Imposed on France it became part of the revolutionary dynamic; take away Rousseauist ideology and Robespierre is not Robespierre and the Revolution is not the Revolution.

Precisely what Robespierre meant by the people differed according to time and circumstances. In the early stages of the Revolution, he used the term "people" Rousseauistically, as when he said in 1790 that "Morality . . . is found only in the mass of the people . . ." He never abandoned that usage, but he applied the term differently in 1792 when he said, "the people, the huge class of workers," had a monopoly on virtue.[22] In a speech to the Jacobins on April 1, 1793 he said, "The Republic belongs only to the people," by which he meant "only to the sans-culottes."[23] In yet another speech to the Jacobins on May 8, 1793 he said, "He who is not for the people is against the people; he who dresses in *culottes dorées* (aristocratic breeches) is the enemy of all sans-culottes."[24] In April and May 1793, when Robespierre made the speeches from which the above quotations are taken, he was aligned with sans-culotte Sections against the Girondins, and, with his approval, the Sections wiped out his enemies in the Convention in the *journées* of May 31 and June 2, 1793. It was while Robespierre and Section leaders were planning that insurrection that he said, in a speech in the Jacobins on April 10, 1793: "The Republic belongs only to the people, to men of all conditions who have pure and elevated souls, to philosophers who are friends of humanity, to the sans-culottes, those in France who take intense pride in their title . . ."[25]

If Robespierre was a devoted follower of Rousseau, so, too, did Mirabeau appear as one when he argued that deputies in the National Assembly spoke in the name of the nation and expressed the general will. The Assembly was the voice of the nation, and "No one can impose any reserves on the nation. No power on earth, not even the executive power has the right to say 'this is my will' to the representatives of the nation."[26] When the Comte de Mirabeau argued on the floor of the Assembly in favor of a suspensive royal veto he did so within the context of Rousseauist theory. In setting forth his case, he said, "the monarch must be regarded as the protector of the people, not the enemy of their welfare."[27] The monarch, as executive, had to intervene in legislation "precisely for the interests of the people" and to declare "the laws to be in harmony with the general will."[28] Adept as Mirabeau was in advancing Rousseauist theory when debating constitutional issues, he made a sharp distinction between the people as an abstract construct and the people of Paris. This was evident after the *journées* of October 5–6, when women of working-class districts of Paris, followed by Lafayette and the National Guard, marched on Versailles and forced the King and Queen to return with them to Paris, where they became virtual prisoners of the people. Mirabeau's response to the episode was to write a secret memoir to the King on October 15, in which he spelled out the obstacles with which the state was confronted and which it must surmount, "if one wants the revolution to be consummated peacefully." The King "was certainly not free to leave Paris," and the Assembly "would not have the power to transfer itself to another city of the kingdom." The problem was Paris, which "has great strength" but "also contains great causes of disorder. Its agitated populace is irresistible." Given food shortage, the coming of winter, and possible bankruptcy Paris could become "a theater of horrors" within the next three months. "Is the King safe?" Mirabeau asked. "I do not believe so. Can even Paris save itself through its own efforts? No: Paris is lost if it is not restored to order, if it is not constrained to moderation."[29]

From the very beginning Robespierre welcomed the Paris insurrection. After the King made a processional visit to the Hôtel de Ville on July 17, in recognition of the political and military consequences of the Paris uprising, Robespierre visited the site of the Bastille, which was already being demolished.

> On the day of the King's journey I was taken there [the Bastille] by a detachment of the good townspeople's militia which had captured it, for after we had left the Hôtel de Ville, the armed citizens escorted deputies whom they met, and wherever we marched we were cheered by the people. How pleasant a place the Bastille is now that it is in the hands of the people. Its cells are empty, and a multitude of men are working ceaselessly to demolish this hateful monument of tyranny. I could scarcely tear myself away from this spot whose aspect gives feelings of pleasure and ideas of freedom to all citizens.[30]

Three days later, on July 20, Thomas-Arthur, Comte de Lally-Tollendal, made a motion in the Assembly calling for order in Paris. Robespierre spoke against the motion. "It is the very insurrection condemned by the motion which has saved the capital and the entire kingdom."[31] According to the *Courier de Versailles*, Robespierre said, speaking "with force against the proclamation of M. de Lally [-Tollendal], what is the result of the Paris uprising? Public liberty, a little spilt blood, a few heads cut off without doubt, but guilty heads."[32] There was further debate in the Assembly after the murders of Foulon and Bertier de Sauvigny on July 22, and again Robespierre defended the people. Writing to his friend A.-J. Buissart about the killing and decapitation of Foulon and Bertier de Sauvigny, he said the people had "punished" their enemies.[33]

Both Mirabeau and Robespierre employed the language and ideas of Rousseau in the early days of the Revolution and both advanced the doctrine of popular sovereignty. Yet Mirabeau saw the King as "the protector of the people" and argued for the royal veto in order that the laws would be "in harmony with the general will." He argued this line out of expediency. As an outspoken critic of the royal veto, Robespierre entered the lists against Mirabeau; he was outwardly respectful to Mirabeau, and polite, but the two men could hardly have been more different, personally and politically. Mirabeau wanted above all to bring the Revolution to closure, and he believed one way to achieve that objective was through cooperation, necessarily secret, with Louis XVI. For this he was paid, which does not seem to have presented him with any problems. He rendered a service in a cause he believed in and for which there was monetary reward. Mirabeau was quick to make accommodations with others when it suited his purposes, whereas the puritanical Robespierre was unyielding when he believed right and wrong were at issue.

As a true believer in the Rousseauist mold Robespierre committed himself utterly to the people, according to his idealized conception of the people. While Mirabeau believed, along with others in the National Assembly, in popular sovereignty, and the general will, he made a sharp distinction between the people as an abstract construct and the Paris populace. Already in September and October 1789 he became fearful of the people of Paris and indeed of Paris itself. The shock waves of the Paris uprising let loose forces that pushed him in the direction of political moderation. He wanted above all to restore stability; here is where he and Robespierre were in opposite camps. One would apply brakes to the Revolution, the other would goad and drive it forward. If Robespierre was polite to Mirabeau, Mirabeau did not find his rival congenial: "He will go far; he believes everything he says."[34]

Robespierre took a Rousseauist line when he argued that deputies in the Assembly were delegates, not representatives. "The members of the legislature are mandatories to whom *le peuple* have entrusted power, but in the true sense one could not say that they represent it."[35] By "it" he means a unitary people that has exercised the *volonté générale*, a sovereign *peuple*. If this was the theory, practice was different. While Robespierre felt elections should be frequent, he opposed the plebescite; once deputies were elected to office, they needed some safeguards in order to carry out their duties as legislators. Addressing fellow deputies in 1789, he said, "You are the Representatives of the Nation, not the mere bearers of instructions."[36] Later, in June 1793, he denied Primary Assemblies the right to meet freely, because doing so would create "pure democracy, a democracy that would not be tempered by the sage laws that alone can make it stable."[37] Ironically, it was Georges-Jacques Danton, the least Rousseauist of revolutionary leaders, who sounded the clearest call for direct democracy, which was to be achieved by delegates subject to instant recall by the sovereign people. According to Norman Hampson, Danton had "an almost instinctive grasp of the new political game."[38] He did not play that game in the Assembly as Mirabeau and Robespierre did, but as the leader of an organization he built in the Théâtre Français district on the Left Bank that was lined up against the municipal government. Again, Norman Hampson stated correctly: Danton "was the inventor of what were to become the tactics of every radical group fighting for its place in the sun: the basis of all authority was the local meeting which claimed to reflect the direct democracy of the sovereign people, even if, in fact, it stood for no more than a militant minority. . . . Throughout the Revolution this was to be the program of the men at the bottom."[39]

The organization Danton helped build, the Cordeliers, had a different makeup than the Jacobin Club that met close to the Manège, the meeting place of the Assembly, on the Right Bank. One club was the hub of a national network of patriotic clubs ultimately numbering some nine hundred; the other was a local organization that developed close ties to the Paris Sections. Danton's strategy was to appeal to local autonomy and denounce municipal despotism; like Robespierre, he constantly invoked the people when doing battle with adversaries, but he did so because it served his purpose rather than from Rousseauist conviction. Robespierre was at one with Rousseau ethically; like his spiritual mentor, he believed passionately in the idea of an exalted people. Danton, by contrast, instinctively took the winning side, covered his tracks, hedged bets, and, when circumstances dictated, threw up a barrage of rhetoric, often violent, that screened his real views. There were times when he appeared to be serving four or five parties or factions at the same time. He almost certainly accepted bribes. Like Robespierre, he was a master of denunciation, but he denounced not from genuine outrage, or paranoia but to gain tactical advantage. It was a device to insulate himself from danger and gather support, as circumstances dictated. Danton was a political realist, a pragmatist, and he was a cynic. He was not given to abstractions, and he did not see moral regeneration as a central or even marginal purpose of the Revolution; he was a master of dissimulation; he wore masks; he bargained and cut deals. Robespierre was as ingenuous as Danton was disingenuous; he was transparent in the Rousseauist manner. When he denounced opponents, he did so out of conviction. For Danton public opinion was a whore, and according to Dominique-Joseph Garat, he said he was driven into the arms of the sans-culottes. As much as Danton's strategies depended on the Paris Sections, and as willing as he was to excuse popular violence, he did not idealize the people, not an idealized Rousseauist *peuple* and not the people of Paris.

One of the Revolution's ironies is that it was Robespierre, an idealist and humanitarian, who opposed the death penalty on principle, and who presided over the Reign of Terror. Had Mirabeau lived longer, there is little doubt that he would either have become an emigré or gone to the guillotine. Danton did go to the guillotine and it was Robespierre who sent him there. For all of the violence of Danton's rhetoric he was a moderate, or perhaps it should be said he became one after achieving his own political objectives. After a political career marked by failure as much as success, Danton was appointed Minister of Justice on August 11, 1792. Having come to power as the result of a Paris *journée*, he was conciliatory toward his old enemies and he wanted to calm the Paris Sections. "When justice comes into action popular vengeance must cease." However, Danton did not try to protect prisoners during the September Massacres when efforts were made to save them, and, according to Mme Roland, he said, "I don't give a damn for the prisoners, let them look after themselves as best they can." Mme Roland was hardly an impartial reporter, but the cynicism she attributed to Danton was not entirely out of character. Such a remark from Robespierre would be unthinkable. Yet, Danton, the cynic, was able to forgive and forget whereas Robespierre, the idealist, was severe and unrelenting when right and wrong were at issue. One favored a policy of conciliation in an effort to end the Terror, the other drove the Terror forward until he was one of its victims.

How is Robespierre, the provincial lawyer from Arras who during the Terror found himself at the center of the Revolution, to be explained? His early life had some striking parallels with that of Rousseau.[40] His mother died when he was six and his father left him a few months later, although he returned sporadically to borrow money from relatives. Like Rousseau, the young Robespierre was raised by relatives. A local canon secured him a scholarship at Louis-le-Grand at age eleven, where he mingled with far wealthier boys, and where he spent twelve years as a student. In the elite world of Louis-le-Grand, Robespierre was something of an outsider. He won three second prizes as a student and upon returning to Arras was elected to a local academy; in a competition sponsored by the Academy of Metz, his essay on "corruption of the blood" won him a second prize in 1784. In 1786, he wrote an essay on illegitimacy in which he said, "Politics itself is nothing but public morality."[41] By this time, he had discovered Rousseau. In 1789, before being chosen a deputy of the Estates-General, and, in response to the political crisis in France, he wrote a scathing attack on the court. "Behold, underneath all that imposing luxury and pretended public wealth . . . the enormous wealth of a few citizens founded on the ruin and wretchedness of all the rest. . . . Behold above all, that lowest

class . . . which pride thinks to stigmatize with the name of people
. . ."[42] While trying to secure his election as a deputy to the Estates-
General, Robespierre wrote a pamphlet, "The Enemies of the *patrie*
Unmasked," in which he warned of great perils: "O citizens, the nation is in danger! Domestic enemies, more dangerous than foreign
armies, are secretly plotting its ruin . . . they are already considering
the martyrdom of all the defenders of the people . . ."[43] Before his election as a deputy to the Estates-General, and before the Revolution
began, Robespierre saw plots and conspiracies; he regarded domestic
enemies as more dangerous than foreign armies, exactly as he would
three years later when war was debated in the National Assembly.
Robespierre even thought of the "martyrdom of all," echoing the ap-
prehensions of Rousseau. Before going to Versailles, Robespierre saw
the world in terms of good and evil, and he saw conspiracies of the
powerful directed against the defenders of the people.

As a deputy to the Estates-General, Robespierre was unknown and
unheralded when that body began its deliberations at Versailles. Along
with other deputies elected to the Third Estate, he was a provincial
lawyer who had been active in local affairs. But for the Revolution he
would in all likelihood have lived out his days in quiet but decent ob-
scurity, doing what was in his power to benefit the weak and defenseless. Robespierre established a reputation as a serious and persistent
speaker in the Assembly.[44] He spoke, not to introduce legislation but on
issues of principle—and to warn of aristocratic plots. His opinions and
alarms carried little weight with the majority of the deputies. His attitude was one of all or nothing; compromise and mediation of differences was outside his modus operandi. On October 20, 1789, he said on
the floor of the Assembly, "Sirs, I will tell you everything: the security
of the state is in peril: a most atrocious conspiracy has been formed.
The nation is threatened once again . . ."[45] On the following day, October 21, he responded to a proposal of moderate critics to draft a martial
law bill after a baker had been lynched by a hungry mob: "All our evils,
including riots, are the result of a conspiracy against public liberty."[46]
Why were the people hungry? he asked, because of powerful enemies of
the state who sought to crush the people and extinguish liberty. What
Robespierre was unable to do, or did not do, was examine conditions in
the marketplace that resulted in the food shortage. Rather, he assumed
there were plots against those who suffered privation and were at the
mercy of prices that drove them to starvation and desperation. In his
view of the world, there was a division between the rich and the poor;
the poor suffered and were victims of the rich and powerful.

After the first upheavals of the Revolution subsided most members
of the Assembly, moderates and those on the Right, wanted the Revo-

lution to be over; it was time for the educated leadership to remake France. Their idea of the people and Robespierre's idea were at variance. If those across a broad spectrum found sovereignty in the people, Robespierre's idea of the people extended to the poor. Given this difference, and given Robespierre's incessant moralizing, it is hardly surprising that he was disliked by his colleagues, in many cases intensely. He did not sit on committees but was, in effect, a moral censor, sitting, listening, passing judgment. It was in the Jacobin Club that he built a following. A German, who also belonged to the Jacobins, Oelsner, said of Robespierre that "he sees only one side of the question he is treating and thinks himself the elect of heaven. He despises everything else. He behaves more like the leader of a religious sect than a political party."[47] Robespierre never saw himself as the head of a political party and rejected not only parties but also factions of all types. Robespierre stood above all else for unity. As a good Rousseauist dedicated to a sovereign people bound together by the general will, political divisions of any type were anathema. But in the face of very real divisions that resulted in conflicts within the revolutionary leadership and within France, he pursued a goal of unity to the very end. Revealingly, the enemies Robespierre feared were often "secret" enemies, not those with whom he was in open conflict. His automatic response was to denounce enemies as traitors. A pamphlet asked the pointed question, "How many 'traitors' did [Robespierre] create by accusing blameless citizens of treason?"[48]

When the National Assembly moved from Versailles to Paris and met in the Manège until permanent accommodations were available in the Tuileries deputies addressed not only fellow deputies when they mounted the rostrum, but also the galleries were open to the public. Some deputies did not care for this arrangement, and, weary of having to compete with noise from the galleries, 120 moderate deputies refused to participate in the proceedings. One deputy, Louis Riqueti, Vicomte de Mirabeau-Tonneau, raised his sword and exchanged insults with a hostile gallery. For Robespierre the gallery was a godsend. His idea of the perfect building for the Assembly was, "a huge and majestic building, open to twelve thousand spectators. Under the eyes of so many witnesses, neither corruption, intrigue nor perfidy would dare show themselves. Only the general will would be consulted. The voice of the nation and of public interest alone would be heard."[49] Robespierre addressed not just deputies in the Manège and people in the gallery, but public opinion. The editor of the *Barbillat* said, "What was remarkable" about Robespierre's speeches "is that they are known in advance, and that the opinions of this famous deputy enjoy prodigious success in all the taverns of the capital before being uttered in the nation's senate."[50]

Robespierre lived on the rue Saintonge, over a mile from the Manège, until the July 17, 1791 Champ de Mars crisis. On that night, Maurice Duplay, who frequently attended Jacobin meetings, offered him a bed in his nearby home on the rue Saint-Honoré. That Robespierre might be arrested or assassinated seemed a real possibility; not only did Robespierre accept the offer but, except for a brief period when he resided with his sister Charlotte, remained there for good. As a master carpenter, Duplay hired about a dozen journeymen and a similar number of apprentices, who worked in a shop that was attached to the house, which they were not allowed to enter. Life in the Duplay household was proper, simple, and respectable. It was located just above the Tuileries, close to the Manège and Jacobins, and far removed culturally and ethically from working-class sections to the east. With those districts, Robespierre had no direct contact; he was not seen in the Saint-Antoine quarter or other sans-culotte districts. He did not attend meetings of the sans-culotte sections and did not wear their clothing. Rather he wore the culottes of ancien régime fashions, and in the mornings he curled his hair. Amid the Duplays, he read aloud the works of Corneille, Voltaire, and Rousseau. His manners were polite; however, he did not have the common touch. Edgar Quinet was not altogether incorrect when he said, "No orator in the world spoke a language less popular, more educated, more studied, than Robespierre. . . . Anyone who attempted to speak the language of the people was immediately and naturally odious to [him]."[51] It was not that Robespierre found either the people or their language odious; what he disliked was anyone who "attempted" to use a language that was not their own, meaning educated people who imitated popular language. For Robespierre, always transparent, this was disingenuous and false. It was the linguistic equivalent of wearing a mask. Robespierre was not of the people and would not pretend otherwise.

If Robespierre achieved a position of leadership in the Jacobins after moderates pulled out in July 1791, he was still an outsider in the Assembly. Paradoxically, it was his very position as an outsider, lecturing his political colleagues, revealing conspiracies, denouncing traitors, and uncovering plots, that worked to his eventual advantage. As the Revolution moved always to the left, he lined up even farther to the left; by taking more advanced and radical positions, he both moved with the Revolution and pushed it forward. He was a disinterested politician unswervingly loyal to the public weal who proposed in May 1791 that members of the Assembly be barred from sitting in the Legislative Assembly. By taking this position, which was approved, he excluded himself from membership. In the debate over war in the Jacobins in the fall of 1791 and spring of 1792, he stood virtually alone, opposed to groups that, divided on other issues, supported war.

Jacques-Pierre Brissot de Warville said war was a national benefit and: "We need treachery on a national scale; our salvation lies that way, for strong doses of poison remain in the body of France, and strong measures are necessary to expel them." He believed that war would force the King to show his true colors; either the king was behind the Revolution or aligned with its enemies: "If he betrays us, the people will be ready." Marie Antoinette's response was: "The fools! Don't they see they are serving our purposes." Louis XVI said, war would discredit the revolutionaries and "the nation will see no other resource but to throw itself into my arms."

Robespierre took a different line. In time of war, "the people forget the issues that most essentially concern their civil and political rights and fix their attention only on external affairs." The real problem, he felt, was internal; it was the enemies within France that must be destroyed. Moreover, war would put generals in power and could result in military dictatorship. Lafayette was the general Robespierre feared most and attacked most savagely in the war debates: "You only want a revolution measured to your aristocratic prejudices and for your personal interests."[53] It was his responsibility to "unmask" Lafayette. According to Robespierre, Lafayette was not only duplicitous but vicious: He had murdered the baker Françoise in the fall of 1789; he was personally responsible for the murder of two men at the Champ de Mars in 1791; he might murder the King in order that he could seize his crown. To vilify Lafayette, Robespierre grossly exaggerated the number of casualties at the Champ de Mars to fifteen hundred (perhaps twelve were killed and thirty or forty wounded), and he later said Lafayette's soldiers not only slaughtered pregnant women in Brabant in the Belgian campaign, but also carried their unborn children on bayonets.

Such rumors had circulated, an index of the hysteria in revolutionary France, and Robespierre repeated the rumors when it served his purpose. He was caught up in the hysteria, and imagined himself the object of assassination. "I am surrounded by enemies, by assassins; but on the day when the daggers reach my breast, that will be when I denounce [Lafayette] and hold him up to public scorn with all my powers."[53] While Robespierre lost the debate on the war, he won the battle. He emerged a prophet as Lafayette defected to Austria and the war proved a disaster, one of the greatest mistakes of the Revolution. The war created pressures that would destroy the Brissotins and put Robespierre in a position of power. The pressures were felt throughout France but were greatest in Paris, which again became the center of *journées*, popular uprisings that drove the Revolution in new and un-expected directions.

It was followers of Brissot, angered over their dismissal by the King, who orchestrated a demonstration on June 20, 1792 when some twenty thousand sans-culottes converged on the Tuileries on the third anniversary of the Tennis Court Oath and one year after the king's abortive flight to Varennes. Robespierre was not among those who or-ganized the June 20 demonstration and even opposed it. The Brissotins who were behind it helped set the stage for the *journée* of August 10 that would spell the end of monarchy and result in their own destruc-tion. As *fédérés* swarmed into the capital in June and July and Paris moved ever closer to insurrection, Robespierre's position changed. Paris was on the verge of an explosion and under these circumstances Robespierre thought of the people as a political force. He called for in-tegrating the armed *fédérés* with the Sections on July 11, and he and the Jacobins aligned themselves with the Sections to destroy monar-chy. He did not enter the streets on August 9 and 10, but he believed in the necessity of insurrection. Only months before, in May and June, he had defended the Constitution, but now he maintained that insurrec-tion was "prescribed" by the Constitution. Believing in the right of in-surrection he cut through the legal barriers that had defined the limits of his political thought. It was in the aftermath of this bloody day, far more violent than July 14, 1789, when Robespierre wrote his only piece of contemporary history, "The Events of August 10, 1792."

He sought out and questioned eyewitnesses, whose comments he pieced together in a three-part account that included anecdotes, his narrative, letters, and documents seized by insurgents in the storming of the Tuileries. The event he discussed was a crucial turning point in the Revolution and for Robespierre personally. As a lawyer, he had stood for the rule of law and defended the Constitution, which the in-surrection he supported destroyed. As a moralist, Robespierre had to justify himself; his world was divided into right and wrong, and there could be no question that in the revolution of August 10 he was on the side of right. The duplicity of the court left the people no choice but to rise up in rightful wrath. "The French people, completely dishonored, oppressed for a long time, felt that the moment had come to fulfill the sacred duty imposed by nature on all living beings, and with even more reason on all nations, of being able to take care of their own preserva-tion by a generous resistance to oppression."[54]

When Robespierre moved from grand abstractions to specific infor-mation, he was less than accurate. He inflated the number of dead Mar-seillais and diminished the number of dead Swiss. Even more revealing was his reduction of the killing of the Swiss to the execution of a few guilty aristocrats: "The people's justice punished, through the chastisement of several counterrevolutionary aristocrats, who dishonored the name of Frenchmen, the eternal impurity of all the oppressors of humanity." In their retribution, he wrote, the people "observed all the forms necessary to protect the innocent."[55]

In the aftermath of the August 10 insurrection, Robespierre called for the opening of Sections to everyone, and for a reconstituted Commune to send delegates to the departments to explain the insurrection. The King was incarcerated in the Temple, and the Assembly had no choice but to call elections to form a convention. The primary elections were held on August 27 and the secondary elections on September 2. It was on that day that Paris, swept by fear, was rent by another wave of violence, the September Massacres that began on the second, lasted until the seventh, and resulted in the death of some twelve hundred prisoners suspected of counterrevolutionary conspiracy, including women and children, priests, and criminals. Robespierre maintained that the September Massacres were of a piece with the *journée* of August 10, and like it they were a justifiable expression of popular justice. Unlike Danton he did not praise the episode, but he did defend it. For this he was repeatedly attacked by Girondins whose ties were with the provinces. Throughout the running conflict between Girondins and Jacobins, the role of Paris in the Revolution was at the heart of the differences between the two factions. More particularly, what separated them was how they viewed the sans-culotte Sections. When the Convention began sitting in September, Robespierre answered Girondin denunciations. In a speech of September 25, he began ironically by thanking his Girondin "accusers," whose "calumny" served the public good, so transparent was their duplicity. "For what is this would-be denunciation if not the clumsy result of the basest of all intrigues? It is I who will disclose the criminal coalition that has long and ceaselessly circulated error and imposture in the eighty-three departments by the periodicals at their disposal." Not content with their efforts to win support in the provinces, the Girondins "ceaselessly calumny the people of Paris;" it was the Convention's responsibility to occupy itself uniquely with the "happiness of a great people and humanity" and to end the "imbecile declarations against the city of Paris."[56]

In the trial of the King, which began on November 23 and was held in the Manège, Robespierre spoke of the people as if they were one. Arguing against sympathy for the King, he said, "this humanity they talk to you about is cruelty toward the people."[57] Within the Convention there was great reluctance to impose the death penalty but in the bitter polemics of the trial Louis XVI was seen as the enemy of the people. It was Robespierre's young colleague and devoted follower Louis-

Antoine de Saint-Just who argued this case against the King most cogently. Louis XVI, the "enemy of the people," was not of the same species as the people; he was a "barbarian." "Louis," he said, was "a stranger in our midst." Building his case against the king in what Albert Camus called his "gallows style," Louis-Antoine-Léon de Saint-Just argued that the people was sovereign, the King was its enemy, and "between the people and its enemies there is nothing in common but the blade." To appreciate the arguments that were advanced, it is important to realize that the trial of the King was public, and that galleries were filled with sans-culotte spectators, armed with pikes. These spectators made their feelings and presence known by applauding speeches they agreed with. Inside this public forum Saint-Just instinctively seized the opportunity. "Since the French people has demonstrated its will [by invading the Tuileries], everything outside the sovereign is the enemy."[58] This was political théâtre; Saint-Just's conquest of the Convention was achieved through the incisiveness and abstract logic of the case he built against the King, through his ability to isolate and compromise his opponents, and by playing to the galleries.

The trial of the King brought into sharp focus the differences between the Girondins and Jacobins, and, in effect, it was an episode in the struggle for power between the rival groups.[59] With their constituencies in the provinces, the Girondins were at a distinct disadvantage. Robespierre said in a speech of January 6, 1793 that a report of Roland was directed "against the people of Paris. . . . When public tranquillity is threatened the Sections of Paris alone maintain it. . . . The Sections, from the beginning of the Constituent Assembly, have maintained tranquillity; they made the revolution [August 10]; they have supported it against all perfidious maneuvers, against all aristocrats, against all who would make trouble. Tranquillity reigns, in spite of some factions, it reigns in the Sections, it is the Sections that maintain it." Robespierre said in the same speech: "It is necessary to return to principles, and to forget men."[60] This is a revealing comment. Robespierre lived, in some measure, in a world of abstractions. When confronted with events in the political world that were incompatible with his idea of how events in that world should transpire, he took refuge in abstractions. Those abstractions were his inventions. In the speech of January 6 he said, "tranquillity reigns" in the Sections, "in spite of some factions." It was as if reality broke in upon his mental construction in the qualifying phrase, "in spite of some factions." In building his own constructions, Robespierre had to arrange the past: the Sections, he said, "made the revolution" on August 10 and then supported it in early September against all aristocrats and troublemakers. By referring to the September Massacres in this way, Robespierre offered a sanitized version of the Revolution's most senseless episode of popular violence.

Food was in short supply in February and March 1793; long lines and high prices led to riots that began on February 25. In a meeting of the Jacobins on February 25, after the first disturbances, Robespierre said, "The people suffer; it has not yet received the fruit of its labor; it is still persecuted by the rich." The rich persecuted the people and authored "perfidious designs" against them. "I have been witness myself to these movements. Beside honest citizens we have seen strangers and wealthy men dressed in the clothing of respectable sans-culottes." It was they who were responsible for the disturbances: "When the people rise up would it not have a goal worthy of itself? Would paltry merchandise be such a goal? It [the people] has taken nothing, for it is valets of the aristocracy in whose hands bread and sugar have been received. . . . The people do not rise up for sugar but to vanquish brigands."[61] In fact, suffering from inflation and food shortages over which the government was unable, or unwilling to exercise control, the people of Paris broke into shops and took what they needed, sometimes leaving behind what they felt was a fair price. Robespierre's mental construction of the people did not allow for conduct of this type; it was yet another perfidious conspiracy of aristocrats.

People were starving and the Revolution was in disarray. The Girondins were still able to muster more votes in the Convention than Jacobins, but the King's trial had weakened their position. As a political body that represented all of France, the Convention was often at odds with the city in which it was situated. Proposals to move the Convention out of Paris had failed, and in the difficult spring of 1793 tensions in Paris mounted, intensified by the high price of bread, military reversals, and counterrevolution in the Vendée. The Convention, divided between Girondins and Jacobins, was paralyzed and ineffective. By the end of March plans for an insurrection against the Convention were under way in Paris Sections. Notified of the plan, Robespierre gave it his support, but, even as he endorsed the insurrection, he was at pains to define its limits. In a speech in the Jacobins on March 29, he set forth his position: "When I propose firm and vigorous measures, I do not propose convulsions which give death to the body politic. I demand that all Sections be alert and identify bad citizens without attacking the inviolability of the deputies. I do not want anyone to touch these fragments of the national representation, but I want to unmask them and deprive them of the ability to do harm."[62]

The insurrection Robespierre supported was to have limited goals and an elevated purpose, as indicated by his remarks on April 1: The "means of defense" necessary to the "safety of the country was to be found in the genius of the people and the virtue of the Convention." A fellow Jacobin exclaimed that it was "In the force of the people!" not the "genius of the people" that the country's safety lay. Robespierre did not accept that viewpoint: "I do not speak through an interpreter, I say only what I want to say. The Republic cannot be saved by a sudden outburst, by a thoughtless and ill-considered movement . . . the most fatal of all measures would be to violate the national representation."[63] Making his position even more clear, he said on April 18: "To purge the Convention of all traitors? This would mean that we would be portrayed as men who want to dissolve the Convention and destroy the moderate members."[64] What he wanted was a "moral" uprising, not the *"insurrection brutale,"* as Jules Michelet put it, that took place in two episodes on May 31 and June 2, 1793.

Sans-culottes with pikes and guns entered the Convention on May 31, took seats by the Montagnards, and listened as a series of demands was debated. The Montagnard goal was to break the parliamentary majority but not at the cost of scuttling parliamentary government. The sans-culottes were less interested in such niceties, and, while they were willing on May 31 to sit and listen to debates, they did not intend to leave matters at that pass. Two days later, on Sunday, June 2, a much larger turnout of sans-culottes appeared at the Convention and subjected deputies, including the Montagnards, to their type of rough treatment. The sans-culottes who occupied the Convention, demanded the arrest of twenty-two Girondins, but Bertrand Barère proposed that they be suspended instead. Sans-culottes listened to the debate on their demands and let it be known that they wanted results, not words from the mouths of deputies. Marie-Jean Hérault de Séchelles, president of the Convention, sent a message to François Hanriot, commander of National Guardsmen lined up outside the Convention, requesting him to end the intimidation of deputies. Hérault could not have enjoyed the reply: "Tell your fucking President that he and his Assembly can go fuck themselves, and if within one hour the twenty-two are not delivered, we will blow them all up."[65] Cannons were lined up at the doors to underscore the message. Barère, in a desperate attempt to retain parlementary integrity, proposed that the deputies leave the hall, a gesture whose purpose was to demonstrate their independence. Outside the Tuileries, Hérault, standing in front of the deputies, met François Hanriot, sitting on horseback in front of armed guards. Hérault asked for the doors of the Tuileries to be free; Hanriot demanded that the twenty-two accused deputies be handed over within twenty-four hours and made cannons ready and pointed them at the Tuileries. The deputies returned to the chamber and voted against the accused.

Robespierre accepted the insurrection of May 31 and June 2, but at a cost. Even before the insurrection took place he gave expression to his weariness. On May 29, he said in the Jacobins that he was "exhausted by four years of revolution and by the oppressive spectacle of the victory of all that is most vile and most corrupt."[66] According to Minister of Justice Joseph Garat, Robespierre said in late March or early April, "I am utterly tired of the Revolution; I am ill; the country was never in greater danger, and I doubt whether it will survive."[67] He had not wanted the Convention to be purged when the people intervened on May 31 and June 2 but it was purged under threat of muskets and cannon. Having supported the insurrection, he was in the difficult position of having to assuage the fears of fellow deputies; on June 8 he assured them there would be no more purges and that those already purged would not be punished. He also opposed the execution of the Queen, but later in the year both Marie-Antoinette and the Girondins would go to the scaffold. The Paris populace put the Montagnards in power in the Convention but this does not mean the Montagnards were free to pursue an independent direction. The Convention had already begun to divest itself of authority in April when it created the Committee of Public Safety, which in time would have full executive power and hold its deliberations in secret. Seven of the nine original members were Centrists; only two were Montagnards. Membership of the Committee would increase and it would come under Jacobin leadership during the summer of 1793. Robespierre was appointed to the Committee on July 27; it was here that he would achieve a position of power and leadership. Up to this point, he had held no government office and had made his presence felt in the Convention as a member of a minority faction. Now it was his turn to parry the thrusts of opposition groups of the Left and the Right. Before he had prodded the Revolution forward as a radical Jacobin who allied with the Paris sans-culottes, but now that he was in office he had to confront the very forces with which he had aligned himself as well as contend with moderates who also opposed him. As a man in the middle Robespierre was never free to chart his own course.

The first group he had to contend with were the *enragés*: Jacques Roux, a former priest, Jean Varlet, Théophile Leclerc, and Claire Lacombe. Active in planning the insurrection of May 31 and June 2, their political views differed from those of Robespierre.[68] Varlet was disenchanted with representative government and argued that voters should have the right to recall those they elected to office at any time. "We cannot help feeling the same distrust even toward those to whom we gave our votes." Varlet's antiparliamentary stance did not endear him to Robespierre. Another problem between Robespierre and the *enragés* was how they regarded violence. As an idealistic member of the Assembly, Robespierre had opposed the death penalty. While he accepted and even justified popular violence after it took place, he was not an advocate of violence. Roux, by contrast, said in March 17, 1792, "Chain [*emigrés*] up and let them be the first to be exposed to the fire of the enemy . . . remember that England saved itself only by making the scaffolds red with the blood of treacherous and false kings." Robespierre wanted to guarantee the safety of the Girondins, but, after the insurrection of June 2, Leclerc called for their execution: "Why are you afraid of a few drops of blood?" Claire Lacombe, in association with the Cordeliers, sent a petition on May 19 to the Jacobins, denouncing the "merchant aristocracy, an insolent caste that wants to put itself in a class with royalty . . . exterminate the scoundrels."[69]

One of the founding members of the *Société des Républicaines Révolutionnaires*, a radical women's club, Lacombe had joined in a savage attack on Théroigne de Méricourt, a Girondin, outside the National Convention on May 15. Opposed to Méricourt's politics, Lacombe and other women stripped her naked and flogged her. Already subject to symptoms of instability, this incident seems to have contributed to Méricourt's descent into insanity.[70] According to some reports, Jean-Paul Marat, who was passing by when Lacombe and other women were beating Méricourt, interceded on her behalf. That Marat would have intervened in this episode is revealing. For all of the violence of his rhetoric, Marat was a man of the Convention, denouncing enemies endlessly but as someone working within the parliamentary system. The *enragés* were outside and hostile to that system. All four of the *enragés* were provincials from educated families who came to Paris during the Revolution and took up the popular cause, but they did so on the opposite side of a barrier that separated them from the Montagnards.[71] This is evident in a speech given by Roux on June 25, 1793 on the plight of the people: "Who among you deputies of the Mountain has visited the third to ninth stories of the houses of this revolutionary city? Had you done so, you would have been moved by the tears and moans of a vast population without bread or clothing, reduced to this state of distress and misfortune by stockjobbing and hoarding, because the laws have been cruel to the poor, because they were made by the rich for the rich."

Back at the Jacobin club, Robespierre vented his anger: "I say that those who go around preaching against the Mountain and against the Convention are the only enemies of the people . . ."[72] Not only did Robespierre call the leader who took up most urgently the sans-culotte cause an enemy of the people but accused him of being an Austrian spy. Robespierre's charges resulted in Roux's imprisonment; it was in prison after a second arrest that he would commit suicide. The next group Robespierre had to contend with was the Hébertists. While Jacques-René Hébert aligned himself with Robespierre and the government after the insurrection of May 31 and June 2, he withdrew his support on August 1 and attacked the government as "a new clique of scoundrels and intriguers." Pressures in Paris were building for another insurrection and Hébert and his ally Pierre-Gaspard Chaumette moved quickly to direct the storm on September 4 when a sans-culotte crowd appeared before the Hôtel de Ville. The crowd shouted that it wanted higher wages and more bread. Chaumette told the crowd, "I, too, have been poor, so I know what the poor are like. Now we have open warfare of the rich against the poor. They want to crush us. Well, we must stop them and crush them ourselves. We have the power." Hébert urged the crowd to go to the Convention the next day to set forth its demands, and on September 5 sans-culottes occupied benches next to deputies. Chaumette said the people demanded "food, and to have it, force for the law!"[73] Among his demands was the immediate establishment of a revolutionary army.

This was not a new idea. Sans-culottes demanded a revolutionary army made up of armed civilians in the insurrection of May 31 and June 2; the demand was accepted, with Robespierre's approval. His idea of a revolutionary army was a reserve army subject to military laws and training, not an autonomous army. Others, including moderate Sections, opposed the plan altogether, and the federalist authorities took up the project for their own ends. Under these circumstances, the plan remained a dead letter. In a meeting of the Jacobin club on September 1, Claude Royer said the federalists were no longer in a position to gain control over a revolutionary army and that the time was right to put the plan into effect. He called for "an *armée révolutionnaire* to spread out through the Republic and eradicate all the germs of Federalism, royalism and fanaticism with which it is still infected . . ." Continuing, he said, "You have made terror the order of the day; what better way to ensure its success than to create an army of 30,000 men, divide it into flying columns and attach a revolutionary tribunal and a guillotine to administer justice to traitors and conspirators alike?" During the insurrection of September 4–5 demands for a revolutionary army were made repeatedly: Chaumette, standing on a table, said, "I demand that the Convention be asked to establish an *armée révolutionnaire*," and Hébert added, "each division, each column should be followed by a guillotine."[74]

The demand for a revolutionary army was connected to the Reign of Terror in these pronouncements, but who was to direct the Terror? Would it be the government that would do so, through its offices? Or would it be armed sans-culottes whose columns were to be followed by guillotines? The real question was who controlled the Revolution. Those with whom Robespierre was allied, the sans-culottes, would gain control of the Revolution if they were to impose terror on France. Robespierre, the friend of the people, had to compete with the people for power—not the moral people of his abstract concept, but the militant sans-culottes of the Paris Sections. The only way for Robespierre to carry out the terror, according to his objectives, was to strip the Paris Sections of their power. The first step in the reduction of the Sections was taken on September 5, 1793, in the Convention, and to the acclaim of the sans-culottes. It was Danton, now a moderate, who introduced a measure to prevent section assemblies in Paris from being in permanent session. Rather, their meetings should be limited, he said, to two a week. His stated reason for the proposal was to prevent the assemblies from falling under the control of aristocrats. For sans-culottes the word "aristocrat" was a buzzword that signified all that was deceitful, traitorous, and conspiratorial; using it in this context, Danton struck a responsive chord. What further added to the appeal of his proposal was a provision to reimburse citizens with forty sous for each meeting they attended. The crowd whistled, cheered, waved, rose to their feet, and threw hats in the air. Danton's gambit worked, and gambit it seems certainly to have been. Limiting sans-culotte assemblies was the first step in the eventual elimination of the assemblies. From this moment on, the Jacobin government moved steadily and surely to reduce the power of the sans-culottes.

Tensions had long been present between Jacobins and sans-culottes. The *bonnet rouge* was adopted as a symbol of liberty at the beginning of the Revolution and it quickly became an obligatory article of clothing for sans-culottes. When sans-culottes tried to force the patriotic symbol on the Jacobins in March 1792, Robespierre and Pétion together opposed the motion. Robespierre said it would "detract from the powerful impression" of the tricolor cockade.[75] Similarly, sans-culottes rejected the use of *vous* in December 1792 in favor of the familiar *toi*, but the view was not shared by either Brissot or Robespierre. When it came to sans-culotte *tutoiement*, (theeing and thouing) Girondin and Jacobin leaders were in agreement. Sans-culotte successes in 1793 brought *tutoiement* into wider usage, but when sans-culottes tried to make it compulsory the Convention refused to comply. Men of the Convention and sans-culotte Sections were separated by manners and culture and after the insurrection of September 5 by politics. It was on the very day of that insurrection, when Danton got a measure through the Convention, limiting sans-culotte assemblies, that suppression of the sans-culottes began. From this initiative sprang a systematic and successful effort to crush the popular movement.

The *enragés* were the first to go. Roux was arrested on September 5 and Varlet on September 18. With the destruction of the *enragés*, the Hébertists became the leaders of the popular cause and henceforth were on a collision course with the Jacobin leadership. Married to a former nun, Jacques-René Hébert was an outspoken dechristianizer, which put him at loggerheads with Robespierre. Hébert carried on a running argument with Danton over subsidies for the *Père Duchesne*, and he carried on a journalistic debate with Camille Desmoulins over dechristianization. He also quarreled incessantly with Pierre Philippeaux, deputy of Sarthe department, over Philippeaux's lack of rigor in the campaign against counterrevolutionaries in the Vendée. After December, Hébert stopped attending meetings of the Jacobins and went instead to the Cordeliers. Robespierre was caught in the middle of factional strife. In December 1793, Danton and Desmoulins argued that the military tide beyond the frontiers had changed in France's favor, that internally the counterrevolution was crushed, and, with these successes, it was time for relaxation of the Reign of Terror.

Desmoulins pushed his case in the *Vieux Cordelier*, and he and Danton worked together on a conciliation committee for a policy of moderation. For his part, Hébert railed against the rich, denounced hoarders and monopolists, and called for sans-culottes to rise up against those responsible for their plight. He said sans-culottes should threaten their oppressors with hanging; these included not only big profiteering farmers but also grocers, wine merchants, and butchers: ". . . little by little the virtue of Saint Guillotine will deliver us from all these devourers of human flesh."[76] People were overheard uttering epithets in cafes and in the marketplace similar to those made repeatedly by Hébert in the *Père Duchesne*. Hébert tried to stir the people and it was not difficult for the Jacobin leadership to see a connection between his diatribes and the murmurings of a hungry populace.

Trying to chart a safe course through the troubled waters of the Terror was no easy task for the Jacobin leadership. On February 26, 1794, Louis-Antoine-Léon de Saint-Just devised a plan to reward sans-culottes by giving them property seized from suspects. Hébert welcomed the plan but also demanded guaranteed work for all. On March 2, Ronsin called for an insurrection in a meeting of the Cordeliers. Hébert opposed Ronsin, and two days later Marat's sister accused him of temporizing and cowardice. When Jean-Baptiste Carrier also joined the call for action Hébert reversed his position, and, in a published account of the Cordelier proceedings that appeared the next day, he was reported to have said that Robespierre the "misled man" had saved the "traitor Desmoulins." The first arrest of the Hébertists took place on March 14 and others were to follow on March 16. To destroy the Hébertists, it was necessary to win the support of men who were reluctant to give it. Some of those who voted against the Hébertists applied pressure on Robespierre to wipe out the Dantonists and this was precisely what happened. Hébert went to the guillotine on March 24 and Danton did so on April 5. Both factions, the Hébertists and Dantonists, were barriers to unity, always the Jacobin goal. The annihilation of one meant the destruction of the other. Bizarrely, the Hébertists were charged with a plot to starve Paris, seize the government, open the prisons, and massacre the representatives of the people. No documents were introduced to buttress the charges. The trial took three-and-a-half days. Robespierre wanted it over and a juror, Antonelle, was arrested to intimidate others on the Revolutionary Tribunal. Ronsin said, "The party that sends us to our death will follow there in turn and it won't be long now."[77] The charges against the Hébertists were completely bogus, as had been those against the *enragés* in 1793. In the judgment of Morris Slavin, the Hébertist purges of March 1794 can be compared to the Moscow trials of the 1930s.

After the purge of the Hébertist leadership, their partisans in the General Council in the Commune were dismissed, as were those from the Ministry of War. These men had helped form a linkage between the Jacobin-dominated government and the Sections, and with their removal the political alliance of Jacobins and Sections was weakened. In the three months following the March purges, some one hundred and fifty Section cadres were removed and many of them were imprisoned by the Robespierrist Convention. Richard Mowery Andrew has described an incident that illustrates the "disaggregation within Revolutionary Paris"—the clearing out of the old Section leadership by the Jacobins.[78] Charles-Marie Lion was removed as police commissioner of the Ponceau Section under the charge of Hébertist sympathies and replaced by Nicolas Gambette, a salaried agent of the government with no ties in the Ponceau Section. Five weeks after his appointment, Gambette appeared at a Section banquet that was to celebrate the French victory on June 26, 1794 at the Battle of Fleurus, and arrested thirteen sans-culottes. With the military victory hopes had risen among sans-culottes for relief from extreme material hardship, for implementation of the Constitution of 1793, and for the rule of popular sovereignty. The Jacobin-dominated Convention had banned spontaneous banquets for fear that they might arouse the Sections, and Gambette's arrest of thirteen sans-culottes in the Ponceau Section was a response to that measure and, as such, part of the crushing of the Sections by the government.

In the aftermath of the March purges of the Hébertists, sans-culotte institutions were stripped of their power and the armed wing of the sans-culottes, the *armée révolutionnaire*, was discredited. The Jacobin leadership during the Terror struck out at its enemies, and in doing so it not only destroyed those who had themselves been at the center of the Revolution, the Girondins and Dantonists, but also those who had played a vital role in bringing the Jacobins to power, the sans-culottes. With the purging of the Hébertists, a decisive blow was struck at the sans-culottes and apathy set in within the Sections. By the summer of 1794, sans-culotte zeal had flagged, and according to Richard Cobb, the firebrands and militants whose fierce patriotism and political intervention had put the Robespierrists in power returned to private life, to their shops, their billiards, their families, their lovers.[79]

The government had crushed the popular movement. In doing so, it gathered power into its own hands, but, through internal struggles and purges, the result was a narrowing of the Terror and fear within a government that carried it out. As faction after faction was destroyed, those who remained in power could not avoid wondering who would be removed from power. The pressures among those who exercised power became intolerable; the struggles within the Committee of Public Safety were not recorded—minutes of its meetings were not kept—but they were fierce, and they took a toll.[80] If the sans-culottes grew weary, so did the Robespierrists who carried out the Reign of Terror. Robespierre himself became ill and stopped attending meetings of the Committee of Public Safety. An atmosphere of fear was pervasive; no one was safe. Finally, on 9 Thermidor (July 27, 1794) members of the Convention struck out against Robespierre, who had made charges of conspiracy within the Convention but had refused to name the conspirators. Placed under arrest and sent to the Luxembourg, he was free by 9:00 P.M. when the turnkey refused to lock him up.

Earlier in the evening the Commune threw its support behind Robespierre and called for an insurrection. The tocsin was sounded at about 7:00 P.M. and some three thousand Parisians gathered at the Place de Grève. Robespierre did not join the insurrection initially out of respect for the Convention, and by the time he did so it was too late. By midnight the crowd at the Place de Grève began to disperse. Inside the Hôtel de Ville at about 1:00 A.M. Robespierre, Georges Couthon, Saint-Just, and François-Joseph LeBas were received by the General Council of the Commune with loud applause, and appeals went out to the Sections—to which sans-culottes were now returning. It was under these circumstances that a letter was sent to Robespierre's own Section, the

Section des Piques: "Courage, patriots of the Pikes Section! Liberty is winning the day! Those men whose constancy had made them feared by the traitors have already been released. Everywhere the people is showing itself worthy of its reputation. The rallying-point is the Commune, where the brave Hanriot will carry out the orders of the Executive Committee which has been set up to save the patrie."[81] Robespierre's signature was the final one on the letter. "Liberty is winning the day!" it had proclaimed. The reality was the isolation and flight of men who had just lost a power struggle in the Convention.

The moment of reckoning was drawing near, but even then Robespierre announced that the people, "showing itself worthy of its reputation," should meet at the Hôtel de Ville to face the traitors who feared them. The ironies of the situation are powerful. Robespierre continued to throw off abstractions about "liberty," "the people," "traitors," and efforts to "save the country." The rhetoric had lost its magic; the members of the Section des Piques, not a sans-culotte section, could not be counted on to support Robespierre. At 2:00 A.M. Vicomte Paul-François-Jean-Nicolas de Barras and Léonard Bourdon sent men to the Hôtel de Ville to seize Robespierre and his twenty two allies who were still laying plans to save the day. Augustin Robespierre tried to escape by a window but fell and was seriously injured. François Hanriot, quite drunk, fell onto a dung heap when he, too, tried to escape by a window. Georges Couthon's frail body was broken and his head gashed when he fell down a flight of stairs in his wheelchair. LeBas blew his brains out with a pistol and Robespierre also turned a pistol on himself but missed aim and fired a charge into his jaw, which he shattered. He was placed on a plank and taken down the great staircase of the Hôtel de Ville. At the bottom of the stairway, where a crowd had gathered, someone raised the arm which Robespierre had used to cover his shattered jaw: "He's not dead, he's still warm," the man commented, while another spectator said jeeringly, "He makes a handsome king, doesn't he." A bystander said, "he should be thrown into the gutter."[82] Someone had Robespierre sit up to keep him alive, the authorities protected him from the crowd, and, when circumstances allowed, he was sent to the Tuileries.

He and the other accused men were then taken to the Conciergerie and appeared before the Revolutionary Tribunal, but no hearings were necessary. The "conspirators" only had to be identified. They were placed in three carts and taken to the Place de la Révolution, from which the guillotine had been removed, however, for this occasion it was restored. Describing the people who lined the streets as Robespierre went to his fate, Louis-Sébastien Mercier wrote: "They mount on the stalls, they crowd the windows and the shop-fronts; the roofs are thick with onlookers of every class who have but one object—to see Robespierre go to his death. . . . Tumult and uproar are all round him, made up of a thousand cries of joy and mutual congratulation." The procession wended its way slowly through the center of Paris for an hour, and, as it approached its destination, it passed along the rue Saint-Honoré, where a large crowd had gathered to celebrate the festive event. It is said that when the procession reached the Duplay house it was drawn to a halt. It was here that Robespierre had read the classics to a family that took pride in their illustrious guest, and here that he had given himself over to his one indulgence, the oranges that he dearly loved. Now, according to Mercier, "a group of women dance to the clapping of hands. And all of them seize the moment to address [Robespierre] by voice and gesture: 'I am drunk with joy at your torment! Go down to Hell with the curse of every wife, of every mother of children.' "[83] As women danced at the entrance to the Duplay courtyard, an urchin with a broom splattered blood, obtained from a nearby butcher shop, on the shutters. The gallows humor of the episode expresses symbolically and perfectly the distance between Robespierre and the people, not the idealized people of his imagination but the real people of Paris. He belonged to one world, one culture, and they to another. The Revolution that had drawn them together drove them apart, and, as Robespierre continued to move down the rue Saint-Honoré after the macabre scene in front of the Duplay house, the procession proceeded ever closer to the guillotine. There the fall of the blade ended the Revolution with which Robespierre had been so closely identified from the beginning. The Reign of Terror was over.

Chapter 5

David and the
Tennis Court Oath

*J*acques-Louis David's *Tennis Court Oath* (fig. 3) was the work of an artist with an ability to "see nobly," to use a term employed by the anonymous author of a 1782 pamphlet, *Sur la peinture*. The article discussed history painters within the privileged sanctuary of the Academy.[1] All of David's talent as a history painter was poured into this scene of contemporary history; the enlightened, high-minded deputies of his painting were seen as men of intellect, principle, and moral vision. That David borrowed from and alluded to Michelangelo's Sistine Chapel ceiling and Raphael's *School of Athens* and *Parnassus* in his *Tennis Court Oath* underscored the grandness of his vision, whose realization was to be achieved on an immense twenty-three feet by thirty-three feet canvas.[2] In contrast to Prieur's narrative and descriptive illustration of the same event, David took liberties in his very different version. He showed the deputies arrayed not along the length of the tennis court, as in fact they were, but along the width. By compressing the figures into the narrower space, David was able at once to show individual figures prominently and to create the tension essential to the drama of the event. Had the figures been spread across the length of the tennis court, as in Prieur's illustration, they would necessarily have been smaller and there would have been an attendant loss of tension.

Prieur's vantage point is to the right of the portrayed scene and midway between the deputies on the floor and the spectators above them. The effect is that he looks down on the deputies, of whom only those on the left are seen in full. David's vantage point is in the exact center of the tennis court and lower than that of Prieur. The result of seeing the deputies who swear the oath from below rather than above is to elevate them and add to their sense of significance.

The deputies in David's patriotic painting swear an oath not to disband, whatever the consequences to themselves, they embrace fraternally, they hold up their hats jubilantly, and they clasp their hands in devout thanks. The powerful rhythms of their arms capture the sense of unity that is a vital part of David's conception. An allegorical gust of wind blows through the gallery on the left, driven by a storm that sends a bolt of lightning through the sky. The bolt of lightning points directly at the upraised hand of Jean-Sylvain Bailly, who receives oaths from the gathered deputies. Bailly is a lightning rod drawing an electrical charge from above—and from the aroused deputies whose outstretched arms express their dedication to the nation. The scene David portrays is charged with the electricity of a new age, receiving light from above. The sky outside the tennis court is stormy, as seen in the far openings in the gallery, on the left, but the storm has already begun to clear. From the bright sky at the near opening of the gallery, light passes into the tennis court, light that is as allegorical as the bolt of lightning. The assembled delegates on whom light shines down from above were men of the Enlightenment, rational members of the educated elite, patriots dedicated to the nation, apostles of a secular faith.

In Prieur's illustration of the *Tennis Court Oath*, Bailly is seen standing on a table with deputies lined up on both sides, as they are in David's version, but there are significant differences in how the two artists arrange the figures. Prieur shows Bailly at the far side of the tennis court, next to a wall and below figures in the gallery above, and the deputies are arrayed in front of him. By rotating the tennis court and placing the deputies within its width rather than across its length, and placing them behind Bailly, David creates an entirely different effect. Bailly does not face the deputies, as in Prieur's illustration, but looks toward the viewing public of the historic event. Only Bailly gazes in the direction of the people; the other figures respond to his initiative, his call for united action.

One of the leaders of the Third Estate, Isaac-René-Guy Le Chapelier, had prepared a text that announced the goals of the deputies who swore the oath: "It is decided that all members of this Assembly will now take a solemn oath not to disperse but to meet wherever circumstances demand, until the Constitution of the realm has been set up and consolidated on firm foundations and that the members, when they have taken the oath, shall confirm their unswerving resolution by their signature, given by each individually."[3] Prieur's illustration of the *Tennis Court Oath* was faithful to this text; the meaning of the event was confined to the participants gathered together within the interior space of the tennis court. By placing Bailly at the head of the deputies and having him look straight ahead, David created an active dynamic between the portrayed scene and his audience.

We, the audience, are drawn into the action, as if we are present in the creation of a new nation, as if we enter into the collective will, as if we are part of the Social Contract. What contributes to this dynamic is the organization of the foreground figures into a semicircle, a compositional device whose effect is to draw the viewer into the action of the scene. The deputies respond to Bailly, Bailly holds his hand upward as he looks at us, and we, too, participate in the birth of a new order. Of the two representations of the Tennis Court Oath, Prieur's and David's, it is Prieur's that portrays the actual event most accurately, and the language used by the artist, narrative and descriptive, is appropriate to that rendering. By contrast, the rhetorical and elevated language of David has been placed in the service of a conceptual scheme that has been imposed on the actual historic event. In David's *Tennis Court Oath*, the theme of unity issues from the collective action of the deputies; it passes from the finite space within which the deputies are seen outward to a nation that is born on this historic occasion.

The theme of David's painting of the *Tennis Court Oath* connects it to his earlier salon painting, the *Oath of the Horatii* (fig. 84), the best-known and artistically the most important of the oath paintings that appeared in France—and elsewhere—in the 1760s, 1770s, and 1780s. Paintings of this type include Gavin Hamilton's *Oath of Brutus* (1763–1764), Benjamin West's *Hannibal Taking the Oath* (1771), Henry Fuseli's *Oath on the Rütli* (1777–81), and Jacques-Antoine Beaufort's *Oath of Brutus* (1771).[4] "The act of taking the oath," as Jean Starobinski has said, "was based on an antique model. At the same time as it inaugurated the future, it also repeated a very ancient archetype for entering into a contract."[5] Rejecting the present, the oath would inaugurate a new age by restoring or regenerating the forms and ideals of the past.

In the political climate of June 1789, amid the hopes and aspirations spawned by the summoning of the Estates-General, a new age was to be created; it was the assembled deputies who occupied a tennis court at Versailles after being shut out of their regular meeting place on June 20 who were its architects. As rendered by David, the oath they swore not to disband until the King transformed the Estates-General into a National Assembly was an act of resolution, achieved with an unswerving sense of purpose; it was an assertion of will worthy of Jean-Jacques Rousseau, whose ideals many of the deputies embraced. The individual deputies in David's *Tennis Court Oath* were drawn by the oath into a collective impulse, as if they became part of the general will.

FIGURE 84. J.-L. David, *Oath of the Horatii*, Musée du Louvre

That David gives prominence to Martin Dauch, the deputy from Castellane at the far right, whose arms are held tightly against his chest, for he refuses to take the oath as one deputy implores him to, underscores the importance of entering voluntarily into the collective action (fig. 85). This point is reinforced by a deputy who exhorts a fellow deputy to leave Martin Dauch to his own devices. One must swear the oath willingly and out of conscience; each deputy, each individual, enters into a collective will volitionally. By pressing his hands against his chest, Dauch creates a dissonance between himself and the deputies whose arms are extended in patriotic oath. Among those deputies are three on the opposite side of the painting, against the wall on the left, who appear to have wandered into the tennis court from David's 1785 Salon painting, the *Oath of the Horatii*, in order that they can again swear a patriotic oath.

The *Oath of the Horatii* can be read as a Rousseauist discourse with men of heroic resolve, swearing a patriotic oath as women abandon themselves to feelings appropriate to their gender. The separation of men and women in the painting is consistent with the writings of Rousseau that assign men to a public sphere and consign women to a private and domestic sphere.[6] By transposing the male figures of the *Oath of the Horatii* onto the *Tennis Court Oath*, David has extended the Rousseauist discourse of his 1785 painting into a work that is Rousseauist at its conceptual core. But is the separation of the male and female figures in the *Tennis Court Oath* part of a Rousseauist discourse? By placing women in the galleries above the male deputies David is adhering to the facts of the event; like other artists, he shows women in the galleries, where they are seen alongside men. The women are not passive spectators and marginalized, as it has been claimed, but, like the men, they are deeply involved in the drama of the event unfolding below them.[7] An older woman with a child in the left gallery looks down with grave mien at the oath-swearing deputies, as does the boy who follows her example (fig. 86). They do so in spite of a gust of wind that blows an umbrella behind the woman inside out and distracts the man who holds it, as well as the person next to him. If the men are distracted, the woman devotes all of her attention to the scene below her. Another woman in the gallery on the left, at the far end, leans forward in order that she can take in fully the momentous event taking place on the floor of the tennis court (fig. 87). The man next to her looks at the curtain that the gust of wind blows into the room rather than downward. On the opposite gallery, women are seen alongside men, and like them they lean forward so they can observe the deputies below them. Of particular interest is the standing woman who holds a hat in her hand, as if in patriotic salute (fig. 88). Next to

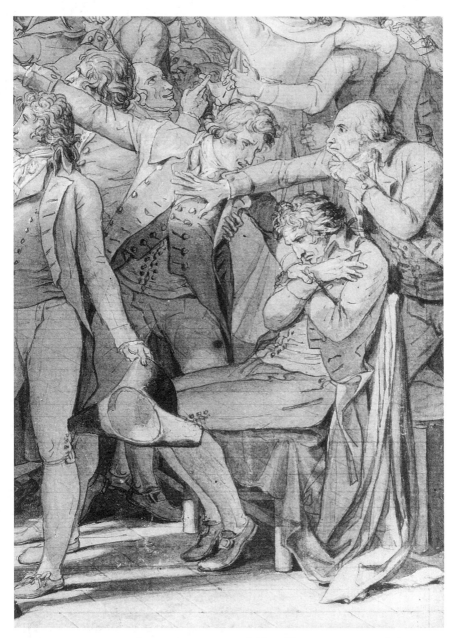

FIGURE 85.   J.-L. David, *Tennis Court Oath* (detail), Musée National du Château, Versailles

FIGURE 86. J.-L. David, *Tennis Court Oath* (detail), Musée National du Château, Versailles

her is a soldier who holds a sword in his hand in a similar gesture. The two arms, those of the woman and the man, are parallel and part of a rhythmic sweep that links them together not only compositionally but also expressively and patriotically. Directly behind these two figures, the soldier and the woman, is Jean-Paul Marat, who inscribes the words "L'Ami du peuple" on a tablet. Thus, the woman is part of a grouping of figures that expresses patriotic devotion. She, along with the other women in David's *Tennis Court Oath*, are not Rousseauist females who inhabited a domestic and private sphere separate from the world of events and politics occupied by public-minded and patriotic men. David had separated men and women into separate spheres, public and private, in the *Oath of the Horatii* (as he did again in *Brutus and the Lictors*) but he has not done so in the *Tennis Court Oath*; it would seem that his patriotic painting of 1790–1792 is Rousseauist in its call for unity, but not in its depiction of female involvement in the birth of a New Order.

FIGURE 87.   J.-L. David,
Tennis Court Oath (de-
tail), Musée National du
Château, Versailles

In fact, female readers, who devoured the novels of Rousseau, were
not limited to passive creatures of a properly ordered Rousseauist world.
Some of the women who responded to Rousseau with such enthusiasm
did so in ways that would have met with his approval. Commenting on
Julie's deathbed scene in *La Nouvelle Héloïse*, Yolande-Martine-
Gabrielle de Polastgron, Comtesse de Polignac wrote, "I dare not tell you
the effect it made on me. No, I was past weeping. A sharp pain convulsed
me. My heart was crushed. Julie dying was no longer an unknown person. I believed I was her sister, her friend, her Claire. My seizure became
so strong that if I had not put the book away I would have been as ill as
all those who attended that virtuous woman in her last moments."[8] Female readers were so overwhelmed by Rousseau's novels that they
wanted to meet the author of *La Nouvelle Héloïse*. Rousseau was
amused that ladies of *le monde*, from a world he denounced, sought his
intimacy. "Women . . . became so intoxicated with the book and with its

FIGURE 88. J.-L. David, *Tennis Court Oath* (detail), Musée National du Château, Versailles

author that there were few of them, even of the highest rank, whom I could not have had, if I had but attempted their conquest."[9]

Yet the women whose feelings were touched by Rousseau were not just society ladies, they were educated readers who helped form the eighteenth-century public. Like men who inhabited the public sphere, women were aware of public issues, and like them were swept up by revolutionary enthusiasm in 1789. Among those carried forward by the patriotic wave were Olympe de Gouges and Mme Roland, both devoted Rousseauists. Another was Mme David, the wife of the artist, who joined a delegation of women on September 7, 1789 that went to the National Assembly to give jewelry to the Nation. All twenty-one women were wives of artists; all were clad in white and wore cockades in their hair. They had prepared a speech which Mme Moitte was to have read, but which the deputy Bouche read instead, owing to an excess of feeling on her part: "The regeneration of the State will be the work of the Representatives of the Nation. The liberation of the State must be the work of all its citizens. When the Roman women presented their jewelry to the Senate, it gave the Senate the gold without which it could not carry out the vow made by Camillus to Apollo before the capture of Veii."[10] The women who performed this patriotic deed were not confined to a narrowly domestic—and Rousseauist—sphere. They were part of the public sphere; they were alert to public issues and swept up by enthusiasm for the Revolution, with which they identified personally and directly. When they said, "The liberation of the State must be the work of all its citizens," they included themselves. By making that identification they crossed the barrier established by Rousseau between the male and female spheres. What they did was to include themselves in the Nation, as citizens, at least by implication. They were, by extension, part of the Social Contract.

It is in this modified Rousseauist context that David has incorporated women into the *Tennis Court Oath*. Yes, there is separation between the male deputies on the floor of the tennis court who swear the oath and the women in the galleries above who observe them doing so, but it is not a Rousseauist separation. Women are seen alongside men in the gallery, and like them they rejoice over the momentous event that unfolds below them. In portraying women in the gallery, David has reported the facts of the event: Prieur also has shown women in the gallery. Yet, David has given them greater prominence than Prieur, and, judging from his preparatory studies, they figure prominently in his conceptualized thinking of the painting.[11] Women play an important role in his conceptual scheme, and in his finished design for the painting; they are part of a patriotic impulse felt by men and women alike. The *Tennis Court Oath* can be read as a Rousseauist discourse, however, by including women as involved observers, it is a discourse that does not observe strict Rousseauist tenets; it can be thought of as an expanded Rousseauist discourse that by including women enlarges the Social Contract beyond limits Rousseau himself would have imposed.

The importance given to the spectators in David's *Tennis Court Oath* anticipated the relationship between the legislature and the public in the meetings of the National Assembly and the Convention during the Revolution. In the ancien régime, government was carried out by the King and his ministers in closed chambers, but this model went into full eclipse in 1789. Government was to be conducted openly, before the people, in conformity with the revolutionary ideal of transparency. For the apostles of Rousseau, candor, openness, sincerity, and directness was a personal ideal; when extended into the political sphere, as it was, it led to a new conceptual framework for government. Government was not to be carried out by groups of officials within narrow spaces and in isolation, but by deputies chosen by the people and in the presence of the people. Already in the sessions of the Estates-General held in the *Salle des menus plaisirs* at Versailles as many as two thousand people sat in galleries to hear the deliberations, and deputies, aware of their presence, addressed them to gain support. When the Assembly moved from Versailles to Paris and met temporarily in the Manège, galleries were open to the public, and when the Convention moved to the Tuileries in 1793, seating for the people was provided. We have seen that Robespierre's idea for the perfect building for the Assembly was, "a huge and majestic building, open to twelve thousand spectators. Under the eyes of so many witnesses, neither corruption, intrigue, nor perfidy would show themselves. Only the general will would be consulted. The voice of the nation and of public interest alone would be heard." Robespierre's Rousseauist idea of the perfect building for the Assembly was in basic agreement with plans for an entirely new building that was to seat the legislature. While never constructed, the several designs submitted for this project conformed to the Rousseauist ideal to which Robespierre had subscribed in his vision of the ideal building for the legislature.[12]

Conceived in the early stages of the Revolution when the Rousseauist ideals of unity and transparency offered a positive vision for the future, David's *Tennis Court Oath* captured the spirit of that moment. Yet the painting was never completed. By the time David abandoned the project in September 1792 a second revolution, that of August 10, had taken place, and beyond it lay factional strife within the revolutionary leadership, counterrevolution, and the Reign of Terror. David moved with the Revolution as it veered to the left, but his friend André Chénier, who returned to Paris in April 1790, after spending three years in London, leaned away from the Revolution. By the time David put aside his twenty-three feet by thirty-three feet canvas, he and Chénier had had a bitter falling out. Chénier and David had met in the 1780s in the Trudaine Circle that assembled in the hôtel of two wealthy brothers in the Place Royale. Charles-Louis Trudaine de Montigny and Charles-Michel Trudaine de Sablière, both classmates of Chénier at the Collège de Navarre, were sons of an intendant of finances who had been a friend of Anne-Robert-Jacques Turgot and was close to the Physiocrats. Those attending gatherings held by the Trudaine brothers were liberal and progressive, and conversation turned often on reform issues. In this milieu, Chénier and David had discussed the role of the artist and the importance of artistic freedom, topics on which they were in full agreement, and which contributed, it seemed, to close personal ties.

Chénier joined the liberal *Société de 1789* in absentia, before returning to France, as a charter member. Made up of 660 members, with an inner circle of eighty-nine, the *Société de 1789* described itself in a April

12, 1790 manifesto as "neither a sect nor a party, but a company of friends of men and, so to speak, agents of social truths."[13] Unique among revolutionary clubs, the *Société de 1789* attracted members from the far Left to the far Right. Among those on the Left were Bertrand Barère and Jean-Marie Collot d' Herbois and on the Right was François-Alexandre-Frédéric de Duc La Rochefoucauld-Liancourt, but most of the membership, including Lafayette, Mirabeau, Bailly, Marie-Jean Caritat, marquis de Condorcet, Pierre-Louis, comte Roederer, and Pierre-Samuel Dupont de Nemours, occupied a broad middle position within the political spectrum, devoted to the Revolution and eager to find broad principles of agreement, such as, "The defense of a free constitution and . . . the perfection of social art."[14] Among those belonging to the *Société de 1789* was the entire membership of the Trudaine circle, including both Trudaines, Louis and François de Pange, Laurent and Françoise Lecolteux, Pierre-Louis de Lacretelle, Claude Emmanuel Joseph Pierre, marquis de Pastoret, Abel de Malartic de Fondat, André Chénier, and probably David.[15] When the *Société de 1789* was founded in the early part of 1790, it was possible for men of different views to come together to discuss politics, under the assumption that while they might disagree on particulars there was enough consensus to make the exchange of ideas useful. This changed as divisions within the Revolution created tensions and conflicts between members of the *Société de 1789*, some of whom dropped out as they found themselves separated by intractable differences with others rather than held together by shared principles and objectives. Finally, after the political shock waves that followed the King's abortive flight to Varennes and the Champ de Mars Massacre in 1791, the members of the *Société de 1789*, who also belonged to the Jacobins, pulled out of that club and joined the Feuillants.

As the leading journalist for the official publication of the *Société de 1789*, initially called the *Journal de la Société de 1789* but renamed the *Mémoires de la Société de 1789* in September 1790, André Chénier wrote a highly polemical piece, "Avis au peuple français sur ses véritables ennemis," in August 1790, in which he called the Revolution "a just and legitimate insurrection," and in the word "insurrection" one of the keys to Chénier's political thought can be found.[16] Chénier favored the breakup of the ancien régime and the end of monarchical despotism, but as a Montesquieuist moderate and admirer of the British constitution, and as an advocate of the rule of law, he wanted stability in order that the Assembly could draw up a constitution. Structurally, the *Avis* was organized into two parts, one calling for the Assembly to frame a constitution, and second, a warning against the forces within France that were a threat to the Assembly. He said of the Assembly that

. . . it is the last anchor that supports us and keeps us from breaking apart. The National Assembly has faults because it is composed of men; because these men, considering how they have been elected, have necessarily been subject to diverse and incompatible interests; because they are fatigued by the vast quantity of work to which the National Assembly has already been subject. But the work already undertaken [by the Assembly] contains the germs of perfection of which it is capable, even as the faults it has committed have prepared it for what it yet has to do. The sovereignty of the nation, the equality of men, and the other immutable bases on which it has built its edifice, assure it a long life, if we do not create obstacles. Thus, it is the unique center around which all honest citizens, all of the French people, should rally. They should do everything possible to complete its great work and to pass it on to hands instructed to receive it, perfect it, and consolidate it.[17]

Among the problems the Assembly faced was a crowd of orators and journalists, a "numerous and terrible race of libelists who know no shame," recognized no limit, and wanted to win the people over to their subversive views:

Trying to determine the source of the suspicion, tumult, and insurrection which have increased so much of late, we must ask if the division of interests, the heat of opinions, the unfamiliarity with liberty are completely natural, or whether they have been considerably heightened, nourished, and spread by a crowd of orators and writers who seem to have organized themselves into a party. All that is good in the Revolution can be attributed to writers, but at the same time one can find in their work many of the evils that threaten us. Moreover, the reason behind their sinister words is all too clear: these men are too obscure, too feeble, to be at the head of a party. We can conclude, then, that they are motivated by greed, or some propensity to do harm. In political revolutions it is not necessary to believe that all who embrace a bad cause and support their deadly opinions are all perverse and motivated by bad intentions. Since most men have strong passions but weak judgment, in tumultuous times they are swept up by the forces of passion, act according to their feelings, and are at the mercy of villainous demagogues (*scélérats habiles*). The wise man, for his part, uses his eyes; he sees what the scoundrels intend to do; he observes their every step and every word, and understands what they are about. And he declares them public enemies whose real purpose is to preach a doctrine detrimental to the public good.[18]

In this passage, Chénier identified two obstacles to the completion of the constitution by the Assembly. First was not only the people, volatile, inflammatory, with a "mass compulsion to commit acts of violence," but also, and this was his main point, "orators and writers" who did everything in their power to agitate the people and goad them into action. As long as the Assembly lived under the threat of subversive writers and orators, who used the people as instruments of their "villainous" designs, it was compromised in its effort to complete the constitution. The "hangman orator" that Chénier hated most was Jean-Paul Marat, but there were other targets as well, including Camille Desmoulins and Jacques-René Hébert.

Warnings against demagogic orators and journalists appeared again in Chénier's *Jeu de Paume*, a poem in twenty-two stanzas dedicated to "Louis David, Painter." Published in March 1791, Chénier presumably wrote the *Jeu de Paume* after he completed the "Avis au peuple français" in August 1790. David had begun work on his *Tennis Court Oath* in the spring of 1790, before Chénier's return to Paris. The two friends had collaborated on an earlier painting, the 1787 *Death of Socrates*, for which Chénier made suggestions that David appears to have followed, and they again collaborated on David's twenty-three feet by thirty-three feet patriotic painting that celebrated an event to which Chénier attached the greatest importance. The first part of Chénier's *Jeu de Paume* celebrated artistic freedom, a principle on which he and David had exchanged views in the *société Trudaine*, as if to stir memories of their earlier friendship, and to reaffirm ideas and goals they shared in common: "Virile liberty is the happy genius of the arts. . . . No talent is born of royal favor."[19] In stanza 14, Chénier gave full voice to the sense of renewal that he associated with the Tennis Court Oath:

> O people twice born! People old and newly born!
> Stock renewed by the years!
> Phoenix risen alive from the ashes of the tomb!
> And hail to you also, bearers of the torch
> That guided our destinies!
> Paris to you holds out its arms, children of our choice!
> Fathers of a people! Architects of laws!
> You who can found, with a firm and sure hand,
> A solemn code for man,
> On all its sacred rights, his ancient and pure charter;
> His sacred rights, born with nature,
> Contemporaries of the eternal.
> You have tamed all. No yoke restrains you,
> Any obstacle lies dead under your blows.[20]
>
> •••
>
> O Peuple deux fois né! peuple vieux et nouveau!
>   Tronc rajeuni par les années!
> Phénix sorti vivant des cendres du tombeau!
> Et vous aussi, salut, vous, porteurs du flambeau

Qui nous montra nos destinées!
Paris vous tend les bras, enfants de notre choix!
Pères d'un peuple! architecte des lois!
Vous qui savez fonder, d'une main ferme et sûre,
Pour l'homme un code solennel,
Sur tous ses premiers droits, sa charte antique et pure;
Ses droits sacrés, nés avec la nature,
Contemporains de l'éternel.
Vous avez tout dompté. Nul joug ne vous arrête.
Tout obstacle est mort sous vos coups.

Then, in the final line of this stanza, Chénier sounded an alarm with the verb *descendre*, a "turning-point, or hinge in the argument of the poem," according to Francis Scarfe. Up to this point in the *Jeu de Paume*, Chénier recalled his earlier friendship with David, alluded to the *Death of Socrates* that they had discussed in the *Société Trudaine*, sang praises to David as an artist, and commented on the great events of 1789, but in stanza 15 he struck a different note:

People! Let us not believe that all is allowed to us.
Fear your avid courtisans,
O sovereign people! A hundred orators who have your ear
Call themselves your friends.
They blow homicidal fires.
Prostituting our rights at the feet of our pride,
Our passions become laws by their doing.
Thought is given over to their cowardly tortures.
Looking for treason everywhere,
For our jealous suspicious, hatreds, perjuries,
They keep on creating dreadful pastures.
Their rags, black with poison,
Are so many gibbets hungering for carnage.[21]

• • •

Peuple! ne croyons pas que tout nous soit permis.
Craignez vos courtisans avides,
O peuple souverain! A votre oreille admis
Cent orateurs bourreaux se nomment vos amis.
Ils soufflent des feux homicides.
Aux pieds de notre orgueil prostituant les droits,
Nos passions par eux deviennent lois.
La pensée est livrée à leurs lâches tortures.
Partout cherchant des trahisons,
A nos soupçons jaloux, aux haines, aux parjures,
Ils vont forgeant d'exécrables pâtures.
Leurs feuilles, noires de poisons,
Sont autant de gibets affamés de carnage.

The warnings of the poem from this point on were substantially the same as in the "Avis au peuple français," but now they were addressed not only to the public but to his friend David.

Some of the figures David chose to show individually in his design for the *Tennis Court Oath* played a leading role in the historic event, such as Bailly, Sieyès, Joseph-Ignace Guillotin, Le Chapelier, Mounier, Barère, Barnave; they occupied prominent positions in the design. Martin Dauch was included because he refused to swear the oath, and Christophe-Antoine, dom Gerle, Henri-Baptiste, abbé Grégoire, and Jean-Paul Rabaut Saint-Etienne, because they symbolized religious unity. Including dom Gerle, who was not a deputy on June 20, in his design was an indication of how willing David was to take liberties in order to achieve the effects he sought. Another example of his taking liberties was the inclusion of Jean-Paul Marat, whom David placed in the upper gallery on the right, inscribing the words "L'Ami du peuple," the title of his radical newspaper, on a tablet (fig. 89). Like dom Gerle, Marat was not present at the Tennis Court Oath. Robespierre was present as the deputy from Arras, but he was unknown at the time, and as

FIGURE 89.   J.-L. David, *Tennis Court Oath* (detail), Musée National du Château, Versailles

such was undeserving of the prominence he received in David's sepia study, if historical accuracy is considered. He and three Left-leaning Jacobins, Jérôme Pétion, François Buzot, and comte Philippe-Antoine Merlin de Douai, were organized into a coherent group whose prominence Chénier could not have appreciated, given the fact that they belonged to a political club he bitterly opposed (fig. 90).

When David first conceptualized the Tennis Court Oath, he saw the event from a 1790 perspective. The theme of unity, central to his conception, was at variance with what some of the figures in the design represented. One group of figures that David used to project the theme of unity, dom Gerle, abbé Grégoire, and Rabaut Saint-Etienne, revealed the divisions within the Assembly when David began work on the painting, *Tennis Court Oath* (fig. 91). The pious and mystical Christophe-Antoine, dom Gerle made a motion in April 1790, while

FIGURE 90. J.-L. David, *Tennis Court Oath* (detail), Musée National du Château, Versailles

FIGURE 91.   J.-L. David, *Tennis Court Oath* (detail), Musée National du Château, Versailles

debate was taking place, on measures affecting the church and clergy; he advocated making Catholicism the state religion. The deputy Louis-Nicolas Ménard compared the response within the Assembly to dom Gerle's motion to an eruption of Mount Vesuvius. Debate over the position of the Catholic Church was highly sensitive and had the potential of being deeply divisive; as it turned out, the Civil Constitution of the Clergy split France in half, and arguably more than any single piece of legislation created a rupture that not only would not mend, but also contained the seeds of conflict between the Revolution and the Counterrevolution. It was dom Gerle, a figure in David's *Tennis Court Oath*, part of a group of three deputies that symbolically represented unity, who added vitriol to the debate in the Assembly on the position of the Church. David's inclusion of dom Gerle in the *Tennis Court Oath* was, therefore, a double falsification. He was not present at the June 20 event, and, by the time David made the decision to include him among the deputies, he had already triggered a scene of anger and contentiousness among deputies, deeply divided on the issue he addressed. What further undercut the theme of unity represented by David's grouping of three clerical deputies was the fact that abbé Grégoire was a staunch patriot with Jansenist leanings; he was utterly opposed to dom Gerle's narrow Catholicism, while Rabaut Saint-Etienne, a Protestant, was opposed by definition to a motion to make Catholicism the official religion of France. The stunning contrast between the idea of unity that dom Gerle, abbé Grégoire, and Rabaut Saint-Etienne purported to project and the reality of disunity and conflict with which they were associated could hardly have been more striking.

If the inclusion of dom Gerle in the *Tennis Court Oath* was at variance with the theme of unity that was at the conceptual core of the painting so, too, was the inclusion of Jean-Paul Marat. That David included Marat in his design was a decision that his friend André Chénier could only have found objectionable. Of all the radical journalists, the "hangman orators," that Chénier despised, none was more prominent than Marat. Chénier went so far as to write an ode, *To Marie-Anne-Charlotte Corday*, in July 1793, eulogizing Marat's assassin. This was fifteen months after the rupture between Chénier and David, but already in the winter of 1790–91, when the two friends discussed David's *Tennis Court Oath* painting, political differences had begun to surface. It is impossible to tell precisely when David chose to include Marat in his design for the *Tennis Court Oath*, but he did a drawing of the radical journalist in the Louvre Sketchbook (folio 35, recto, fig. 92), which contained what must have been some of David's final thoughts before bringing his ideas together in the sepia study.

The earlier Versailles Sketchbook contains two preparatory studies of Robespierre. In the first of these drawings (folio 52, verso, fig. 93), Robespierre is shown as an antique warrior, nude, helmeted, and surrounded by virile warriors whose raised swords are signs of Spartan *vertu* and patriotic dedication. He is seen alongside Mirabeau, who stands behind him with raised sword. In the next study (folio 53, recto, fig. 93), Mirabeau stands in front of Robespierre, and in that drawing Mirabeau raises his right hand upward, without the sword, as he swears the oath. In the sepia study David has separated Robespierre from Mirabeau and has placed Gérard, a farmer who wears clogs, between the two leaders. Rather than being connected to Mirabeau in the sepia study, the figure of Robespierre is part of a compositional grouping that includes the Left-leaning Jacobins, Pétion, Buzot, and Merlin de Douai.

Among the studies by David for the *Tennis Court Oath*, the one that shows Robespierre as an antique warrior is exceptional. That David would have depicted the radical Jacobin in this way signifies an interest, an attachment, that is singular. In this connection, it is important to note that Robespierre is not among those who answered David's invitation to pose for him in his studio, located close to the Manège, the meeting place of the Assembly deputies. This was in spite of the fact that the Jacobins gave their support to the *Tennis Court Oath*, after

FIGURE 92.   J.-L. David,
Study, Louvre Sketch-
book, for Tennis Court
Oath, Musée du Louvre

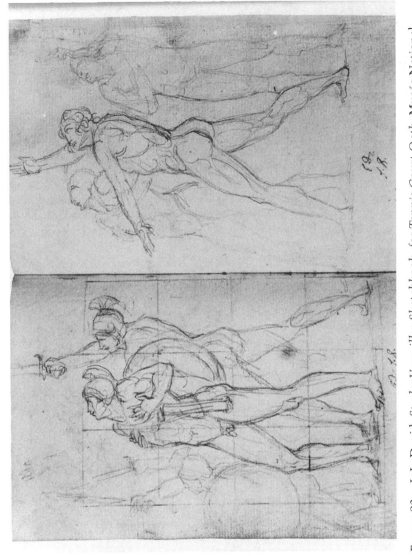

FIGURE 93. J.-L. David, *Study, Versailles Sketchbook, for Tennis Court Oath*, Musée National du Château, Versailles

David had attended several of their meetings. David had become friendly with Edmond-Louis-Alexis Dubois-Crancé and Barère, but not, at this time, in the winter of 1790–91, with Robespierre. Standing behind Robespierre in the sepia study is Dupont de Nemours, like David a member of the *Société de 1789*, who answered David's request and posed for him in his studio. Yet Dupont is far less prominent than Robespierre in the sepia study, whom he stares at intently (fig. 90).

At the time of the Tennis Court Oath, Dupont was a celebrated writer, a renowned Physiocrat, the former secretary of the Assembly of Notables, and author of the lengthy *cahier* of Nemours. By contrast, Robespierre was an unheralded and virtually unknown deputy from Arras. Yet in the sepia study only the head of Dupont was shown, in contrast to the full figure of Robespierre. Even in his secondary role Dupont de Nemours was a striking presence because of the direction in which his head was turned and because his intense stare was fixed on Robespierre. While Dupont swore an oath with his right hand, his attention was directed not at Bailly but at a deputy who inspired grave concern. That concern was a result of David's projecting conflicts within the Assembly after deputies swore the Tennis Court Oath onto his portrayal of that event. Also, the heroic stature of Robespierre, as seen in the preparatory studies in the Versailles Sketchbook, suggested that David was drawn to the radical Jacobin before he entered his orbit in the spring of 1792. Given Robespierre's prominence in the sepia study of the *Tennis Court Oath*, André Chénier could have been aware of his friend's attraction to a leader whose views he opposed, and that awareness could help explain the warning signals sent up by Chénier in the last eight stanzas of his poem, *Jeu de Paume*.

Unlike André Chénier, whose position as a moderate remained constant, David's political views changed. By the time he completed his sepia study in May 1791, his perspective was different from when he began work on the project. Having begun with a conception that celebrated the "*révolution heureuse*," as he saw the Revolution in the spring of 1790, when he was in Nantes, his perspective shifted as he saw the historic event through the lens of subsequent factional strife and political turmoil.[22] It was as if political sparks from 1790 and 1791 landed on a painting that celebrated the 1789 Revolution. If those sparks captured tensions that were an essential part of the ongoing revolution, they were in conflict with David's original conception.

That he included sans-culottes, wearing *bonnets rouge* in the gallery on the left, behind Horatii-like deputies and soldiers with muskets, is another of the liberties taken by him in the sepia study. Compressed into the tight space of the gallery, the sans-culottes are a dark and glowering presence, their rough features in striking contrast to the soldiers in front of them and even more to the lovely, wide-eyed youths to their left (fig. 94, 95). Crouched behind the well-coiffed and elegantly dressed deputies, whose outstretched arms betoken patriotic dedication, the sans-culottes are unable even to see the historic event that unfolds before them. They are screened off from that event, literally, by the deputies who rise above the space to which they have been confined. Yet sans-culottes are there, anachronistically, in the wings, put there by David with the knowledge that they would soon emerge as a decisive force in the Revolution. And David has included the same Jean-Paul Marat whom André Chénier despised in the sepia study; he has placed him opposite the sans-culottes in the upper gallery, where he inscribes the words "L'Ami du peuple" on a tablet.

FIGURE 94.   J.-L. David, *Tennis Court Oath* (detail), Musée National du Château, Versailles

FIGURE 95.   J.-L. David, *Tennis Court Oath* (detail), Musée National du Château, Versailles

Whatever strains may have developed between David and Chénier by the time David completed the sepia study, they remained friends until April 1792. As late as March 1792 David accepted a commission from the King to paint *Louis XVI showing the Constitution to his Son*. Just before its dissolution on September 29, 1791, the Assembly had asked the King to have a painting made, portraying "the moment when, having accepted the Constitution, he is showing his royal assent to his son, the Prince Royal."[23] The painting, which was to be placed in the "meeting room" of the Assembly, would express the King's support of the Constitution, a matter of obvious concern to the National Assembly.

France was about to become a constitutional monarchy under a King whose own actions denoted something less than loyalty to the government he would soon head. At this point, there was little for the King to do but make the best of circumstances, and he not only agreed to commission the painting, but also, after first giving the commission to Adélaide Labille-Guirard, asked David to create the painting. The radical press attacked David for accepting the commission, and at that point, on March 24, 1792, Chénier responded to David's critics in an article in the *Supplement au Journal de Paris*.[24] David had agreed to undertake a project that served the very principles to which Chénier was committed; never an admirer of Louis XVI, Chénier nonetheless believed the surest way to achieve political stability was through constitutional government, for which monarchy was essential.

David never completed the *Louis XVI* project. After doing a number of sketches for the painting, he abandoned it, for he underwent a decisive change in political direction. Four drawings in the Louvre Sketchbook represented different compositional approaches to *Louis XVI showing the Constitution to his Son*, and two of the following three studies showed allegorical figures bearing pikes and phrygian caps, symbols of the Revolution. Having moved away from his original ideas in studies that were no longer suitable for the commissioned painting, David dropped the project. He was now actively involved in a project that made continued work on the *Louis XVI* painting impossible. It was while David was doing preparatory studies for the *Louis XVI* project that he, along with Chénier's brother, Marie-Joseph-Blaise, and the composer François-Joseph Gossec became involved in a festival for the Châteauvieux regiment. The harsh repression of enlisted men who had mutinied against officers in August 1790 was followed by fierce debate in the press. That debate was a defining moment of the Revolution, because it crystallized so sharply differences between rival groups. What added fuel to the debate was the fact that both those who supported rehabilitation of the Swiss regiment and those who opposed it could build cases in their favor. The issues were not clear cut, and as charges and countercharges were made attacks became increasingly personal and acrimonious.

André Chénier and his brother Marie-Joseph had already had a public falling out over André's anti-Jacobin philippic, "On the Cause of the Disorders that trouble France and impede the Establishment of Liberty," which appeared on February 26, 1792, two weeks after the opening of Marie-Joseph's *Caius Gracchus*. Strongly supported by Jacobin backers, the play still hung in the balance with the public, and anxious not to be mistaken as the author of his brother's polemical piece, Marie-Joseph Chénier sent a notice to several journals dissociating himself from the article: "I hereby declare that I had no part in the creation of this article, that it expresses an opinion directly contrary to my own, that I take pride in being a member of the Society of the Friends of the Constitution, sitting at the Jacobins in Paris." An anonymous writer published a piece on March 1 defending André and taking Marie-Joseph to task, and from that point on relations between the two brothers became more strained. On March 7, André explained in the *Journal de Paris* that Marie-Joseph would "continue to find the devotion one owes to a brother and the esteem due to a man of his talents"; he also responded to charges made against him during the previous week in the Jacobin press. The situation in the first week of March was that André Chénier, having attacked the Jacobins, was in turn the object of their journalistic counter-attacks, and what complicated matters was a debate between his brother and him that spilled, through the press, into the public arena. Having been accused of being a "creature" of the government André insisted, "I frequent the meetings of no club; that I am attached to no society, to no person of power, to no political party."[25] For his part, Marie-Joseph announced publicly and boldly that he belonged to the very club, the Jacobins, against which his brother's attacks had been made. As much as the two brothers tried to retain proper relations and express mutual respect, they were separated by such sharp political differences that all that was needed for a breach was a divisive issue. The Châteauvieux festival was that issue.

It was on March 24 that David, Marie-Joseph Chénier, Collot d'Herbois, Jean-Lambert Tallien, and Théroigne de Méricourt presented a petition to the Commune requesting official support for a festival in honor of the forty members of the Swiss regiment who had been consigned to galleys but set free according to the terms of an amnesty decreed by the Assembly. When André Chénier read that the Commune accepted the petition, he was quick to respond. He wrote an article in measured terms in the *Journal de Paris* on April 2 that maintained there was little public enthusiasm for the festival and that honoring the Swiss was a mistake. At the same time that Chénier exercised restraint, arguing against the festival, he was outspoken in denunciations of the Jacobins who sponsored it, and whose "absurdities" and "lies" he deplored. Responses to Chénier in the radical press were swift and vitriolic. Marat, Hébert, and Jean-Louis Carra all attacked Chénier; what added fuel to the fire was a published speech given by Collot d' Herbois in the Jacobins on April 4 that called Chénier a police spy, a sycophant, a false and perfidious writer, and a sterile poet. The people were wiser than Chénier, Collot said, and scorned him. Continuing, he denounced Chénier and Jean-Antoine Roucher, another opponent of the festival, with a fiery example of Jacobin oratory: "Cruel egotists! Your lies are powerless to deprive the people of their good will towards the Châteauvieux soldiers. You're too weak to stop the fête we're preparing for these heroes. It will be like the people themselves—simple, expressive, frank, and majestic. Since I know the efficiency of the patriotic societies directing it, I assure you that it will be remarkable, well-ordered, fraternal, and law-abiding. Then, when it is in the past, I intend to show my personal respect for our laws by appearing before a court of justice to bring against Messrs Roucher and André Chénier a charge of cowardly calumny." Responding to Collot in the *Journal de Paris* on April 10, Chénier said:

> Collot d'Herbois is the one whose dissatisfaction is expressed with most rage and bitterness. He has indeed proved that the abuse showered upon me is in essence stupidity. I shall not try to rival him in eloquence. But he threatens to bring charges of cowardly slander against me in a court of justice! I call upon him to fulfill his threat, the outcome of which I anticipate with tranquillity or, to be more exact, with impatience. The world will be told of the calumnies of which he calls me guilty. And the world will see whether or not I am a coward, I who, alone and without aid, have denounced before all France a small set of mountebanks who wander through the realm in the name of Liberty and disguise with the expression WILL OF THE PEOPLE their capricious and tyrannical ambitions. Collot has said that I'm a hypocrite, that I don't believe a word of what I write, that I belong to a party, that I'm the agent and instrument of intriguers, etc. All these imputations admit of only one response: M. COLLOT D'HERBOIS HAS LIED.[26]

Four days later, on April 15, the festival that Marie-Joseph Chénier and Jacques-Louis David organized—for which they also provided songs and decorations—was held in Paris. On that same day, André Chénier published the "Hymn to the Swiss of Châteauvieux." According to Andrew Scarfe, Chénier's journalistic style had changed in the course of bitter polemical exchanges with the radical press. "He had cut out the flowers of rhetoric which decorated his early, more leisurely articles, while broadening his vocabulary to match the coarseness of his opponents—which was to give edge later, to his *ïambes*, which are such a curious mixture of noble and vulgar images and vocabulary."[27] The "Hymn to the Swiss of Châteauvieux," the first of Chénier's *ïambes*, written in a new verse form for this occasion, expressed Chénier's rage:

> Forty murderers [the Swiss soldiers] beloved of Robespierre,
>> Will be raised on our altars.
> O arts, who give life to canvas and stone,
>> hasten to render immortal
> The great Collot d'Herbois, his Helvetian clients,
> This forehead, which gives heroes
> Virtue, taverns, and the help of pikes,
> People heaven with new stars,
> O ye, children of Eudoxus, Hipparchus, and Euclid . . .[28]
>
> •••
>
> Quarante meurtriers, chéris de Robespierre,
>> Vont s'élever sur nos autels.
> Beaux-arts, qui faites vivre et la toile et la pierre,
>> Hâtez-vous, rendez immortels
> Le grand Collot d'Herbois, ses clients helvétiques,
>> Ce front qui donne à des héros
> La vertu, la taverne, et le secours des piques,
>> Peuplez le ciel d'astres nouveaux,
> O vous, enfants d'Eudoxe et d'Hipparque et d'Euclide . . .

The last line referred to David, Marie-Joseph Chénier, and the composer Gossec who were responsible for the artistic arrangements of the Châteauvieux festival.

Chénier's attacks on the Jacobins continued throughout the spring and into the summer of 1792 until, finally, with the storming of the Tuileries, he went into hiding. For his part, David abandoned work on the *Tennis Court Oath* in the wake of the political explosion of August 10 and the tremors that continued into September. It was in the month of September, when prisoners were slaughtered, that he set aside the project in which he had invested so much time, but whose message of unity and renewal through constitutional government was hopelessly incongruous in a Revolution that was torn by violence, factional strife, and popular fear and anger. Some of the heroes of the *Tennis Court Oath* were no longer heroes, and others would soon become enemies of a Revolution that had traveled far from the goals and ideals of 1789.

At the time of his decision to abandon the *Tennis Court Oath*, David had sketched in nude figures on the twenty-three feet by thirty-three feet canvas and painted the faces of four delegates, Barnave, Mirabeau, Gérard, and Dubois-Crancé. After entering into correspondence with the King, Mirabeau died in April 1791. Initially an outspoken voice against despotism, he became a moderate and as such was an enemy of the Left in the Assembly. His remains were removed from the Panthéon when his correspondence with the King was discovered after the storming of the Tuileries. Barnave sided with the people in 1789 and defended the savage murder of Foulon and Bertier ("is their blood therefore so pure?") but ended up a moderate. Assigned to escort the King and Queen from Varennes to Paris, he sympathized with their plight and carried on a correspondence with Marie-Antoinette which, like that of Mirabeau, was discovered after the storming of the Tuileries. He was arrested and executed during the Reign of Terror. Dubois-Crancé was a king's musketeer before the Revolution, became a Jacobin, but clashed with Robespierre and conspired in his downfall on 10 Thermidor. Gérard, the last of the four deputies whose faces were painted on David's canvas, was conspicuous in 1789 for his attire and manners. A farmer and deputy from Rennes, he stood out among his civilized colleagues because of his rusticity; in the sepia study, he wore wooden clogs. Never an important political figure in the Assembly he soon dropped from sight.

To the left of Mirabeau, Barnave, Dubois-Crancé and Gérard was the group of Jacobin figures that included Pétion and Robespierre. Jérôme Pétion de Villeneuve became mayor of Paris after Bailly; he ended up siding with the Girondins against Robespierre. Denounced by Jacobins, he escaped from Paris and committed suicide in June 1794. Standing next to Pétion is his friend Buzot, who also committed suicide. Seated next to Pétion and to his left was Sieyès, who considered himself fortunate to survive the Terror. "I have survived" ("J'ai vécu") was his comment. To the left of Sieyès were the three figures representing religious unity, dom Gerle, Rabaut Saint-Etienne, and Grégoire. Of these, one, Rabaut Saint-Etienne, went to the guillotine. Rising above the figure of Rabaut Saint-Etienne was the figure of Bailly, sketched in white chalk, an ironically (and appropriately) ghostly apparition. Bailly became the enemy of the people when he called in troops that fired on a crowd in the Champ de Mars on July 17, 1791; for his execution, the guillotine was moved to the Champ de Mars in 1793. A red flag, the symbol of order, had been raised before troops fired on the people, and a red flag was now "attached to the back of the carriage, and dragged to the place of execution." It was then burnt in front of Bailly before he was decapitated. Among the other figures in David's *Tennis Court Oath* to be executed were Le Chapelier (who, along with Barnave drafted the Tennis Court Oath) and Jacques-Guillaume Thouret. Dr. Joseph-Ignace Guillotin, another deputy in David's *Tennis Court Oath*, was imprisoned; however, he was fortunate not to be executed by the instrument whose use he advocated for humane reasons. Dominique-Joseph Garat, seen below Le Chaplier on the left-hand side of the sepia study, succeeded

Georges-Jacques Danton as Minister of Justice, was arrested for Girondist sympathies, released when Robespierre interceded on his behalf, and turned against Robespierre on 9 Thermidor. Pierre-Louis, comte Roederer, opposite Garat on the right-hand side of the painting, came under suspicion when he urged Louis XVI to take refuge in the Manège on August 10; he went into hiding until after the fall of Robespierre. Other deputies included by David, who ran afoul of the Revolution they heralded in 1789, were Louis-Marie de La Réveillière-Lépeaux and Jean-Denis, Comte Lanjuinais, both of whom went into hiding when they were proscribed after the *journée* of June 2, 1793. Dupont de Nemours fled France and the Revolution to America.

The female figures in David's *Tennis Court Oath* were part of his liberal conception of the event he portrayed. Women played an active role in the circles in which David moved in the 1780s, and, as we have seen, Mme David, in an act of patriotic dedication, was among those who gave jewels to the Nation in September 1789. Educated, publicly aware women were drawn into the Revolution in its early, liberal phase but they were excluded from politics during the Reign of Terror. Among the profounder ironies of the Revolution was the fate of women, devoted followers of Rousseau, who were excluded from politics by the Jacobins. Women proclaimed their rights in feminist manifestoes at the beginning of the Revolution, they formed their own political clubs, and they attended meetings of the Assembly and the Convention. In October 1793 J. B. Amar, a leading Jacobin, raised three questions in a meeting of the Committee of General Security: "(1) Must assemblages of women meeting in popular societies be permitted? (2) Can Women exercise political rights and take an active part in government affairs? (3) Can they deliberate in political or popular gatherings?"[29] The Committee said no to each of these questions: women were not to have an active political voice. Seen through the prism of women's political suppression during the Terror, the female figures in David's *Tennis Court Oath*, who look down from galleries at oath-swearing deputies, belonged to a particular historical moment, one in which women were entering the political arena.

When artists' wives offered their jewels to the Assembly in September 1789, a contemporary said of the patriotic deed that it was "associated with dawning Liberty . . . Liberty is going to create . . . a new society and new models."[30] Among the new models was one that included women in the Nation. The female figures in David's *Tennis Court Oath* can be seen within that context. In 1790–1791, while working out the design for his twenty-three feet by thirty-three feet painting, David showed women caught up in patriotic fervor, much as his own wife was in September 1789. However, his marriage ended in divorce in 1794; he was part of the Jacobin leadership that crushed the women's movement during the Terror.

The language of David's *Tennis Court Oath*, elevated and heroic, was not only more than a product of the artist's academic training, but it also partook of the public ethos of the time. Members of the liberal elite, who swore the Tennis Court Oath, were educated in the classics and lived in an exalted world that was consistent with their idealized vision of antiquity. Patriotic loyalty and stoic sacrifice were part of that vision. Men utterly dedicated to the 1789 Revolution went to the guillotine during the Terror, some of them singing the "Marseillaise." Revolutionary leaders, who became victims of the Terror, typically maintained self-control at the time of their death. As members of the elite, it was important for them not to experience physical humiliation in front of the people. Even as they died, they were members of a public that was far removed from the world of the populace. The same was true of royalists. Reports indicated that when royalists feared arrest they made no effort to flee or resist but stayed on their estates "to await their fate," and when they went to the guillotine they were imperturbable.[31] The stoic aloofness with which they faced death resembled the calm detachment of revolutionaries, Girondins and Jacobins alike, who experienced the same fate.

When debate took place as early as 1789 on use of the guillotine, there was fear that the machine might "excite the horrible curiosity of the people." If the guillotine was adopted for humanitarian reasons, it also allowed greater control of audiences when it became the killing machine of the Terror. Contemporary accounts described crowd passivity when victims of the Terror went to the guillotine, but they also described a contrary atmosphere of festivity, with singing, dancing, and jocularity. As much as the authorities tried to restrain crowds, they were not always able to do so, particularly when victims showed signs of weakness. Members of the elite sometimes committed suicide rather than experience public degradation, and those who were condemned tried to remain calm and aloof as they went to the guillotine. Their death, stoic, dignified, Roman, would give no pleasure to the populace.

Robespierre, seen as an ancient warrior in one of David's studies for the *Tennis Court Oath*, did not take hemlock, as he said he might in a meeting of the Jacobins on the night of 8 Thermidor, but he did attempt suicide after one o'clock on the morning of 10 Thermidor. Having shot himself in the jaw, he was placed on a plank, as we have seen, and, covering his shattered face with his right arm, he was carried down a flight of stairs below which a crowd had gathered in front of the Hôtel de Ville. He was taken to the Tuileries, his body was laid out on a table in the *salle d'audience*, and a box with scraps of army bread was placed under his head as a pillow, where he lay half-conscious for an hour. He still had on his blue coat and nankeen breeches, but someone unbuckled his garters and pulled down his stockings. Robespierre thanked him courteously for the kindness. He placed a leather bag on his shattered jaw, which continued to bleed, and then he applied scraps of paper to it, which men, watching him, gave to him. A surgeon, who came to dress his wounds, found his jaw fractured and his mouth filled with loose teeth. He placed a key in Robespierre's mouth, removed the teeth, bound the wound, and placed a bowl of water at his side. After washing himself, while no one was paying much attention, Robespierre sat up on the table, pulled up his stockings, and seated himself in a chair. He then asked for more water and clean linen. Throughout the episode, in the midst of unspeakable pain, he had uttered no cries, showed no signs of pain or distress, and conducted himself with control, dignity, and rectitude. Only the bandaged jaw, blood-splattered clothing, and livid complexion indicated the refinements of pain he had undergone.

Ever fastidious, even in the throes of excruciating pain, he maintained a proper bearing and exhibited no signs of weakness. Observers commented on the absence of any signs of suffering. He then endured the hour-long passage from the Conciergerie to the Place de la Révolution, seated in a tumbrel, "His head . . . wrapped in a dirty, blood-stained clout, which half conceals the pallid and ferocious face." Along the way "Tumult and uproar [were] all around him, made up of a thousand cries of joy and mutual congratulation." As he was strapped to the board of the guillotine, Sanson tore the bandage from his face. Robespierre shrieked from pain. The crowd in the Place de la Révolution cheered as it heard the thud of the blade and Sanson held up the severed head of the Incorruptible Robespierre. According to Mercier, the applause lasted for fifteen minutes. This was a crowd that Robespierre was unable to control. The stoicism of his death was in grim contrast to the popular festivity that surrounded it. According to Lynn Hunt when she comments on the "false consciousness" of revolutionaries, Karl Marx wrote that "in the classically austere traditions of the Roman republic its gladiators [bourgeois revolutionaries] found the ideals and the art forms, the self-deceptions that they needed in order to conceal from themselves the bourgeois limitations of the content of their struggles." Like Rousseau, Robespierre admired and strove to emulate the stoicism of the ancient Greeks and Romans; he suffered cruelly from the pain of a shattered jaw and went resolutely to the guillotine, but not as a bourgeois revolutionary. His forbearance rested on a code of behavior common to the ancien régime public.[32]

David, a devoted follower of Robespierre, was not among those executed on 10 Thermidor. The artist whose paintings captured the Spartan virtue of the revolutionary elite had said he would take hemlock with Robespierre, but he claimed afterwards that he became ill and was unable to attend the fateful meeting of the Convention on 9 Thermidor. David's absence from that meeting undoubtedly saved his life. André Chénier was less fortunate. After the August 10 insurrection, he left Paris for Marly, fearing that his outspoken opposition to Jacobins made him politically suspect. This was indeed the case. Having joined his friends the Trudaines in the country outside Paris for several weeks, he returned to the capital but abandoned journalistic forays against radicals, for he could no longer denounce without putting himself at risk. His position became ever more precarious during the Reign of Terror; when he was arrested by chance on March 7, 1794, he was taken to the Luxembourg, then to the offices of the Committee of General Security, and finally to Maison Lazare, recently made over from a monastery to a prison. After several months detention, he was sent before the Revolutionary Tribunal, where charges were made that applied not to him but to his brother Sauveur, also an inmate at the Maison Lazare. When Chénier explained that the charges were made against the wrong person, he was charged again, along with twenty-five others, and like them he was found guilty and sent to the guillotine. When the death sentence was read to Chénier on 7 Thermidor (July 25, 1794), the day before Robespierre's fateful speech to the Convention, he is said to have exclaimed, "The miserable assassins!" His friend Jean-Antoine Roucher replied, "Now then, Chénier, my friend, *du calme.*"[33] Some reports say that Chénier and Roucher recited Racine to each other as they rode in a tumbrel to be executed. Chénier went to his end with the dignity appropriate to someone of his education, breeding, and station. Opposed to Robespierre as he was, he maintained a similar dignity when he went to the guillotine a mere three days before the Jacobin leader came to the same end.

Having abandoned the *Tennis Court Oath* after the August 10 insurrection and the ensuing September Massacres, and after his election to the Convention, David had less time to paint. During the twenty-two months between cessation of work on the painting and the fall of Robespierre, David became involved in the politics of the Revolution as a Jacobin, a member of the Convention, a member of the Committee of General Security, the Committee of General Instruction, and the Revolutionary Tribunal. Administrative duties occupied much of his time: attending meetings, drafting reports, giving speeches. As Pageant Master of the Revolution, he orchestrated a host of festivals that were an integral part of Robespierre's effort to galvanize public support for the Revolution and to forge the people into an indivisible Nation. His only paintings during this period of twenty-two months were done in conjunction with revolutionary festivals. In every respect, his life as an artist and participant in the Terror connected him to the Jacobin leadership that dominated the Revolution from the time of the August 10 insurrection to the fall of Robespierre. The farther David moved to the Left, the more he was drawn into radical politics and into the Terror, and the more removed he was from the moderate liberalism he and his former friends had embraced at the beginning of the Revolution. Some of those friends emigrated, others were arrested and executed, including both Trudaine brothers, André Chénier, and Lavoisier, whose portrait, *M and Mme Lavoisier* (fig. 96), David had exhibited in the 1789 Salon and whose wife had been his student.[34] The twenty-three feet by thirty-three feet painting, which commemorated the ideals David's friends had advocated, was rolled up and put into storage, a mute reminder of transformations that placed a bottomless gulf between David and his former friends. The canvas that was placed in storage had six holes in it. At the time of the Storming of The Tuileries the *Tennis Court Oath* painting was in the deconsecrated church of the Feuillants, which David used as a studio, and was close to The Tuilleries Palace. Swiss Guards who took refuge there on August 10 were slaughtered by insurrectionists who tore the canvas with bayonets as they carried out reprisals.[35] The painting was later cut into four sections, a

FIGURE 96. J.-L. David, *M and Mme Lavoisier*, Metropolitan Museum of Art, New York

FIGURE 97. F. Gérard, *The French People demand Removal of the Tyrant in the Insurrection of August 10*, Musée du Louvre

commentary of sorts on the failed project, as were the bayonet holes in the canvas.

Yet, oddly, the *Tennis Court Oath* continued to exert an influence on artists who were close to David during the Terror. Among those who felt that influence were two of David's students who presented works for the great *concours* of the Year II (1794).[36] Instigated by the Committee of Public Safety, artists who submitted paintings were asked to portray the great events of their time. Among the artists who submitted works for the *concours* was David's brilliant twenty-four-year-old student, François Gérard. His painting, *The French People demand Removal of the Tyrant in the Insurrection of 10 August* (fig. 97) was one of two prize-winning works, awarded by a jury that did not include David. This work was clearly in the debt of David's *Tennis Court Oath*. As William Olander has shown, Gérard retained the pyramidal structure of his master's great unfinished painting, but he did so after splitting the composition in half, retaining only the right-hand part: "The forced unity of the *Oath of the Tennis Court* could not play a part here, for what we are witness to is the power of 1794 being born in the figures of the *Sans-culottes*, represented as the harbingers of light into the corrupt realm of darkness, which was, in this case, the revolutionary government itself."[37] In David's patriotic painting, movement was directed toward the center, with Bailly's outstretched hand as its focal point, a compositional feature that was at one with David's conception of the event he strove to commemorate. The unity of David's work has been replaced by Gérard's "activated, dispersed and fragmented composition." Angry sans-culottes burst into the *Manège*, the meeting hall of the Assembly, their arms held forward not (as in David's work) to swear a patriotic oath but to denounce the King and Queen, who had taken refuge in the recorder's box; they can be seen behind its bars.

The fierce resolution of the sans-culottes is in contrast to the collapse of the deputies seated between them and the King and Queen. The deputies hold their heads in dismay and turn away from the sans-culottes, as if recoiling from their shock waves, and sit in stunned silence. While powerful rhythms mark the forceful entry of the sans-culottes into the *Manège*, the deputies, who preside over the Assembly's proceedings, are compositionally fragmented. There are pockets of darkness in the galleries where deputies are standing, as if they were "cast into villainous shadows." An oil study on paper for Gérard's *The French People* brings out the symbolic importance of light and darkness in the artist's conceptual scheme.[38] In this study, the *Manège* is a realm of darkness, into which light is admitted through the sans-culottes, whose figures stand out thanks to the passage of light that illuminates the space they occupy.

If David's *Tennis Court Oath* anticipated a new relationship between the legislature and the people, Gérard's *concours* painting can be seen as a later commentary on that scheme. It was in the very building in which Gérard's *The French People demand removal of the King* was set, the *Manège*, that the Rousseauist model of a legislature open to the people was applied when the National Assembly moved to Paris in October 1789. The people who attended meetings of the Assembly limited themselves to the role of spectators until August 10, although not necessarily quiet spectators, but, in the bloody aftermath of the storming of the Tuileries, they entered the *Manège* to demand the removal of the King. They occupied the meeting place of the Convention—it was now located in the Tuileries—in the *journée* of May 31–June 2, 1793 and again in the *journée* of September 5 of the same year. The intimidation of the legislature in its meeting place by the people turned the Rousseauist ideal of open, transparent government inside out. Rather than being open to the people, the legislature was exposed to invasion by the people.

Even as Gérard followed David's *Tennis Court Oath* design, he did so in ways that were consistent with his own purposes: The event he por-

FIGURE 98.
J. Masquelier, *Legislative Assembly in the Manège*, Musée Carnavelet

trayed was politically explosive and his design dramatized that fact. David lowered the ceiling and galleries of the tennis court to project a sense of unity; Gérard took similar liberties in depicting the interior of the *Manège,* but for a contrary reason, to create dissonance. Lowering the galleries allowed him to intensify the contrast between the people in the galleries and the deputies below them on the floor of the *Manège.* The extent to which Gérard lowered the ceiling and galleries of the Manège was evident when his study, *The French People demand removal of the King,* was compared to J. Masquelier's illustration, *Legislative Assembly in the Manège* (fig. 98), which showed the interior of the Manège in what were presumably its actual proportions. (The Manège no longer stands.)

The standing deputies in Gérard's study are seen as an orderly group whereas the people in the gallery directly above them sit, stand, move about, and above all give themselves over to spontaneous feelings, waving, leaning forward, and, in one instance, holding up a child so it can see the tumultuous scene below. With one exception, the people in the gallery wear the attire of ordinary people—working people: The exception is a man in a coat and tophat who bolts for an opening, as if he had wandered into a space that was not where he belonged. Under the gallery filled with a demonstrative populace are deputies who wear coats and tophats, or raise their hats in salute to the people who have forcefully entered the *Manège.* Even as several of the deputies salute the people, others look apprehensively toward the King and Queen who have taken refuge behind the bars of the *logographe.* The King tries to reassure the Queen but she, aware of the danger, looks straight at the sans-culottes who point at her with outstretched arms. The sans-culottes who hold their arms outward in this way are derived from the deputies in David's *Tennis Court Oath.* In David's patriotic painting outstretched arms express the Rousseauist ideal of unity; in Gérard's *concours* study outstretched arms are expressions of sans-culotte anger and as such they are a stunning commentary on the disintegration of the earlier ideal.

Somewhat incongruously, Gérard's fierce sans-culottes, dressed raggedly or wearing trophies of slain Swiss Guards, are accompanied by women. By the spring of 1794, when Gérard began work on his *10 August,* the political role of women had been sharply curtailed, and yet in his patriotic painting they are shown center stage, along with the men. Another oil on canvas study, different from the one discussed above, suggests why Gérard may have decided to include women in his painting.[39] In this study (see fig. 99), women are seen on the far left, behind the militant sans-culottes whose forceful gestures are reminiscent of the patriotic males in David's *Oath of the Horatii.* As in the *Horatii,* the male figures are organized into bold and powerful diagonals, whereas the female figures behind them are grouped into curvilinear

FIGURE 99.   Author's drawing of the left-hand side of a Gérard study for *August 10*. The study from which I made this drawing is in a private collection; all efforts to locate the owner failed; and unable to reproduce the work I resorted to the only possible device, drawing the relevant part of Gérard's study myself. As in David's *Oath of the Horatii* and *Brutus and the Lictors* women collapse under the weight of female grief. Compare my drawing after Gérard's study with David's two paintings, and particularly the female figures in *Brutus and the Lictors*.

forms. While the female figures bear some similarity to those in the *Horatii*, they resemble the women in *Brutus and the Lictors* (fig. 100) even more closely. The woman at the far left of Gérard's oil on canvas study, who holds another woman who leans on her, is derived from David's painted image of Brutus's wife who supports her two daughters. Like David's females in both the *Horatii* and *Brutus*, Gérard's female figures sink under an unbearable weight.

That Gérard alluded to the work that catapulted his master to a position of preeminence among the French school of artists, the *Horatii*, and to his 1789 Salon painting, the *Brutus*, was a thoughtful touch by a student who appreciated the continuing support of his mentor. He also included women because something within him responded to the spectrum of feelings they expressed. A comparison of the oil on canvas study and the finished study showed how Gérard had second thoughts about the women he was to include in the painting. Rather than retain the collapsing female behind the helmeted sans-culotte, Gérard in-

FIGURE 100. J.-L. David, *Brutus and the Lictors*, Musée du Louvre

serted a woman whose hand was placed approvingly on the shoulder of a barefoot boy, who holds a sword in emulation of the armed men; behind her were the same women in the oil study, only now the one that is derived from David's *Brutus* held her arm upward in a gesture that connected her to the males in front of her. If in his second thoughts Gérard decided to emphasize the theme of militancy within the groups of female figures, his original conception suggested a different perspective, one that separated the male from the female and brought out the emotional burdens of women when confronted with violence. Judging from what we know about Gérard, this was his most authentic response to the scene he portrayed. When he returned to France in 1793 after two years in Italy, (his birthplace), David secured him a position as a juror on the Revolutionary Tribunal, which exempted him from military service; he attended meetings only twice, giving ill health as the reason for his customary absence. Temperamentally, Gérard was ill-suited for the political role in which he had been cast during the Reign of Terror. In a perceptive discussion of Gérard, Walter Friedländer wrote: "The likable, gracious, and elegant character of [his] art had no connection either with the political or the heroic, and he could not, like David, attain his full stature in those fields. . . . In his whole style and feeling Gérard is much more a painter of women." Given his propensity for the delicate and sentimental, it is hardly surprising that Gérard changed artistic direction completely after the Terror, taking up a "graceful, rather idyllic manner, somewhat in the spirit of earlier decades of the eighteenth century. The brutal gestures demanded by his own time were alien to him."[40] The fall of Robespierre prevented the public exhibition that, according to official plans, was to have been held after the *concours*. Among the works never completed was Gérard's prize-winning entry. Conceived during the Terror, it was abandoned after the Terror.

Another work undertaken for the *concours* by a student of David, and also derived from the master's *Tennis Court Oath*, is Pierre-Etienne Le Sueur's *Execution of the Tyrant, 21 January, 1793* (fig. 101). Set in the Place de la Révolution, where Louis XVI was executed, the figures in Le Sueur's composition give themselves over to saturnalian rejoicing as the head of the dead monarch is held up for all to see. With one exception, all contemporary accounts, republican and royalist alike, describe the scene of Louis XVI's execution as one of silence. At the most, a few spectators might have tossed their hats in the air, but calm prevails in the Place de la Révolution. In the words of a royalist account, "a gloomy silence reigned everywhere; but this was a silence like the silence of a tomb." A republican account also comments on the crowd's silence, and explains it as a result of female weakness. Only one account, that of Rony l'Aîné, departs from all others and describes a scene of rejoicing and dancing.

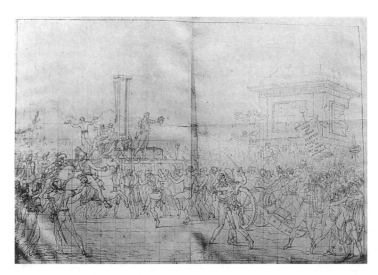

FIGURE 101.   P.-E. LeSueur, *Execution of the Tyrant,* January 21, 1793, Bibliothèque Nationale, Paris

This account matches exactly with Le Sueur's *Execution of the Tyrant*, and, according to Daniel Arasse, it is probably derived from that work and is not a description of the actual scene of the King's execution.[41] What would appear to be accurate accounts agree with Isidore-Stanislas Helman's engraving, *Execution of Louis Capet in the Place de la Révolution* (fig. 102), which shows two rows of soldiers arrayed in a semicircle around the guillotine and behind them people holding their hats upward. This illustration is in striking contrast to Le Sueur's *Execution of the Tyrant*, whose point of departure is his mentor David's *Tennis Court Oath*. As in David's *Tennis Court Oath* patriots hold one another in fraternal embrace, and, as in that work, there is a note of incongruity on the right-hand side of the composition. Taking the place of Martin Dauch in Le Sueur's *Execution of the Tyrant* is a recalcitrant member of the crowd, looking away from the head of the decapitated King in spite of the entreaties of two youths. There is reason to divert one's eyes from the grisly scene on the scaffold, one might think, but this is shown as an aberration, not as a normal response. By turning away from the severed head of the King, this figure places himself outside the patriotic crowd that is unified by festive rejoicing. Not to rejoice after the guillotine has done its deadly work was to isolate oneself from a great public event. Truly, this work belongs to the Reign of Terror. Another figure in Le Sueur's *Execution of the Tyrant* also connects the work to the Terror—and to David's *Tennis Court Oath*. To the left of the recalcitrant member of the crowd is a helmeted warrior who holds his

FIGURE 102.   Engraving by I.-S. Helman, after Charles Monnet, *Execution of Louis Capet in the Place de la Révolution*, Bibliothèque Nationale, Paris

sword to his chest, derived from the figure of Robespierre in David's patriotic painting. That this is Le Sueur's most literal reference to David's work can be explained in part by the contemporary political scene.

Some of David's major figures—Bailly, Mirabeau, Barnave, Pétion—had run afoul of the Revolution and been discredited, executed, or committed suicide. Le Sueur could hardly have paraphrased these figures from his master's *Tennis Court Oath*. But not Robespierre. He was not only politically active, but the dominant figure of the Revolution, and it was he who presided over the Terror, of which Le Sueur's *Execution of the Tyrant* can be regarded as an allegory. Like Gérard's *The French People*, it was never completed and is known only by the drawing now in the Bibliothèque Nationale.

Just as politics forced David to abandon his *Tennis Court Oath* so did it make his two students, Gérard and Le Sueur, abandon projects for the great *concours* of the Year Two (1794). In the case of Le Sueur, the figure appropriated most directly from the master's patriotic painting, Maximilien Robespierre, came to the same fate as other revolutionary leaders in David's *Tennis Court Oath*. The same logic, central to the politics of the French Revolution, that led to David's abandonment of his ambitious painting resulted also in the abandonment by two of his students of ambitious, large-scale projects undertaken at the height of the Terror.

The story of David's *Tennis Court Oath*, then, is an extended one that includes not only the period of more than two years David spent on the preparatory studies and then on the huge canvas, but also the period after its abandonment, when two of his students drew inspiration from it in their own patriotic paintings. This story is a running commentary on the Revolution.

When David began work on the *Tennis Court Oath* in the spring of 1790, he referred, in a speech in Nantes, to the Revolution as *"heureuse"*; he partook of the widespread feeling of euphoria that followed the great events of the previous summer, and he drew from that reservoir of feeling as he set to work on the project. By the time he abandoned it in September 1792, events had overtaken the project and subverted its theme of patriotic unity. Henceforth, David, himself a member of the Convention, a Jacobin, a *Montagnard*, and a Robespierrist, organized festivals that strove to mobilize public support for the Revolution. In the twenty-two month period between his abandonment of the *Tennis Court Oath* and the fall of Robespierre, he painted only three works, all done in connection with the revolutionary festivals that he planned. The last of these works, *Joseph Bara*, was abandoned after the Convention turned on Robespierre on 9 Thermidor. Begun during the Terror, it was a casualty of the Terror. The politics of the French Revolution prevented completion of David's *Tennis Court Oath*, two paintings derived from it by his students, and the last of his three paintings of revolutionary martyrs.

Chapter 6

Robespierre, David, and Revolutionary Festivals

Ought there to be no entertainments in a republic? On the contrary, there ought to be many. It is in republics that they were born, it is in their bosom that they are seen to flourish with a truly festive air. To what peoples is it more fitting to assemble often and form among themselves sweet bonds of pleasure and joy than to those who have so many reasons to like one another and remain forever united? We already have more of these public festivals; let us have even more. . . . But let us not adopt . . . exclusive entertainments. . . . It is in the open air, under the sky, that you ought to gather and give yourselves to the sweet sentiment of your happiness.

—*J.-J. Rousseau,* Lettre à d'Alembert sur les spectacles, *1758*

There is, however, a type of institution which should be considered as an essential part of public education, and which pertains necessarily to the subject of this report. I wish to speak to you of national festivals. . . . Man is the greatest object produced by nature, and the most magnificent of spectacles is that of a great people assembled together. One could never speak without enthusiasm of . . . national festivals.

—*Robespierre's Report to the Convention on Religious and Moral Ideas and Republican Principles, and on National Festivals, May 7, 1794*

The National Convention has charged me to present my ideas on the plan for the festival in honor of [Joseph] Bara and Agricol Viala. Citizens, I will try to help you understand better your own sentiments and at the same time show the world that you want the nation to experience a complete moral regeneration.

—*David's report to the Convention on the Festival for Bara and Viala, July 11, 1794*

In the first of the above quotations, taken from the *Lettre à d'Alembert sur les spectacles*, Rousseau proclaims the importance of festivals to people living under the republican form of government. He had recently returned to Geneva, and he and the citizens of that city, he wrote, "Need not have recourse to the games of the ancient Greeks; there are modern ones which are still in existence, and I find them precisely in our city."[1] When Genevans participate in festivals, they are "lively, gay, and tender; their hearts are then in their eyes as they always are on their lips; they seek to communicate their joy and their pleasures. They invite, importune, and coerce the new arrivals and dispute over them. All the societies constitute but one, all become common to all."[2] The second quotation is from a long—to some it must have seemed inordinately long—report to the Convention given on May 7, 1794; it includes recommendations for festivals to be held thirty-six times annually, one for each *décadi*.

It was Robespierre who made the report, and Georges Couthon urged that it be translated into all languages and disseminated throughout the universe. As a disciple of Rousseau, Robespierre felt that festivals were a source of harmony and unity. "Bring men together and you will make them better, for when men are brought together they will try to please one another, and they will only be able to please by those qualities that make them estimable. Give to their reunion a grand moral and political motive and love of honest deeds will enter with pleasure into all hearts, for men do not come together without pleasure." While the festivals of ancient Greece had put on display the talent of athletes, poets, and orators, the French people would give their assemblies a broader purpose and greater significance. "A system of well organized national festivals would offer at once the most gentle of fraternal ties and the most powerful means of regeneration."[3] When Robespierre gave his report to the Convention, he had already collaborated on festivals with Jacques-Louis David, whom he mentioned by name. David's report on the Festival of Bara and Viala, made in the Convention two months later, on July 11, 1794, and from which the third quotation is taken, was a result of that collaboration. The festival for which David was making plans was to honor two youthful martyrs of the Revolution, Joseph Bara and Agricol Viala. "These two young soldiers, at age thirteen, have equalled the heroes of antiquity, devoting themselves generously to the liberty of their country." With the example of such heroes, the people "can march in their footsteps, carrying gravely in its heart a scorn of death [and] hatred of crowned brigands." The remains of the young martyrs would be carried by mothers and young soldiers; "the French people, holding the palms of victory in its hand, will be the ornament of this touching ceremony."[4]

Lofty and elevated as these three pronouncements on festivals were—those of Rousseau, Robespierre and David—each had a dark underside. Rousseau's *Lettre à d'Alembert sur les spectacles*, from which his discussion of festivals is taken, marked his definitive break with the Encyclopedists. Rousseau had returned to Geneva in 1754, where Voltaire also took up residence. Deeply attached to théâtre, Voltaire launched a campaign to overturn Geneva's laws proscribing it; in 1757, he persuaded d'Alembert, editor of the *Encyclopédie*, to insert a passage in his article on Geneva, suggesting that it should have a théâtre. In early 1758, Rousseau protested against any efforts to end Geneva's ban on théâtre. The work in which he argued his case, the *Lettre à d'Alembert*, was highly polemical; it was a work that not only drove a wedge between Rousseau and the Encyclopedists, but also, as Allan Bloom said, was "like a morality play, entitled 'The Spirit of the Enlightenment against the Spirit of Republican Virtue.' "[5] In arguing against théâtre for Geneva, Rousseau asked what type of entertainments were best for the people of that city. In doing so, he built an elaborate case against théâtre and, at the end of his work, he argued in favor of civic festivals, which had long been celebrated in Geneva and were also important in antiquity. In making his case, Rousseau argued that théâtre favored manners over morals, undermined civic duty, undercut family and religion, weakened citizenship, and had as its goal creating taste. Attuned to the courts of Europe, théâtre was a source of corruption. "Look at most of the plays in the French théâtre; in practically all of them you will find abominable monsters and atrocious actions, useful, if you please, in making the plays interesting and in giving exercise to the virtues; but they are certainly dangerous in that they accustom the eyes of the people to horrors they ought not to know and to crimes they ought not to consider possible."[6] To expose the people to théâtre was to expose them to fanaticism, for "Once fanaticism exists, I can see only one way left to stop its progress . . . one must leave philosophy behind, close the books, take the sword, and punish the imposters."[7] In his diatribe against théâtre, Rousseau presented himself as a censor who took the high moral ground; the assumption throughout the *Lettre* was that virtue was on his side. This would not have pleased those he argued against; the vehemence of his language was tantamount to throwing down the gauntlet. For Rousseau, a théâtre in Geneva was like a disease from Paris that would contaminate his city. It was his self-appointed task to stop the contagion, to prevent the "big-city monkeys" from poisoning the simple, virtuous ways of the Genevan people. The *Lettre à d'Alembert* was more than polemical; it was a declaration of war. Rousseau's argument in favor of festivals was part of a direct assault on writers, the Encyclopedists, with whom he had maintained close ties but from now on were on the far side of a barrier he constructed.

Rousseau's argument in favor of festivals followed an attack on adversaries and, similarly, Robespierre's 1794 proposal for thirty-six annual festivals followed attacks on political opponents. Since the fall of 1793, Robespierre had been locked in bitter conflict with dechristianizers who had closed local churches, ridiculed priests, and desecrated holy objects. No friend of priests or Christianity, Robespierre, a deist in the mold of Rousseau, was offended by the coarseness of the campaign; he was opposed to it on political grounds. He felt that dechristianizers were driving an even deeper wedge into a France already rent by counterrevolution. Rather than pursue a religious policy that was divisive, he favored one that would further unity, and it was to that end that he gave his report to the Convention on Religious and Moral Ideas and Republican Principles, and on National Festivals. "The idea of the Supreme Being and immortality of the soul is a continual call to justice; it is therefore social and republican." Atheism, by contrast, was "a system of conspiracy against the Republic." The conspirators had nothing to put in the place of what they were destroying. All they had to offer was "chaos, emptiness, and violence. They would scorn the people too much so they could persuade them; rather than enlighten them they only wished to irritate them, frighten them, or deprave them."[8]

In a sense, what Robespierre accomplished in his report to the Convention was to reenact the conflict between Rousseau and his adversaries. Among those who set the stage for the Revolution, he said, were renowned "men of letters who, by virtue of their influence on public opinion, began to exert influence on public affairs." Their influence was not always positive. The Encyclopedists were made up of a "few worthy men and many ambitious charlatans. . . . This sect, in political matters, always fell short of the rights of the people; with regard to morals it went far beyond the destruction of religious principles. Its leaders sometimes declaimed against despotism while they received pensions from despots. They wrote books against the court and at the same time dedicated their works to kings. They were proud in their writings and grovelled in ante-chambers. This sect propagated with much zeal the opinion of materialism that prevailed among the great and the clever." Those who belonged to this party developed a "practical philosophy that reduced egoism to a system, regarded human society as a *guerre de ruse*, success as the rule of right and wrong, honesty as a matter of taste or propriety, and society as the patrimony of adroit rogues." Many of this sect had "intimate connections with the house of Orléans," and "the English constitution was the *chef-d'oeuvre* of politics and the *maximum* of social happiness." During the Revolution they entered the ranks of moderates, at which time they revealed their true colors: "They have opposed the Revolution from the moment they feared it would raise the people above all private vanities; some have employed their cleverness to adulterate republican principles and to corrupt public opinion; they have prostituted themselves to factions and especially the house of Orléans; others have taken refuge in a base neutrality. Men of letters in general have dishonored themselves during the Revolution." Lined up resolutely against the sophisticated but shallow men of letters before the Revolution, Robespierre wrote, was Rousseau. "Among those who, in the period of which I speak . . . [was] a man who, by elevation of soul and grandness of character, showed himself worthy of being preceptor of the human race. He attacked tyranny openly; he spoke with enthusiasm of the Deity; his manly and probing eloquence painted in brilliant colors the charms of virtue, and he defended the consoling dogmas given by reason for the support of the human heart. The purity of his doctrine . . . drew the hatred and persecution of rivals and false friends. Ah! If he had witnessed this Revolution, of which he was a precursor, and which has placed him in the Panthéon, who would doubt that his generous soul would have embraced with transport the cause of justice and equality!"[9]

Robespierre could reasonably have seen a connection between the dechristianizers and the Encyclopedists; what was revealing was his indictment of both. Not content to argue against dechristianization on political grounds, he connected the advocates of that policy to eighteenth-century men of letters before whom Rousseau had thrown down the gauntlet in the *Lettre à d'Alembert*. Robespierre not only embraced the ideas of Rousseau, but like his spiritual mentor took the high moral ground when doing battle with others. And just as Rousseau saw himself as a victim of conspiracies, so did Robespierre level charges of conspiracy against his antagonists. "You have already been struck, no doubt, with the ease with which so many men who betrayed their country have embraced the sinister opinions I combat." For Robespierre, the Revolution was a morality play and those on the wrong side of the moral fence were "enemies of the people," "aristocrats," "fanatics," part of a "counterrevolutionary malignity" and the "authors of a criminal plot."[10] Even as Robespierre pursued a policy that had as its goal unity rather than divisiveness, he turned his adversaries, real or imagined, into monsters of deceit, deception, perfidy, and treason against the state. The conclusion of his report, a recommendation for thirty-six national festivals that were to further revolutionary unity and solidarity, was preceded by an attack on enemies that was a reenactment of Rousseau's *Lettre à d'Alembert*.

David's report to the Convention on the Festival of Bara and Viala is yet another morality play. "Today, representatives of the people, your efforts are directed toward morality, and you have felt how important it is to lead men back to truth. To attain this goal I think it will be useful to compare despotic government with the one you have established, a division between vice and virtue. Men are only what government makes them . . . Despotism diminishes and corrupts public opinion . . . it carefully proscribes all virtues and to guarantee its sway it makes its way with terror, dresses itself in fanaticism, and wears the hat of ignorance. Everywhere base and perfidious treason hold forth, followed by death and devastation . . . [despotism] lives in darkness and meditates crime [committed against] its unfortunate victims, whose blood it sucks. Ingenious in its tortures, it raises Bastilles; in moments of leisure it invents punishments and rests its eyes on the spectacle of cadavers immolated by its fury."

On the other side of David's moral fence was "democracy, [which] takes counsel only from nature, to which it ceaselessly restores men. Its purpose is to render [men] good, to make them love justice and fairness. It is [that form of government] that inspires the noble disinterest that elevates souls and renders them capable of undertaking and executing grand causes."[11] The dark underside of David's report to the Convention was the Reign of Terror, which was in full swing but was soon to end: the festival for Bara and Viala had been scheduled for 10 Thermidor, the very day that Robespierre went to the Guillotine. It was never held.

David's report of July 11 to the Convention shared a moral dualism with Robespierre's report of May 7. In both, the Revolution, the embodiment of good, was contrasted to the forces of evil. Also noteworthy was David's remark: "Men are only what government makes them." The festivals on which Robespierre and David collaborated were more than patriotic celebrations; their purpose was to mobilize political support and beyond that to regenerate society. In part, Robespierre's interest in festivals was not only a function of revolutionary politics, of which it was a strategic component, but it also drew from the moral headwaters of Rousseau. The connection between Rousseau, Robespierre, David, and festivals was direct, and it was a connection that explained much about the relationship between ideas and the politics of the French Revolution.

As formulated by Rousseau and appropriated by his followers during the French Revolution, the patriotic festival was part of a new system of belief, a new religion as some historians would have it.[12] For Rousseau, politics was about morals, for the purpose of government was the transformation of human nature. At the core of this essentially religious conception was the idea—it would become a passion during the Revolution—that this world can be re-formed, made anew, cast in a different mold. Bound up with this faith were revolutionary cults, rituals, symbols, martyrs, even a new calendar to separate the New Age from the previous Christian Age. The Festival of the Supreme Being, held in Paris on June 8, 1794, embodied the articles of the new revolutionary faith. Revolutionary festivals were not mere patriotic exercises that endeavored to inculcate support for the Revolution but had the larger and more lofty goal of creating a new species of humanity. Rousseauist ideas of virtue were at the core of this conceptual system.

The Revolutionary festivals favored by Robespierre not only can be traced back to a model articulated by Rousseau in the *Lettre à d'Alembert*, but also they were a logical outgrowth of the civil religion ideal in Book 4, chapter 8 of the *Social Contract*. In the final chapter of his political treatise, Rousseau established a dichotomy between the old religion, Christianity, and the civil religion that was to take its place. A society of true Christians, Rousseau said, "would not be a society of men."[13] The Christian, for whom getting to heaven was the main goal, could not devote himself to and fight for the state against its enemies. "Suppose your Christian republic were face-to-face with Sparta or Rome: the pious Christians will be beaten, crushed and destroyed. . . . But I am mistaken in speaking of a Christian republic; each of these terms excludes the other. Christianity preaches only servitude and dependence. . . . True Christians are made to be slaves; they know it and are scarcely concerned; their short life is of little value in their eyes."[14] Rousseau said that some claim Christian troops were excellent; he denied it. With the victory of Christianity in the Roman world, "Roman valor completely disappeared." Citizens should, of course, be free to worship according to their conscience, but what was of greatest concern to Rousseau was devotion to the state. "Far from binding the hearts of the citizens to the state [Christianity] has detached them from all earthly things. I know of nothing more contrary to the social spirit."[15] As for the dogmas of civil religion, they "ought to be simple, few in number, enunciated precisely and without explanation or commentary. The existence of a powerful, beneficent, provident, all-caring divinity, the life to come, the happiness of the just, the punishment of the wicked, the sanctity of the social contract and the laws: These are its positive dogmas."[16] Within the new civil religion, enunciated by Rousseau, revolutionary festivals had a natural and logical place.

From the very beginning of the Revolution, the summer of 1789, there were spontaneous festivals that grew out of popular gatherings when the French countryside was gripped by the Great Fear. Villagers mutilated or destroyed traditional symbols, tore pews out of churches, and pulled down weathercocks. Swept up in patriotic enthusiasm, they wore cockades, planted maypoles and liberty trees, and forced neighboring villages to do the same. Knives were pulled and sometimes used; violence could and did erupt in the midst of village celebrations. Popular festivals held spontaneously throughout France as the nation was gripped by the Great Fear did not sit easily with those concerned with order and stability. One response to popular festivals was the organization of federative festivals by units of provincial National Guardsmen in an effort to keep forces of disorder in check. On November 29, 1789 some twelve thousand National Guardsmen from Vivrais and Dauphiné pledged an oath of mutual protection and brotherhood, an initiative that was duplicated by National Guardsmen across France. Out of local federations came local festivals whose military character reflected the makeup of the organizers. This included not only National Guardsmen and officers in the regular army, but others who also played a role in the festivals, for example, mayors, local dignitaries, and the like. The predominant role of the military was evident in the processions of guardsmen in federative festivals, in the blessing of flags, and swearing of oaths, sometimes with swords in hand. Defensive as local federative festivals were, they also drew from a patriotic impulse that was at the heart of a Revolution whose ideals were being celebrated. Both popular village festivals and those organized by National Guardsmen and local officials combined an element of fear with celebration of the defeat of despotism and the birth of a new order. Even as the two types of festivals shared these features, they differed in the scripts they followed and the groups that provided the initiatives. Between the two types of festival was a barrier that extended backwards in time from the Revolution into the society and culture of the ancien régime, one separating the public from the populace.

Out of the federative festivals in the provinces came the idea for a national festival to be held in Paris, the July 14, 1790 *Fête de la Fédération* whose oath-taking ceremony was synchronized to coincide exactly with thousands of local festivals throughout France. A procession began at the Porte Saint-Denis in the north of Paris, proceeded along the rue Saint-Denis, moved along the rue Saint-Honoré, crossed the Place Louis XV, and ended up at the Champ de Mars in a day of continuous rain. The Assembly had approved the festival on June 7, and for some two weeks throngs of Parisians worked feverishly to make ready for the event. It has been estimated that between 300,000 and 400,000 were present in Paris for the festival, many having traveled to the capital from all over France to celebrate the grand public event. The *Fête de la Fédération* was a public event in the sense that it not only took place in public spaces and was attended by people of all stations, but also in the sense that it bore the stamp of those who organized it. While announcements proclaimed that everyone took a place in the national festival "without distinction of age, sex, or fortune,"[17] this was not entirely the case. The same line that separated active from passive citizens was typically followed in the July 14 federative festivals; passive citizens observed ceremonies officially celebrated by active citizens. According to Mona Ozouf: "The people joined in only as gatecrashers."[18] Ozouf also said that the federative festivals were part of a single stereotype. It was this model, shorn of the parody and violence of popular festivals in provincial France, that was followed on July 14, 1790. The *Fête de la Fédération* was "profoundly conservative," defensive, and rooted in fear at the same time that it harbored utopian hopes of a new future. It was necessary to bring the Revolution to closure; ultimately this was the central purpose of the July 14 patriotic celebration.

Lafayette was a strong supporter of the *Fête de la Fédération*. As master of ceremonies, he administered an oath that those attending the festival swore, "to be forever faithful to the nation, the law, and the King."[19] Mirabeau, who hoped to use the festival to rally allegiance to the King, was another supporter, even though he resented Lafayette's role. An elaborate system of symbolism was devised for the festival that included clasped hands, triangles, obelisks, pyramids, altars of the *patrie*, angels, compasses—motifs taken from antiquity and Christianity alike—to assure the widest possible support. The goal was one of maximum identification. Oaths were taken and speeches delivered that proclaimed the festival "completes the edifice of our liberty" and puts "the final seal on the most memorable of revolutions."[20]

Unity was the goal of the *Fête de la Fédération*, the assimilation of all into a nation, breaking down barriers that were a legacy of the ancien régime. A Rousseauist impulse that fed into the national patriotic festival on July 14 was unmistakable, but at the same time the festival served the purposes of those who organized it, and on this occasion it was to bring the Revolution to closure. To say that the *Fête de la Fédération* failed to achieve that objective is to utter the obvious, however, it was possible in July 1790 to hold a national patriotic celebration that elicited genuine and widespread enthusiasm and was free of controversy. This was decidedly not the case a year later, on July 11, 1791, when a festival was held to commemorate the pantheonization of Voltaire. At the time of Voltaire's death in 1778, the Catholic Church had refused him burial in consecrated ground, but with the Revolution efforts were made to undo the wrong, and after a law was passed in November 1790, requiring priests to swear an oath to the

Constitution, a delegation went to the Commune, requesting that offi-
cial steps be taken to reclaim Voltaire's body. Out of these efforts came
Voltaire's pantheonization and the Festival of Voltaire. Conditions in
France were markedly different for this festival than for the *Fête de la
Fédération* held a year earlier. Louis XVI had made his abortive flight
to Varennes weeks before the Festival of Voltaire, and, a few days after
it was held, Lafayette's guards fired on a crowd at the Champ de Mars.
Lafayette had presided over the earlier festival; now he was aligned
with the forces of reaction. Louis XVI swore to uphold the Constitution at the *Fête de la Fédération*; when the Festival of Voltaire was
held, however, efforts were under way to abolish monarchy. Between
the two festivals latent conflicts within France had been hardened by
the Civil Constitution of the Clergy. The Revolution was more divided
in July 1791 than July 1790, particularly over religion, and traditional
Christians regarded the Festival of Voltaire as an affront. Pamphlets
about the festival disagreed sharply over the event. To those supporting
the festival, it was a great success: "The most beautiful and imposing
of festivals," in the opinion of the *Chronique de Paris*, and according
to the *Courier de Provence*, "never was a pomp more brilliant or more
solemn." By contrast, the Marquis de Ferrières called it a "kind of
farce" and another aristocrat ridiculed it as "a foolish carnival." Mme
de Genlis dismissed the festival as the "most foolish, abominable and
ridiculous absurdity that was ever seen in Paris . . ."[21]

The Festival of Voltaire was the first of the Revolutionary festivals
in which David was involved. While David has sometimes been cred-
ited with the design of the triumphal *char* that conveyed Voltaire's remains to the Panthéon, contemporary documents do not support this
claim. According to an official program of the festival prepared by
Joseph Charron, it was Jacques Célerier, who had designed the triumphal arch on the Champ de Mars for the *Fête de la Fédération*, who
"made the drawing of the chariot."[22] David did collaborate in plans for
the festival by offering drawings and tracings of classical objects that
he had done as a student in Rome to help in the design of costumes,
musical instruments, and other objects that constituted the festival's
mise en scène. Those responsible for organizing the festival understandably wanted to include David not only because of his artistic
stature and prominence as a patriot, but also because of his influence
on a revival of Voltaire's *Brutus* in November 1790. David helped the
actor Talma design his clothing for the play, had him cut his hair short
in good antique fashion, and loaned his bust of Brutus, a copy of an antique sculpture, to the production. Moreover, in the last line of the
play, the actor Vanhove, who took the part of Brutus, slumped in his
chair in a position the audience was able to recognize as patterned after

the figure of Brutus in David's painting; as he did so four lictors in the background bore the body of Brutus' son, Titus, across the stage, in direct imitation of David's painting. Subsequent performances of Voltaire's *Brutus* included the reenactment of David's painting; in this way, David continued to be associated with Voltaire's *Brutus*, and with Voltaire, as plans moved forward for the Voltaire festival.

It was in November 1790 that the Marquis de La Villette gave a speech to the Jacobins, urging national recognition for the transfer of Voltaire's remains to Paris. In subsequent meetings of the Jacobins, others supported Voltaire's pantheonization, including Anacharsis Clootz, Marie-Joseph Chénier, and Camille Desmoulins. Robespierre was not among those in the Jacobins who gave vocal support to the Festival of Voltaire. Soon to become a strong adherent of revolutionary festivals, Robespierre had not yet lined up in that direction; he had not played a role in organizing the July 14, *Fête de la Fédération*, and he did not speak on behalf of the festival.

Other leaders seized on festivals as vehicles to mobilize support for the Revolution before Robespierre. Among those who did so was Mirabeau, in his *Discours sur l'éducation nationale*, published posthumously in 1791 and written between September 1790 and April 1791. Mirabeau proposed festivals based on those of antiquity that would be devoted to "the cult of liberty, the cult of law." It was not enough to persuade man to obey the rule of law, it was necessary to make him want to do so, and this could be achieved through appeal to emotions that festivals were capable of stirring. Man, Mirabeau said:

> obeys his impressions more than his reason. It is not enough to show him the truth, the capital point is to make him passionate for her. It accomplishes little to serve him in his immediate need, if one does not seize hold of his imagination. It is a question less of convincing him than of moving him, less of proving to him the excellence of the laws which govern him, than to make him love them by means of his lively and emotional feelings . . .[23]

In this appeal, Mirabeau envisaged festivals as a way to mold a citizenry, a good Rousseauist intention, but according to Mirabeau's particular agenda, that of a moderate who sought political stability in order that the National Assembly could complete the Constitution; who allied himself secretly with the King; and upheld the sanctity of and obedience to the law. Mirabeau wrote that while festivals had "worked wonders" for the ancients, Roman triumphal ceremonies had encouraged "the avid fury of a conquering people," a response that he preferred to avoid. Nor did he want festivals to allow saturnalian celebrations that could serve as an invitation "to recall in an illusory way the primal equality of men."[24] At the center of Mirabeau's thinking about festivals was control and the regulation of all details to achieve his ideal of order. Conceptually, what he hoped to achieve through festivals was unity; recognizing tensions and conflicts within France and within the Revolution, he sought, to the extent it was possible, to resolve them. The absorption of differences was at the core of Mirabeau's conceptual scheme for festivals.

The July 14, 1790 *Fête de la Fédération* had been congruent with those intentions, but this was decidedly not the case for two festivals held in 1792, the year after Mirabeau's death, the Festival of Châteauvieux, and the Festival of Simonneau. These festivals marked an irreparable break within the revolutionary leadership; they also marked a permanent divide within the Revolution itself. The Festival of Châteauvieux was sponsored by the Jacobins, and the Festival of Simonneau was organized by moderates who were opposed to the Jacobin agenda. These festivals served political agendas in direct conflict with one another, as was reflected in public statements by those who organized them, and by the orchestrated polemics in the radical and conservative press on both.

When Robespierre issued a call for national festivals on February 10, 1792 in a speech to the Constituent Assembly, he did so within the context of debate on the war. As he did throughout that debate, he maintained that France's real enemies were internal, not external. "I am going to propose," he began, "the means to save the *patrie*, to smother the civil war and foreign war by confusing all the plans of our internal enemies."[25] Besides taking defensive measures, such as organizing the *gardes-françaises* and maintaining constant vigilance in the Sections of Paris, it was essential that the entire nation be regenerated. This could be done by following the sage wisdom of Rousseau: "I am going to propose simple and grand measures that will rapidly propagate the public spirit and the principles of the Revolution."[26] National festivals dedicated to the people, to equality, and to humanity, would serve this end. "Our national festivals should be embellished with objects that will make them worthy of their purpose." Among the models to be emulated were those of Rousseau, Voltaire, and David, the creators of the *Social Contract, Emile*, the tragedy of *Brutus*, the painting of *Brutus*, the *Death of Socrates*, and the *Tennis Court Oath*. "These are the models that belong to the French people." If the Assembly did as Robespierre suggested, it would "see the French people appear again in all its majesty, peaceful, but imposing; generous, indulgent, but ready to strike a blow . . . at the first cry of violated liberty. . . . Join together, unite . . . and all the tyrants of the earth will turn pale on their tottering thrones."[27] The Revolution was in peril, but means were at hand to strengthen the *patrie*; patriotic festivals would further that end.

It was when Robespierre issued a call for national festivals that he first referred to David in a speech to the Convention. He had seen David in the Jacobins in June 1790, when the artist attended several meetings to solicit support for the *Tennis Court Oath*. David became a member of the Jacobins at the end of 1790, but this was when moderates still made up a significant part of the membership. He attended only three meetings of the Jacobins in 1791, and this was when artistic matters were discussed. There was no evidence of contact between David and Robespierre in 1790–91, and as we have seen, Robespierre did not accept David's invitation to deputies of the Third Estate to pose for him in his studio adjacent to the Manège for the *Tennis Court Oath*. Yet, judging from preparatory studies in the Versailles Sketchbook and from Robespierre's prominent position in the 1791 sepia study for the *Tennis Court Oath* David admired Robespierre. Now, in February 1792, Robespierre referred to David in a speech in which he spoke of festivals. The time was drawing near for Robespierre and David to begin collaboration on revolutionary festivals—but it had not yet arrived.

On March 3, 1792, three weeks after Robespierre's speech to the Constituent Assembly, the *Courier de Paris* announced: "The King is having himself painted handing the Constitution to his son the Prince Royal. He has requested the patriotic brush of the celebrated David."[28] On September 29, 1791, the Constituent Assembly had urged the King to have a portrait made of himself, accepting the Constitution and showing it to his son so it could be placed in the hall where members of that body met. When David's role in the project was announced on March 3, he came under heavy attack from the radical press. To accept the commission was to identify with political moderates, which David was still able to do at this point in the Revolution. André Chénier wrote an article in support of David's Louis XVI commission that appeared in the *Supplément au Journal de Paris* on March 24, 1792. It was on that day that David, M.-J. Chénier—André's brother—Collot d'Herbois, Jean-Lambert Tallien, and Théroigne de Méricourt presented a petition to the Commune, requesting permission for the Festival of Châteauvieux. David had changed camps: he no longer lined up with André Chénier and the moderates but with radicals who were on the opposite side of the political fence. The Festival of Châteauvieux resulted in a falling out between David and André Chénier; it set the stage for David's jacobinization. He and Robespierre were, so to speak, now thrown together.

The March 24 petition for the Châteauvieux festival proclaimed: "This touching festival will be everywhere the terror of tyrants, the hope and consolidation of patriots. This festival which civism and the fine

arts are going to render memorable . . . [will be] the triumph of the martyrs and the cause of the people."[29] The reaction in the conservative
press was immediate and sharp. André Chénier called the Swiss "insub-
ordinate and rebellious . . . murderers . . . public enemies,"[30] and the
moderate Feuillant Club argued against the project. In a meeting of the
Jacobins on April 6, Robespierre said, "David and other artists will
have the pleasure to see their talent contribute to the triumph of liberty. Nothing will prevent the soldiers of Châteauvieux and the people
from triumphing next Monday."[31] The festival, even before it was held,
became a symbolic battlefield between Jacobins and Feuillants. Pressing his case against opponents on April 6, Robespierre asked the Jacobins to present a petition to the municipality that would order removal of busts of Lafayette and Bailly from the Commune. Robespierre
continued his support of the Châteauvieux festival in meetings of the
Jacobins on April 8, 9, 11, 13, and 14. These meetings were given to debate on many topics, but in every case Robespierre turned at some
point, and with characteristic fervor, to the Châteauvieux festival.
Having recommended national festivals to fellow Jacobins on February
10, before plans for the Châteauvieux festival had been announced, in
April he pressed home his case in support of a festival that David, the
artist he had already singled out as a good patriot, was organizing.

Efforts were made to block the Festival of Châteauvieux right up to
the day on which it was held. The day was bright and clear, and perhaps 100,000 (400,000 by some contemporary accounts, surely exaggerated) turned out for the celebration. People from working-class districts constituted most of the crowd; joining them in a procession were
members of the Châteavieux regiment, National Guardsmen, and Jacobins. David designed the large triumphal *char* that bore a statue of
Liberty and was adorned with bas relief sculptures of Brutus sentenc-
ing his sons to death and William Tell aiming a javelin at an apple on
the head of his son. The chariot, according to a contemporary account,
was drawn by "twenty democratic horses" who did not hold their
heads high, whose "manes were not plaited with gold, nor adorned
with white plumes," and "walked rather ploddingly."[32] The procession
paused at the site of the Bastille and then proceeded to the Hôtel de
Ville, where Pétion was joined by Robespierre and Danton. Continuing
towards its final destination, the Champs de Mars, the procession
passed through the Place Louis XV (see fig. 70), where it came to the
large equestrian statue of Louis XV that was crowned with a *bonnet
rouge* and blindfolded for the occasion. The festival was deliberately
provocative, and those who opposed it were indignant. Reports of the
radical press were favorable and those of the conservative press were
hostile. Brissot de Warville wrote: "Nothing could be more beautiful

than this festival because nothing is more beautiful than a great mass of men animated by the same sentiments of patriotism and of fraternity . . ." By contrast, the *Journal générale de France* said, "nothing could be as shabby as this . . . noisy and picturesque mob . . . of the very poorest inhabitants." In the opinion of Robespierre, the Festival of Châteauvieux was "simple and sublime."[33]

Not content to protest against a festival supported by the Jacobins, the Feuillants organized another festival that had as its purpose respect for the law (see fig. 71). Quatremère de Quincy, David's companion in student days at Rome, now a staunch Feuillant, presented a report to the Assembly on May 12, calling for a festival that was given official approval. This festival was in honor of Louis Simonneau, the mayor of Etampes, who was killed by peasants on March 3, 1792, when he refused to fix grain prices. Those who opposed the Festival of Châteauvieux seized on the Simonneau incident as the occasion for a counter festival. Orchestrated by Quatremère de Quincy, it was held on June 3. Members of the National Guard were prominent in the procession, underlining the theme of order that was central to the event. "The most curious item in the procession," according to an account in *Révolutions de Paris*, was "a kind of shark raised aloft on the end of a pikestaff; the sea animal had its mouth open and was showing its teeth; on its body was written, "Respect for the law." At the rear of the procession was a colossal statue of the law, "represented by a seated woman, leaning on the tablets of the rights of man . . ." The account in the *Révolutions de Paris*, clearly hostile, drew attention to the final stage of the festival when the procession ended at the Champ de Mars, where a picture of Simonneau's death was hung from a palm tree: "One thing worth observing . . . is that the organizers chose precisely the front of the altar of the fatherland . . . by which, on July 17, Bailly and Lafayette came and, in the name of martial law, shot down the patriots gathered on the altar."[34]

Different as the two festivals may have been in style and purpose, they shared some common characteristics. Both were draped in a high sense of purpose and reflected ideas and attitudes of the public-minded leaders who organized them. This was in marked contrast to festivals held in villages and towns throughout France from 1789 on that not only employed burlesque and parody, but also drew from the conventions and traditions of popular culture. Improvised festivals not held under official auspices acted out scenarios that included mud, manure, saints surrounded by nettles, kings and popes astride animals with Bibles tied to their tails, goats pulling feudal insignias, donkeys harnessed with episcopal ornaments, a calf's heart bearing an inscription, identifying it as the heart of an aristocrat, a fat pig, representing the

king with a nanny goat as his "execrable companion," bishops mounted
backwards on donkeys, women flogging saints' statues, and revellers
dressed in clothing stolen from churches.[35] Motifs in these festivals
drew from a repertoire of cuckolds and village dolts that were part of an
ancient popular lore. Like the carnival celebrations they mimicked they
were potentially explosive. Parody could lead to rioting and violence.
Unlike official festivals, they were spontaneous, free, and unleashed
pent-up feelings. Popular festivals were cut from one piece of cloth; official festivals were measured out from a different piece. Official festivals reflected the elite makeup of the revolutionary leadership. This
was true of the *Fête de la Fédération*, the Festival of Châteauvieux, the
Festival of Simonneau, and subsequent official festivals. Neither David
nor Quatremère de Quincy, organizers of two 1792 official festivals, allowed the events they orchestrated to be spattered by the mud of popular festivals. Divided as the two organizers were politically, they were of
one mind in maintaining proper standards of decorum in the festivals;
they refused to descend to the low, common, and obscene. Both stood
for control. Moreover, both employed allegory, which set their festivals
apart from the parody, pungency, and crudeness of popular festivals. In
all of these respects, David and Quatremère brought elite habits of
mind and standards of taste to the festivals they orchestrated.

After the Châteauvieux Festival the next Jacobin festival orchestrated by David was held in commemoration of a revolutionary martyr,
Louis-Michel Le Peletier de Saint-Fargeau, who was assassinated on
January 20 by a former royal guard, because he had voted for the death
of Louis XVI. Barère moved in the Convention for the pantheonization
of Le Peletier on January 21, and M.-J. Chénier recommended that
David and Gossec organize the funeral procession. Robespierre, not
content just to support Barère's motion, wanted to eulogize the fallen
martyr. "Peletier," he said, "was a noble; Peletier held a leading place
in one of the most powerful bodies under the monarchy [Avocat in the
Châtelet of Paris]. Peletier enjoyed an immense fortune, and yet from
the beginning of the Revolution he was a defender of popular principles, and he was one of the most zealous founders of the Republic."[36]
Beside supporting Barère's motion for Le Peletier's pantheonization,
Robespierre joined him in a call to search the houses of those suspected
of harboring emigrés; he believed it imperative to "avenge the assassinated patriot."[37] For the funeral procession organized by David, Le
Peletier's body, its torso uncovered, was put on a couch that was placed
on a pedestal in the Place Vendôme, where a statue of Louis XIV had
stood before being pulled down after the storming of the Tuileries.
David put steps around the pedestal from which candles and large
burners wafted incense.

David proposed on January 25, the day after Le Peletier's pantheonization, that "a marble monument [be created] to show posterity how Le Peletier looked as you saw him yesterday, when he was being carried to the Pantheon." Then David decided to do a painting of Le Peletier, which he described in a speech to the Convention on March 29:

> I shall have done my duty if one day I cause an aging patriarch, surrounded by his large family, to say, "Children, come and see the first of your representatives to die for your freedom. See how peaceful his face is—when you die for your country, you die with a clear conscience. Do you see the sword hanging over his head by just a hair? Well, children, that shows how much courage Michel Le Peletier and his noble companions needed to rout the evil tyrant who had oppressed us for so long, for, had they set a foot wrong, the hair would have broken and they would all have been killed. Do you see that deep wound? You are crying, children, and turning your heads away! Just look at the crown; it's the crown of immortality. The nation can confer it on any of its children; be worthy of it."[38]

It is clear from David's description of the painting that he was already at work on it. The history of the painting was peculiar. Originally it hung on the wall of the Convention, behind the President, where it was joined later by David's second martyr painting, *Marat Assassinated*, but it was returned to David in 1795, after the fall of Robespierre. David subsequently sold the painting to Le Peletier's daughter, who came bitterly to oppose everything the Revolution stood for; she destroyed the painting of her father, and purchased all available copies of P. A. Tardieu's engraving of the work and destroyed them as well. All that now remains of what must have been one of David's most deeply felt and finest paintings is a single, tattered Tardieu engraving and a drawing of the work by Anatole Devosge (figs. 103, 104). From the mutilated print and the drawing, one can at least see how David designed the first of his martyr paintings. As he indicated in his speech to the Convention on March 29, a sword hangs "by a thread" over the body of Le Peletier. The sword pierces a piece of paper, a ballot that reads I vote the death of the tyrant. Blood drips from the sword and the white sheets on which the martyr lies would have been streaked with blood. Both the drawing and engraving show the open wound on Le Peletier's side, but it is the engraving that captures most graphically the torn flesh, from which blood flows onto the sheets. Below the wound is the clenched, powerful fist of Le Peletier, which contrasts with the expression of calm on the dead martyr's face.

The image of Le Peletier was steeped in traditional Christian imagery. The recumbent figure of the revolutionary martyr alluded to Christ as a Man of Sorrows, but at the same time the seminude and

FIGURE 103.   P. A. Tardieu, *Engraving of David's Le Peletier de Saint-Fargeau*, Bibliothèque Nationale, Paris

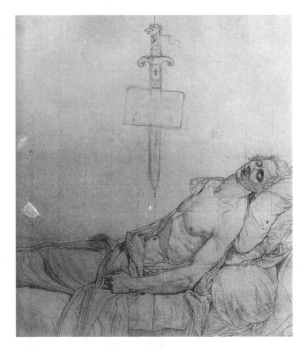

FIGURE 104.   A. Devosge, *Drawing of David's Le Peletier de Saint-Fargeau*, Musée des Beaux-Arts, Dijon

well-muscled body drew from the antique tradition of deathbed figures whose sculpted images were statements on posterity. The idealized face of Le Peletier, calm in repose, was an object of veneration, whereas the powerful torso, massive forearm, and clenched fist evoked Spartan manliness. Devoted to the Spartan ideal, as a good Rousseauist, Le Peletier favored an educational program that would separate boys from girls, submit boys to strict discipline, and form them into citizens willing to make all necessary sacrifices to the state. In his painting, David represented Le Peletier as manly and forceful, and calm and serene: the clenched fist projected his Spartan quality and the beatific face, consistent with Christian iconography, expressed a calm that is associated with the Passion of Christ. In countless images, reaching back to the Middle Ages, the crucified Christ is seen as serene in the knowledge that his suffering offers new hope to humankind. This was the very message, albeit within the context of a new religious system, that of the revolutionary religion, that came through in David's beatific image of Le Peletier.

David organized another Jacobin festival for a fallen revolutionary on April 28, 1793, in the midst of a bitter struggle in the Convention between Girondins and Jacobins. This festival was in honor of Claude Lazowski, a wealthy Pole, who was a devoted Jacobin. Robespierre regarded him as a close friend, for he played an active role in the *journées* of June 20, 1792 and August 10, 1792. In the factional strife that followed the King's execution, Lazowski had been conspicuous in anti-Girondin riots held on March 8–10, 1793. Pierre-Victurnien Vergniaud denounced him in the Convention on March 13, and called for his arrest. Marat defended Lazowski the next day, and, when Robespierre tried to speak on his behalf, he was denied the floor in what must have been a very heated meeting of the Convention. Then, on April 22, Lazowski died unexpectedly under what some believed were suspicious circumstances, perhaps poisoning. This was in the direct aftermath of an unsuccessful attempt by Girondins on April 13 to arraign Marat on charges of treason. It was on the same day that Marat was acquitted, April 24, that Robespierre delivered a eulogy on Lazowski at the Convention. "I was the intimate friend of Lazowski. I have known his entire soul. I have mourned Lazowski for two days and all the faculties of my soul are absorbed in my regrets for the immense loss to the Republic occasioned by his death."[39] In the midst of his speech one of the galleries in the Convention collapsed under the weight of too many bystanders, but the audience still "waved their hats in the air, and swore to avenge [Lazowski's] death."[40] However deeply Robespierre felt the loss of Lazowski, his eulogies on his behalf, both before and after his death, must be seen within the context of bitter factional strife in the Convention. So, too, must the funeral celebration in honor of Lazowski that was orchestrated by David. When the funeral was held on April 28, popular societies and sans-culotte Sections turned out in full force. With music by François-Joseph Gossec, sounding of the tocsin, pikes, and cannons in the procession, it achieved its objective which was to stir the populace. Lazowski's remains were put to rest before the Tree of Fraternity in the Place du Carrousel, where he had raised the cry of insurrection on August 10. David's orchestration of the ceremony was deliberately provocative and at one with the line taken by Robespierre in his speech to the Jacobins as plans were under way for the *journées* of May 31 and June 2 that would destroy the Girondins.

The next of the funerals David organized was for Jean-Paul Marat. When Charlotte Corday, a supporter of the Girondins, came to Paris to murder Marat, her purpose was to put the Revolution back on track. Having welcomed the Revolution in 1789, she remained firm in her support, however, her backing led to quarrels with her father over politics. Out of desperation, she took up residence in June 1791 with a spinster aunt in Caen. In May 1792, she wrote a letter, describing an incident in the nearby village of Verson. Local National Guardsmen tried to find local priests, who had refused to swear the oath of loyalty called for by the Civil Constitution of the Clergy. Fearing for their lives, the priests fled the area and as a result the Guardsmen sacked a chapel and took some fifty people, mostly women, prisoner. They not only bound the women with rope and forced them to walk to Caen, but they cut off the hair of a curé's sister and that of a canon's mother, and branded several women. Writing of the incident, Charlotte Corday said: "You ask me what happened at Verson. Every imaginable abomination. About fifty people were beaten and their hair cut off. It seems that it was largely women they had a grudge against. Three of them died a few days later. The rest are still ill . . . Among the women were the Abbé Adam's mother and the curé's sister." Corday felt the Jacobins had derailed the Revolution, and it was the demagogic Marat that she held most responsible. A Norman aristocrat by birth and a descendant of Corneille, she lived in a world of heroic idealism. "In Sparta and Athens there were many courageous women," she wrote, before going to Paris on July 11 to kill Marat on the floor of the Convention.[41] The event, as she imagined it, was to be public, it was to be exemplary, it was to result in her death on the spot, and it was to bring an end to revolutionary violence. The actual event turned out otherwise: Suffering from a fatal skin disease, Marat was confined to a bath in his house in the Cordeliers district, and it was there that Corday murdered Marat; far from putting an end to revolutionary violence, the deed unleashed further violence. According to J. M. Thompson, "Charlotte's deed was the prelude, not to a Girondin peace, but to a Jacobin vendetta."[42]

It was Marat who had nominated David to the Convention; when Girondins tried to arraign Marat for treason in April 1793, David stood up in the Convention and said, "I demand that you assassinate me. I am also a virtuous man . . . liberty will triumph."[43] Robespierre was less enthusiastic about Marat than David. At the time of Marat's impeachment, he said, "I am quite able to appreciate Marat's worth; and I say that, whilst he has been guilty of some errors of fact, and some faults of style, his opponents are conspirators and traitors." Continuing, Robespierre described Marat as "a man whose mistakes I have never shared."[44] Thrown together in the Jacobins by the force of circumstances, Robespierre and Marat were not close personally. They are known to have met together privately on only one occasion. Robespierre did not join the rush of praise for Marat in the Convention on July 14, the day after his murder, but limited himself to calling for an inquiry into the circumstances of his death.

In a meeting of the Jacobins that night he expressed surprise, undoubtedly mixed with annoyance, over all that had been said that day in the Convention about Marat's poverty, his paper, L'Ami du peuple, and about plans for a funeral in his honor. Robespierre did not view a public funeral for Marat with favor: "It is not necessary now to give the people the spectacle of a public funeral, but when the Republic is finally victorious."[45] Robespierre scoffed at the idea of burying Marat next to Mirabeau, but Pierre-Louis Bentabole felt otherwise. Marat would be buried there, he said, "in spite of those who are jealous of him."[46] The pressure for a public funeral for Marat was irresistible; it offered Jacobins an occasion to use it for their own ends. On July 15 the Convention entrusted David and Nicolas-Sylvestre Maure with responsibility for the funeral. Before it was held, Marat's body was placed in the Church of the Cordeliers, where members of the Convention, representatives of the Sections and political clubs, and enormous crowds came to pay their respects. By the time Marat's body was placed on display it had begun to decompose, and under the circumstances David's and Maure's elaborate funeral plans had to be abandoned. When the modified procession was held on the night of July 16 it made its way to the sound of muffled drums and accompanied by torches. According to David Dowd, Marat's funeral "was no crude incitement to mass vengeance";[47] this was not a provocative event; it was not designed to stir popular anger. Paris remained in the throes of a protracted political crisis and the most urgent need was for stability. Thus, Jacobin funerals could follow markedly different scripts.

In April 1793, the public funeral for Lazowski had been deliberately provocative; it was held as plans for a Paris insurrection were under way and in honor of a Jacobin who had been active in bringing sans-culottes into the streets for revolutionary journées. Moreover, Robespierre, a friend of Lazowski, threw the full weight of his support

behind his funeral. Three months later, in July 1793, the political landscape was different, and now the need was for calm in the Sections, not
a call to arms. When a public funeral was held in honor of Marat, it was
not provocative, and it was held in spite of Robespierre's reservations.

In a July 14 speech in the Convention, Guiraud called not only for
Charlotte Corday's death but for torture worse than death. In that same
speech he said, "Where are you, David? You have transmitted to posterity the picture of Le Peletier dying for his country, and here is another painting for you to do." David replied, "Yes, I will do it."[48] He
had visited Marat in his home the day before his death, where, as he described the visit, "I found him in a striking position. He had beside him
a wood block with paper and ink on it, and his hand, hanging over the
bath-tub, wrote down his latest thoughts for the people's safety. . . . I
thought it might be interesting to show him in the position I found
him, writing for the people's happiness."[49] In his painting, *Marat Assassinated* (fig. 105), David took liberties to heighten the effect he
hoped to achieve. He wanted to project an image of Marat as the friend
of the people. When Charlotte Corday was arrested, a letter that she
had written earlier in the day but had not shown to Marat was found
tucked into her dress. In a slightly amended form, it was read at a
meeting of the Convention; it was this letter that David showed in the
dead hand of Marat, smeared by his own blood. The original version of
the letter ended with the sentence, "I am wretched; that alone gives
me a right to your protection." In the version David heard in the meeting of the Convention, the letter stated: "I need only make you see how
wretched I am to have a right to your esteem." In the painting, David
added changes of his own to heighten the effect he strove for. It reads:
"It is enough for me to be truly wretched to have a right to your kindness."[50] Through David's verbal amendment, the duplicity of Charlotte Corday had been heightened; she was seen to have appealed to the
"kindness" of the man that she had killed with her knife.

The liberties taken by David in *Marat Assassinated* may be regarded as part of the painting's rhetoric, as part of an argument to sway
and influence, to mold opinion, and as such it can be placed within the
context of revolutionary propaganda. But more important was David's
authentic personal feeling, which he transferred to the painting. *Marat
Assassinated* like *Le Peletier de Saint-Fargeau* was a work of idealism.
Both revolutionary martyrs, as chance had it, were known for their ug-
liness, but in David's pristine and elevated paintings they were physi-
cally transformed, their features were smoothed over and made worthy
of veneration. In David's first martyr painting, the sword that took Le
Peletier's life pierced the piece of paper on which he had written the
words, "I vote for the martyr's death." The sword dripped blood on Le

FIGURE 105.   J.-L. David, *Marat Assassinated*, Musées royaux des Beaux-Arts, Brussels

Peletier's well-muscled body, above the gaping wound. In *Marat Assassinated*, the bloody knife used by Charlotte Corday rested beside Marat's hand, which still held the pen he had used to write a widow, whom he offered support through a gift of revolutionary assignats. Blood was not only on the blade of the knife but the handle as well, as if to drive home the point that Corday, the assassin had blood on her hands, the blood of a martyr. Marat's blood flowed freely from the wound below Marat's collarbone, the wound that caused his death. It flowed down the chest of Marat, onto the sheet that lined the tub, and into the bath water, making the water blood red. Brilliantly conceived and executed, *Marat Assassinated* was arguably David's masterpiece, its greatness achieved in spite of the painting's falsifications.

Like *Le Peletier de Saint-Fargeau*, *Marat Assassinated* draws from traditional Christian iconography. The image of Marat is derived from the figure of Christ taken from the cross, of which there are countless examples, although necessarily only the upper part of the body is seen. That the water is blood red is visually striking and symbolically significant: David's original title for *Marat Assassinated* was *Marat a son denier soupir*, which links the painted image to the body, and blood of Christ and the Eucharist. Daringly, David presents Marat, a revolutionary martyr, as a figure of religious veneration, an icon of worship. The wound in Marat's chest, as Charles-Pierre Baudelaire said, is a sacrilegious wound; offsetting it is the white turban, suggesting a halo.

The starting point of David's next festival, the August 10, 1793 Festival of Unity and Indivisibility, begins on May 30, when the Paris Sections demanded a festival on the anniversary of the storming of the Tuileries. The Convention approved the measure the next day, the day of the May 31 insurrection, while sans-culottes were lined up in its meeting place in the Tuileries. David was given responsibility for the festival and he presented a long report to the Convention on July 11, describing in close detail the five stages of the day-long ceremony. The first stage began with a gathering at the site of the Bastille; the procession then moved to the boulevard Poissonière, where the events of October 5 and 6, 1789 were commemorated; it traveled next to the Place de la Révolution, where Louis XVI had been guillotined and where the "immortal and imperishable *journée*" of August 10 was celebrated; it proceeded then to the Place des Invalides, where a colossal statue of Hercules, symbolizing the French people, dealt blows to monsters of federalism; and finally, at the end of the day, the procession moved to the Champ de Mars, where the people swore an oath to the new Constitution, ate a frugal meal, and watched a pantomime reenactment of the bombardment of Lille.[51] What is striking about David's orchestration of the event was the avoidance of the storming of the Tuileries a year earlier that was the occasion of the ceremony. This was not accidental.

The period between the sans-culotte demand on May 30 for the Festival of Unity and the time of its celebration on August 10 was troubled. Girondin deputies fled Paris after the June 2 *journée* and joined forces with the counterrevolution in the south of France; losses were inflicted on revolutionary armies by Vendéan rebels in the west; Austrian armies captured French fortresses in the north; and in Paris, on the floor of the Convention, *enragés* attacked the government for its inability to provide cheap bread and, as Jacques Roux put it, for supporting laws that were "cruel to the poor, because they have been made by the rich and for the rich." Roux lectured the Convention on its failings on June 25; Danton's moderate government fell on July 10; Marat was murdered on July 13; Robespierre was appointed to the Committee of Public Safety on July 27; and on August 11 he told the Jacobins that the Constitution, promulgated on the previous day, during the Festival of Unity and Indivisibility, would have to be suspended. Robespierre began his speech to the Jacobins with dire warnings: "Friends of liberty, I have come to warn you that the moment has arrived when the full truth must be known if the *patrie* is to be saved by all remaining measures. . . . Our armies have experienced new reversals; our enemies are more audacious than ever; all our problems are rooted in the same source, villainy and treason . . ."[52]

The Festival of Unity and Indivisibility was a Rousseauistic morality play adapted to the period in which it was planned and held. "Magnanimous and generous people," David said during introductory remarks of his July 11 report, "people truly worthy of liberty, French people, it is you that I offer as a spectacle in the eyes of the Eternal. In you alone He recognizes his own work; He sees men and brothers as equal, as if they issued from Divine hands."[53] Elevated sentiments, these, worthy of Rousseau, and when the August 10 festival began at the site of the Bastille, renamed the Champ de Réunion, the space was planted in trees and shrubs, as if to evoke the spirit of Rousseau. A cantata by Gossec with a text based on Rousseau's *Profession du Foi d'un Vicaire Savoyard* was sung first, and then Marie-Jean Hérault de Séchelles, president of the Convention, received and drank a cup of water that issued from a Fount of Regeneration represented by an allegorical figure of Nature (fig. 106). He then passed the cup to eighty-six old men, representing each of France's departments. This took place on the site of the Bastille, but the ceremony omitted all reference to the heroism and violence of July 14.

David organized this stage of the festival around symbols and allegories that were far removed from the historical event associated with the

FIGURE 106.   Helman Engraving of Monnet Drawing, *The Fount of Regeneration on the Ruins of the Bastille*, Bibliothèque Nationale, Paris

space on which it was held. The second stage of the festival was held on the rue Poissonière where women of Paris had gathered on October 5 before marching to Versailles. As Simon Schama has written, "The disturbingly potent image of belligerent *poissardes* astride their cannon [were] carefully neutralized in conformity with standard Rousseauan-Jacobin doctrine on the wife-mother role for women patriots. The authentic women of October were replaced by prettified actresses whose brows were crowned with laurel and who were told . . . 'Let all the martial and the generous virtues flow together in your maternal milk and in the heart of the nursing women of France.'"[54] At the next stage, the crowd gathered at the Place de la Révolution, where Louis XVI had been guillotined. To get there it passed around the Place du Carrousel, which a year earlier had been littered with bodies in the aftermath of the Storming of the Tuileries. This space was avoided. The focal point of stage three of the festival was the pedestal that once bore the large equestrian statue of Louis XV, around which scepters, crowns, and orbs were scattered, the attributes of monarchy. As in the first two stages, allegory replaced the historically specific; attention was not focused on the execution of the King or the violence of August 10; allegory was the instrument by which history was transformed into a morality play. An Allegory of the French people made another appearance in stage four at the Place des Invalides, where a gigantic statue of Hercules, stood on a mountain built specially for the festival, smashing with his club the monsters of federalism that writhed at his feet (fig. 107).

When David planned the Festival of Unity and Indivisibility, parts of the south of France were securely in the hands of Girondin federalists

FIGURE 107.   Anonymous Engraving, *The French People overwhelming the Hydra of Federalism, Festival of Unity*, August 10, 1793, Musée Carnavelet, Paris

and revolutionary armies were incurring punishing defeats in the west. An accurate response to the crisis of summer 1793 was Robespierre's speech to the Jacobins on August 11: "Our armies have experienced new reversals; our enemies are more audacious than ever," not David's allegorical portrayal of victory over federalists in the penultimate stage of the August 10 festival. At the end of the fifth and final stage of the daylong festival, the crowd was entertained by a mock bombardment of Lille; a special fortress was built between the Seine and the Champ de

Mars. Beyond the frontiers, revolutionary armies were being routed; in the center of Paris, in entertainment, France was triumphant. Projecting such an image was not cheap. Altogether, the Festival of Unity and Indivisibility cost 1,200,000 livres, no small outlay in a time of severe hardship in Paris and throughout France. Propaganda was expensive, but to the Jacobins it was worth the price. And it was the genius of David—in this context the word has an ironic twist—that served the Jacobin cause.

Neither David nor Robespierre played any role in the next revolutionary festival, the November 10, 1793 Festival of Reason. This festival was an episode in a campaign to dechristianize France, which began in the fall of 1793 and continued into the spring of 1794. In September, Joseph Fouché, a representative on mission sent into central France to enforce government policy, launched a campaign against Christianity. Himself a former priest, Fouché denounced "religious sophistry" on September 22 and inaugurated a civic religion that included a "Feast of Brutus." An opponent of clerical celibacy, Fouché ordered priests who refused to marry to adopt orphans or support the aged. On October 10 he issued a decree forbidding the practice of any creed except that of universal morality, and Christianity was banned. Other representatives on mission followed Fouché's lead.

In Quimper, a village in Brittany, a certain Dagorne, one of a team of three officials, occupied the marketplace when local peasants came together for market day, and in full public view he subjected holy vessels to "the most obscene and disgusting profanation."[55] Among the more zealous dechristianizers were soldiers in the revolutionary army. When an army of two thousand arrived in Auxerre, cannoneers smashed in church doors and destroyed sacred images. A crucifix was then carried around town to be spat upon. A soldier cut off the nose of a quarryman who refused to participate in the profanation. As representatives of the government and soldiers of the Revolution attacked churches, villagers in provincial France were encouraged to act out an ancient anticlericalism. Local festivals were held, drawing from traditional practices, that mocked the pope and included donkeys dressed in bishops' robes. Churches were vandalized, windows smashed, and bells melted down and made into cannon. The tide of dechristianization passed from provincial France to the capital, and on November 7, Jean-Baptiste-Joseph Gobel, the bishop of Paris, appeared before the Convention, resigned his office, and gave up his insignia.

Three days later the Festival of Reason was held in Notre Dame, which was renamed the "Temple of Reason" and was decked out in classical trappings appropriate for the occasion. A mountain was built where the high altar had stood, and sitting atop the mountain was a temple of philosophy. From the top of the temple, in the midst of a ceremony that included patriotic maidens dressed in virginal white, emerged a female wearing the *bonnet rouge* and representing Liberty. At the end of the ceremony the actress, citizeness Maillard of the Paris Opéra, who had taken the role of Liberty, accompanied officials of the Commune to the Tuileries, where they were welcomed by the Convention. The ceremony first given at Notre Dame was repeated in the presence of the Convention, and after it was completed and the president and secretaries kissed the goddess of Reason fraternally the members of the Convention marched to Notre Dame, "in the midst of general enthusiasm and joyful acclamations."[56] Not all members of the Convention were enthusiastic about the Festival of Reason or the dechristianization campaign. Robespierre was deeply offended, and argued against dechristianization on November 21: "What right," he asked, did the dechristianizers have attacking "the liberty of cults in the name of liberty, attacking fanaticism with a new fanaticism?" The Convention should never support the "false measures" of dechristianization. "Atheism is *aristocratic*; the idea of a Supreme Being who responds to oppressed innocence and punishes triumphal crime is popular."[57] Among the dechristianizers were political rivals, Jacques-René Hébert and some of his followers, with whom Robespierre was locked in a struggle for power. When Robespierre first spoke out against the dechristianizers, he did so as a voice in the wilderness. The dechristianization campaign grew out of some of the deepest forces within the Revolution, and received impetus from the revolutionary calendar decreed by the Convention in October. As William Doyle has written, "The new republican calendar marked a further stage in the divorce between the French state and any sort of religion."[58] Opposing dechristianization, Robespierre took up a cause that put him in direct conflict with powerful rivals.

Committed to festivals as a means to regenerate the people—according to his lights—Robespierre was not well disposed to the use of festivals by rivals as instruments of their purposes. November 1793 was not a good festival month from Robespierre's viewpoint. Besides the Festival of Reason in Paris, a festival held in Lyons was also objectionable. Lyons had thrown up the banner of counterrevolution on May 29, 1793, but the rebellious city was retaken on October 9 by an army sent from Paris. A festival was held in the following month to commemorate a local Jacobin, Joseph Chalier, who had been executed in the aftermath of the May 29 rebellion. Strictly loyal to Paris Jacobins, Chalier had strong support in the capital. Among those who praised Chalier was Robespierre, but he did so with less enthusiasm than a fellow member of the Committee of Public Safety, Jean-Marie Collot d'Herbois. For Robespierre loyalty to Chalier was dictated by circumstances, but to Collot Chalier was a genuine hero. Both men were fanatics. According to D. M. G. Sutherland, Chalier, a "crazy demagogue," had declared that "nine hundred victims would be executed . . . and their bodies thrown into the Rhône."[59] Collot, determined to punish Lyons, explained that after evacuating most of the Lyonnais, "it will be easy to make the city disappear, and to say with truth, 'Lyons is no more.' "[60] Describing the festival he gave in commemoration of Chalier shortly after his arrival in Lyons on November 4, Collot said, "all hearts swelled, the silence of sorrow was interrupted by cries a thousand times repeated: 'Vengeance! Vengeance!' " He added: "We swear it, the people will be avenged; our severe courage will reply to their just impatience; the soil that was reddened by the blood of patriots will be overturned; everything raised by crime and vice will be annihilated."[61] An eyewitness described the violence that surrounded the festival: "To purge the earth and the place where the last remains of this great man were to repose, ten heads were immolated yesterday, and perhaps ten more will die tomorrow."[62] Another eyewitness drew up a report on the festival: "The most remarkable facts are first that an ass was dressed as a Monseigneur. A mitre and cross and all the finest pontifical garments were put on him. And church vases of gold and silver were carried before the ass. And along the way incense was burnt for him. And they said vessels were broken on the tomb."[63] According to R. R. Palmer, the "crude impieties" of the Chalier festival were in direct opposition to Robespierre's policy of respecting the objects of Catholic worship. Collot was an ally of the Hébertists and a dechristianizer, and in Lyons he organized a festival whose impieties and mockeries went against the wishes of Robespierre.

While records are not extant of the meetings of the Committee of Public Safety on which both Collot and Robespierre sat, the festivals that each sponsored say much about their differences—and conflicts. Collot organized the Chalier festival not only to grind in the message of repression to the once rebellious people of Lyons, but also within the context of Parisian politics. On December 1, he sent a letter to the Convention that was accompanied by a bust of Chalier, along with his mutilated head, which had been severed only after repeated blows from the guillotine.

> Citizen colleagues, we are sending you the bust of Chalier and his mutilated head, as it was when it emerged for the third time from below the axe of his ferocious murderers. When one seeks to move your sensibilities, uncover this bloody head to the eyes of the pusillanimous men who see only individuals; recall them by this energetic language to the severity of duty and to the impassiveness of the national representation. . . . No indul-

gence, citizen colleagues, no delay, no procrastination in the punishment of crime, if you wish to produce a salutary effect.[64]

When Collot's letter arrived in Paris, Georges-Jacques Danton and the Indulgents were gaining support for relaxation of the Reign of Terror. Federalists in the south were all but crushed and beyond the frontiers the military tide ran in France's favor. Robespierre opposed the Hébertist type of terror, which sowed fear and furthered divisions by its excesses, and he was receptive, if only briefly, to pleas for moderation. So, too, was the Convention, which arrested Charles-Philippe Ronsin, an Hébertist commander of the revolutionary army, and François-Nicolas Vincent, Hébert's ally in the War Office, on December 17. Four days later, Collot returned to Paris from Lyons to do battle with the Indulgents on their own ground. He arrived a day after the Commune held a festival in honor of Chalier, in which the mutilated head of the dead man, placed under a black veil, had been paraded through the streets of Paris. This was an Hébertist festival, a type that Robespierre opposed; it was given when he was wavering between a policy of moderation and continuation of the Terror.

Robespierre was at a critical turning point at the end of December 1793, as was the Revolution. As the dominant figure on the Committee of Public Safety, he was the creator or the architect of policies that had achieved great successes, both within France and in the war beyond her borders against foreign powers arrayed against the Revolution. The representatives on mission had faced colossal problems, but they had carried out their work with resolution, force, and a measure of success that, given the time they had been allowed, is difficult for the historian, even now, to grasp. In some measure, the successes resulted from sheer exertion of will. With the fall of Toulon, the last center of the counter-revolution had been crushed, apart from the Vendée, and revolutionary armies had achieved victories that turned the tide of war in France's favor. So why not relax the Terror? Why not consolidate the hard-earned gains, as the Indulgents argued circumstances now made possible? Cogent as Danton's arguments were, they were not entirely disinterested. Revelations of corruption within the government would soon come out that would compromise Danton, and, for now, buying time could best be achieved through a relaxation of revolutionary vigilance.

The main problem for Robespierre was the political struggle between the Dantonists who favored conciliation, and the militants on the far left, Collot d'Herbois, Jean-Nicolas Billaud-Varenne, and their Hébertist allies in Paris. However great the Revolution's successes had been there were still problems, not in the south and not beyond the borders, but in Paris. When Robespierre committed himself to continuing the Terror—he did so with the support and undoubted encouragement of Saint-Just, who returned to Paris from Alsace in the first week of January—he placed himself on a collision course with the competing groups, the Dantonists and Hébertists, whose internecine conflicts were instrumental in continuation of the Terror. They were consumed by the engine for which they provided the fuel. Their destruction did not end the Terror; not only did the Terror continue, but it accelerated, as legislation swept away limits previously placed on the Revolutionary Tribunal. First, in the laws of April 16 (27 Germinal) and 8 May (19 Floréal), the Revolutionary Tribunal was given exclusive jurisdiction over cases of counterrevolutionary crime. Then came the law of June 10 (22 Prairial), whose fourth article expressed a decisive shift in the Tribunal's mission from one that was judicial to one that was political. Its mission now was "to punish the enemies of the people." This legislation allowed arrests on the grounds of mere denunciation; the accused were denied the assistance of attorneys; and they could not testify on their own behalf. Therefore, the death curve rose sharply in June and July of 1794. Robespierre, who presided over the session of June 10 in the Convention, did not hesitate to justify its measures: "We shall brave the perfidious insinuation of excessive severity with which some have sought to attack measures prescribed by the public interest. This severity is redoubtable only to conspirators, only to enemies of the law."[65]

It was when Robespierre committed himself to continuation of the Terror at the end of December 1793 that he entered into the closest working relationship with David. In a *Report on the Principles of Revolutionary Government* delivered to the Convention on December 25, he announced continuation and intensification of the Terror: ". . .only good citizens deserve public protection, and the punishment of the people's enemies is death."[66] This was the day after Barère had announced on the floor of the Convention that Toulon had fallen to a revolutionary army; on the same day David presented a plan to the Convention for a Festival of the Taking of Toulon. David's program was accepted the next day and was praised that night in the Jacobins, particularly by Augustin Robespierre, Maximilien's brother. Held on December 30, the festival was a victory celebration with military panoply suitable for the occasion. Soldiers from the fourteen armies of the Republic and captured battle flags were followed by girls in white with tricolor sashes and members of the Convention who marched *en masse*, held together by a tricolor ribbon. All of this was accompanied by salvoes of artillery, the sound of trumpets and drums, and patriotic songs. If the festival was to be "a triumph of the Mountain party," it also strove to stir patriotic feeling and to solidify support for the Revolution. Its celebratory character was in marked contrast to the provocative festival for Chalier held ten days earlier, which was staged in spite of Robespierre's opposition to festivals of that type.

The Festival of the Taking of Toulon was not Robespierre's only response to the festival for Chalier. On December 15, five days before the Festival for Chalier, Barère read a report to the Convention by General Desmarres that described the death of Joseph Bara, a thirteen-year-old who had been killed in the Vendée by Chouan rebels when he refused to give them horses. "Yesterday this brave child was surrounded by brigands and chose to die rather than give them the two horses he was leading."[67] Robespierre was quick to see the propaganda value of the incident, and on December 28 he requested a Panthéon burial for the boy martyr. This was eight days after the Chalier festival and two days before the Festival of the Taking of Toulon. In his speech to the Convention, Robespierre transformed the circumstances of Bara's death. Desmarres had said the boy was killed rather than give up the horses he was leading, but in Robespierre's version Bara was "Surrounded by brigands who threatened to kill him and ordered him to cry 'Long live the King!'" It was under these circumstances, Robespierre reported, "he died shouting 'Long live the Republic!'" Continuing his freely invented version of Bara's death, Robespierre said: "This small child supported his mother on his earnings; he divided his loyalties between his filial affections and his country. It would be impossible to find a more perfect example to kindle the love of glory, country, and virtue in young hearts."[68]

That Robespierre called for Bara's pantheonization eight days after the festival for Chalier was not accidental. Revolutionary martyrs were used to further political objectives, and Chalier served the purposes of Collot and his Hébertist allies. The December 20 Chalier festival could ignite sparks of protest in sans-culotte Sections that Robespierre wanted to extinguish. Under these circumstances, the boy martyr Joseph Bara was perfectly suited to Robespierre's objectives. What Robespierre wanted was to dampen the spirit of faction, to find a symbol of unity, to honor a hero who was outside politics. Such a hero was Joseph Bara, a boy who had no political past, was beyond controversy, and with whom all good revolutionaries could identify. After calling for Bara's pantheonization, Robespierre recommended that David arrange the funeral ceremony, but as of yet without establishing a fixed timetable. On February 4, 1794, *Le Républicain* reported the death of Agricol Viala, a boy who was killed in Marseilles, a center of counterrevolution, and as plans moved forward for a festival to honor Joseph Bara they now included Viala.

As plans for the Bara and Viala festival were moving forward, Robespierre gave a report to the Convention on May 7 that called for national festivals. He had argued in favor of national festivals on February 10, 1792 in a speech to the Legislative Assembly, before becoming involved in the various festivals in which he and David worked together, Jacobin festivals, the first of which was the Festival of Châteauvieux. Jacobin festivals had particular agendas and assumed different forms; they were determined by the circumstances that brought them about. They could be provocative or conciliatory; they could stir the Sections or try to maintain calm in the Sections; they could be held at Robespierre's behest or with his approval, or they could be held against his wishes. Always they grew out of political divisions within the Revolution; they reflected the ongoing conflict between competing factions. If they aimed for national unity that was but a secondary objective, subordinate to the more immediate goal of mobilizing support against rival groups and enemy forces. While Robespierre had favored national festivals with the Rousseauist objective of achieving unity within a patriotic citizenry as early as February 1792, conditions were not right at that time for that model to be imposed. Much had changed when Robespierre advanced a proposal in May 1794 for Rousseauist national festivals. In March and April of 1794 forces on both the Left and Right of Robespierre, the Hébertists and Dantonists, had been destroyed, the counterrevolution had been largely crushed, and the tide of war now ran in France's favor. Under these circumstances, Robespierre was in a position to push for and achieve his plan for national festivals.

His May 7 *Report on Religious and Moral Ideas and Republican Principles*, referred to at the beginning of this chapter, struck a positive note at the very outset, as if to proclaim the Revolution's successes. As the "clamor of our victories resounds throughout the world" the "legislators of the French Republic, with new solicitude, watch over themselves and their country, and strengthen the principles upon which its stability and its happiness must depend." As he laid out a moral vision that offered hope for a better future, Rousseau was his guide: "Nature tells us that man was born to be free, and the experience of centuries shows him to be a slave. His rights are written in his heart, and his humiliation in history." The founders of the French Republic should not despair over past crimes against humanity but recognize that the world had changed, thanks to the achievements of the human mind, scientific progress, and the torch of reason. The French people in particular had led the way, having "outdistanced by two thousand years the rest of the human race . . . Europe is on its knees before the shadows of the tyrants whom we are punishing." Only France, "This delightful land which we inhabit, and which nature caresses with special affection, is made to be the domain of liberty and happiness; this sensitive and proud people were indeed born for glory and for virtue." But the reign of virtue that was the unique achievement of the French people was opposed by the "unceasing efforts of the kings leagued against us, and of all the conspirators, to perpetuate among us the prejudices and vices of the monarchy." The Revolution, in all of its glory, was confronted by enemies, the "tyrants" beyond the frontiers of France, the despot monarchs of the world, and "conspirators" within France who "regretted the passing of the old regime" and tried to "enchain" the French people, "by means of subversion, revolt, and corruption of their morals." The internal enemies of whom he spoke were the dechristianizers who "plotted in the darkness of night" against the Convention. The "atheism" of the dechristianizers was "linked to a system of conspiracy against the republic." The dechristianizers "raised immorality not only into a system but into a religion . . . and attempted to extinguish all generous sentiments by their example as well as by precepts." It was the wish of these wicked people that "not a single good man remained on earth, so they would never encounter a single accuser." Robespierre regarded dechristianizers as enemies of the state, and he felt there was but one response to their nefarious plots, belief in the Supreme Being and "the immortality of the soul," which was a "continual recall to justice, and, therefore, was "social and republican." At the end of his speech, Robespierre called for "a system of well organized national festivals [that] would be at once the sweetest bond of fraternity and the most powerful bond of regeneration." Of the thirty-six festivals called for by Robespierre, the first was to be the Festival of the Supreme Being and Nature (Article XV). "All of our festivals," Robespierre said, "should be celebrated under the auspices of the Supreme Being; let them be so consecrated."[69]

Robespierre's report to the Convention that ended with a call for national festivals was surely motivated, in part, by tactical considerations, but more importantly it offered a moral vision that revealed the extent of Rousseau's influence on Robespierre's thought. It can be regarded as part of the Rousseauist discourse that passed through and helped give shape to the Revolution. The victory of Rousseau over Montesquieu in 1789 meant more than instituting a unicameral rather than a bicameral legislature; its results extended beyond the forms of government and passed into the minds of the men who dominated the Revolution.

This is what comes through in Robespierre's May 7 report to the Convention, with its moral polarities that separated the righteous from the unrighteous, men of patriotic virtue from those who "betrayed their country" with "criminal plots," the "Enemies of the people, whoever you may be."

It is useful to contrast this mode of discourse, this way of organizing the world, with the Montesquieuist mode and its very different mental scheme. Montesquieu had said, "Great God, how can we possibly be always right and others always wrong." Uneasy about true believers and absolutes of right and wrong, he was disposed to look at issues from different perspectives, and to develop forms of compromise between those who had different agendas and viewpoints. Moreover, he was aware of dangers inherent in the exercise of power: "Every man with power is led to abuse it. He presses on until he encounters some limit. Who would have thought it, *vertu* itself needs limits." Placing limits on virtue was not a formula Robespierre was disposed to follow, above all not during a revolution, when, as he said in his February 5, 1794 *Report on the Principles of Political Morality*, "virtue . . . without terror is fatal; terror . . . without virtue is impotent."[70] The Terror was accelerating, particularly after the law of June 10 that swept aside the last vestiges of judicial protection offered those accused of crimes against the Revolution. Robespierre's plans for national festivals that were to achieve a goal of Rousseauist unity were set against the backdrop of the Terror and its rapidly accelerating death curve.

When Robespierre gave his report to the Convention, David had already completed plans for the Festival of the Supreme Being. He gave a very detailed report on the festival to the Convention on May 7, and, in the following weeks, he headed a team of artists, sculptors, and carpenters, one of whom was Maurice Duplay, Robespierre's landlord, that built the props for the grand celebration. When the day of the festival arrived on June 8, 20 Prairial in the revolutionary calendar, the weather was clear and beautiful. Parisians from the forty-eight Sections went to their headquarters; at a given signal, they proceeded to the Tuileries gardens. Awaiting arrival of the people, inside the Tuileries palace, were members of the Convention. Upon receiving word that they should join the people below, deputies, led by Robespierre, who happened to be president at the time, entered the garden and took seats in an amphithéâtre specially installed for the occasion. In front of the amphithéâtre was a statue of Atheism surrounded by figures of ambition, discord, and misery. Robespierre began a speech but, before completing it, he set a torch to the symbolic statues, which disappeared into nothing. "From the debris rose a calm and serene figure of Wisdom."[71] Robespierre then completed his speech, which brought to a close the first stage of the ceremony. The crowd then dispersed to the sounds of a "simple joyous song" and proceeded to the Champ de Mars, not by chance but according to David's carefully devised plan. A squadron of cavalry, drummer boys, students from the Institute of Music, men and women from twenty-four of the sections, members of the Convention and—in the middle of the procession for the sake of symmetry—a cart drawn by eight oxen and laden with allegorical paraphernalia, more drummers, men and women from the remaining twenty-four Sections, a carriage filled with blind children singing a hymn, and finally, at the rear of the procession, another squadron of cavalry, made their way from the Tuileries to the Champ de Mars in David's masterpiece of organization. At the head of the several hundred members of the Convention was Robespierre. Arriving at the Champ de Mars, the various contingents arrayed themselves, again according to plan, around a mountain built for the occasion. The mountain was decked with a Liberty Tree at the peak and covered with rocks, shrubbery, and paths; next to the mountain was a column that bore a statue of Hercules (fig. 108). Members of the Convention made their way by path to the summit, selected groups occupied places on the mountain below the summit, and the people of Paris gathered below. The people heard well-rehearsed members of the Convention sing the "Marseillaise," and, when prompted to join in, they sang the final refrain of Rouget de Lisle's patriotic anthem, swearing annihilation of crime and tyrants. After a final artillery salvo, the crowd departed as men, women, and children returned to their Sections and their homes.

The allegorical statue of Hercules, which towered over the crowd in the Champ de Mars, is known only through contemporary illustrations which indicate that it was derived, in part, from Michelangelo's

FIGURE 108.   Engraving published by Chéreau, *The Mountain erected on the Champ de Mars for the Festival of the Supreme Being*, June 8, 1794, Bibliothèque Nationale, Paris

David. This Hercules, of the finest artistic pedigree, was far removed from a club-wielding figure that had appeared in a contemporary print after David gave a speech in the Convention in November 1793 on plans to create a Hercules monument on the Pont Neuf where the Henri IV equestrian statue had been torn down. The editor of the radical *Révolutions de Paris* wrote in an editorial that he looked forward to a competition that would determine the type of Hercules that would appear on the monument. "No doubt, among the models entered in the competition, we will prefer the one which best projects the character of a sans-culotte with its figure of the people."[72] A contemporary engraving, "Le Peuple mangeur de Rois" (fig. 109), which shows a rough, bearded sans-culotte smashing a king with his club, is such an image. Adapted to a popular and sans-culotte revolutionary perspective, this club-wielding figure was an inversion of David's classical conception of an heroic Hercules. And it was that idealized conception, judging from contemporary illustrations, that was realized in the Hercules figure that towered over the passive audience in the last stage of the Robespierrist Festival of Reason on June 8, 1794.

R. R. Palmer has said of the Festival of the Supreme Being that, "it is more than likely" that Robespierre "had never been so happy as on that day." Palmer also explains that, according to some reports, "certain members of the Convention, marching behind their president in the front row on 20 Prairial, purposely lagged behind so that Robes-

FIGURE 109. Anonymous Engraving, *Le Peuple mangeur de Rois*, Musée Carnavelet, Paris

pierre would seem to be hurrying forward in a desire to march alone."[73] After power struggles with rival factions, Robespierre had destroyed enemies and emerged victorious over the dechristianizers, but all of this had been achieved at a cost. Those who had been among the Revolution's prominent leaders were some of its recent victims. Clear and beautiful as June 8 was, the Festival of the Supreme Being had a dark underside. In his finest moment, Robespierre presided over a grand Rousseauist spectacle, surrounded by the Convention, a throng estimated, undoubtedly with exaggeration, at a half million, and by scores of soldiers, musicians, and all of the costumes and theatricality of the day. Yet, Robespierre's end was near. The next festival that he planned, the Festival of Bara and Viala, originally scheduled for June 18 but rescheduled for July 28 (10 Thermidor), was not held. Robespierre's hold on power seemed unshakable; in fact, those close to him, leaders of the Convention, were apprehensive. Men they had known, friends in some cases, no less devoted to the Revolution than they, had gone to the guillotine. Were they safe? What were they to do? What some did was plot against Robespierre. Always imagining conspiracies, this time there was one, and, in a fateful meeting of the Convention on July 26, Robespierre made the terrible mistake of refusing to name conspirators after leveling charges of conspiracy. Thus did he seal his own fate.

Scheduled to be held on July 28, beginning at "three hours after noon," the festival for Bara and Viala was cancelled[74] under the auspices of Billaud-Varenne, who led the attack on Robespierre on July 27: "There can be no doubt that the festival planned for tomorrow was a tactic encircling the Convention and the Committees under the pretext of holding maneuvers for the young soldiers in front of the Convention."[75] After the festival cancellation, Robespierre and his followers were arrested; the only procession held on July 28 was the one that moved from the Conciergerie to the Place de la Révolution. The entoriage passed by the Duplay residence along the way amid popular revelry, and culminated in Robespierre's execution.

While the festival for Bara and Viala was not held, the project left behind two artifacts of the abortive event: David's July 11 report to the Convention on the festival and his unfinished painting, *Joseph Bara* (fig. 110). Contemporary illustrations of the death of Bara showed Chouans cutting down the thirteen-year-old boy (figs. 111, 112), but David departed almost completely from the historical circumstances of his death and showed not the boy martyr, who fights against counterrevolutionaries in the Vendée, but a nude, androgynous youth, who ecstatically clasps the tricolor in the moment of death. The pristine figure of the youth was in contrast to the language of David's July 11 report to the Convention:

Figure 110. J.-L. David, *Joseph Bara*, Musée Calvet, Avignon

FIGURE 111.   Anonymous Engraving, *Heroic Death of Young Bara*, Bibliothèque Nationale, Paris

Despotism attentuates and corrupts public opinion. . . . It proscribes without care all of the virtues and to assure its empire is preceded by terror and envelopes itself with fanaticism and wears the hat of ignorance. Everywhere squinting and perfidious treason follows it, and death and devastation. It meditates its crime in darkness and forges the chains of its unfortunate victims, from whom it sucks blood. Ingenious in tormenting [its victims], it builds Bastilles; in moments of leisure it invents torments and feasts its eyes on the scene of cadavers immolated by its fury.[76]

The intemperance of David's language in his report to the Convention is in striking contrast to the pristine figure of Joseph Bara in the painting he was working on at the time of his speech. Eschewing the violence that found expression in his speech, he portrayed the beautiful image of a youth, seemingly more female than male. It is an image that evokes sympathy, not one that expresses hostility or anger, and in that respect it is strangely at odds with David's speech given to the Convention. The moral qualities of the painting are at odds with the intemperance of the speech; between the speech and the painting there is what one might call a "principle of disjunction."

A principle of disjunction was at work at another level in David's *Joseph Bara.* For the Robespierrist leadership the Revolution was about

FIGURE 112.
P.-L. Debucourt, *The Death of Bara*, Bibliothèque Nationale, Paris

openness, the tearing away of masks; it was a discourse in Rousseauist transparency. For revolutionaries transparency was about openness, the dissolution of differences, the breaking down of barriers that in ancien régime society consigned people to different ranks and stations. Transparency was about simplicity; it was a positive, Rousseauist ideal that rejected the artificial forms of a fallen, corrupt society. Openness, simplicity, and unity were integral to the revolutionary idea of transparency, and it was that idea that was at the conceptual core of David's *Joseph Bara*. David's androgynous youth dissolved the most fundamental of barriers, that between the male and the female. It is impossible to say for certain that David did not intend to paint clothes over the boy martyr, but even if he planned on doing so, and the odds are against it, there were no genitalia in the painting. Besides dissolving the most fundamental of barriers, David created a figure whose simplicity and openness was congruent with the Rousseauist idea of transparency.[77]

The iconic figure of Joseph Bara expressed, in all of its pristine beauty, one of the central ideals of the Revolution, Rousseauist transparency, to which Robespierre was devoted. Devoted to virtue as Robespierre was, he did not hesitate to falsify facts when it suited his purposes. Departing from the report of Bara's death, sent to the Convention by General Desmarres in December 1793, Robespierre turned the episode into a Rousseauist moral tale: "This small child supported his mother on his earnings; he divided his loyalties between his filial affections and his country. It would be impossible to find a more perfect example to kindle the love of glory, country, and virtue in young hearts."[78] When Desmarres heard about Robespierre's fabricated version of Bara's death, and the festival planned in Bara's honor, he wrote another letter to the Convention, hoping to set the record straight: "I think [Bara] should be shown as he was when he received the final blows, on foot, holding two horses by the reins, surrounded by brigands, and replying to the men who had come forward to try and make him give up the horses: 'You [fucking] brigand, give you the horses, the commander's horses, and mine? Certainly not?' Those were the words, repeated several times, that cost him his life."[79] This was not how David portrayed Joseph Bara; the pristine youth of his painting meshed with the ideas of Robespierre, but they were at odds with the actual circumstances of Bara's death. Between abstractions and facts there was a discrepancy, a principle of disjunction, but this had been true of the Rousseauist revolutionary discourse from the beginning. It was true as well of the Revolutionary festivals orchestrated by Robespierre's collaborater, Jacques-Louis David.

Conclusion
David, Prieur, and the Tragedy of the French Revolution

*B*oth David and Prieur were arrested after the Reign of Terror. David was arrested and incarcerated twice, first on August 2, 1794, when he was sent to the Hôtel des Fermes and then transferred to the Luxembourg. He was released provisionally on December 26 but arrested again in the aftermath of the 20 Prairial (June 8) uprising in May 1795, along with former members of the Committee of General Safety and others associated with the Terror. A few days before his first arrest, he told his sons that Robespierre would be denounced as a villain (*scélerat*) and described in the most odious terms, but that they should believe none of it, for history would do him full justice.[1] During the two periods of incarceration, David sang a different tune. His longest defense was a formal response to charges against him by the Museum Section on May 2, 1795, when he explained that he had indeed been a follower of Robespierre, and like others he had marched "in the revolutionary line traced by the dominant opinion of the period." He had not known of the "surreptitious views" of Robespierre, but his eyes had since been opened, and he had severed ties "with the men whose company I kept before my detention."[2] Throughout his incarceration, David protested innocence: To the extent that he had been wrong it was because of "the excess of my love for *la patrie*"; he had lacked understanding but had a "righteous heart"; and "One could never reproach me for any reprehensible deed because my intentions have always been just." Comparing himself to Hippolyte in Racine's *Phèdre*, and quoting a line of that work, he said, "The day is no more pure than the depth of my heart."[3]

Prieur was arrested in the aftermath of the food riots in April 1795, along with Fouquier-Tinville. The former head of the Revolutionary Tribunal had been arrested earlier, on August 1, 1794, but was released and then arrested again by a government that was shaky after the disturbances of 12 Germinal (April 10). Fouquier-Tinville was associated with the worst excesses of the Terror, and, to appease public opinion, he was put on trial, found guilty, and sent to the guillotine on May 7, 1795. As a member of the Revolutionary Tribunal, Prieur was caught in the backdraft of hostility directed at Fouquier-Tinville; he went to the guillotine on the same day. The thirty-nine day trial of those arrested after the April 1795 uprising was dominated by Fouquier-Tinville, whose precise memory enabled him to answer many of the charges against him. The trial of Prieur appears to have been swift. Denying the charge against him that he had insulted those brought before the Revolutionary Tribunal, Prieur acknowledged that he had drawn the heads of the accused. He did not respond to the specific charge of drawing heads covered with blood, saying that his drawings were but *"cochonneries"* and *"petites bêtises."*

As chance had it, Prieur made this flippant remark at almost the precise time that David was preparing a response to charges made against him by the Museum Section. David wrote on May 3, four days before Prieur's execution, that "my crimes, in effect, were horror of tyranny and oppression, hatred of ambition, injustice, falsehood, and charlatanism." It was to the Convention that he addressed his remarks, and to the members of that body he said, "You have spoken of my crimes, while for my part I have spoken of your virtue."[4] David was as self-righteous speaking in his own defense as Prieur was cheeky, answering charges of misconduct as a member of the Revolutionary Tribunal. David was released, resumed his career as an artist, continued to draw students into his orbit, became court painter for Napoléon, and died thirty years later in Brussels, a political emigré forced from France after the Hundred Days. That Prieur went to the guillotine was not only because of the particular circumstances surrounding his arrest and trial, but also because he lacked the influence the well-connected David was able to exert on his own behalf.

The historian G. M. Young has written that "the real, central theme of History is not what happened, but what people felt about it as it was happening."[5] Among the many illustrators who depicted the events of the French Revolution, it is Prieur whose own responses come through most vividly. It is useful to think of him as a rhetorician whose language is his art, and whose images are projections of his own attitudes, feelings, and responses to the great events of the Revolution.[6] A good part of the interest in Prieur's tableaus lies in their partisanship, much as the same can be said of the journalism of a Marat or an Hébert, to mention but two writers who come to mind while trying to locate approximate counterparts for Prieur. The importance to the historian of Marat and Hébert is not just what they said but how they said it, and the same may be said of Prieur. Another obvious connection between Prieur and his journalistic counterparts, Marat and Hébert, is that both he and they identified with the popular revolution.

Each did so in his own way. Marat retained a classical diction even as he gave himself over to outpourings of anger, directed at the enemies of the people. Hébert, by contrast, adopted an artificially popular journalistic style that was heavily laced with *foutres* and *bougres*, and whose syntax and diction was far removed from that of Marat.[7] For his part, Prieur had an ability, unique among illustrators not only to capture the movements and body language of the populace, but also to project in his images the actual sense of a revolutionary *journée*, including its violence and sardonic humor.

Prieur did not often give full rein to his ability to express the violence and sardonic humor of Paris crowds when stirred to political action. He did so only briefly, while depicting the Paris Insurrection of July 12–14 and its aftermath on July 22. Portraying the events that saved the Revolution, Prieur unleashed a unique ability to portray the anger of Paris crowds and its bloody consequences. From there on, he portrayed the people in action but without incorporating explicit, graphic violence into his drawings. In his illustration of the most violent and politically explosive of all Paris *journées*, that of August 10, 1792, he viewed the scene from afar, and in doing so avoided the bloodshed that figures so prominently in the illustrations of other artists. Other artists depicted savage fighting, the mutilation of bodies, and the terrible toll in human life in the Place du Carrousel. To do so, their perspective was up close. Prieur viewed the fighting from afar and portrayed the scene as if it were a battlefield. His illustration showed the overwhelming force of the insurgents as they stormed the Tuileries, but it left out the butchery that was depicted by other artists and in some cases was central to their rendering of the event.

When illustrating the revolutionary violence—the popular violence—of July 1789, Prieur pulled out the stops, but, when portraying the much greater violence of August 1792, he retreated, literally; he established distance between himself and the savage fighting in the Place du Carrousel. Identifying with the popular revolution in 1789, he compiled a visual record of its successes. He continued to identify with the popular cause when he portrayed the much greater violence of August 1792, but, rather than unleash a talent for depicting violence, he took a different tack and presented the scene formalistically, with the enemies of monarchy achieving a signal victory. His last drawing, *Massacre of Prisoners at the Abbaye*, showed just and angry Parisians administering justice to enemies of the Revolution. Having identified with the popular cause at the beginning of the Revolution, Prieur still did so in his last illustrations for the *Tableaux historiques*, which portrayed the events of August and September 1792; however, now he held a talent in check that under different circumstances, three years earlier, he briefly unleashed.

If Prieur illustrated scenes of the Revolution in his own manner, David placed his brush in the service of the Revolution. A frustrated and bitter member of the Academy in 1789, he was recognized as a patriot artist from the beginning and was carried to altogether new heights of success by a *"révolution heureuse"* whose great achievements he proclaimed as an artist.[8] Nothing could have been more natural and obvious for David than to place his brush in the service of a Revolution that offered him fame and recognition. Moreover, as a history painter, who catapulted himself to a position of leadership among the artists of his generation in the Salons of the 1780s, and specialized in patriotic subjects, he was perfectly situated to portray the great events of the Revolution. From the deeds of antiquity to the deeds of the present it was an easy step, and it was one that David took with assurance and an authentic sense of patriotic commitment in the *Tennis Court Oath*. The high rhetoric of that work was a direct outgrowth of David's training as an academician; his elevated language was the perfect vehicle to portray the patriotic ideals of the deputies who dedicated themselves to the formation of a new order.

The *Tennis Court Oath* is the only painting by David that shows Paris workers who would, in time, become sans-culottes. Confined to the galleries on the left, where only their faces are seen, they are a glowering presence, all but hidden from sight, but they are there nonetheless, placed there by David in recognition of the role they would play several weeks later in the Paris uprising that saved the Revolution.

As an artist who placed his brush in service of the Revolution, David limited himself to portraying the heroic deeds of revolutionary leaders and to commemorating martyrs of the Revolution. His perspective was elevated and as such part of what one might call a "public discourse." It was not that he was oblivious to the role of the populace in the Revolution but that he chose, as an artist, not only to portray men of enlightened principle, but also those who gave themselves to the Revolution as martyrs. His position may be likened to that of Robespierre, whom he considered a hero. Robespierre saw the populace as a political force in the Revolution and allied with the Sections, but, as a member of the revolutionary leadership, he inhabited a mental landscape different from that of the populace. He spoke a different language from that of the sans-culottes, and he lived apart from *le peuple*.[9] All of this applies to David as well. At no point did he view the Revolution from the perspective of the street.

Of David's revolutionary paintings only one survived in its finished state, *Marat Assassinated*; it portrayed a revolutionary leader whose excesses Robespierre regretted. David demanded that he be assassinated with Marat when he was impeached and he swore to take the hemlock with Robespierre when he faced a crisis in the Convention. The two men David hero-worshiped were known to have met separately on but one occasion. Such were the complications of the Revolution, when men and women had to make difficult personal choices and difficult political decisions. This was certainly true of David.

He began but never completed two portraits in 1791, *Mme Pastoret* (fig. 113) and *Mme Trudaine* (fig. 114), both friends from the liberal circles in which he had moved at the end of the ancien régime and in the first two years, or so, of the Revolution. These paintings captured the

FIGURE 113. J.-L. David, *Mme Pastoret*, Art Institute, Chicago

FIGURE 114.   J.-L. David,
Mme Trudaine, Musée du
Louvre

tensions of the two women; they were also a projection of his own tensions. Done during the emotionally burdensome period when David
was moving toward the Jacobin Left, the two portraits projected the uneasiness David felt in the presence of friends whose politics he had once
shared but was in the process of abandoning. A yet more direct record of
the burdens David suffered was the 1791 *Self Portrait* (fig. 115). According to Schnapper, the portrait showed David's troubled expression, di-
sheveled hair, and his "haunted intensity of . . . gaze." Already in the
sepia study of the *Tennis Court Oath*, completed in May 1791, David
had given prominence to those on the Left that his close friend André
Chénier opposed, and he went so far as to include Marat in the design,
a radical journalist that Chénier abominated. David's role in the
Châteauvieux festival was the decisive event in David's jacobinization,
and it resulted in a complete rupture with André Chénier. Chénier and
both Trudaine brothers were to go to the guillotine during the Terror.
So, too, did Antoine-Laurent de Lavoisier, the liberal and enlightened
scientist whose magnificent portrait, with his wife, a former student of
David's, was exhibited in the 1789 Salon (fig. 96).

FIGURE 115. J.-L. David, *Self Portrait*, Galeria degli Uffizi

William Doyle has written that the Revolution was "in every sense a tragedy."[11] It was certainly a tragedy for Prieur; it cost him his life. The first commentators for the *Tableaux historiques* also paid with their lives: Fauchet, a Girondin, went to the guillotine and Chamfort, a Jacobin, who was imprisoned, died of complications from attempted suicide. In his very first illustration, the *Tennis Court Oath*, Prieur showed Bailly receiving oaths from assembled deputies. A special gallows was installed in the Champ de Mars for Bailly's execution. Among the figures who appeared in Prieur's pictorial account of the Paris Insurrection was the young firebrand Camille Desmoulins, who went to the guillotine during the Terror, as did his wife, who tried to save him. Another figure in Prieur's tableaus illustrating the Paris Insurrection was the reactionary duc du Châtelet, who swallowed glass and smashed his head against a wall in an effort to kill himself after being arrested and imprisoned. He failed in that effort and went to the guillotine. Lafayette, who appeared in several of Prieur's tableaus, ended up in an Austrian prison. Louis XVI and Marie-Antoinette, also the subjects of Prieur's tableaus, went to the guillotine.

Prieur's pictorial record of the Revolution is one of popular protest and popular violence; it is a record of the events that made the Revolution revolutionary. Marxist historians have tended to accept revolutionary violence as a necessary price for the Revolution's achievements, but post-Revisionist historians seem less inclined to do so. Prieur, like the Marxists, saw violence as a necessary part of the Revolution. He did not sanitize the violence but showed it in all of its explosiveness. He also brought out the popular character of revolutionary violence; he did not hesitate to portray atrocities. Is his record of the Revolution one of tragedy? He would not have said so. There is tragedy, but it lies in the unseen and subsequent consequences of the deeds he portrayed in his tableaus; it lies not only in the Terror but the hunger and smashed hopes of a populace whose active intervention in the Revolution Prieur illustrated so vividly. That he was arrested in the aftermath of 1795 food riots is an example of the Revolution's tragic side. The illustrator, who compiled a unique record of the people's role in the Revolution, went to the guillotine in the aftermath of a popular disturbance in 1795, after he had been forced from the political arena. The destructive forces of the Revolution continued after the fall of Robespierre and Prieur was one of the victims.

If the Revolution was a tragedy for Prieur, what did it mean to the sans-culottes he portrayed in his illustrations for the *Tableaux historiques*? Jean-Louis Ménétra, the glazier who wrote a *Journal of My Life*, described what it meant to him. He was fifty-one in 1789 and, as he put it, was "enjoying myself and watching my days go by when the French Revolution came suddenly and revived all our spirits And the word liberty so often repeated had an almost supernatural effect and invigorated us all[.]" If the Revolution started favorably for Ménétra, he did not see it this way after he lived through it and experienced its twists and turns:

Everything moved forward . . . and all the ills came to a head Murder
drowning everything was allowed Intriguers monopolized all the offices
Good men could only mutter for if they spoke they were lost Hatred
vengeance everything was permitted and nobody dared open his mouth or
even dared to refuse the positions delegated to him in the assemblies.

Ménétra himself became a militant in his Section and was a member of numerous revolutionary committees. This led to attacks against
him by others: "I was informed of all the plots against me So I stayed
on my guard(.)" His accusers "thought I was done for but I kept my
wits about me," and "I continued along my way(.)" Looking back on
the Revolution after the coup of 18 Brumaire Ménétra said:

When I am with old friends . . . We recount what we have seen what we
have felt the good and the evil that the Revolution has done all the as-
saults the days the nights the punishments and the fate of our unfortunate
friends who perished in the time of Terror when good men feared for their
lives We are beginning to see the twilight of the times in which our fathers were happy.

His only hope was that his children would be happy, and that "I may
see them in my old age free of the suffering that the Revolution has
made us all feel(.)"[12] And it was on this note that he ended his *Journal*.
If Prieur did not survive the Revolution, Ménétra did; he regarded it as
a tragedy.

David also survived the Revolution. Among the Revolution's victims were David's liberal friends from the Trudaine circle and the radical Jacobins he sided with during the Terror. All of them were consumed by the Revolution. It would be hard to consider the Revolution,
in personal terms, as anything but a tragedy for David. More important
to the purposes of this study is what David's art said about the Revolution. Swept up in the euphoria of the 1789 Revolution, David undertook a project, the *Tennis Court Oath*, that was to commemorate the
patriotism of deputies committed to the creation of a new order.
Never, it seemed at the time, was a moment so propitious for enlightened change. The deputies portrayed by David in the *Tennis Court
Oath* came out of the eighteenth-century public; they were dedicated
to the public good. What happened to the deputies who figured most
prominently in David's patriotic canvas was a commentary on the failure of the 1789 dream of a better world; it was a commentary on the
tragedy of the French Revolution.

Notes

Preface

1. The one known exception is a drawing in the Royal Library at Windsor, cat. No. 3140, reproduced and discussed in *The French Drawings*, 62–63. This work, a 135 mm. X 163 mm. drawing in black chalk, contains an inscription on the back of the mount: "Denier dessin de Prieur, fameux Jacobin, membre et Juré du tribunal révolutionnaire, guillotiné avec fouquier tinville le 18 floréal l'an 3ᵉ de la république. ce dessin represente une des victimes dont il jugeoit 60 à mort, par jour. ce cannibal se plaisoit a dessiner la figure de ceux qu'il envoyoit à l'Echaufaux." The catalogue entry, no. 350, in *The French Drawings*, says "There is no reason to question the attribution of the Windsor drawing to [Pricur]." A recent trip to the Library of Congress undertaken to see if some Prieur drawings might be in a special 1802 edition of the *Tableaux historiques* yielded some remarkable results, but it did not turn up any unknown works by Prieur. Claudette Hould brought to my attention the possibility that a particular set of the *Tableaux historiques* in the Rosenwald Collection at the Library of Congress might contain original drawings, which it did, some twelve or so in all, but all were by Prieur's successors; none were by Prieur.

2. Gary Apgar identifies the works on David done in connection with the 1789 David exhibit in Paris in "Jacques-Louis David."

3. David was first arrested in the immediate aftermath of 10 Thermidor, released, and then arrested again after the uprising of 1 Prairial (May 20, 1795); Prieur was arrested after the bread riots of 12 Germinal (April 1, 1795) that led to an attack on the Convention.

4. Even as I depart from the Marxist conceptual scheme, I see the Revolution in terms of group conflict that in some basic ways is similar to the Marxist analysis. Tony Judt has described how François Furet has "removed from the center of our historical concerns the old insistence on social categories and conflicts, and replaced it with an emphasis upon the political debates and outcomes of France's revolutionary past . . .," Judt, "On François Furet."

5. Thomas Crow constructed a Habermasian public sphere in *Painters and Public Life* which played a crucial role, according to Crow, in David's prerevolutionary Salon paintings, particularly the *Oath of the Horatii*. Crow continued his study of David in *Emulation*, but in this work the relationship between the art public and David has been replaced by a study of the close and often complicated personal relationships between David and his students. As important as *Painters and Public Life* is, I was critical of the case Crow built between the art public and David's *Horatii* in my *Jacques-Louis David*. If Crow's focus shifted from the public sphere to private relationships in his study of David during the Revolution, I have given the public—and populace—a central position in this study of David and Prieur.

Introduction

1. In his polemical writings against the Marxist interpretation of the Revolution, François Furet makes a distinction between Marx and his twentieth-century followers, most notably about Albert Mathiez, Georges Lefebvre, and Albert Soboul, whom he calls "Neo-Jacobins." Furet, himself a former Marxist, uses Marx in building his case against later historians who flew his banner. He also makes a distinction between early Marx, the Marx of 1843–49, and the later Marx. See *Interpreting the French Revolution*, esp. 118–31, his piece on Marx in *A Critical Dictionary*, 972–979, and *Marx and the French Revolution*. One example of how historians have departed from the Marxist scheme is Guy Chaussinand-Nogaret, who sees the nobility as a force of progressive change in *La Noblesse au XVIII siècle*. For a recent study of the bourgeoisie, see David Garrioch, *The Formation of the Parisian Bourgeoisie*.

2. Taylor, "Non-Capitalist Wealth."

3. Cobban, *The Social Interpretation*. Cobban's 1954 inaugural lecture "The Myth of the French Revolution," reprinted in *Aspects*, first challenged the Marxist interpretation. See William Doyle, "Myth for Myth."

4. Baker, *Inventing the French Revolution*.

5. Furet, *Interpreting the French Revolution*, and Gauchet, *La Révolution des droits de l'homme*.

6. Darnton, *The Forbidden Best-Sellers*.

7. Other studies on public opinion include Baker, "Public Opinion as Political Invention," *Inventing*: 107–99; Ozouf, "L'Opinion publique," in *The French Revolution and the Creation of Modern Public Opinion*, 419–34; Doyle, *Origins of the French Revolution*, 78–95; Gordon, "Public Opinion and the Civilizing Process in France"; Chartier, *The Cultural Origins of the French Revolution*; and Van Kley, "In Search of Eighteenth-Century Public Opinion." Framed differently, but indispensable, is Higonnet, "Sociability, Social Structure, and the French Revolution." See also, Higonnet, *Class, Ideology and the Rights of Nobles*.

8. Darnton, *Forbidden Best Sellers*, 172.

9. Farge, *Subversive Words*.

10. This point is made by P. N. Furbank in "Nothing Sacred."

11. Quoted in Payne, *The Philosophes and the People*, 8. Chartier, *Cultural Origins*, explains that eighteenth-century editions of the *Dictionnaire universal* retained the same negative view of the people as the 1690 edition.

12. Quoted in Payne, *The Philosophes and the People*, 7.

13. Cowell, *Cicero and the Roman Republic*, 326.

14. Ibid, 327.

15. Brown, *A History of Private Life*, 240.

16. Machiavelli, The *Prince*, 51.

17. See Martines, *Power and Imagination*, 45–71.

18. Castiglione, *The Book of the Courtier*, 101.

19. Ibid., 105.

20. Ibid., 53.

21. Ibid., 52.

22. Braudel, *The Mediterranean*, 755–56. It was during the period of Braudel's monumental study, the reign of Philip II, that a new genre of literature appeared, the picaresque novel, which portrayed the world of the dispossessed. Having appeared first in Spain, it was taken up throughout much of Europe and continued into the eighteenth century. This literature offered historians a vivid picture of life among the poor, the dispossessed, and the desperate; it may be contrasted to other genres of literature such as the pastoral novel and the *nouvelle* that represented the elite. As Auerbach has shown in *Mimesis*, the trend from the sixteenth to the eighteenth century was for the people to disappear from elevated literature, and for that literature to reflect the mores of sophisticated audiences. For a brief but trenchant account of the picaresque novel see Davies, *Europe: A History*, 535–36.

23. Braudel, *Capitalism and Material Life*, 121–91.

24. Elias, *The Civilizing Process, Power and Civility*, and *The Court Society*. For a useful critique of Elias see Gordon, " 'Public Opinion' and the Civilizing Process." A work that gets at some of the social and cultural transformations bound up with the new system of manners, but from a very different point of departure from that of Elias, is Auerbach's *Mimesis*. For the new system of manners that took hold in seventeenth-century France see Magendie, *La Politesse mondaine*. Also useful is Lough, *An Introduction to the Seventeenth Century*. I might also mention Roberts, *Morality and Social Class in Eighteenth-Century French Literature and Painting*, 25–43. Most importantly, see *A History of Private Life: Passions of the Renaissance*. A recent and valuable study is Vidal, *Watteau's Printed Conversations*, which offers a different perspective of the civilizing process.

25. Quoted in Gay, *Voltaire's Politics*, 220–21.

26. Quoted in Hampson, *The Enlightenment*, 160.

27. Quoted in Echeverria, *The Maupeou Revolution*, 161.

28. Quoted in Gay, *The Enlightenment*, 519.

29. Quoted in Payne, *The Philosophes and the People*, 160.

30. Quoted in Merrick, "Family and Festivals," 601.

31. Gay, *The Enlightenment*, 519. For Rousseau's conflicted ideas on the people see Crocker, "Rousseau and the Common People."

32. Rousseau, *The Social Contract*, 40.

33. Quoted in Payne, *The Philosophes and the People*, 25.

34. Ibid., 25.

35. For a discussion of the public as a mental landscape see Jacob, "The Mental Landscape of the Public Sphere."

36. See Lougee, *Le Paradis des Femmes*.

37. Quoted in Adam, *Grandeur and Illusion*, 69.

38. Goodman, *The Republic of Letters*.

39. Quoted in Jones, *Reform and Revolution in France*, 74.

40. Ozouf, "L'Opinion Public," 772.

41. Bell, *Lawyers and Citizens*.

42. Montesquieu, *Oeuvres complètes*, 572.

43. The above quotations are from Cobban, *A History of Modern France*, 127.

44. Echeverria, *Maupeou Revolution*, is a fine study of this episode.

45. Ibid., 27.

46. Ibid., 27.

47. Ibid., 74.

48. Ibid., 75.

49. See Maza, *Private Lives and Public Affairs*.

50. Chartier, *Cultural Origins*, 27.

Chapter 1: The Paris Insurrection

1. Mercier, *Le Tableau de Paris*, 1273–76.

2. Paul Kennedy, in *Preparing for the Twenty-First Century*, sees the French Revolution against a background, not of bourgeois capitalism but urban and rural problems created by the pressures of demographic change. See pp. 3–4. This is precisely what is happening in today's world: As greater wealth is being generated, the gap between rich and poor has in-

creased; people pour into cities where they become a problem for authorities whose task it is to maintain order.

3. For eighteenth-century Paris see Chagniot, *Nouvelle histoire de Paris*; Tulard, *Nouvelle histoire de Paris*; Roche, *The People of Paris*; Reinhard, *Nouvelle histoire de Paris*; Rice, *Thomas Jefferson's Paris*; Andrew, "Paris of the Great Revolutions"; and Jordan, *Transforming Paris*, 13–40.

4. For an historian's view of construction projects in eighteenth-century Paris, see Cobban, *A History of Modern France*, 36–49. For works that deal with the architectural development of the capital see Braham, *The Architecture of the French Enlightenment*; Sutcliffe, *Paris: An Architectural History*, 1–77; Loyer, *Paris in the Nineteenth Century*, 1–106; Picon, *French Architects and Engineers*; Hermann, *Laugier and Eighteenth Century French Theory*; and Vidler, *Claude-Nicolas Ledoux*. A study that put the architectural transformation of Paris in a larger context, and from which I derived much benefit, is Kostoff, *The City Assembled*. Hoycraft, *In Search of the French Revolution*, 16, estimates that over half of the geographical area of neighborhoods such as Saint-Germain is made up of inner gardens that cannot be seen from the street. When staying on the rue du Bac in the 1950s, before the street was transformed, I could see interior gardens from the bedroom window of the eighteenth-century building. Two centuries after the construction of the building, there was a striking contrast between the bustle and noise of the street and the quiet and repose that pervaded the interior gardens.

5. Duby and Mandrou, *A History of French Civilization*, 351. Cobban says colonial trade increased from some 40 million livres in 1716 to 204 in 1756, *History of Modern France*, 38–39. See also Cameron and Freeman, "French Economic Growth," 3–30, and Aldrich, "Late Comer or Early Starter?" 89–100.

6. Labrousse, *La crise de l'economie français à la fin de l'Ancien Régime et au début de la Révolution*. See also Lefebvre, *The Great Fear of 1789*.

7. For a discussion of France's struggle with agricultural self-sufficiency see Fernand Braudel, *The Identity of France*, 369–399.

8. See Hufton, *The Poor of Eighteenth-Century France*.

9. Quoted in Kaplow, *France on The Eve of Revolution*, 111.

10. Quoted in Roche, *The People of Paris*, 10.

11. Quoted in Solomon, *Mozart*, 53.

12. Quoted in Kaplow, *France on The Eve of Revolution*, 112.

13. On the policing of Paris see Williams, *The Police of Paris*; Godechot, *The Taking of the Bastille*, 69–86 and passim; and Chagniot, *Paris et l'Armée*. Garrioch, *Neighbourhood and Community in Paris*, 210–19, discusses the tightening of authority at the local level.

14. Williams, *The Police of Paris*, 12.

15. See Schwartz, *Policing the Poor*, and Adams, *Bureaucrats and Beggars*.

16. For the gardes-françaises see Chagniot, *Paris et l'Armée*. For the role of the military in the defense of Paris see Scott, *The Response of the Royal Army to the French Revolution*.

17. Farge and Revel, *The Vanishing Children of Paris*, 34.

18. For studies on violence and the fear it spawned see Farge, *Fragile Lives*; Hufton, *The Poor of Eighteenth-Century France*; Schwartz, *Policing the Poor*, Williams, *The Police of Paris*; and Adams, *Bureaucrats and Beggars*. All address the issue of public and official fear of the populace.

19. Farge and Revel, *The Vanishing Children of Paris*, 8–9.

20. Ibid., 25.

21. Rose, *The Making of the Sans-Culottes*, 13, writes that "Relationships within the guilds were often far from idyllic. The acquisition of mastery was often expensive and hedged about with restrictions, and increasing numbers of journeymen were no longer able to look forward to independent status. Some set up, illegally, as *chamberlains* and competed with the genuine masters. Others began to rebel against the patriarchal atmosphere of the workshops." Mercier commented in the *Le Tableau de Paris* on rebelliousness of journeymen. One result of discontent was strikes, discussed by Rudé, *The Crowd in the French Revolution*, 21. Adding to tensions was the use of guilds as a device for controlling journeymen and apprentices. See Reinhard, *Nouvelle histoire*, 81. For more on the ossified guild system see Kaplow, *The Names of Kings*, 34–38.

22. Farge and Revel, *The Vanishing Children of Paris*, 108.

23. Ibid., 108.

24. Ibid., 109.

25. Ibid., 121.

26. See Van Kley, *The Damiens Affair*; Merrick, *The Desacralization of the French Monarchy*; and Chartier, *The Cultural Origins*, 111–35.

27. Cobban, *History of Modern France*, 126.

28. Chartier, *Cultural Origins*, 116.

29. Ibid., 116.

30. Ibid., 116.

31. Ibid., 117.

32. For a discussion of the Place de Grève see Tilly, *The Contentious French*, 42–57, and passim; and Garrioch, *Neighborhood and Community*, 230–40.

33. Tilly, *The Contentious French*, 49.

34. Ibid., 50.

35. Ibid., 116.

36. For discussion of the Palais-Royal see Billington, *Fire in the Minds of Men*, 25–33; and Isherwood, *Farce and Fantasy*, 217–49.

37. Quoted in Godechot, *The Taking of the Bastille*, 57.

38. Quoted in Isherwood, *Farce and Fantasy*, 249.

39. For a discussion of Orléans's political role before and during the Revolution, see Kelly, "The Machine of the duc d'Orléans and the New Politics."

40. Young, *Travels in France*, 104–5.

41. For a useful discussion of the Paris Insurrection see Solé, *Questions of the French Revolution*, 60–71.

42. See Cleary, *The Places Royales*, 298–429.

43. Quoted in Chartier, *Cultural Origins*, 123.

44. Isherwood, *Farce and Fantasy*, 137.

45. Ibid., 139–40.

46. Farge, *Fragile Lives*, 204–25.

47. Ibid., 30.

48. Ibid., 30.

49. Beside Isherwood, *Farce and Fantasy*, see Root-Bernstein, *Boulevard Theater and Revolution*.

50. Lucas, "The Crowd and Politics."

51. Garrioch, *Neighbourhood and Community*.

52. For a superb account see Godechot, *The Taking of the Bastille*. A different perspective is offered by Schama, *Citizens*, 369–425.

53. Godechot, *The Taking of the Bastille*, 208.

54. Ibid., 309. Godechot includes part of Pitra's eyewitness account in an appendix, 308–20. For the full text see Flammermont, *La Journée du 14 juillet 1789*.

55. Ibid., 319.

56. Quoted in Baker, *Inventing the French Revolution*, 95.

57. Ibid., 97.

58. See footnote 7, introduction.

59. Bosher, *French Revolution*, 45. See also, Schama's comments in "Caste, Class, Elites, and Revolution."

60. Quoted in Roche, *People of Paris*, 220.

61. Ménétra, *Journal of My Life*, 182.

62. Darnton, *The Great Cat Massacre*, 75–104. For the urban populace see Roche, *The People of Paris*; Doyle, *Origins of the French Revolution*, 178–91; Rudé, *The Crowd in History*, and *The Crowd in the French Revolution*; Hufton, *The Poor of Eighteenth-Century France*; Cobb, *The Police and the People*; Schwartz, *Policing the Poor*; Lemoigne, "Population and Provisions in Strasbourg"; Trenard, "The Social Crisis in Lyons."

63. See Cashmere, "The Social Uses of Violence in Ritual." See also Darnton, *The Kiss of Lamourette*, 3–20, which is a reprint of an article that first appeared in the *New York Review of Books* (January 19, 1989); 3–10. Foucault, *Discipline and Punish*, 3–69, describes public executions in eighteenth-century France. What Darnton and Foucault bring out is the use of public violence by the monarchy, of which the execution of Damiens is the most remarkable and frequently cited example.

64. Studies of popular culture include Bakhtin, *Rabelais and his World;* Davis, *Society and Culture,* esp. 97–123, and 152–87; Ladurie, *Carnival in Romans;* and Burke, *Popular Culture in Early Modern Europe.* Kaplow, *France on the Eve,* 100–6, contains a 1655 Resolution of the Doctors of the Sorbonne that condemns "the impious, sacrilegious, and superstitious practices carried on among the journeymen saddlemakers, shoemakers, tailors, and hatmakers, when they induct journeymen . . ." The Sorbonne doctors concluded that "these journeymen's organizations give rise to several types of disorder. (1) Some of the journeymen fail to keep the oath they take to be loyal to the master . . . (2) they injure and persecute the poor boys of the trade . . . (3) they participate in many debaucheries, impurities, drunkenness, etc., etc . . ." Tilly, "Charivari, Repertories, and Politics," discusses the potential for violence still contained in popular festivals in the nineteenth century. Citing Faure, *Paris Carême-prenant,* Tilly writes that "the folklore of Mardi Gras survived into the nineteenth century. In 1830 and, especially in 1848, Carnival and Revolution linked arms to dance in the streets." Weber, *Peasants into Frenchmen,* 377–406, discusses popular festivals in the nineteenth century. The connection between popular festivals and political protest in the French Revolution has not received the attention it deserves.

65. Farge and Revel, *Vanishing Children of Paris,* 56.

66. See Tilly, *The Contentious French,* 217–244.

67. Ibid., 230.

68. *Chronicle,* 321.

69. Manceron, *Blood of the Bastille,* 437.

70. Ibid., 447.

71. These quotes are from Shafer, "Bourgeois Nationalism in the Pamphlets," 31–50.

72. Quoted in Lucas, "The Crowd and Politics," 451.

73. Quoted in Furet's article on Barnave in *Critical Dictionary,* 187.

74. Ibid., 193.

75. Singer, "Violence in the French Revolution."

76. See Girodet's sketch that shows on pikes the heads of de Launay, Foulon, Berthier de Sauvigny, and the heart of Berthier de Sauvigny, fig. 31.

77. Burke, *Popular Culture*, argues for attenuation; Isherwood, *Farce and Fantasy* for vitalization.

Chapter 2: Jean-Louis Prieur and the *Tableaux historiques*

1. Nolhac, *Tableaux de Paris*, introduction.

2. Hould, *Images of the French Revolution*, 82.

3. Ibid., 86.

4. Nolhac, *Tableaux de Paris*, introduction. See also Legrand, *Inventaire général des dessins*, 524–25.

5. For the additional one drawing see footnote 1, preface.

6. According to an entry on a drawing presumably by Prieur, Blunt, *French Drawings in the Collection of His Majesty*, 62.

7. The quotations are from *Le Tribunal Révolutionnaire de Paris*, vol. 2, 191, 323.

8. See note 1, preface.

9. I am greatly in the debt of Claudette Hould for sending me the commentaries for the first fifty tableaus of the *Tableaux historiques*. Dr. Hould also offered important suggestions to me in my work on Prieur at a conference held at the University of Saskatchewan, Regina, in September 1996.

10. Michelet, *History of the French Revolution*, 213.

11. The duc du Châtelet was the son of Voltaire's intellectual companion, Mme du Châtelet. It was he who introduced the motion in the Assembly on the night of August 4 to confiscate the property of the Catholic Church. He did so after the Archbishop of Chartres introduced a motion to abolish hunting rights.

12. Godechot, *Taking of the Bastille*, 183.

13. The illustration in fig. 3 is from Berthault's engraving; Prieur's drawing is one of five drawings, not reproduced in Nolhac, and apparently lost. The others are tableaus 17, 42, 60, and 62; when reproduced here they are from Berthault's engravings.

14. This is from Desmoulins' letter to his father, written four days later. For this episode see Manceron, *Blood of the Bastille*, 495–503; and Michelet, *History of the French Revolution*, 150–51.

15. Godechot, *Taking of the Bastille*, 189.

16. *Images de la Révolution française*, cat. nos. 762–66.

17. Godechot, *Taking of the Bastille*, 189.

18. Braham, *The Architecture of the French Enlightenment*, 196.

19. Godechot, *Taking of the Bastille*, 217.

20. Tackett, *Becoming a Revolutionary*, 162–68, describes responses at Versailles to news of the Paris Insurrection.

21. Michelet, *History of the French Revolution*, 207.

22. Ibid., 210.

23. Lucas, "The Crowd and Politics," 442–46.

24. Beik, *Urban Protest in Seventeenth-Century France*, shows how retribution was at the core of urban protest in the seventeenth century. This was also true in the eighteenth century.

25. Restif, *Les Nuits*, 251.

26. For a discussion of Bertier de Sauvigny and his family see Guillaume de Bertier de Sauvigny, *Le Comte Ferdinand de Bertier*, 1–18. This account is a rebuttal of Michelet's portrayal of Bertier.

27. Jones, *Reform and Revolution in France*, 124–27.

28. See Adams, *Bureaucrats and Beggars*.

29. Michelet, *History of the French Revolution*, 213.

30. Ibid., 212.

31. Restif, *Les Nuits*, 255.

32. Rudé, *The Crowd in the French Revolution*, 56.

33. Schama, *Citizens*, 447.

34. Adams, *Bureaucrats and Beggars*, 221.

35. Restif, *Les Nuits*, 252.

36. Schama, *Citizens*, 446.

37. Ibid., 446–47.

Chapter 3: Jean Louis Prieur and the *Tableaux historiques*:

1. Hould, *Images of the French Revolution*, 185.

2. Quoted in Shapiro, *Revolutionary Justice in Paris*, 63. I am in Barry Shapiro's debt for this fine study, which I follow closely in my discussion of the Fayettist government and the justice it dispensed. For Lafayette, I have followed, Gottschalk, *Lafayette in the French Revolution*.

3. Ibid., pp. 61, 64.

4. Ibid., p. 68.

5. Ibid., 68.

6. Quoted in Doyle, *The Oxford History of the French Revolution*, 120–21.

7. Quoted in Munro and Scraise, *Paris, City of Revolution*, 42.

8. Quoted in Schama, *Citizens*, 466.

9. Hould, *Images of the French Revolution*, 229.

10. Shapiro, *Revolutionary Justice*, 169.

11. In piecing together the February Lyons riot and the riot in Montauban in May, I have used Godechot, *The Counter Revolution*, 149–55, 236–41; Lefebvre, *The French Revolution*, vol. 1, 141–43; Sutherland, *France*, 107–22; and Reinhardt and Cawthon, *Essays on the French Revolution*, 3–63.

12. Hould, *Images of the French Revolution*, 227.

13. Ibid., 231.

14. Ibid., 323.

15. Ibid., 233.

16. Quoted in de La Fuye and Babeau, *The Apostle of Liberty*, 140.

17. Ibid., 140.

18. Schama, *Citizens*, 541.

19. This tableau is incorrectly dated April 6; the actual date of the incident was May 3.

20. Schama, *Citizens*, 549.

21. Ibid., 557.

22. Berthault's engraving does not show the King holding a bottle in his right hand.

23. Schama, *Citizens*, 564.

24. Prieur did not do the illustration for tableau 64, *Taking of Jalès by Patriots*. He would do five more illustrations, the last of which, *Massacre of Prisoners*, was not included in the *Tableaux historiques*.

25. For songs and revolutionary patriotism see Mason, *Singing the Revolution*. The arrival of "La Marseillaise" in Paris is discussed pp. 97–98.

26. See Mercier, *Tableau de Paris*, v. 2, 121–25.

27. Quoted in Schama, *Citizens*, 630.

28. The figure in Prieur's illustration, who wears a hat and points accusingly at traitors, resembles a contemporary drawing of Maillard by Gabriel in the Musée Carnavelet, reproduced in Favier, *Chronicle of the French Revolution*, 286.

29. Another possible reason for the publishing of Swebach-Desfontaine's version rather than Prieur's was a falling out between Prieur and his collaborators in the *Tableaux historiques*. Claudette Hould, who has studied the documents pertaining to this publishing project exhaustively, has told me we simply do not know precisely when, or under what circumstances, Prieur left the *Tableaux historiques*. He would seem, on the basis of his illustrations, to have remained sympathetic to the popular cause when those of a more moderate persuasion responded differently. He continued to move to the Left politically after other artists took his place as illustrator of the *Tableaux historiques*. He could, then, have been at loggerheads with others associated with the project, and this could help explain why Swebach-Desfontaine's illustration of the *September Massacres* was used instead of Prieur's.

30. *Tableaux historiques de la Révolution française*, vol. 3.

31. Hould, *Images of the French Revolution*, 86.

32. Tourneaux, *Bibliographie de l'histoire*, 56.

33. Ibid., 35.

34. Hould, *Images of the French Revolution*, 86.

35. See Kates, *Cercle Social*.

36. Chamfort, *Products of the Perfected Civilization*, 192, 194, 196.

37. Ibid., 270.

38. Ibid., 198.

39. Ibid., 96.

40. For a discussion of this print see Kennedy, *Cultural History*, 267.

Chapter 4: Robespierre and the People

1. The above quotations are from Hampson, *Prelude to Terror*, 100.

2. Quoted in Baker, *Inventing the French Revolution*, 94.

3. Hampson, *Prelude to Terror*, 75.

4. Ibid., 74.

5. Quoted in Hampson, *Will and Circumstance*, 11.

6. Ibid., 10–11.

7. Ibid., 75.

8. In fact, parties emerged from the beginning of the Revolution, "but they never had been accepted as a natural part of the political process," Hunt, Lansky, and Hanson, "The Failure of the Liberal Republic," 738.

9. Quoted in Hampson, *Will and Circumstance*, 30.

10. Robespierre, *Oeuvres de Maximilien*, vol. 3, 371.

11. Quoted in Carol Blum, *Rousseau and the Republic of Virtue*, 72. For Rousseau's political ideas see Cobban, *Aspects of the French Revolution*, 136–91, and for Rousseau and his influence on the Revolution see Mc-

Donald, *Rousseau and the French Revolution,* and Barny, *Rousseau dans la Révolution.*

12. Hampson, *Prelude to Terror,* 102.

13. Ibid., 101.

14. Ibid., 109.

15. Robespierre, *Oeuvres de Maximilien,* vol. 3, 407.

16. For a discussion of those usages see Payne, *Philosophes and People,* 7–17.

17. Quoted in Lefebvre, *The Coming of the French Revolution,* 222.

18. Doyle, *Oxford History,* 124.

19. Quoted in Thompson, *Robespierre,* 69.

20. For Rousseau's involvement in Genevan politics see Palmer, *The Age of Democratic Revolution,* vol. 1, 111–39.

21. Robespierre, *Oeuvres de Maximilien,* vol. 3, 406–8. The republican tradition of political thought, to which Rousseau was connected and from which he drew, was at least in some of its modes archaic, backward looking, inimical both to liberal individualism and capitalism, and consistent with a conservative outlook. Some of its adherents, like Rousseau, favored Sparta over Athens, placed great emphasis on civic virtue, and could even maintain a "decidedly reactionary tone." This quotation is from Wood, *Creation of the American Public,* 59. See also Pocock, *The Machiavellian Moment,* "The Machiavellian Moment Revisited," and *Virtue, Commerce, and History;* Rodgers, *Republicanism: The Career of a Concept;* Dworkin, "Liberalism"; Mouffe, "Democratic Citizenship"; Appleby, *Liberalism and Republicanism;* and Pincus, "Neither Machiavellian Moment nor Possessive Individualism."

22. Quoted in Thompson, *Robespierre,* 244.

23. Robespierre, *Oeuvres de Maximilien,* vol. 9, 217.

24. Ibid., 488.

25. Ibid., 377.

26. Quoted in Hampson, *Prelude to Terror,* 106.

27. Beik, *French Revolution,* 98.

28. Ibid., 99.

29. Ibid., 120–23.

30. Quoted in Matrat, *Robespierre*, 62.

31. Robespierre, *Oeuvres de Maximilien*, vol. 6, 40.

32. Ibid., vol. 6, 40.

33. Matrat, *Robespierre*, 62–3.

34. Quoted in Furet, *Critical Dictionary*, 301.

35. Quoted in Cobban, *Aspects of the French Revolution*, 148.

36. Ibid., 149.

37. Ibid., 149.

38. Hampson, *Danton*, 30–31.

39. Ibid., 33–4.

40. The book that brings out this connection best is Blum, *Rousseau and the Republic*.

41. Quoted from Hampson, *The Life and Opinions of Maximilien Robespierre*, 16. This book brings out the problematic dimension of Robespierre through dialogue between voices that represent different viewpoints. Getting Robespierre right is a problem, certainly for this author, and I am relieved to say even for as fine an historian as Hampson. If he did not pass open judgment on Rousseau his viewpoint does come through. I should like to think the same applies to this chapter.

42. Ibid., 30.

43. Ibid., 42.

44. He spoke 276 times in the Convention, which in a list of speeches given by deputies placed him number 20. For a list of speeches given by leading deputies see Tackett, *Becoming a Revolutionary*, 321–22.

45. Robespierre, *Oeuvres de Maximilien*, vol. 6, 118.

46. Ibid., 122.

47. Quoted in Hampson, *Robespierre*, 82.

48. Ibid., 83.

49. Quoted in Matrat, *Robespierre*, 76.

50. Quoted in Furet, *Critical Dictionary*, 301.

51. Ibid., 307.

52. The quotes on the war debate are from Jordan, *The Revolutionary Career*, 184–8.

53. Robespierre, *Oeuvres de Maximilien*, vol. 8, 268.

54. Ibid., vol. 4, 351.

55. Ibid., 354–55.

56. Ibid., vol. 9, 15.

57. Quoted in Blum, *Rousseau and the Republic*, 179.

58. Ibid., 175.

59. For the Jacobins see Brinton, *The Jacobins, Critical Dictionary*, 704–51; Kennedy, *The Jacobin Clubs*, and for the Girondins see, Sydenham, *The Girondins*.

60. Robespierre, *Oeuvres de Maximilien*, vol. 9, 216–17.

61. Ibid., 274–5.

62. Ibid., 348.

63. Ibid., 354–5.

64. Ibid., 451.

65. Quoted in Schama, *Citizens*, 723.

66. Ibid., vol. 9, 538.

67. Quoted in Jordan, *Revolutionary Career*, 150.

68. See Slavin, *Making of an Insurrection*.

69. Quoted in Furet, *Critical Dictionary*, 337–9.

70. For a discussion of the beating incident see Kelly, *Women of the French Revolution*, 89–90, and for Méricourt's insanity see Schama's moving account in *Citizens*, 873–75.

71. Hébert is said to have been very polite according to Slavin, *The Hébertistes*, 17.

72. Quoted in Furet, *Critical Dictionary*, 340.

73. Ibid., 365–68.

74. These quotations are from Cobb, *The People's Armies*, 223.

75. Quoted in Soboul, *Parisian*, 223.

76. Slavin, *Hébertists*, 42.

77. Ibid., 232.

78. Andrews, "Paris of the Great Revolutions," 107–8.

79. Cobb, *The Police and the People*, 84–94.

80. Still one of the best books on the Committee of Public Safety is Palmer, *Twelve Who Ruled*. In trying to find one's way through the Terror, Palmer is a useful guide, although his propensity to explain the Terror in the light of circumstances some historians, François Furet most notably, refuse to accept.

81. Thompson, *Robespierre*, 577.

82. Ibid., 578–9.

83. Mercier, *The Picture of Paris*, 255.

Chapter 5: David and the *Tennis Court Oath*

1. For the pamphlet *Sur la peinture* see Crow, *Painters and Public Life*, 107–8, 182–5.

2. For a discussion of David's use of Michelangelo and Raphael see Lee, "Jacques- Louis David: The Versailles Sketchbook." Dorothy Johnson, *Jacques-Louis David*, examines David's elevated style in a discussion of his corporal aesthetic, 11–69. I am indebted to Bordes, *Le Serment du Jeu de Paume* and "J.-L. David's 'Serment du Jeu de Paume'." for my discus-

sion of David's *Tennis Court Oath*. See also Wisner, *The Cult of the Legislator*, 99–124.

3. Quoted in Schnapper, *David*, 104.

4. For a discussion of these oath paintings see Rosenblum, *Transformations*, 162–65.

5. Starobinski, *1789: The Emblems of Reason*, 102.

6. See Landes, *Women and the Public Sphere;* Blum, *Rousseau*, 119–26; Steinbrügge, *The Moral Sex*, 54–82; Kates, *Monsieur d'Eon Is a Woman*, 166–71; and Hufton, *Women & the Limits of Citizenship*.

7. The women in the galleries were seen as marginalized in a paper delivered at a Colloquium in Honour of James A. Leith, Symbols, Myths, and Images of the French Revolution in Regina, Saskatchewan, in September 1996 by Weston, "1791: The Past in the Service of the Present."

8. Quoted in Darnton, *Great Cat Massacre*, 243.

9. Ibid., 246.

10. Quoted in Hould, *Images of the French Revolution*, 187.

11. See Louvre Sketchbook, folios 15–24, reproduced in Bordes, *Le Serment*, figs. 176–88.

12. Leith, *Space and Revolution*, 67–117, discusses plans for the National Assembly's new building that was never constructed.

13. Scarfe, *André Chénier*, 220.

14. Smernoff, *André Chénier*, 114.

15. Bordes, *Le Serment*, notes that the address of David on the list of members is not that of J.-L. David, but Wisner, "Jacques-Louis David and André Chénier," 529–44, reasons plausibly that the name was that of J.-L. David.

16. Chénier, *Oeuvres complètes*, 199.

17. Ibid., 212–13.

18. Ibid., 206–7.

19. Bordes, *David*, 155 (stanza 1).

20. Ibid., 159–60 (stanza XIV).

21. Ibid., 161 (stanza XVII).

22. David's remarks in Nantes are reproduced in Bordes, *Le Serment*, 29–30.

23. Ibid., 78.

24. Ibid., 166–73. Bordes includes eight articles in various journals on the *Louis XVI* painting.

25. The above quotations are from Loggins, *André Chénier*, 158–60.

26. Ibid., 162–69.

27. Scarfe, *André Chénier*, 270.

28. Ibid., 272.

29. Quoted in Blum, *Rousseau and the Republic*, 213.

30. Quoted in Herbert, *David, Voltaire, BRUTUS*, 52–53.

31. For discussions of how the condemned went to their death see Arasse, *The Guillotine and the Terror*, 105–18; and Outram, *The Body and the French Revolution*, 106–23.

32. The Marx quotation is in Hunt, *Politics, Culture, and Class*, 22.

33. Quoted in Scarfe, *André Chénier*, 363.

34. For a fine article on David and the Lavoisiers see Vidal, "David among the Moderns."

35. Lee, *David*, 144.

36. For the *concours* of the Year II see Olander, *Pour transmettre à la postérité*.

37. This quote is taken not from Olander's dissertation but from Wintermute *1789: French Art During the Revolution*, 37. For those unable to see the complete dissertation, the excerpt in the catalogue edited by Wintermute is most useful.

38. This study, in a private collection, is reproduced in Wintermute *1789: French Art During the Revolution*, 223.

39. Also in a private collection, this study is reproduced in Ibid., 220.

40. Friedländer, *David to Delacroix*, 38–41.

41. Arasse, *The Guillotine and the Terror*, 71–2, and appendix 5, 191–2. Arasse mistakenly attributes Le Sueur's *Execution of the Tyrant* to Peyron. The two quotes describing the crowd's silence are from Arasse, p. 60.

Chapter 6: Robespierre, David, and Revolutionary Festivals

1. Rousseau, *Politics and the Arts*, 126.

2. Ibid., 127.

3. Robespierre, *Oeuvres de Maximilien*, vol. 10, 458–459.

4. Wildenstein, *Documents*, cat. no. 1096, 108–10.

5. Rousseau, *Politics and the Arts*, xv.

6. Ibid., 33.

7. Ibid., 31.

8. Robespierre, *Oeuvres de Maximilien*, vol. 10, 452–3.

9. Ibid., 454–55.

10. Ibid., 456–457.

11. Wildenstein, *Documents*, cat. no. 1096, 108–10.

12. For a recent discussion of this subject see Leith, "On the Religiosity of the French Revolution." See also Brinton, *A Decade of Revolution*, 142–63.

13. Rousseau, *Oeuvres complètes*, vol. 3, 465.

14. Ibid., 467.

15. Ibid., 465.

16. Ibid., 468.

17. Ozouf, *Festivals and the French Revolution*, 59.

18. Ibid., 59.

19. Quoted in Dowd, *Pageant-Master of the Republic*, 46.

20. Quoted in Ozouf, *Festivals and the French Revolution*, 32–3.

21. Quoted in Dowd, *Pageant-Master of the Republic*, 51–2.

22. Herbert, *David, Voltaire, BRUTUS*, n. 81, 143.

23. Ibid., n. 84, 143.

24. Quoted in Ozouf, *Festivals and the French Revolution*, 65.

25. Robespierre, *Oeuvres de Maximilien*, vol. 8, 181–2.

26. Ibid., 179.

27. Ibid., 180–81.

28. Quoted in Bordes, *Le Serment*, 78.

29. Quoted in Dowd, *Pageant-Master of the Republic*, 56.

30. Ibid., 56.

31. Robespierre, *Oeuvres de Maximilien*, vol. 8, 251.

32. Quoted in Ozouf, *Festivals and the French Revolution*, 68.

33. Quoted in Dowd, *Pageant*, 62.

34. Quoted in Ozouf, *Festivals and the French Revolution*, 69–72.

35. For popular festivals see ibid., 83–105.

36. Robespierre, *Oeuvres de Maximilien*, vol. 9, 250.

37. Ibid., 249.

38. Quoted in Schnapper, *David*, 151.

39. Robespierre, *Oeuvres de Maximilien*, vol. 9, 472.

40. Thompson, *French Revolution*, 330.

41. Roberts, *Jacques-Louis David*, 78–82.

42. Thompson, *French Revolution*, 402.

43. Wildenstein, *Documents*, cat. no. 428, 50.

44. Thompson, *Robespierre*, 328–29.

45. Robespierre, *Oeuvres de Maximilien*, vol. 9, 624.

46. Ibid., 624.

47. Dowd, *Pageant-Master of the Republic*, 106.

48. David, *Le Peintre Louis David*, 141.

49. Ibid., 142–43.

50. Schnapper, *David*, 155–60.

51. Wildenstein, *Documents*, 155–60.

52. Robespierre, *Oeuvres de Maximilien*, vol. 10, 61.

53. Wildenstein, *Documents*, 53.

54. Schama, *Citizens*, 749.

55. Quoted in Palmer, *Twelve Who Ruled*, 217.

56. *French Revolution*, ed. Beik, 271.

57. Robespierre, *Oeuvres de Maximilien*, vol. 10, 196.

58. Doyle, *Oxford History*, 260.

59. Quoted in Schama, *Citizens*, 727.

60. Quoted in Palmer, *Twelve Who Ruled*, 165.

61. Quoted in Germani, "Robespierre's Heroes," 139.

62. Quoted in Palmer, *Twelve Who Ruled*, 164.

63. Ibid., 164.

64. Quoted in Germani, "Robespierre's Heroes," 140.

65. Quoted in Furet, *Critical Dictionary*, 141.

66. Quoted in Thompson, *French Revolution*, 439.

67. Quoted in Sloane, "David, Robespierre and the 'Death of Bara'," 144–45.

68. Ibid., 146–47.

69. Robespierre, *Oeuvres de Maximilien*, vol. 10, 452–59.

70. *The Old Regime*, ed. Keith Michael Baker, 374.

71. Wildenstein, *Documents*, cat. no. 968, 97.

72. Quoted in Hunt, *Politics, Culture, and Class*, 107.

73. Palmer, *Twelve Who Ruled*, 332–33.

74. This was the time indicated in David's July 11 report to the Convention. As plans for the festival moved forward, David's plan was modified, including the time. See Wildenstein, *Documents*, cat. nos. 1113, p. 112, 1117, p. 112.

75. Quoted in Crow, *Emulation*, 184.

76. Quoted in Schnapper, *David*, 162.

77. For all of his devotion to Spartan manliness and his subordination of women to men, Rousseau was, in some respects, most attuned to the female. Hence, the appeal of his novels and their tender sensibility to women readers. Julie, the heroine of *La Nouvelle Héloïse*, was a projection of Sophie d'Houdetot, by whom Rousseau was smitten when he wrote the novel, and she was a projection of Rousseau. Rousseau made lace, like women, and sometimes dressed like women. See Blum, *Rousseau and the Republic of Virtue*, 84–85. Sophie d'Houdetot, who lived until 1813, belonged to a circle during the Revolution that gathered at the home of Mme Hélvetius at Auteuil. Others in the circle included Pierre Cabanis, Constantin de Volney, André Chénier, and Condorcet and his wife. Mme d'Houdetot's verdict on Rousseau was that "he was a pathetic figure and I treated him with gentleness and kindness. He was an interesting madman." The quotation is from Johnson, *Intellectuals*, 27.

The advocate of transparency, Rousseau's duplicities are beyond reckoning. This is not to say that the ideal of transparency was a fabrication; rather it grew out of his own inner divisions, which he never resolved. As much as he believed in the removal of masks, he was given to subterfuges and disguises, or perhaps it should be said multiple personas. His sexual ambiguity can be seen as one of the seedbeds of his ideal of transparency. I am not claiming that David made this connection when he conceptualized his painting of Joseph Bara. David's most problematic work, *Joseph Bara* can be seen as an expression of the burdens he was under when he worked on it, as I argued in my *Jacques-Louis David*, 84–91, and as Crow does in *Emulation*, 177–78. Here I am following a suggestion made years ago by

Simon Schama that David's *Joseph Bara* can be seen as an expression of Rousseauist transparency. It was with no small measure of trepidation that I have tried to develop the idea suggested by Schama. This is particularly so when I argue that David's dissolving the boundaries between the male and female in *Joseph Bara* is congruent with the Rousseauist idea of transparency. With this aside I rest my case.

78. Quoted in Schnapper, *David*, 162.

79. Desmarres subsequently went to the guillotine.

Conclusion

1. Wildenstein, *Documents*, cat. no. 1124, 113.

2. Ibid., cat. no. 1198, 123–32.

3. Ibid., cat. no. 1145–6, 116–17.

4. Ibid., cat. no. 1190, 123.

5. Young, *Victorian England*, vi.

6. See Roberts, "The Visual Rhetoric."

7. Popkin, *Revolutionary News*, 145–68.

8. David used the phrase *"révolution heureuse"* in a speech in Nantes in March 1790. For the quotation see Roberts, *Jacques-Louis David*, 51.

9. Elie Faure has written that David "did not hear the clatter of the people's clogs on the paving stones, the roar of the *sectionnaires* cannon. He did not look at the steaming heads on the end of pikes, nor the streams of blood in the street." This passage, from Faure's *Histoire de l'art*, is quoted in a forthcoming article in *French Historical Studies* by Wisner, "The Genesis of Jacques-Louis David's *Intervention of the Sabine Women*."

10. Quoted in Schnapper, *David*, 186–87.

11. Doyle, *Oxford History of the French Revolution*, 425.

12. Ménétra, *Journal*, 217–38.

Bibliography

Adam, Antoine. *Grandeur and Illusion: French Literature and Society, 1600–1715.* Translated by Herbert Tint. New York: Basic Books, 1972.

Adams, Thomas McStay. *Bureaucrats and Beggars: French Social Policy in the Age of Enlightenment.* New York: Oxford U. Press, 1990.

Aldrich, Robert. "Late Comer or Early Starter? New Views on French Economic History." *Journal of European Economic History* 16 (1987): 89–100.

Andrew, Richard Mowery. "Paris of the Great Revolutions: 1789–1796." In *People and Communities in The Western World.* Edited by Gene Brucker. Homewood, Ill., Georgetown, Ont.: Dorsey Press, 1976.

Apgar, Gary. "Jacques-Louis David (1748–1825) . . . a critical view." *Apollo* 127 (May, 1993): 304–6.

Appleby, Joyce. *Liberalism and Republicanism in the Historical Imagination.* Cambridge, Mass.: Harvard U. Press, 1992.

Arasse, Daniel. *The Guillotine and the Terror.* Translated by Christopher Miller. London, New York, Victoria, Markham, Auckland: Penguin, 1989.

Auerbach, Erich. *Mimesis: The Representation of Reality in Western Literature.* Translated by Willard Trask. Princeton: Princeton U. Press, 1953.

_____. *Scenes from the Drama of European Literature.* Minneapolis: U of Minnesota Press, 1989.

Baker, Keith Michael. *Inventing the French Revolution: Essays on Political Culture.* Cambridge, Eng., New York, Port Chester, Melbourne, Sydney: Cambridge U. Press, 1990.

_____. See *The French Revolution and the Creation of Modern Political Culture,* vols. 1, 4.

Bakhtin, Mikhail. *Rabelais and His World.* Translated by Helene Iswolsky. Indiana: Indiana U. Press, 1984.

Barny, Roger. *Rousseau dans la Révolution: le personnage de Jean-Jacques et les débats du culte révolutionnaire (1787–1791)*. Oxford: Voltaire Foundation, 1986.

Beik, Paul H. See *The French Revolution*.

Beik, William. *Urban Protest in Seventeenth-Century France: The Culture of Retribution*. New York: Cambridge U. Press, 1997.

Bell, David A. *Lawyers and Citizens: The Making of a Political Elite in Eighteenth-Century France*. Oxford, New York: Oxford U. Press, 1994.

Bertier de Sauvigny, Guillaume de. *Le Comte Ferdinand de Bertier et l'enigme de la Congrégation, 1774–1791*. Paris: Presses Continatales, 1948.

Billington, James. *Fire in the Minds of Men: Origins of the Revolutionary Faith*. New York: Basic Books, 1980.

Blanc, Olivier. *Last Letters: Prisons and Prisoners of the French Revolution 1793–1794*. Translated by Alan Sheridan. New York: The Noonday Press, 1989.

Bloom, Allan. See Rousseau, *Politics and the Arts*.

Blum, Carol. *Rousseau and the Republic of Virtue: The Language of Politics in the French Revolution*. Ithaca and London: Cornell U. Press, 1986.

Blunt, Anthony. See *French Drawings in the Collection of his Majesty*.

Bordes, Philippe. *Le Serment du Jeu de Paume de Jacques-Louis David. Le peintre, son milieu et son temps*. Paris: Editions de la Réunion des musées nationaux, 1983.

_____. "J.-L. David's 'Serment du Jeu de Paume': Propaganda without a cause?" *Oxford Art Journal* 3 (1981): 19–25.

Bosher, J. F. *The French Revolution*. New York, London: Norton, 1988.

Braham, Allen. *The Architecture of the French Enlightenment*. Berkeley, Los Angeles: University of California Press, 1980.

Braudel, Fernand. *The Mediterranean and the Mediterranean World in the Age of Philip II*. Translated by Siân Reynolds. 2 Vols. New York, Evanston, San Francisco: Harper & Row, 1975.

_____. *Capitalism and Material Life, 1400–1800*. Translated by Miriam Kochan. New York, Evanston, San Francisco, London: Harper & Row, 1973.

_____. *The Identity of France: Vol. II, People and Production*. Translated by Siân Reynolds. New York: Harper & Row, 1990.

Brinton, Clarence Crane. *The Jacobins: An Essay in the New History*. New York: Macmillan, 1930.

_____. *A Decade of Revolution, 1789–1799*. New York and Chicago: Harper & Row, 1934.

Brown, Peter. "The Wellborn Few." See *A History of Private Life*, vol. 1.

Burke, Peter. *Popular Culture in Early Modern Europe*. New York: Harper & Row, 1978.

Cameron, Rondo, and Charles E. Freeman. "French Economic Growth: A Radical Revision." *Social Science History* 7 (Winter, 1983): 3–30.

Cashmere, John. "The Social Uses of Violence in Ritual: *Charivari* or Religious Persecution." *Journal of European Quarterly* 21, No. 3 (July, 1991): 291–319.

Castiglione, Baldesar. *The Book of the Courtier*. Translated by Charles S. Singleton. Garden City: Anchor Books, 1959.

Chagniot, Jean. *Paris et l'Armée au XVIIIe Siècle*. Paris: Economica Library, 1985.

_____. *Nouvelle histoire de Paris: Paris au XVIIIe siècle*. Paris: Hachette, 1988.

Chamfort, Sébastien Roch Nicolas de. *Products of the Perfected Civilization: Selected Writings of Chamfort*. Translated by W. S. Merwin. New York: Macmillan, 1960.

Chartier, Roger. *The Cultural Origins of the French Revolution*. Translated by Lydia G. Cochrane. Durham and London: Duke U. Press, 1991.

Chaussinand-Nogaret, Guy. *The French Nobility in the Eighteenth Century: From Feudalism to Enlightenment*. Translated by William Doyle. Cambridge: Cambridge U. Press, 1985.

Chénier, André. *Oeuvres complètes*. Edited by Gérard Walter. Paris: Pléiade, 1958.

Chronicle of the French Revolution: 1788–1799. Directed by Jean Favier. London: Chronicle Publications 1989.

Cleary, Richard Louis. *The Places Royales of Louis XIV and Louis XV*. 2 vols. Ann Arbor, Mich.: U. of Michigan, 1986.

Cobb, Richard. *The Police and the People: French Popular Protest, 1789–1820*. London: Oxford U. Press, 1970.

_____. *The People's Armies: The armées révolutionnaires, instruments of the Terror in the Departments April 1793 to Floréal Year II*. Translated by Marianne Elliott. New Haven and London: Yale U. Press, 1987.

Cobban, Alfred. *A History of Modern France, Vol. 1: Old Régime and Revolution, 1715–1799*. Harmondsworth, Eng.: Penguin, 1957.

_____. *The Social Interpretation of the French Revolution*. Cambridge, Eng.: Cambridge U. Press, 1964.

_____. *Aspects of the French Revolution*. New York: Norton, 1968.

Cowell, F. R. *Cicero and the Roman Republic*. Harmondsworth, Eng.: Penguin, 1956.

Crocker, Lester G. "Rousseau and the Common People." *Studies in the Eighteenth Century*. Vol. 3. Edited by R. F. Brissendon and J. C. Eade. 73–93. Toronto and Buffalo: U. of Toronto, 1976.

Crow, Thomas. *Painters and Public Life in Eighteenth-Century Paris*. New Haven and London: Yale U. Press, 1985.

_____. *Emulation: Making Artists for Revolutionary France*. New Haven, London: Yale U. Press, 1995.

Darnton, Robert. *The Great Cat Massacre and Other Episodes in French Cultural History*. New York: Vintage, 1985.

_____. *The Kiss of Lamourette: Reflections in Cultural History*. New York: Norton, 1990.

_____. *The Forbidden Best-Sellers of Pre-Revolutionary France*. New York: Norton, 1995.

David, Jules. *Le Peintre Louis David 1748–1825*. Paris: Harvard, 1880.

Davies, Norman. *Europe: A History*. New York: Harper & Row, 1988.

Davis, Natalie Zemon. *Society and Culture in Early Modern France*. Stanford, Conn.: Stanford U. Press, 1979.

Dowd, David. *Pageant-Master of the Republic: Jacques-Louis David and the French Revolution*. Lincoln, Neb.: U. of Nebraska Press, 1948.

Doyle, William. *Origins of the French Revolution*. Oxford: Oxford U. Press, 1980.

_____. "Myth for Myth: The Rise and Fall of the Declining Bourgeoisie." *The Consortium on Revolutionary Europe Proceedings*. 306–19. Athens, Georgia: Univ. of Georgia Press, 1983.

_____. *The Oxford History of the French Revolution*. Oxford, New York: Oxford U. Press, 1990.

Dworkin, Ronald. "Liberalism." In *Liberalism and its Critics*. Edited by Michael J. Sandel. New York: New York U. Press, 1984.

Duby, Georges, and Robert Mandrou. *A History of French Civilization: From the Year 1000 to the Present Day*. Translated by James Blakely Atkinson. New York: Random House, 1964.

Echeverria, Durand. *The Maupeou Revolution: A Study in the History of Libertarianism France. 1770–1774*. Baton Rouge, Louisiana, London: Louisiana State U. Press, 1985.

Egret, Jean. *The French Prerevolution, 1787–1788*. Translated by Wesley D. Camp. Chicago: U. of Chicago Press, 1977.

Elias, Norbert. *The Civilizing Process: The History of Manners*. Translated by Edmund J. Jephcott. New York: Urizen, 1978.

_____. *Power and Civility. The Civilizing Process, Volume II*. Translated by Edmund J. Jephcott. New York: Pantheon, 1982.

_____. *The Court Society*. Translated by Edmund J. Jephcott. New York: Pantheon, 1983.

Eroticism and the Body Politic. Edited by Lynn Hunt. Baltimore and London: Johns Hopkins U. Press, 1991.

Essays on the French Revolution: Paris and the Provinces. Edited by Steven G. Reinhardt and Elisabeth A. Cawthon. Arlington, Texas: U. of Texas, 1992.

Farge, Arlette. *Fragile Lives: Violence, Power and Solidarity in Eighteenth-Century Paris*. Translated by Carol Shelton. Cambridge, Mass.: Harvard U. Press, 1993.

_____. *Subversive Words: Public Opinion in Eighteenth-Century France*. Translated by Rosemary Morris. University Park: Penn State U. Press, 1994.

Farge, Arlette, and Jacques Revel. *The Vanishing Children of Paris: Rumor and Politics Before the French Revolution*. Translated by Claudia Miévilla. Cambridge, Mass.: Harvard U. Press, 1991.

Faure, Alain. *Paris Carême-prenant du Carnivaal à Paris au XIXe siècle 1800–1914*. Paris: Hachette, 1978.

Favier, Jean. See *Chronicle of the French Revolution*.

Foucault, Michel. *Discipline and Punishment: The Birth of the Prison*. Translated by Alan Sheridan. New York: Random House, 1969.

French Art During the Revolution. Edited by Alan Wintermute. New York: Colnaghi, 1989.

The French Drawings in the Collection of His Majesty the King at Windsor Castle. Anthony Blunt. Oxford, London, New York: Phaidon, Oxford U. Press, 1945.

The French Revolution. Edited by Paul Beik. New York, Evanston, London: Harper & Row, 1970.

The French Revolution and the Creation of Modern Public Opinion (vol. 1): *The Political Culture of the Old Regime.* Edited by Keith Michael Baker. Oxford: Pergamon Press, 1987.

_____. (vol. 2): *The Political Culture of the French Revolution.* Edited by Colin Lucas. Oxford: Pergamon Press, 1989.

_____. (vol. 3): *The Transformation of Political Culture.* Edited by François Furet and Mona Ozouf. Oxford: Pergamon Press, 1989.

_____. (vol. 4): *The Terror.* Edited by Keith Michael Baker. Oxford: Pergamon Press, 1994.

Friedländer, Walter. *David to Delacroix.* Translated by Robert Goldwater. Cambridge, Mass.: Harvard U. Press, 1952.

Furbank, P. N. "Nothing Sacred." *New York Review of Books,* 42, No. 10 (June, 1995): 51–55.

Furet, François. *Interpreting the French Revolution.* Translated by Elborg Forster. Cambridge, London, New York, New Rochelle, Melbourne, Sydney: Cambridge U. Press, 1981.

_____. *Marx and the French Revolution.* Translated by Deborah Kan Furet. Chicago and London: U. of Chicago Press, 1988.

_____. *The French Revolution 1770–1814.* Translated by Antonia Nevill. Oxford, Cambridge, Mass.: Blackwell, 1990.

_____. and Ozouf, Mona. *A Critical Dictionary of the French Revolution.* Translated by Arthur Goldhammer. Cambridge, Mass.: Harvard U. Press, 1989.

_____. See *The Political Culture of the French Revolution,* vol. 3.

Fuye de La, Maurice and Emile Babeau. *The Apostle of Liberty: Life of La Fayette.* Translated by Edward Hyams. New York: T. Yoseloff, 1956.

Garrioch, David. *The Formation of the Parisian Bourgeoisie, 1690–1830.* Cambridge, Mass.: Harvard U. Press, London, 1996.

_____. *Neighbourhood and Community in Paris. 1740–1790.* Cambridge, Eng.: Cambridge U. Press, 1986.

Gauchet, Marcel. *La Révolution des droits de l'homme.* Paris: , 1988.

Gay, Peter. *Voltaire's Politics: The Poet as Realist.* Princeton: Princeton U. Press, 1959.

Germani, Ian. "Robespierre's Heroes: The Politics of Heroization During the Year Two." *The Consortium on Revolutionary Europe Proceedings.* 132–56. Athens, GA.: Univ. of Georgia Press, 1988.

Godechot, Jacques. *The Taking of the Bastille July 14th, 1789.* Translated by Jean Stewart. New York: Scribner, 1970.

_____. *The Counter Revolution: Doctrine and Action 1789–1804.* Translated. by Salvator Attanasio. London: Routledge & Kegan Paul, 1972.

Goodman, Dena. *The Republic of Letters: A Cultural History of the French Enlightenment.* Ithaca and London: Cornell U. Press, 1994.

Gordon, Daniel. "'Public Opinion' and The Civilizing Process in France: The Example of Morellet." *Eighteenth-Century Studies* 22, No. 3 (Spring, 1989): 302–28.

Gottschalk, Louis R. *Jean-Paul Marat: A Study in Radicalism*. New York: U. of Chicago Press, 1966.

_____. *Lafayette in the French Revolution: From the October Days Through the Federation*. Chicago: U. of Chicago Press, 1973.

Gottschalk, Louis R. and Margaret Maddox. *Lafayette in the French Revolution: Through the October Days*. Chicago: U. of Chicago Press, 1969.

Habermas, Jürgen. *The Structural Transformation of the Public Sphere: An Inquiry into a Category of Bourgeois Society*. Translated by Thomas Burger and Frederick Lawrence. Cambridge, Mass.: M.I.T. Press, 1989.

Hampson, Norman. *The Enlightenment*. Baltimore: Penguin, 1965.

_____. *The Life and Opinions of Maximilien Robespierre*. London: Duckworth, 1974.

_____. *Will and Circumstance: Montesquieu, Rousseau and the French Revolution*. Norman, Okla.: U. of Oklahoma Press, 1983.

_____. *Prelude to Terror: The Constituent Assembly and the Failure of Consensus, 1789–1791*. Oxford and New York: Blackwell, 1988.

_____. *Danton*. Oxford: Blackwell, 1988.

Herbert, Robert. *David, Voltaire, BRUTUS and the French Revolution: An Essay in Art and Politics*. New York: Viking, 1967.

Hermann, Wolfgang. *Laugier and Eighteenth-Century French Theory*. London": A. Zwemmer, 1962.

Higonnet, Patrice. *Class, Ideology, and the Rights of Nobles during the French Revolution*. Oxford: Oxford U. Press, 1981.

_____. "Sociability, Social Structure, and the French Revolution." *Social Science: An International Quarterly of the Social Sciences* 56, No. 1 (Spring, 1989): 99–125.

A History of Private Life (vol.1): *From Pagan Rome to Byzantium*. Edited by Paul Veyne. Translated by Arthur Goldhammer. Cambridge, Mass., London: Harvard U. Press, 1987.

_____. *Passions of the Renaissance*. Edited by Philippe Ariès and Georges Duby. Translated by Arthur Goldhammer. Cambridge, Mass., London: Harvard U. Press, 1989.

_____. *From the Fires of the Revolution to the Great War*. Edited by Michelle Perot. Translated by Arthur Goldhammer. Cambridge, Mass., London: Harvard U. Press, 1990.

Hould, Claudette. *Images of the French Revolution*. Quebec, Canada: Musée du Québec, 1989.

Hoycroft, John. *In Search of the French Revolution: Journeys Through France*. London: Secker & Warburg, 1989.

Hufton, Olwen H. "Women in Revolution 1789–1796." *Past and Present* 53 (November, 1971): 90–108.

_____.*Women & the Limits of Citizenship in the French Revolution*. Toronto, Canada: U. of Toronto Press, 1992.

_____. *The Poor of Eighteenth-Century France: 1750–1789*. Oxford: Clarendon Press, 1974.

Hunt, Lynn. *Politics, Culture, and Class in the French Revolution*. Berkeley, Los Angeles: U. of California Press, 1984.

_____. *The Family Romance of the French Revolution*. Berkeley and Los Angeles: U. of California Press, 1992.

Hunt, Lynn, David Lansky, and Paul Hanson. "The Failure of the Liberal Republic in France, 1795–1799: The Road to Brumaire." *Journal of Modern History* 51, No. 4 (Dec., 1979): 734–59.

Images de la Révolution française. Bibliothèque Nationale Videodisc, Catalogue 3 vols. Paris: Bibliothèque Nationale, Pergamon, 1990.

Inventaire général des dessins École française XIII de Pagnest à Paris de Chavannes. Coordinated by Catherine Legrand, assisted by Varena Forcione, Véronique Goarin, Catherine Scheck. Paris: Bibliothèque Nationale, Pergamon, 1997.

Isherwood, Christopher. *Farce and Fantasy: Popular Entertainments in Eighteenth-Century Paris*. New York, Oxford: Oxford U. Press, 1986.

_____. *Force*

Jacob, Margaret C. "The Mental Landscape of the Public Sphere: A European Perspective." *Eighteenth-Century Studies* 28, No. 1 (January, 1994): 95–113.

Johnson, Dorothy. *Jacques-Louis David: Art in Metamorphosis*. Princeton: Princeton U. Press, 1993.

Johnson, Paul. *Intellectuals*. New York, London: Harper & Row, 1990.

Jones, Peter M. *Reform and Revolution in France: The Politics of Transition, 1774–1791*. Cambridge, Eng.: Cambridge U. Press, 1995.

Jordan, David P. *The Revolutionary Career of Maximilien Robespierre*. Chicago: U. of Chicago Press, 1989.

_____. *Transforming Paris: The Life and Labors of Baron Hausmann*. New York, London: Free Press, 1995.

Judt, Tony. "On François Furet (1827–1897)." *New York Review of Books* 44, No. 17 (November 6, 1997): 41–42.

Kaplow, Jeffrey. *The Names of Kings: The Parisian Laboring Poor in the Eighteenth-Century*. New York: Basic Books, 1972.

_____. *France on the Eve of Revolution*. New York: Wiley, 1971.

Kates, Gary. *The Cercle Social, the Girondins, and the French Revolution*. Princeton: Princeton U. Press, 1985.

_____. *Monsieur D'Eon Is a Woman: A Tale of Political Intrigue and Sexual Masquerade*. New York: Basic, 1995.

Kelly, George Armstrong. "The Machine of the duc d'Orléans and the New Politics." *Journal of Modern History* 51, No. 4 (December, 1979): 667–84.

Kelly, Linda. *Women of the French Revolution*. London: Hamish Hamilton, 1987.

Kennedy, Emmet. *A Cultural History of the French Revolution*. New Haven and London: Yale U. Press: 1989.

Kennedy, Michael L. *The Jacobin Clubs in the French Revolution: The First Years*. Princeton: Princeton U. Press, 1982.

_____. *The Jacobin Clubs in the French Revolution: The Middle Years.* Princeton, N.J.: Princeton U. Press: 1988.

Kennedy, Paul. *Preparing for the Twenty-First Century.* New York: Random House, 1989.

Kostoff, Spiro. *The City Assembled: The Elements of Urban Form Through History.* Boston, Toronto, London: Little Brown, 1992.

Labrousse, C. E. *La crise de l'economie français à la fin de l'Ancien Régimé et au debut de la Révolution, Vol. 1: La Crise viticole.* Paris: Presses universitaires, 1943.

Ladurie, Emmanuel Le Roy. *Carnival in Romans.* Translated by Mary Feeney. New York: George Braziller, 1979.

Landes, Joan. *Women and the Public Sphere in the Age of the French Revolution.* Ithaca and London: Cornell U. Press, 1988.

Lee, Simon. *David.* London: Phaidon, 1999.

Lee, Virginia. "Jacques-Louis David: The Versailles Sketchbook." *The Burlington Magazine* Part 1 (April, 1969): 197–208, Part 2 (June, 1969): 360–69.

Lefebvre, Georges. *The French Revolution: From its Origins to 1793.* Translated by Elizabeth Moss Evanson. London and New York: Columbia U. Press, 1962.

_____. *The French Revolution: From 1793 to 1799.* Translated by John Hall Stewart and James Friguglietti. London and New York: Columbia U. Press, 1964.

_____. *The Coming of the French Revolution.* Translated by R. R. Palmer. Princeton: Princeton U. Press, 1967.

_____. *The Great Fear of 1789: Rural Panic in Revolutionary France.* Translated by Joan White. Princeton: Princeton U. Press, 1982.

Leith, James A. *Art as Propaganda in France, 1750–1799: A Study in the History of Ideas.* Toronto, Canada: U. of Toronto Press, 1965.

_____. "On the Religiosity of the French Revolution." *Culture and Revolution.* Edited by George Levitine. 171–85. State College, PA: Pennsylvania State U. Press, 1989.

_____. *Space and Revolution: Projects for Monuments, Squares and Public Buildings in France, 1789–1799.* Montreal, Kingston, London, Buffalo: McGill U. Press, 1991.

Lemoigne, Y. "Population and Provisions in Strasbourg in the Eighteenth Century." *New Perspectives on the French Revolution: Readings in Historical Sociology.* Edited by Jeffrey Kaplow. 47–67. New York: John Wiley & Sons, 1965.

Lévêque, Jean-Jacques. *L'art et la Révolution française, 1789–1809.* Neuchâtel, Suisse: Ides et Calandes, 1987.

Loggins, Vernon. *André Chénier: His Life, Death, and Glory.* Athens, Ohio: Univ. of Georgia Press, 1965.

Lougee, Carolyn C. *Le Paradis des Femmes: Women, Salons, and Social Stratification in Seventeenth-Century France.* Princeton: Princeton U. Press, 1976.

Lough, John. *An Introduction to the Seventeenth Century.* London: Longmans, 1954.

Loyer, François. *Paris in the Nineteenth Century: Architecture and Urbanism.* Translated by Charles Lynn Clark. New York: Abbeville Press, 1989.

Lucas, Colin. "The Crowd and Politics between *Ancien Regime* and Revolution in France." *Journal of Modern History* 63, No. 2 (September, 1988): 421–57.

_____. See *The Political Culture of the French Revolution*, vol. 2.

Luckett, Thomas Manley. "Hunting for spies and Whores: A Parisian Riot on the Eve of the French Revolution." *Past and Present* 156 (August, 1997): 116–43.

Machiavelli, Niccolò. *The Prince*. Translated and edited by Robert M. Adams. New York: Norton, 1977.

McDonald, Joan. *Rousseau and the French Revolution*. London: Athlone, 1965.

McMahon, Dennis M. "The Birthplace of the Revolution: Public Space and Political Community in the Palais-Royal of Louis-Philippe-Joseph d'Orléans, 1781–1799." *French History* 10, 1 (March, 1996): 1–29.

Magendie, Maurice. *La Politesse mondaine et les théories de l'honnêtété en France au XVIIᵉ siècle de 1600 à 1660*. 2 vols. Paris: F. Alcan, 1925.

Manceron, Claude. *Blood of the Bastille, 1787–1789: From Calonne's Dismissal to the Uprising in Paris*. Translated by Nancy Amphoux. New York: Simon and Schuster, 1989.

Martines, Lauro. *Power and Imagination: City States in Renaissance Italy*. New York: Knopf, 1979.

Mason, Laura. *Singing the Revolution: Popular Culture and Politics, 1787–1799*. Ithaca and London: Cornell U. Press, 1996.

Mathiez, Albert. *The French Revolution*. Translated by Catherine Alison Phillips. New York: Grosset & Dunlap, 1964.

Matrat, Jean. *Robespierre, Or the Tyranny of the Majority*. London: Angus and Robertson, 1975.

Maza, Sarah. *Private Lives and Public Affairs: The Causes Célèbres of Prerevolutionary France*. Berkeley, Los Angeles, London: U. of California Press, 1993.

Ménétra, Jacques Louis. *The Journal of My Life*. Edited by Daniel Roche, Foreword by Robert Darnton. Translated by Arthur Goldhammer. New York: Columbia U. Press, 1986.

Mercier, Louis-Sébastien. *Le Tableau de Paris*. 2 Vols. Edited by Jean-Claude Bonnat. Paris: Mercure de France, 1994.

_____. *The Picture of Paris*. Translated by Wilfrid and Emilie Jackson. New York: Dial Press, 1929.

Merrick, Jeffrey W. *The Desacralization of the French Monarchy in the Eighteenth Century*. Baton Rouge, Louisiana, London: Louisiana State U. Press, 1990.

_____. "Family and Festivals: Social Integration and Disintegration in Morellet's Critique of the French Revolution." *History of European Issues* 17, No. 5 (1993): 599–614.

Michelet, Jules. *History of the French Revolution*. Translated by Charles Cocks. Chicago and London: U. of Chicago Press 1967.

Montesquieu, Baron de la Brède. *Oeuvres complètes*. Preface by Georges Vedel. Notes by Daniel Oster. Editions du Seuil: Macmillan 1964.

Mouffe, Chantal. "Democratic Citizenship and the Political Community." In *Dimensions of Radical Democracy: Pluralism, Citizenship, Community*. Edited by Chantal Mouffe. London: Routledge, Chapman & Hall, 1992.

Munro, Jane, and Scraise, David, see *Paris, City of Revolution*.

Ninth of Thermidor: The Fall of Robespierre. Edited by Richard Bienvenu. New York, London, Toronto: Oxford U. Press, 1968.

Nolhac, Pierre de. *Tableaux de Paris pendant la révolution française (1789–1792), soixante-quatre dessins originaux de J.-L. Prieur*. Paris: Le livre at l'estampe, 1902.

_____. *Inventaire général des dessins*.

Oeuvres de Maximilien Robespierre. Edited by Marc Bouloiseau, Georges Lefebvre, Jean Dautry, and Albert Soboul. 10 vols. Paris: 1963–1968.

Olander, William. *Pour transmettre à la postérité: French painting and the Revolution, 1794–1795*. Ann Arbor, Mich.: U. of Michigan, 1984.

Outram, Dorinda. *The Body and the French Revolution: Sex, Class and Political Culture*. New Haven and London: Yale U. Press, 1989.

Ozouf, Mona. *Festivals and the French Revolution*. Translated by Alan Sheridan. Cambridge, Mass., London: Harvard U. Press, 1988.

_____. "L'Opinion Public." In *The French Revolution and the Creation of Modern Public Opinion* vol. 1: 419–34.

Palmer, R. R. *Twelve Who Ruled: The Year of the Terror in the French Revolution*. Princeton: Princeton U. Press, 1941.

_____. *The Age of Democratic Revolution: A Political History of Europe and America, 1760–1800, The Challenge*. Princeton: Princeton U. Press, 1959.

Paris, City of Revolution. Edited by Jane Munro, and David Scraise. Cambridge, Eng.: Cambridge U. Press, 1989.

Parker, Harold T. *The Cult of Antiquity and the French Revolution*. Chicago: U. of Chicago Press, 1937.

Payne, Harry G. *The Philosophes and the People*. New Haven and London: Yale U. Press, 1976.

Picon, Antoine. *French Architects and Engineers in the Age of Enlightenment*. Translated by Martin Thom. Cambridge, Eng.: Cambridge U. Press, 1992.

Pincus, Steve. "Neither Machiavellian Moment nor Possessive Individualism: Commercial Society and the Defenders of the English Commonwealth." *American Historical Review* 103 (June, 1998): 705–36.

Pocock, J. G. A. *The Machiavellian Moment: Florentine Political Thought and the Atlantic Republican Tradition*. Princeton: Princeton U. Press, 1975.

_____. "The Machiavellian Moment Revisited: A Study in History and Ideology." *Journal of Modern History* 53 (March, 1981): 49–72.

_____. *Virtue, Commerce, and History: Essays on Political Thought and History, Chiefly in the Eighteenth Century*. Cambridge, Eng.: Cambridge U. Press, 1985.

Popkin, Jeremy. *Revolutionary News: The Press in France, 1789–1799*. Durham, London: Duke U. Press, 1990.

Prieur, Jean-Louis. See *Tableaux historiques de la Révolution française*.

Reinhard, Marcel. *Nouvelle histoire de Paris: La Révolution, 1789–1799*. Paris: Hachette, 1971.

Reinhardt, Steven G., and Cawthon, Elisabeth A., see *Essays on the French Revolution: Paris and the Provinces*. Arlington, Texas: Texas A&M Press, 1992.

Restif de la Bretonne. *Les Nuits de Paris*. Translated by Linda Asher and Ellen Fertig. New York: Random House, 1964.

Rice, Howard C. *Thomas Jefferson's Paris*. Princeton: Princeton U. Press, 1976.

Roberts, Warren. *Morality and Social Class in Eighteenth-Century French Literature and Painting*. Toronto, London: U. of Toronto, 1974.

_____. *Jacques-Louis David, Revolutionary Artist: Art, Politics, and the French Revolution*. Chapel Hill, North Carolina: U. of North Carolina, 1989.

_____. "The Visual Rhetoric of Jean-Louis Prieur." *Canadian Journal of History/Annales canadiennes d'histoire* 32 (December, 1997): 415–36.

Roche, Daniel, *The People of Paris: An Essay in Popular Culture in the 18th Century*. Translated by Marie Evans and Gwynne Lewis. Berkeley, Los Angeles: U. of California Press, 1987.

Rodgers, Daniel T. "Republicanism: The Career of a Concept." *Journal of American History* 79 (June, 1992): 11–38.

Root-Bernstein, Michele. *Boulevard Theater and Revolution in Eighteenth-Century Paris*. Ann Arbor, Mich.: U. of Michigan, 1984.

Rose, R. B. *The Making of the Sans-Culottes: Democratic Ideas and Institutions in Paris, 1789–92*. Manchester: Manchester Press, 1983.

Rosenblum, Robert. *Transformations in Late Eighteenth-Century Art*. Princeton: Princeton U. Press, 1967.

Rousseau, Jean-Jacques. *Oeuvres complètes*. 5 vols. Edited by Gagnebin, Raymond. Gallimard, 1959–95.

_____. *Politics and the Arts: Letter to M d'Alembert on the Theatre*. Translated by Allan Bloom. Ithaca: Cornell U. Press, 1968.

_____. *The Social Contract*. New York and London: Everyman, 1950.

Rudé, George. *The Crowd in the French Revolution*. Oxford: Oxford U. Press, 1959.

_____. *The Crowd in History, 1730–1848*. New York: Wiley & Sons, 1964.

Scarfe, Francis. *André Chénier: His Life and Work, 1762–1794*. Oxford: Oxford U. Press, 1965.

Schama, Simon. "Caste, Class, Elites, and Revolution." *Consortium on Revolutionary Europe*. 36–47. Athens, Georgia: 1982.

_____. *Citizens: A Chronicle of the French Revolution*. New York: Knopf, 1989.

Schnapper, Antoine. *David*. Translated by Helga Harrison. New York: Alpine, 1982.

Schwartz, Robert M. *Policing the Poor in Eighteenth-Century France*. Chapel Hill, North Carolina, London: U. of North Carolina Press, 1988.

Scott, Samuel F. *The Response of the Royal Army to the French Revolution: the Role and Development of the Line Army, 1787–93*. Oxford: Oxford U. Press, 1978.

Shafer, Boyd C. "Bourgeois Nationalism in the Pamphlets on the Eve of the French Revolution." *Journal of Modern History* 10 (1938): 31–50.

Shapiro, Barry. *Revolutionary Justice in Paris: 1789–1790.* Cambridge, Eng.: Cambridge U. Press, 1993.

Singer, Brian C. J. "Violence in the French Revolution: Forms of Ingestion/ Forms of Expulsion." *Social Science: An International Quarterly of the Social Sciences* 56, No. 1 (Spring, 1989): 263–93.

Slavin, Morris. *The Making of an Insurrection: Parisian Sections and the Gironde.* Cambridge, Mass., London: Harvard U. Press, 1986.

_____. *The Hébertistes to the Guillotine: Anatomy of a "Conspiracy" in Revolutionary France.* Baton Rouge, Louisiana: Louisiana U. State Press, 1995.

Sloane, Joseph. "David, Robespierre and the 'Death of Bara.'" *Gazette des Beaux Arts* 74 (September, 1969): 143–60.

Soboul, Albert. *The Parisian Sans-Culottes and the French Revolution 1793–4.* Translated by Gwynne Lewis. Oxford: Clarendon Press, 1964.

Smernoff, Richard A. *André Chénier.* Boston: Twayne, 1977.

Solé, Jacques. *Questions of the French Revolution: A Historical Overview.* Translated by Shelley Temehin. New York: Pantheon, 1989.

Solomon, Maynard. *Mozart: A Life.* New York: Harper Collins, 1996.

Starobinski, Jean. *The Emblems of Reason.* Translated by Barbara Bray. Charlottesville: U. of Virginia Press, 1982.

Steinbrügge, Liselotte. *The Moral Sex: Women's Nature in the French Revolution.* Trans. by Pamela E. Selwyn. New York: Oxford U. Press, 1995.

Stone, Bailey. *The Genesis of the French Revolution: A Global-Historical Interpretation.* Cambridge: Cambridge U. Press, 1994.

Sutcliffe, Anthony. *Paris: An Architectural History.* New Haven, London: Yale U. Press, 1993.

Sutherland, D. M. G. *France 1789–1815: Revolution and Counterrevolution.* New York: Oxford U. Press, 1986.

Sydenham, M. J. *The Girondins.* London: U. of London Press, 1961.

_____. *The French Revolution.* New York: Capricorn Books, 1966.

Tableaux historiques de la Révolution française. 3 vols. Paris: Auber, 1802.

Tackett, Timothy. *Becoming a Revolutionary: The Deputies of the French National Assembly and the Emergence of a Revolutionary Culture (1789–1790).* Princeton: Princeton U. Press, 1996.

Taylor, George V. "Non-Capitalist Wealth and the Origins of the French Revolution." *American Historical Review* 72 (January, 1970): 469–96.

Thompson, J. M. *The French Revolution.* New York, Oxford: Oxford U. Press, 1966.

_____. *Robespierre.* Oxford and New York: Blackwell, 1988.

Tilly, Charles. "Charivari, Repertories, and Politics." In *French Cities in the Nineteenth Century.* Edited by John M. Merriman. New York: Hutchinson, 1981.

_____. *The Contentious French: Four Centuries of Popular Struggle.* Cambridge, Mass., London: Harvard U. Press, 1986.

Tourneux, Maurice. *Bibliographie de l'histoire de Paris pendant la Révolution française.* Paris: Impremerie Nouvelle, 1890.

Trenard, L. "The Social Crisis in Lyons on the Eve of the French Revolution." *New Perspectives on the French Revolution: Readings in Historical Sociology.* Edited by Jeffrey Kaplow. 68–100. New York: Wiley & Sons, 1965.

Le Tribunal Révolutionnairre de Paris. 2 vols. Edited by Emile Compardon. Paris: Henri Plon, 1886.

Tulard, Jean. *Nouvelle histoire de Paris: La Révolution.* Paris: Hachette, 1989.

Van Kley, Dale K. *The Damiens Affair and the Unravelling of the Ancien Régime, 1750–1770.* Princeton: Princeton U. Press, 1984.

_____. "In Search of Eighteenth-Century Public Opinion." *French Historical Studies* 19, No. 2 (Spring, 1995): 215–26.

Vidal, Mary. *Watteau's Painted Conversations: Art, Literature and Talk in Eighteenth-Century France.* Princeton: Princeton U. Press, 1992.

_____. "David among the Moderns: Art, Science, and the Lavoisiers." *Journal of the History of Ideas* 56, No. 4 (October, 1995): 595–624.

Vidler, Anthony. *Claude-Nicolas Ledoux: Architecture and Social Reform at the End of the Ancien Régime.* Cambridge, Mass.: MIT Press, 1990.

Weber, Eugen. *Peasants into Frenchmen: The Modernization of Rural France, 1870–1914.* Stanford, Conn.: Stanford U. Press, 1976.

Weston, Helen. "1791: The Past in the Service of the Present." Paper presented on Symbols, Myths, and Images of the French Revolution. Regina, Saskatchewan, 1996.

Wildenstein, Georges. *Documents complémentaires au catalogue de l'oeuvre de J.-Louis David.* Paris: Foundation Wildenstein, 1973.

Williams, Alan. *The Police of Paris.* Baton Rouge: Louisiana State U. Press, 1979.

Williams, Gwyn A. *Artisans and Sans-culottes: Popular movements in France and Britain during the French Revolution.* New York: Norton, 1969.

Wintermute, Alan. *1789: French Art During the Revolution.* New York: Colnaghi, 1989.

Wisner, David. "Jacques-Louis David and André Chénier: The Death of Socrates, The Tennis Court Oath, and The Quest for Artistic Liberty (1787–1792)." *The Consortium on Revolutionary Europe Proceedings.* 529–44. Athens, Georgia: Univ. of Georgia Press, 1986.

_____. *The Cult of the Legislator in France 1750–1830: A Study in the Political Theology of the French Enlightenment.* Oxford: Voltaire Foundation, 1997.

_____. "The Genesis of Jacques Louis David's *Intervention of the Sabine Women*: An Essay in historical Re-enactment." Forthcoming article in *French Historical Studies.*

Wood, Gordon J. *The Creation of the American Republic, 1776–1787.* New York: Norton, 1969.

Young, Arthur. *Travels in France during the Years 1787, 1788, and 1789.* Intro. by Jeffrey Kaplow. Garden City, N.J.: Doubleday Anchor, 1969.

Young, G. M. *Victorian England: Portrait of an Age.* London: Oxford U. Press, 1960.

Index